Witchdoctor Kahuna Healer, Unfiltered Original Philosophy, Folklore, and Techniques in Ancient Hawaiian Healing with Soul Retrievals, Psychic Surgery, Past Life Healing, Herbal Medicine, and Story © 2025 Aly Cardinalli LLC, Texas, United States

Text © 2025 Aly Cardinalli, First Edition

Cover: *Kapua Accepts Kanaloa's Healing Waters in Milu* designed by Aly Cardinalli

Paperback ISBN 979-8-9920110-5-0

e-book ISBN 979-8-9920110-4-3

No portion of this book may be reproduced in any form without written permission from the publisher or author, except as permitted by U.S. copyright law.

This publication is designed to provide accurate and authoritative information in regard to the subject matter covered. It is sold with the understanding that neither the author nor the publisher is engaged in rendering legal, investment, accounting or other professional services. While the publisher and author have used their best efforts in preparing this book, they make no representations or warranties with respect to the accuracy or completeness of the contents of this book and specifically disclaim any implied warranties of merchantability or fitness for a particular purpose. No warranty may be created or extended by sales representatives or written sales materials. The advice and strategies contained herein may not be suitable for your situation. You should consult with a professional when appropriate. Neither the publisher nor the author shall be liable for any loss of profit or any other commercial damages, including but not limited to special, incidental, consequential, personal, or other damages. All Rights Reserved. No part of this publication may be reproduced or transmitted in any form or by any means, electronic or mechanical, including photocopy, recording or any other information storage and retrieval system, without prior permission in writing from the publisher.

Illustrations by Aly Cardinalli

Be the first to know: www.alycardinalli.com

WITCHDOCTOR KAHUNA HEALER
BOOK 2

UNFILTERED ORIGINAL PHILOSOPHY, FOLKLORE, AND TECHNIQUES IN ANCIENT HAWAIIAN HEALING WITH SOUL RETRIEVALS, PSYCHIC SURGERY, PAST LIFE HEALING, HERBAL MEDICINE, AND STORY

ALY CARDINALLI

WWW.ALYCARDINALLI.COM

Trigger Warning

This book contains dark themes and content that may be distressing or triggering for some readers. Topics covered include various forms of abuse including domestic abuse, violence, non-consensual acts, the occult, addiction and substance abuse, exorcism, demonic possessions, sexual themes, monsters, demonology, hauntings, psychopomps, deities, spirits, ghosts, spirit walking, witchcraft, soul retrievals, past life regression, conjuring entities, psychological distress and diagnosis, damaged souls, soul removals, coffins and burials, death, cultural oppression, and other dark subject matter. This book is based on real experiences, unedited cultural stories, and true stories. Reader discretion is advised. If any of these topics are likely to cause emotional discomfort or distress, it's recommended to approach this book with caution or consider choosing a different reading option. Your well-being is essential. For exact details on the content of this book, please visit the author's website.

Disclaimer

The author and publisher make no representation or warranties with respect to the accuracy, applicability, fitness, or completeness of the contents of this book. The information contained in this book is strictly for educational purposes. Therefore, if you wish to apply ideas contained in the book, you are taking full responsibility for your actions. There is no guarantee that your life will improve in any way using the techniques, ideas, and information presented in the book. Self-help and improvement potential are entirely dependent upon the person using the concepts and techniques. Your level of improvement in attaining results depends on the time you devote to developing skills, your commitment to learning the ideas, techniques, principles, and skills mentioned, and your personal belief system. The author and publisher assume no responsibility for any of your actions, whether you use the information for positive or negative purposes. As always, the advice of a competent professional should be sought. The information contained in these pages is not meant to substitute for the advice of health or mental health professionals. Readers should use discretion before performing any rituals or spells. The author is not liable, or in any way responsible, for any actions that the readers may take as a result of the information contained in this book. The reader is encouraged to cast spells and work with spirits responsibly.

Downloadable Bookmark

QR for Bookmark on Book Characters

Author's Note

The names and various personal information have been changed to keep my students' and clients' lives private. Information in this book has been collected from the sources listed in the bibliography. The absence of individual citations is for the flow of learning, not to claim credit for others' information. This is simply a stylistic choice and not an attempt to claim copyright. Please do read the books referenced, as they have amplified my journey and knowledge. My knowledge comes from the authors who have preceded me. We should always celebrate those who laid the foundations that we build on. I hold you all in the highest regard.

"I am sorry for the hypothetical person who has the task of organizing the occult movement, for occultists of different schools cannot be induced to cooperate. Any technique which differs from that which they are used to is suspect; any unfamiliar contact is black. The great majority of the heads of schools that I have known have sat each in his own circle of light and damned everybody else."
- Dion Fortune's Psychic Self-Defence

Why This Format And Why We Tell the Story

Hawaiian Pronunciation
A, as in water
E, as in convey
I, as in unique
O, as in note
U, as in Luke

In the captivating realm of witchdoctors, a profound and sacred connection exists. We serve as the conduits between the spirit world and the web of our existence, holding the key to healing and understanding. This mysterious quilted existence and how to mend it is how we will embark on our journey of exploration, focusing on the enigmatic and often misunderstood topic of the kahuna.

At the heart of this connection lies the well-being of spirits and the profound journey towards wholeness. This encompasses present vitality and extends to the remnants of past afflictions. It is through the preservation of our own humanity, our harmonious alignment, and with the spirit of all things that we achieve this profound sense of wellness.

In the pursuit of this equilibrium, we sail on a journey of mystic energy healing, meditation, talking, and natural medicine, all while utilizing the art of storytelling.

Consider the power of a dance that embodies the anguish of a woman who has lost her child. In that moment, the fragile nature of a baby's mortal existence is laid bare before us. Or perhaps, the haunting melody of a heart-rending ballad that stirs memories of love and desolation within our own souls. When we surrender to the universal urge to dance in joyous celebration, or find our hearts gripped by fear while watching a terrifying film, we become one with the spirit of storytelling. It is through this profound connection that communication transcends all beings, be they spirit or human.

To omit storytelling from our teachings would amount to cultural erasure. Through the narratives we share, we convey the timeless wisdom of our craft. I impart my teachings by interweaving them with real-life anecdotes and cultural mythologies from the Hawaiian library, offering insight into the healing of spirits, ourselves, and others, alongside the sacred practice of spirit removal.

In our craft, storytelling reigns supreme. By providing glimpses into our practice, we weave that quilt with understanding. Whether through mythical tales or personal experiences, we strive to reinforce the lessons we bestow. Thus, you gain fragments of anecdotal evidence that attest to the efficacy of our methods.

While each witchdoctor's experiences are unique, we diligently strive to pass down our knowledge and methodologies. To support your journey, I provide a bibliography of resources where you may cross-reference the wisdom I share within these pages.

I understand that many students harbor concerns about the validity of the literature they encounter. I encourage you to cross-reference, explore further, engage with practitioners, or seek guidance from teachers and students at the esteemed BearBridge Academy of Witchcraft and Psychic Development, where I humbly serve as the Headmaster. We aim to present reliable, well-researched, and cross-referenced information. Spells, rituals, and secrets hold little meaning without a contextual foundation.

Within the realm of witchdoctors, storytelling plays a significant role. Through storytelling, we impart wisdom, communicate our experiences, and reinforce the teachings of our craft. I share stories of healing, spirit removal, and personal anecdotes to provide a context for understanding the intricacies of our practice.

Storytelling ingrains the context necessary to navigate the intricacies of our craft. It is both my teaching style and an integral aspect of my cultural heritage. Thus, within these books, I expand upon the lessons through the captivating medium of storytelling.

To omit the stories would extract the very soul from our teachings, leaving behind a hollow shell devoid of context and the elusive "how" to conquer the tempestuous facets of our craft. Similarly, neglecting lessons would provide only a fleeting glimpse into the realm of an exorcist. But when combined, they unveil the finer details that lie hidden within the ethereal canvases of our work.

The elements contained within these pages unfold in a symphony of knowledge, each layer building upon the next. Begin with the alphabet, progress to simple words, and then venture into more potent linguistic entanglements: complex sentences, paragraphs, and themes. Even if you are already well-versed in certain areas, such as spirit-walking or hedgewitchery, I implore you to immerse yourself in the practical reacquaintance of these teachings. Uncover additional approaches that enrich your existing understanding, granting you skills from a practitioner deeply intertwined with these sacred practices.

As you explore deeper into the realm of witchdoctors, I implore you to follow my example. Resist the urge to simply "tell" and instead embrace the transformative power of sharing. Unleash your own stories, your triumphs, folklore, and even your failures. By acquiring this book, you have already assumed the mantle of a hero dedicated to preserving and honoring our craft. For that, I extend my deepest gratitude.

Mythology holds a central role in shamanism across various cultures for several pivotal reasons. Folklore is a vital aspect of the shamanic tradition that encapsulates the spiritual, cultural, and existential frameworks within which shamans operate.

Mythology provides a cosmological map that outlines the structure of the universe, the nature of the spiritual world, and the relationships between different spiritual entities. These myths offer a framework for understanding how the world works from a spiritual perspective, guiding shamans in their interactions with the spirit world.

Myths help legitimize the role of the shaman within the community. By tying shamans to the foundational myths of a culture, these stories establish and reinforce the shaman's authority and duties. Additionally, as these myths are passed down through generations, they ensure the continuity of shamanic knowledge and practices.

Myths serve as educational resources that impart wisdom, moral values, and practical knowledge to the community. They often contain lessons about the consequences of moral choices, the importance of balance and respect in one's interaction with nature, and the protocols for engaging with the spiritual world.

In many shamanic cultures, the storytelling done by shamans is part of the healing process. Myths can offer psychological comfort, hope, and pathways to understanding personal or communal crises. They help individuals connect their personal experiences to larger spiritual and cultural narratives, which can be profoundly healing.

Myths often prescribe the rituals that shamans perform. They provide the narratives that make rituals meaningful and effective, explaining why certain actions, words, and objects are used in ceremonies. This not only guides the shaman but also helps the community understand and participate in the rituals more fully.

In many traditions, the knowledge of myths themselves is considered a source of spiritual power. Shamans often gain power through their intimate knowledge of myths, which enables them to navigate the spirit world, command spiritual entities, and perform miracles or magic.

Myths help define the identity of a community by telling stories about its origins, heroes, and important spiritual beliefs. Through shared mythology, a community can reinforce its cultural identity and cohesion, with the shaman often playing a central role in this process by recounting and embodying these myths.

Myths allow shamans and their communities to understand and engage with concepts that transcend ordinary experience. They provide a narrative form to abstract spiritual and metaphysical ideas, making them accessible and actionable within the shamanic practice.

By anchoring shamanic practice in a rich bed of mythology, these narratives explain and guide the shaman's actions and connect the individual to a broader communal and cosmic reality. This deep integration of mythology and shamanism underscores the profound human need to find meaning and order in the universe through narrative.

The Stories:

You'll read about the various stories from Hawaiian lore. I have taken the unedited version of these stories. The versions that take out the editing done by our current judgment on sex, sexuality, healing, and culture that were not present at that time. Many of the stories we hear today are edited for "white consumption."

This means… You might be uncomfortable at times. There will be murder, non-consensual sexual acts, homosexuality, genderfluid work, resigned belief of illness and death, unconventional love themes, and dark tones, including depression, grief, anger, and lust. The Hawaiian people recognize all aspects of the human condition, even if they are kapu. They still exist, and therefore, they exist here as well.

Table of Educational Content

First
- Shaman, Witchdoctor, or Kahuna: Recognizing the Call

Part 1: Ho'omanamana and Spirit Travel
- Huna and New Age Hawai'i
- The Hawaiian Tenets & Kapu
- The Shamanic Transformation
- Spirit Walking: The Practice of Shamanic Journeying
- Traveling in Spirit

Part 2: The Biology and Parts of the Soul
- Mana Check
- The Three Parts of the Soul
- Biology of the Three Parts of the Soul
- How Reincarnation Works With the Parts of the Soul

Part 3: Hilina'i: Psychic Surgery & Belief

- Hilina'i, Belief, and Medicine
- Spiritual Illness Test
- Psychic Surgery
- Cord Cutting and the Flow of Mana
- Hands That Heal the Soul
- Heal It And Let It Go
- Borrowing from Taoism: Li (Why Are You So Pretty?)
- Thoughts on Reiki
- Healing Spirits

Part 4: Aumakua & Soul Retrievals

- Cursing the Self (Yes, The Problem Is You), Thought Implantation, and Psychic Attack: Ho'upu'upu, Ho'opi'opi'o
- Spiritual Bypassing and How to Deal With Failure
- Healing Aumakua: Soul Retrieval Diagnosis
- Soul Retrieval Process
- Wala'au or Stay Sick
- Healing With Stories: Catharsis
- Life Balance
- Ho'oponopono & Healing Your Crowd
- Notice Others

Part 5: Uhane & The Body
- Breath in Polynesian Philosophy: Energetically Designed to Heal
- Herbs, Medicine, Nutrition
- Aromatherapy

Part 6: Unihipili & Past Life
- Trigger Unihipili Healing With Past Life Regression: The Akashic Records
- Past Life Healing
- Music in Healing: Power of Song, Prayer, and Dance
- Releasing Into Water and Receiving From Trees
- The Stone in the Jar, Grief in Hawai'i

Final
- The Proof Is In the Fruit

Author Bio
Bibliography and Cited Sources

Table of Narrative Content

First
- A Witch And A Priest
- Rough Encouragement

Part 1: Ho'omanamana and Spirit Travel
- The Tribe's New Witchdoctor
- The First Kahuna
- A Shark Boy Named Nanaue
- My Shamanic Death
- Hi'iaka's Epoch of Lohiau and Pele
- A Father Travels to Milu

Part 2: The Biology and the Parts of the Soul
- Maui and The Quest For Fire, The Quest For Life
- Creation Story and Pele's Hawai'i Home
- Setting a Demon Free

- Scolding From An Oni

Part 3: Hilina'i: Psychic Surgery & Belief
- May's Misuse
- Ego and D'artanian's Damage
- Psychic Surgery and Cancer
- Namaka'okaha'i and Kanaloa: Guardians of the Flow
- Kapua Accepts Kanaloa's Healing Waters
- Skeletal Gazelle Bird
- Strong Woman Doesn't Need Healing
- Advanced Certification Weekend
- Arianrhod Grandmother Spider Teotihuacan Yevabog

Part 4: Aumakua & Soul Retrievals
- Lucifer's Forgiveness
- Being Sick is How I Experience Love
- La'ieikawai, La'ielohelohe, The Rainbow, and The Song
- The Death of Souls of 2020
- Fluff's Failure or What Happens If You Don't Send The Soul Fragments Back
- I'll Talk, But No Therapy
- Stalkers on Maui
- If Your Life Had No Meaning, Would You Let A Demon Drive?
- Pele and Kamapua'a

Part 5: Uhane & The Body
- The Story of the Ipu

- How The Work of Plant-Healing Came To Be

- You're Not Sick, The Doctor Is Making You Sick

Part 6: Unihipili & Past Life Healing
- Maui Slows Down The Sun

- Blasphemous Blogger

- Pele and Poliahu: Fire and Snow

- Step Kick

- The Story of Laka and The Gift of Hula

Final Thoughts
- La'amaomao and Passing The Wind

Author Bio

Bibliography and Cited Sources

Witchdoctor Kahuna Healer

CHARACTERS:

Haumea - Goddess of Birth
Hi'iaka'akapoli'opele (Hi'iaka) - Youngest Sister of Pele, Goddess of Healing and Dance.
Hina - Goddess of the Moon
Hinenuitepo - Primordial Womb Goddess of the Underworld
Hopoe - Hi'iaka's consort and spirit of pono (righteous) messages
Kahoupokane - Goddess of Snowstorms
Kalei - The beautiful woman that Kamohoali'i seduces to have his half-human child
Kamapua'a - Pig God and of the Rainforest
Kamoho'ali'i - The Shark God (Pele, Namaka, and Hi'iaka's older brother)
Kanaloa - God of Magic and the Veil between the Ocean and the Underworld
Kane - God of the Sky
Kanekua'ana - Sleeping Water Lizard Dragon
Kapua - First Healer Through Water & Kualana's sister
Ku - God of War
Kualana - A young male loving chief
Kukala Ohia - Hi'iaka's canoe to guide her home
La'amaomao - Goddess of the Wind
Laka - Goddess of Inspiration
Lehua - A woman devoted to her love, Ohia - transformed into a flower
Lilinoe - Goddess of the delicate mist on Mauna Kea
Lohiau - Prince of Kaua'i
Lono - God of agriculture
Lonopele - The chief of Kahiki (Tahiti), brother to Pa'ao
Maui - Demi-god of Pure Will
Namaka'okaha'i (Namaka) - Goddess of the Ocean Waters
Nanaue - The demi-god child of Kamoho'ali'i
Ohia - A man devoted to his love, Lehua - transformed into a tree
Pa'ao - Fisherman (the first Kahuna)
Paka'a - La'amaomao's Son, the Steward of the Ipu
Papa - Earth Mother
Pele - Goddess of the Volcano and Fire
Pili & Nolo - Lizard Dragons of Maui
Poliahu - Snow Goddess
The Menehune - The little people of Hawai'i
The Mo'o - Giant Water Sex Lizard
Waiau - Goddess of cold waters
Wakea - Sky Father

First

A Witch and a Priest

Characters
Me
Namaka'okaha'i - Goddess of the ocean
Father Mark - Methodist priest, a friend of mine
Pele - The volcano goddess
Kamapua'a - The pig god of rainforests
Mauna - mountain
Kanaloa - God of Magic and the Veil between the Ocean and the Underworld

    I was raised in Hawai'i and with Hawaiian culture for a big chunk of my life. I clarify this because there is a fundamental difference between living in a place, like most people who are not born Hawaiian, and being part of the culture itself. These are vastly different experiences. Most outsiders admire and slurp up what they can of Hawaii, but those people only taste the Hawaiian ways as a delicious beverage. The beverage of our culture that the foreigner tastes is actually the blood that runs through the bodies of those raised in indigenous cultures. This is my blood.
    Along the way, I learned the Hawaiian stories and bathed in our mysticism as regularly as I could. I believed in Pele and her wrath. I believed in Kamapua'a and his animals. I watched out for the menehune and feared the night marchers. But I had no Hawaiian blood, so why would these unbelievable gods choose me as a priest for them? They wouldn't, and they didn't, so I kept dancing and teaching instead. I thought the door to becoming a priest was closed to me because I didn't hear from the Hawaiian gods, which meant that I could not officially be

a kahuna in my life. I saw signs from Namaka'okaha'i and signs from Pele, but that didn't make me special. Not special enough to represent the gods. I could do the other eight areas, but the part associated with the Hawaiian gods was not open to me.

My parents divorced when I was tiny. My mother married the most amazing man, Pops. He will always be the most important and influential man in my life. Pops had a lot of health issues, mostly with his heart. We went on vacation to Kauai with the cousins when I was about eight years old, and then to Maui. My family decided we were moving. After conducting some research, which included examining the schools and their cultures, I realized this was not the best fit for me.

My sister was much darker than I was and could have been accepted as a local person, but I was pale and had light hair and green eyes. There was rightful discrimination against white presenting people because of the atrocities that had taken place in Hawaiian history by the United States, which illegally seized Hawaii as a state, and because of the land lost to wealthy interests. Also, the Hawaiian language was illegal for some time, and hula was considered vulgar until the 1950s and 1960s, when mainland America made money off of a bastardized version of the sacred movement and spirituality.

The school system in Hawai'i was terrible, rated 50th in the country, with only a 50% graduation rate in many areas. My parents decided that we would live in Northern Nevada and that I would go to public school, which was rated as one of the top schools in the nation at the time. When we were not in school, we would go "home" to Maui.

There was another person at my high school in a similar situation. I think his name was Kimo. I don't remember which island he went home to, but we both spoke Standard American English on the mainland and switched back to Pidgin English when we were back home.

We got a condo in South Kihei/Wailea and shared it with Pop's twin brother, Uncle Don. Uncle Don stayed there during the school year, or at least visited and enjoyed the condo, and we went back home to Maui at Christmas, Easter, every break, and during the summers. If there was a long period of time, we could go home; we did.

My mother decorated the Nevada house with Hawaiian things, and we had Hawaiian music playing all the time. I was immersed in the Hawaiian culture, be it in Nevada or Hawai'i. When I started dancing at 13, my life drastically changed. I started working professionally as a dancer at 16, which meant I had no life outside of school studies and dancing.

Most kids in middle and high school enjoy the world around them. They become one with the state they live in and identify with that precisely. I missed out on that. The only thing I identified as a Nevadan was the Friday night football games, where I would support my friends on the football team. I was an out gay kid in high school, and half of the football team were people who accepted me and took care of me and my safety. Otherwise, my home state was inside the dance studio (which could have been located anywhere in the world, staring at the walls, mirrors, and other dancers) and Hawai'i Nei.

I might as well be in Hawai'i when I was in Nevada because I was either in school or in the studio. You can take that and plop it in any location and make minimal changes, but the music, culture, and life within me were Hawaiian. Thanks, Mom and Pops, for that gift.

When we went home, we were hanai into a family in Keanae. The Pahukoa family. Hanai means someone adopts you as family. Pops and Uncle Jimmy were like brothers. Auntie Phyllis and my mother were pretty close. But it was my new cousins that made life amazing. When we were back on Maui, we spent time with the Pahukoas in Keanae, and many of my memories that aren't in a dance studio were there on the peninsula or at their plantation.

> My being was Hawaiian, even if my blood wasn't. Like a wolf raised by cats, I was a cat, but aware that I looked like a wolf, I smelled like a wolf, and I would always be a wolf.

As much as my culture and my faith are wrapped up and tangled in the old Hawaiian ways, I still do not call myself Hawaiian. Hawaiian is a race that is slowly dying off. However, no Hawaiian can tell me that this isn't my culture, my home, or my essence. My spirit was as Hawaiian as anyone because I prayed to Pele and Kamapua'a. I listened for the souls of the water. I looked for menehune. And above all, I respected (and still do) the mana in all things. I cry at the Mauna and fear the Kai, in awe of the ocean's beauty, strength, and grace. I'm a local boy, and my spirit belongs to the aina.

In fact, many of my local friends turn to me to talk to the spirits of the aina (land), as they recognize that who I am, my connection to our home, and my spirit are not of my making. If we all had our eyes closed and felt each other's souls, I was kanaka maoli. My skin color and sea-weed-green eyes were not of my making, but my spirit was cultivated by allegiance, diligence, and aloha.

My essence was built on the foundations of connection, authenticity, humility, and industry. My work ethic was strong and honest, and I loved connection. It's why I loved faith and the gods, and although I didn't hear from the Hawaiian ones, eventually I was given the blessing of hearing from others. I still received signs that the Hawaiian gods accepted me as ohana; I just needed to mind my place and be a healer and whisperer to the spirits.

This then takes us to this story.

Father Mark came to me for help. It was a Tuesday evening. We sat on his deck under a beautiful awning. He brought me a glass of red wine and one for himself. Father Mark was dressed in khaki shorts with a light green polo, barefoot, perfect for this June day.

Father Mark had lost a relative and reached out to me to help him contact his loved one. That kind of mediumship was always difficult for me, but for him, I did it. I'm not naturally a death medium, so I need tools to help me connect to the departed.

I believe that priests, healers, teachers, and artists help remind us of our humanity. They are the real people who prevent war and strife. Helping Father Mark through his grief so that he could be valuable to his flock was important to me. I didn't like the work of talking to the human dead because it tired me out quickly. After I had talked to his late relative, we kicked back and enjoyed the sunset.

"I'm surprised you would come to a witchdoctor, Father. Doesn't your book... like Deuteronomy, say you should hunt us down and kill us?" I asked, peering over my glass of wine. I adjusted in my seat. I had overdressed, which was the usual for me, but that didn't make him uncomfortable. I wore a dark purple loose-woven sweater. In case we were inside, I'd be warm, but if we were outside, I'd have the circulation. I wore long slacks with my 2" Cuban-heeled Mary Poppins style shoes. I was sticking to the seat cushion, so I took it out from under me and repositioned it as a back pillow.

"Yeah, but that's Old Testament," he excused. I giggled.

"I'm glad we are doing this over a wine date," I said. "I've never been on a date with a priest before," I teased. Father Mark didn't have a problem with me being gay or married to a man. It was nice building a relationship with a straight man who also loved faith. I held up my glass to clink his, "From one follower of gods to another." He didn't move. He just stared into his glass. I looked over his glass to see if I could look into his eyes, "Did I say something wrong?"

He stared down into the red of his drink and didn't speak for a while. "I think..." he started and stopped, his voice choking.

"Take your time, dear," I said. I put my glass down on the side table between us. I put my hand on his shoulder and tilted my head to try to look into his eyes. "You don't have to hurry. I'm here to help." A lovely cool breeze went through his deck ceiling fan. I welcomed the air. The sun was about to set, changing the mood from refreshing to ominous. Dusk does that. It's a time of transition.

"Do you believe in god, Aly?" He asked me.

"Do you mean your God?" I asked for clarification. "Yes, but I don't work with Him. Like the Hawaiian gods, I believe in them, but don't have access. From what I understand, the Christian God is more of an observer, right?"

Father Mark pondered this. "What do you mean?" He asked.

"Well, your priests..." I stopped myself. "Ok, I may say something, from my limited knowledge and observation, that might be offensive, Father. I don't mean to be disrespectful in my observation. May I say what I've observed?" I asked.

"Of course, you can," Father Mark's tone changed to a behind-the-confession-voice.

"Ok," I said. I picked my glass back up, took a sip of wine, and placed it back down on the table between us. "Your priests tell parishioners that if they reach out to your God that He'll answer. But I don't believe that's how your book actually reads. I think your book talks about incredible lessons and stories, but the only time your God shows up is when there is something major. He doesn't actually answer everyone's prayers, and he stays back, just watching. So why do the priests tell the parish one thing, but your actual holy book assumes another? I think it kind of sets people up for..."

"I've lost my faith, Aly," he said suddenly, cutting me off.

I stopped. I realized I had gotten on my teaching soapbox and needed to redirect to a person in need.

I studied him, allowing the silence to fill the air. He felt like shame to me. When I psychically read people, even against my will, when I'm connected to them, listening, and caring, I feel in my physical body what they feel. Through my skin and my blood, I sank in his shame. As he looked down at the rim of his wine glass, I furrowed my eyebrows, studying what I felt was his. Shame. In my own skin, I felt that his skin felt wet and clammy under his arms. He felt cold, but the kind of cold that is just on the edge of discomfort. His chest felt heavy right behind his sternum, like a giant potato pressing down on his stomach. I felt a tingle in my/his legs, running through those nerves. This was what shame feels like. I then noticed tears that quietly pulled at his cheek.

"Why do you feel shame?" I asked.

"Don't do that!" He chided. "Don't jump right in and do that thing that you do."

"I'm sorry," I said sincerely. I paused, again, and tried a different approach to helping Father Mark. "Do you want to tell me how you lost your faith, father?"

"Just call me Mark. With you, just Mark. I might as well be honest somewhere." He took a deep breath and wiped away his tears. He put his glass down on the table next to mine and crossed his legs. He looked up at the awning. "When Melony died, I asked God why. I have counseled so many people who have lost loved ones, and my answer was that they were with God or no longer in pain, or that loss is part of a greater plan. Something I've always been told to say. But I haven't ever heard God. I've never felt his voice, his knowledge, his reasoning. I'm lying to people, Aly. I'm a fake. A phony. I don't know what I'm doing. I've just had faith, but then Melony died, and…" He trailed off for a moment to gather himself. "I don't know. So, I asked God. I waited for hours in the chapel. I just waited. I did this for weeks, and nothing. I stared up at Jesus, and I felt nothing… I miss her so much. Why won't God comfort me? Why won't he tell me he's here? Priests are supposed to speak directly to God for the flock. He has never spoken to me. Never in seminary. Never in service. And he won't know …even when I question my faith in him."

"Can I ask," I said carefully, "why are you coming to me? I'm sure that other priests could help you, maybe even better than I can? They may be more equipped than I am. I'm happy to help in any way I can, but why not turn to others who do speak to your God?"

"Judgement, Aly." He said. He uncrossed his legs and leaned forward onto his thighs, resting his forearms on his legs and cradling his face.

"From fellow priests?" I asked.

"Yes. There are a lot of aires, as you say. I don't know if any of them talk to God either. I don't know if they are playing some holy pyramid scheme, but I do love my faith, at least I did. And I love my parish, and I love the Bible. But how can I speak *for* God if he doesn't speak *to* me? How can I promote a God who won't tell me why he takes my only family away?" Father Mark sobbed.

All I could say was, "Oof."

He cried softly for about fifteen seconds. Took a deep, labored breath, adjusted his shoulders, and controlled the natural way his body wanted to grieve by stuffing it into a cage covered by the Priest's collar.

"The other priests may want my place or could use this, a weakness, to get ahead or hurt me. There are conniving people hiding everywhere, Aly. I'm fifty years old. Some of these young priests are opportunistic and waiting for an opportunity. I can't go to them for help when many are wolves after my flock. And I didn't know where to turn." He said. "I can't believe I've gone to a..." he trailed off. He was looking off, into the walls of his house.

"Witch," I said.

"Yeah. I'm sorry."

"It's ok, Fathe... er... Mark... just Mark." I was so awkward. "So, how can I help? What do you want me to do?" I asked.

"Connect me to God," he looked down at the floor and then into my eyes.

"Um, what?" I said.

"I know you talk to Gods; I've seen you do it. I've read about people like you. Oracles, they used to be called. Medicine men, or whatever. Talk to God and ask him why he won't talk to me or connect me to God or..." his voice hitched, and he started to sob. He was desperate. He put his face into his hands. I stood up and walked over to this broken man and kneeled before him. I wrapped my arms around his torso and hugged him tight while he cried.

Holding him, I could feel his aka reaching, desperately searching. Tendrils of his unique, beautiful soul stretching for communication of the divine and coming up short. His soul felt anguished, thousands of tiny pieces reaching and finding nothing. His spirit wrapped around mine, finding some peace in my genuine comfort. He was meant to talk to God. His spirit showed me that, constantly searching for the connection.

"Mark, I will try," I said. He held his breath and looked at me. "I don't know your God, and I don't think he will answer me. I don't think that would be the best approach, but I can try to repair you, ok? Try to repair your own connection?"

"I was never connected to him," Mark said.

"I don't believe that. I just think the way he talks to you is different. Right now, I just need to mend you, then we will find the way He speaks to you, ok?" I said confidently.

"Ok, what do I need to do?" He asked.

I instructed, "Scoot forward. I'm going to sit behind you." He moved to the edge of the chair and sat up, wiping his face.

"You do talk to gods, don't you?" He pressed.

I smiled. "Um, yes, but it isn't something I lead with on dates," I joked. He breathed more regularly. He planted his feet evenly on the floor. I put my foot behind him on the seat and stood on the chair over him. I then sat on the back of his chair, my knees behind his back. "Is this going to hold both of us?" I asked.

"Yeah, I'm more worried about what the neighbors will think," he laughed. He looked around past his covered porch, more concerned with how my work would turn out than with any gossip that might spread.

"They will think that you have lost your connection to your faith. You brought over a witch, liquored him up, and forced him to make love to your spirit." I said.

"You're going to do what?" He said.

"I'm just kidding," I said. I took a deep breath. Once I felt my own spirit steady, I put my right arm around his chest, landing my right hand on his heartbeat. I put my left hand on his head, in his hair, just above his ear. I held him there.

"Should I close my eyes?" He asked.

"It doesn't matter. Just sit still for me." I felt his aka, the lost ones, move toward me. I kept my constitution as welcoming as possible so his spirit would stay calm for the healing. His energy looked weak, depleted. The cords that reached from his aumakua and his unihipili were shredded, damaged. I let go of his heart and head. I pulled his broken aka together and began to sew and stitch, as the spirits had taught me as a child (which is amazingly anecdoted by other kahuna in writings). I pulled his frayed spirit and mended, taking parts of mine and sewing them into the frayed parts of his...

"Aly, I feel warm," he said.

"Hush, Mark, I'm almost done." With my eyes closed, I pulled and stitched the pieces of his soul, but I honestly didn't know if it would work. I braided his broken pieces together, the ones that weren't connected to anything, the cords frayed from fear, shame, trauma, disappointment, self-loathing. I made a long tunnel, reaching upwards, towards where the Christian God was supposed to be. I funneled my hands toward the sky. With my breath, I blew up into the clouds nine times. Pushing his energy upwards, hoping like a lasso that his reach would snag a Christian God. Now, I needed help, divine intervention. This priest was healed, but still without connection.

I put my right arm back around him into a hug, holding his heartbeat, and my left arm back into his head. *Kanaloa*, I prayed in my head, *please take his cords and connect him to his God. If you hear my prayer, this will help many people. Thank you for your connections, laughs, lessons, and paths. If you deem him unworthy or that this is part of his path, I humbly recognize this as your choice. I now give this over to you. Thank you, Amene.*

Just then, we caught the scent of the ocean air in the suburban inlands of Maryland.

"You're done," I said, and I let go of him. I stood up on the chair. "Now, let's see what happens," I jumped off his chair and took him by the wrist. He stood up and followed me into his house. My instinct, my knowing, told me what to do, and I just listened. I obeyed the knowing, the cunning, that the gods gave me to do.

I walked past his desk, past the dining room, and to a bookshelf in his living room. I let go of him and searched for... the Bible. I took it out and held it in my hand. "Ha!" I said.

"What?" He stood behind me and watched, mystified.

"No flames." I laughed hard. "Nah, nah, just kidding, ok, follow me." I took him by the wrist, again, pulling him down his hallway, so he wouldn't have a choice. I walked him into his bedroom.

"Aly? What are we doing?"

"Just trust me, Mark." He let go and turned on the light switch.

"No, keep it off," I said. Nighttime was coming. He stared at me, hovering his hand over the light switch.

"Are you..."

"Seducing you?" I smiled greatly and laughed so hard. "No, but that would go with the stereotype and stories your people say about us witches. Harlots! No, but if you tell anyone about my seductions, can you make me sound amazing? Haha!" I sounded crazed, but I felt so strong about what to do. He was connected. I could feel it. I saw his spirit was no longer searching. It was calm and at rest. A beautiful, soft pale blue aura radiated off his worried mind; he just needed to listen. "Just turn off the light and come over to me. We need to see if your God will answer." Father Mark turned off the light and walked over to the bed. "Sit on the floor, with your back to the nightstand."

"Ok," he did.

"Hug your knees," I said and took a step back. He did. "What if," I began, "what if what I had done to you was to speed up your life? You will die within minutes." I paused. Unmoving, I stared at him. He looked up at me, stunned. I used a cold, authoritative tone, void of empathy. This apathetic tone was what I used when putting a spell out into the world over the ingredients. "If this is the end, you in the dark, on the floor, hugging your knees, and I standing over you, a witch, holding *your* Bible... This is the end of Mark." Void of care, I continued my orders, "Close your eyes, Mark. Close your eyes and listen. What happens?"

Mark closed his eyes, confused and thrown by what was happening. He opened his eyes and said, "Wait, did you curse me?"

"Close your eyes!" I bit, "and listen, or you will die. You will die here and now, and I will walk out of your home. Someone will find your dead body, cold and alone, in the dark of your room. Close your eyes." He stared at me, not knowing if what I was saying was the truth or hypothetical. I knew this was unkind, but I couldn't show my hand to him. I needed this to work. I felt his fear rise. Now we are ready. "Good, you're beginning to feel afraid. Now. Close. Your. Eyes." He did.

He was still for about thirty seconds, his spirit reaching up to the sky. I took a step forward and handed him his Bible. He took it from me and kept it in his hand. His eyes stayed closed. A few moments later, Mark hugged it. He breathed in with a gasp and looked down at his book. He opened it up and read out loud: "Be strong and courageous; do not be frightened or dismayed, for the Lord your God is with you wherever you go."

He dropped his legs to his side as he read in the darkness of his room.

"Aly..." he said.

"Yes?" I waited, tears filled my eyes. He glowed. His faith was repaired. He felt fresh like spring, and his heart sang with joy. I don't know what was happening to him, but it looked like someone's prayer might have been answered. "You have to be a kind of psychic to hear directly from spirits. You can be deaf and blind and still be the perfect representative for your god. You just need a kind of... Braille."

His eyes welled.

"I am a messenger of his word, and his word is here, in front of me, the whole time. God will speak to me through his words." He stood up and hugged me hard.

"I feel him, Aly. I feel God."

"I know," I hugged him back.

He towered over me at 6'2". With my heels on, I stood at a reasonable 5'7". He hugged me harder than anyone had ever hugged me before. "Thank you," he whispered. Tears choked my voice.

"You're welcome, Father." I could feel him smile into my shoulder.

"How can I ever repay you?" He asked.

"First, let go. You might break one of my ribs." He did, laughed, and held me in front of him. He held my arms and kept me there.

"How much money can I give you? For your service? You charge, don't you? I need to pay you or whatever you want..." He asked.

"For others, yes, I would charge for my services, but I think there is something bigger here than you and I will ever understand. Why would the follower of the old ways be allowed to mend a follower of the new? Just help more people find faith: real faith, Father. Not like your co-workers. Like you. Help people who are also in the darkness. And can you also help break down the hatred toward those who are not like them, break down the hate towards people like me? If a witch and a priest can be friends and help each other, then anything is possible."

"Amen," he said.

On my way out, I said, "Mark, your church's exorcisms are barbaric. If you need help, please reach out to me, even if the church is not aware."

"Alright, Aly, and for the record, some of your spells are barbaric. We can accomplish some of the same things with prayer."

"Fair. That's fair. Let's finish that wine sometime, Father?"

He corrected: "Mark, to you, Aly."

Father Mark wasn't the only priest who had come to knock on my witchdoctor door. They know I'm not going to judge. I'm just going to heal, and so should you. Finding faith is essential to our spiritual health. We have been spiritual creatures since the beginning of time. We need to believe in something greater than ourselves, giving over to the fact that we will never truly be in control of our lives in this chaotic reality: God, the gods, science, the spirits, the flow of life in all things, anything. Have faith because faith gives us solace, comfort, and direction in a directionless, lonely world. Without faith, we leave ourselves open to so much pain and possible spiritual hostility.

Faith is the number one way to refill your mana, cleanse your soul, and repair your aka. Imagine a warrior never getting medical attention, just hoping he will heal independently. Maybe he will, and perhaps he will get scars. Or perhaps our hypothetical warrior will get an infection? Or will he sit in a static state of injury because he never gets a chance to heal fully? Faith heals. Father Mark was frayed, like that wounded spiritual warrior, honestly trying to help people and carry their burdens. You, too, are a warrior in this terribly hostile world. Faith will heal you.

Shaman, Witchdoctor, or Kahuna: Recognizing the Call

With the death of many of the Hawaiian ways, this book is an integration of those ways with the Neolithic techniques and philosophies of other cultures. Here, because of the loss and assimilation of the Hawaiian ways, you'll learn an integrated process to healing, rooted in the animistic ways of witchdoctors everywhere, with a focus on Hawaiian. We are continuously surprised by how similar the shamanic traditions are, with interconnected realities, the parts of the spirit, the acknowledgment of entities and the supernatural, and the mindfulness that health is the integration of smooth life and spirituality.

Remember that it was illegal to "be Hawaiian" in any authentic way; therefore, the indigenous peoples of the Hawaiian Islands were forced into assimilation, relinquishing their ethnic and cultural identities to become more mainstream. Naturally, with how rich the Hawaiian culture stands, many of those ways bled into the colonized culture as well. For instance, the word taboo made its way from the Hawaiian Islands. Its origin is the word *kapu*, which means "a hidden set of rules in order to avoid misgivings."

The term "witch-doctor" originated in 19th-century England, and its usage continued. A witchdoctor is a practitioner who combines elements of shamanism, healing, spirituality, and mysticism in their practice. While the term "witchdoctor" is not specific to any one culture, it is often associated with indigenous or traditional healing practices.

A witchdoctor is part of the shamanic community. A witchdoctor isn't only someone with bones through their nose, wearing animal skin. A Voodoo priest calling on the power of their ancestors or the gede to help in healing is also a witchdoctor. The rootworker who gives you advice on the plants that you should put in your garden to keep evil away is also part of the witchdoctor family.

When the white man came to Hawai'i to discover the beliefs, rituals, and "savageness," they ascribed the term for all of the different healers as "witchdoctors," our experts, the Kahuna. It was a derogatory term, one I hope to reclaim and celebrate, bringing all the different faith healers under one beautiful umbrella term.

Witchdoctors are skilled in various areas, including shapeshifting or storytelling, healing, psychic mediumship, acting as a mediator between spirits and communities, and guiding individuals through life transitions. They may utilize a combination of spiritual rituals, herbal remedies, energy work, and intuitive abilities to facilitate healing and spiritual growth. It is important to note that witchdoctors are not necessarily Wiccans or practitioners of witchcraft, and the term primarily denotes their role as healers and spiritual guides. Similarly, the concept of the rootworker emerged from the spiritual practices of Fon faith healers who were forced into slavery in the Southern United States. Witchdoctors are shamans, simply put, and we can affectionately say that Kahuna are as well.

A shaman is a term used to describe a spiritual practitioner who acts as an intermediary between the physical and spiritual realms, providing healing, guidance, and protection within their community. The concept of shamanism dates back to ancient times and is found in every indigenous culture across the world. To understand the role and significance of a shaman, let's explore the historical context and the diverse practices associated with this ancient tradition.

Shamanism can be traced back to Neolithic faith systems, representing one of the oldest known spiritual practices. The term "shaman" itself originated from the Tungus people of Siberia, who used it to describe their spiritual leaders and healers. However, similar practices and concepts can be found in indigenous cultures ranging from the Americas to Africa, Asia, and Australia.

In many indigenous societies, the shaman is known as a medicine man or woman. These individuals possess deep knowledge of herbal medicine, rituals, and spiritual teachings. They have the ability to enter altered states of consciousness, often through the use of drumming, chanting, dancing, or ingesting sacred plants. These altered states allow the shaman to communicate with spirits, seek guidance, and access hidden realms beyond the ordinary human experience.

Shamans function as intermediaries between the physical and spiritual worlds, bridging the gap and maintaining balance within their communities. They are believed to have the ability to journey to other realms, retrieve lost souls, and communicate with nature spirits, ancestors, and deities. Through their connections with the spiritual realm, shamans acquire knowledge, power, and healing abilities to address physical, emotional, and spiritual ailments.

The role of a shaman varies among different cultures and regions. In some societies, the shaman may primarily focus on healing practices, using spiritual energies and rituals to alleviate illnesses and restore harmony. This involves diagnosing ailments, performing ceremonies, and providing herbal remedies or energy work to rebalance the individual. Shamans are often sought after for their ability to heal physical and psychological illnesses that conventional medicine may not fully address.

In addition to their healing roles, shamans also serve as spiritual guides and advisors within their communities. They are consulted for divination, wisdom, and guidance in making important decisions or resolving conflicts. Shamans may perform rituals, ceremonies, or rites of passage to mark significant life events, such as birth, marriage, or death.

They also play a vital role in communing with the natural environment, ensuring the well-being of both the community and the land.

It is crucial to note that shamanism is deeply rooted in animistic beliefs, which recognize the spiritual essence in all things. This spiritual worldview acknowledges the interconnectedness of all beings and the importance of maintaining harmony with nature and the spirit world. Shamans hold the responsibility of maintaining this balance, acting as stewards of the natural world and transmitting ancestral wisdom to future generations.

One type of shamanic practitioner (or modern word, "witchdoctor") is Kahuna. The term "kahuna" originates from Hawaiian culture and refers to an expert, practitioner, or master of a specific field of hidden knowledge or expertise. These individuals were highly respected within their communities and played significant roles in various aspects of Hawaiian life.

In ancient Hawaiian society, kahuna were revered for their specialized knowledge and skills in fields such as healing, spirituality, navigation, agriculture, and warriorship. They held a crucial role in preserving and passing down the traditions, customs, and wisdom of the Hawaiian people. The knowledge possessed by kahuna was considered sacred, and their expertise in these intricate areas of life was held in high regard.

One of the most well-known types of kahuna was the "kahuna la'au lapa'au," the healer or herbalist. These kahuna specialized in traditional medicine, using a range of plant-based remedies and spiritual practices to help restore balance and promote healing in individuals. Kahuna la'au lapa'au possessed extensive knowledge of herbs, plants, and their medicinal properties, as well as the spiritual aspects of healing.

Another important category of kahuna was the "kahuna kalai wa'a," the canoe builder and navigator. These experts were responsible for constructing canoes and possessing the navigational skills necessary for long-distance voyaging. Kahuna kalai wa'a had a deep understanding of the natural elements, celestial navigation, and the art of building seaworthy vessels. Their expertise was crucial for the exploration and settlement of new lands, as well as maintaining connections between different Hawaiian islands.

Kahuna also played a vital role in spiritual practices and ceremonies. The "kahuna pule" were the religious leaders and priests who conducted rituals, offered prayers, and invoked blessings. Their knowledge of spiritual traditions and connection with the divine allowed them to guide and facilitate communal spiritual experiences. Kahuna pule were seen as intermediaries between the human and spiritual realms, ensuring harmony and balance within the community.

In addition to their specific areas of expertise, kahuna were often recognized for their overall wisdom and ability to provide guidance in various aspects of life. They were sought after for counsel, problem-solving, and decision-making, as their depth of knowledge and experience made them trusted advisors within their communities.

The term "kahuna" itself carries profound meaning as it represents an individual who possesses hidden knowledge and expertise. This hidden knowledge is built upon a deep connection to ancestral wisdom, spiritual practices, and lived experience, not acquired through academic study. The role of a kahuna was not taken lightly and often involved extensive training, initiation rituals, and adherence to strict codes of conduct.

Although the traditional role of kahuna has evolved over time, and some aspects of their practices have been lost, their legacy continues to be recognized and respected in Hawaiian culture. The concept of a kahuna as an expert in hidden knowledge remains an essential aspect of the cultural heritage and represents the rich tapestry of Hawaiian wisdom and spirituality.

Kahuna were esteemed practitioners who possessed specialized knowledge and expertise in various fields. Their status as experts of hidden knowledge was derived from their dedication, training, and connection to ancestral wisdom. They played significant roles in healing, navigation, spirituality, and other aspects of Hawaiian life. The term "kahuna" carries profound meaning, representing the wisdom and expertise held by these revered individuals in Hawaiian culture.

Understand that being part of an indigenous culture goes beyond simply living in a place. It requires a deep understanding and connection to the cultural practices and traditions that are ingrained in one's blood. I was fortunate to be raised in Hawai'i and exposed to Hawaiian culture, which has informed my practice, but I also draw from my African heritage and European influences, while living and thriving in the mainland United States of America.

This book serves as a foundation, blending ancient shamanic wisdom with contemporary tools and skills. By practicing in this manner, you become part of the Black, Indigenous, People of Color (BIPOC) community in spirituality, preserving the sanctity of indigenous traditions while dismantling colonial influences that have eroded cultural authenticity. Why am I blending aspects and practices with the Ancient Ways of Hawai'i? Easy, colonizers villainized, deleted, and eradicated many of these ways. They are gone. Some are reconstructed with the work of authors in the late 1800s, and even today, some are still putting pieces together from hula and folklore. However, some things are gone forever, so we can look to the healing modalities of other Polynesian, eastern Asian, and Micronesian philosophies.

I invite you to join us in this important work, preserving and transmitting the sacred knowledge of our ancestors. Together, we can ensure that the practice of witchdoctors remains true to its origins and inclusive of all legitimate practitioners who embody all nine essential areas of expertise, even if some of them are transplants from neighbors.

Originally, Hawaiian society had many Kahuna, who individually had expertise in one specific area. As time continued through colonization, the Kahuna had to adopt several roles with the eradication of the culture. To truly embody the roles of the kahuna, you must possess a specific set of skills and abilities, including:

1. *Shapeshifting or storytelling*: The ability to transform or weave narratives that convey wisdom and understanding.

2. *Healing*: Utilizing various methods to facilitate physical, emotional, and spiritual wellness.

3. *Psychic mediumship*: Connecting with spirits and navigating out-of-body experiences.

4. *Peacemaker or priest*: Intermediary between spirits and communities.

5. *Guide*: Help individuals through transitions and stages of life.

These skills are essential for kahuna, who take on the role of healers and teachers. However, there is a scarcity of practitioners who possess these abilities in their entirety. Oftentimes, individuals may excel in one or two areas while lacking proficiency in others.

You may wonder why, despite my deep connection to Hawaiian traditions, I call myself a witchdoctor instead of a kahuna. While the kahuna is indeed an avatar of witchdoctor, practicing all nine areas specific to the Hawaiian culture is a prerequisite for using that title. I don't only use Hawaiian. I am mixed in my practice. My healing methods are primarily Hawaiian, which is why we get a book on this specifically. But my witchcraft draws from Hoodoo and Italy. My spirit travel work from Italy. My faith practice from the Druids. I was raised with many different areas of practice, and those cultures all inform me in different ways. Because I don't work only in Hawaiian with the nine areas of practice (although I must say that my storytelling and teaching practice are also Hawaiian-influenced).

I am mindful of cultural appropriation and ensure that I practice with respect and within the context of my own indigenous heritage. Because a kahuna, in today's standards, needs to be able to accomplish all nine areas in Hawaiian tradition in order to call themselves a kahuna, I cannot.

However, if we were back 1,000 years ago, I would have had the title for my individual expertise.

A Kahuna Has These Qualities

Loss of sense of self: Sacred sites have an intoxicating ability to absorb us completely. We are drawn into these places, desiring to merge and become one with them, to dissolve and disappear into their essence. Alternatively, we long to carry the intoxicating feeling or ecstasy they evoke within us, cherishing it throughout our lives as a cherished memory.

Mental calm: Typically, our busy and restless minds slow down, and our inner chatter subsides. We no longer fret over things, and our logical thinking takes a backseat, allowing our intuitive and creative side to take the lead. We begin to perceive colors, shapes, relationships, and overall patterns in a heightened manner.

Transcendence and immanence: Power spots can evoke a paradoxical sensation of simultaneous transcendence and immanence. We feel transported beyond the present moment and location, connected to the vast universe surrounding us. At the same time, we also experience the concentrated power of that universe condensed right where we stand. Time and space lose their hold on us as we become intoxicated by the sacred, perceiving the vastness of creation while also sensing the Creator's presence in the smallest of details.

Interspecies communication: It is not uncommon to find ourselves able to communicate with other species in a power spot. We can understand the messages conveyed by the wind rustling through the trees, the rhythmic sound of water flowing over stones, and even the melodies sung by birds. We have a profound understanding of their communication directed towards us or about us.

Physical transparency: In certain parts of the landscape, or even within hidden corners of it, there may be a sense of transparency, where we perceive it as more pure and diaphanous. It's as if a veil has been lifted, allowing us to see the invisible worlds of color and form beyond. We feel the cosmic energy or divine power of the universe flowing through trees and rocks, with a celestial light illuminating everything, seemingly emanating from within.

Feelings of unity: Another sign of being in a sacred location is the overwhelming sensation of being connected to something greater than ourselves. We experience a sense of awe, joy, or a deep sense of rightness, where everything seems to be in perfect harmony and alignment. It's as if we feel that everything is right in the world.

If this is all that was needed, I'd adopt the full title of Kahuna. But since we are only looking through the lens of healing, I offer you specifically the Kahuna Healer.

Recognizing the Call to Kahuna Healing

A common sign of being called to healing work is repeated health obstacles. With personal pain, we are reminded of the urgency to help others get out of theirs, creating a continuous supply of empathy, and the guidance to help the client with strength, grit, and fortitude to overcome the difficult and painful coat of what healing actually means. And with so much suffering in pain, losses, illnesses, heartbreak, and the numerous other forms of suffering, we wonder why compassion for others is so uncommon. The witchdoctor cannot lose this compassion for the pain of others.

If you feel a deep and powerful attraction towards shamanism, it is possible that you are being called to this path. Here are some signs that may indicate this calling:

- You frequently have mysterious and inexplicable experiences

- You have undergone a profound near-death encounter

- You have embarked on many out-of-body journeys

- People often seek your guidance and advice

- Others find it effortless to trust and confide in you

- You find solace and renewal in the embrace of nature

- You possess empathic abilities, easily sensing and understanding others' emotions

- You have a heightened intuition, perceiving thoughts and ideas beyond the surface

- You possess vivid memories of past lives as a shaman, seer, or healer

- You excel in problem-solving using your intuition

- Your creativity flows abundantly

- You have the ability to control and direct your dreams

- You are capable of perceiving spiritual energies

- You can communicate with animals and understand their messages

These are just a few signs that suggest a calling towards shamanism. The fact that you are reading this book is already evidence of it. The transition into being a shaman is accompanied by death or near-death, or extreme fear. From then on, you will develop your spirit support system and spirit family. As you learn to travel out of your physical body, the dream-state (journeying/spirit walking/ecstasy) will be a means of communication with these spirits.

Types of Kahuna

Remember that a kahuna simply means someone who is an expert in hidden knowledge. As time shifted from expert to someone who was an expert in hidden spiritual knowledge, the kahuna was separated into many different specialities. Much like an exorcist, having specific, unique individual skills for which that one person prefers to extract spirits, a kahuna can be any of these experts:

Kahuna kaula - Prophet

Kahuna wehe wehe - Dream interpreter

Kahuna kilo kilo - Reader of skies and omens

Kahuna 'ana 'ana - Users of death magic and sorcery (also called: ho'okalakupua, poko'i, mo'okiko)

Kahuna kuehu - One who drives off evil spirits (exorcist)

Kahuna ninau 'uhane - One who speaks to spirits (cryptozoologist)

Kahuna papalua - psychic

Kahuna 'ea - One who could raise the dead (necromancy)

Kahuna la'au lapa'au - Herb doctor (talks to plants)

Kahuna la'au kahea - Faith healing

Kahuna haku mele ula - Makers of chants and music

Kahuna wanana ikeau'okamanawa - Reader of weather signs

Kahuna kukei' wana'ao - Expert storyteller

Kahuna hui - Leads functions and ceremonies for royalty or the elite.Kahuna koho (noho) - Recurring temporary spiritual possession, usually by a higher power, without willful control of the medium.

Can you be more than one? Yes. Just remember that you would probably only address yourself as a kahuna, and others would describe you based on what you can do. You offer the service, but you don't brag about yourself. You just supply.

Rough Encouragement

"There's something I haven't told you," said the horse.
"What's that?" said the boy.
"I can fly, but I stopped because it made other horses jealous."
"Well, we love you whether you can fly or not."
<u>The Boy, the mole, the fox, and the horse</u> by Charlie Mackesy

My friend Lia was Hawaiian. She knew peripherally of the old ways, and she was one of the few people who knew about my sensitivities. By that time, I had my interaction with "The Monster," and was fully practicing secretly as a witchdoctor. She told me that the land had chosen me to fulfill the old ways. That I was meant to fulfill certain spiritual Hawaiian duties because of my curses and my gifts. She pushed me hard, which led me to tell her that she needed to focus on herself, on being a real version of herself instead of the spotlight version she presented to everyone else. I was mean. She replied:

> You're a hypocrite, Aly. You tell everyone to follow their true selves, but look at you! You hide! You hide who you are! There aren't people left who can do what you do, and you're shameful! You should be shame for not embracing who you are and for hiding yourself. You push anyone away who gets too close and sees you. Well, it's a shame.

Lia was right. I pushed her away because she saw who I was, and it scared me. We stopped speaking after that email. Only recently did I have the opportunity to see her again. She stopped by a friend's house, whom I was visiting back on Maui. It had probably been five or six years since we had seen each other. Honestly, I didn't expect to see Lia ever again. She knocked on the door, and I opened it, surprised that she, of all people, was standing there.

We looked into each other's eyes. Instantly, all was forgiven. She walked in the door and grabbed me tightly. We hugged. We just stood there hugging and crying.

I whispered through the tears, "I'm sorry."

"No, I'm sorry," She said.

"You were right, and I'm so sorry," I said.

Even writing this, my eyes fill with tears. Lia was so brave to tell me how it is. She was my roughest cheerleader for something extremely scary and hard to accept. How do you accept that you are a spirit catcher? A spirit healer? An exorcist? A psychic medium? How? She accepted me and my purpose long before I did. And when I have moments of doubt, I remember Lisa, that it's ok to follow a destiny you yourself might not understand.

I honestly owe her a huge "thank you" for my career. She saw in me the old kahuna ways, the ones that were dying off, and it didn't matter to her what my blood said. She said it wouldn't matter to anyone who was truly Hawaiian. The land chose me, and now I had an obligation to uphold. She was rough with me regarding my purpose. When we sat there that day, I told her I had switched careers and was working in the old ways, teaching and practicing. Lia was so proud of me. I told her that I owed her a huge thank you. That I would never have been doing this completely if it weren't for her.

All of you reading this book who are learning these old ways... it wouldn't be possible, I wouldn't have been brave enough without her. May you also have a Lia who sees your potential and helps you uncover the uncomfortable layers that stand in the way of becoming your truest self.

Part 1

Ho'omanamana and Spirit Travel

The Tribe's New Witchdoctor

Characters:
The Girl
The Kahuna

Children who displayed exceptional talent in a specific craft or profession were nurtured and guided towards it, often leading to them becoming kahuna. This recognition was based on the child's innate mana, or spiritual power. No one was inherently born a kahuna, although there may be signs of aptitude. It was a title that could only be attained through rigorous training and the application of dedicated studies. While some sources suggest a training period of 20 years before "graduation," the duration of training likely varies depending on the specific profession (and we know that there are going to be folks who read this book one time and say "I'm a kahuna, too..." ok, Becky).

In some cases, older individuals also sought out kahuna for their teachings, indicating a lifelong learning process. Before training commenced, the candidate or their family would present gifts to the kahuna teacher. These offerings, such as pigs, fine sleeping mats, and other valuable items, were considered necessary and can be seen as a form of tuition to honor the teacher's knowledge and expertise.

Imagine a tribe, and it can be anywhere in the world. In this tribe, there is a witchdoctor/faith healer/kahuna, someone who oversees the spiritual education of the community, remembers stories, dances, and songs that help teach connection to others, their mortality, ethics, and relatability to human experiences, someone who is connected to the spirit world and gives divine guidance through divination, handles the physical, mental, and spiritual health of the community, and manages supernatural balance. All the other tribe members have their jobs as well. They build boats, or houses, or make cloth, and some fish, or hunt.

In the village, there are the children, and as the children grow, they are observed by the tribe. The tribe recognizes each child's natural aptitude, encouraging these strengths to help them feel fulfilled in life.

In this story, there is a cloth maker and a farmer. This couple has a little girl. This girl looks off into the distance, daydreaming. She wakes with nightmares, and those nightmares have a tendency to come true. She loves to spend time in the garden, gently petting the plants and singing to them.

During a time of harvest and gathering, the local witchdoctor sings and dances a dance about the plants, giving their soul energy to the tribe who consumes them. Everyone celebrates in the harvest, except the little girl. The little girl is sad. She is sad because she feels the pain of the plants as they are pulled from the Earth. While everyone celebrates, the girl keeps her hands in the soil and wishes to pull the love and kindness of the soil into the empty spaces where the harvest used to be. She longs to mend her loneliness and mourns for the spirit's life within the plants. She seems to be talking to herself, but the kahuna could see that she is talking to the spirits of the now-dead harvest.

The next day, the witchdoctor goes to the cloth maker and the farmer and explains that their daughter needs to become the next kahuna healer and begin her transition. They are terrified. They know that if their daughter does not succeed in the shamanic transformation, she will likely die; however, the kahuna is old and has not seen the potential in any of the tribe's children in decades. They agree. It is what is best for everyone.

The kahuna finds the little girl playing by a stream, talking to herself. The kahuna sees that she is singing and talking to the spirits in the water, encouraging them to jump and play with her song. He sits next to her.

Even though she didn't know it, by interacting with the spirits, consoling the plants, and dancing with the sun, her spirit is also preparing for the imminent transition ahead. Her seedling mind and sweet constitution can't comprehend what is ahead of her, but her spirit knows. That's why the kahuna then explains to her the path she has to take. The girl is ten years old, and when she turns thirteen, she will need to undergo her rite of passage, the shamanic transition.

Over the next three years, the girl learns stories, songs, and dances. She learns about the healing properties of herbs, mud, and the weather. She learns how to talk to the spirits and how to get them to follow her. She also learns that her ability to connect to others, to heal them, would not happen unless her soul was inverted, done with death, terror, fear, or torment.

Her thirteenth birthday decides to show its ugly face, but the village celebrates the once ostracized girl, for, with hope, she will be the one to continue to save, love, and care for them all. They know that she will be changed forever, and soon, so they took the time to let her be a normal little girl. Even in her youth, the little girl didn't have many friends, none living anyway, but the community of children is kind and celebrates her, anyway. They are taught that one day they will need her services as a healer, as a guide, and as a storyteller.

The night of the ceremony, the moon hides from witnessing a young child's death. The winds sing the dirge of ominousness, granting permission for the event. As the festivities come to an end, the whole village walks to the edge of the clearing. They face the forest. They look into its darkness. It is time. The little girl has to have her first shamanic death. She says goodbye to her family and takes the witchdoctor by the hand. The two odd spirit-talkers walk into the night, into the jungle.

Stepping over branches and moss, the witchdoctor guides the child to the middle of the jungle, where wild animals hunt and dominate the property. He sits the child down, where she can be viewed plainly by every animal resident. Her heart thuds, and she closes her eyes. She says a prayer to the gods, to the spirits of the jungle, and to her ancestors to watch over her this night. That she may be blessed to live. The winds laugh at her request. Her heart pounds against her little chest so hard that her clothes dance to the wind's song.

The kahuna bends down, hugs her tight, and blindfolds the child. She hears his stillness standing over her. He relieves a final breath, and although he attempts to cloak his own resignation to the possibility of her death with supportive confidence, she hears the subtle doubt escape stealthily from his mouth. That all her training could possibly be for nothing. That she could not be chosen to serve her tribe, and instead will be a helpless sacrifice to the wild. Then, he leaves her.

The little girl has to stay there and survive the night. She hears the horrors of roars, screams, and clawing from the vicious animals of the night. She continues her focus in connection, looking in, looking into her mana. Her fear grows so greatly, she decides she will likely die enduring this unknown. Her heart beats with anxiety for several hours, bestial cacophonous hours.

A tear soaks into her blindfold. She starts to hum. She sings to the animals, the predators, the venomous residents. Her song has no words, a sudden power song that comes from deep behind her sternum but floats velvety through her high and juvenile vocal cords. It's gentle. It's reassuring for both her and the jungle. The hum is a song of a warm, loving embrace, like the notes are the strings in a fabric that blankets us in an embrace, surrounded by the adoring love of your family. Her song is love wrapped in love and made with love.

She trusts and hums. She makes connections with all life as a creature who belongs with the wild, can care for the wild, and be exempt from its treachery; it is time to be accepted in humble vulnerability and trust.

In a moment of loss in focus, from exhaustion for having to be so diligent and only a child, she allows the parasitic thought of the hesitation in the kahuna's last breath, and it distorts her focus, her song. A quiver invades her hum like a crack in the foundation of the fortress of training she presents the spirits, making the offering fragile.

In the new song, she hears a prowl. She feels the life forces in the ground-cover's leaves; each life within each leaf like glowing beacons. One by one, each life extinguishes and breaks and dies under the giant depression of weight from something hooved. She hears a puff escape through the whistle of tusks, low to the ground, and traitorous. She hears it charge, and overcome with fear, she faints.

Upon this fainting spell, something happens to the little girl. She became so deeply terrified by the very real likelihood of being mauled, poisoned, or killed, and with the incredibly fast approach of a jungle's occupier, that her spirit was scared to death. Her lifeless body lies gently on the ground-covering. The little girl is so dainty and small for thirteen, she barely makes an impression in the leaves as they hold her in comfort for failing her test.

The boar walks around the little girl, huffing. She lies down by the girl's body, as if the beast knows a secret no one else has access to and wants to be the first to reveal the forest's magic.

The winsome little girl, lifeless, is not lifeless.

Her spirit, instead of escaping and going to the lower world to greet her ancestors, grows into something very tiny within her body. This small light of her soul doesn't take human form like a ghost. It becomes a tiny firelight and moves to her center. Her soul collects so densely in her chest that any psychic would say that her torso glowed brightly in the moonless sky. The fibers of her soul start to fold, and as they fold, they invert.

The once human-shaped webbed soul of a little girl reaches and claws out as tendrils. Her soul has inverted, and she has transitioned.

In her sleep, the girl leaves her body and looks down at her physical soul's need to reach and connect. She sees the cords of her body like tentacles instead of a net. Her spirit feeds a local plant and is fed by some moss. Delicate, almost invisible tendrils connect her to her parents, her tribe, and the spirits of the streams. She steps back into her body, and, leading with her small hand, sits up, blindfolded, and pets the dangerous female boar.

She continues to pet the boar and begins her song, her hum, a transformed maturity and confidence that lulls the pig to sleep. This giant animal, comforted by her song, huffs a "see?" to the rest of the forest, closes her eyes, and revels in the first gift the little girl has to give.

As the pig goes to sleep, the little girl stands, keeping her blindfold on. She can feel the energy and spirit in all things, so much clearer than the beacons of light she saw in the plants. She takes a step and watches the world around her take shape in her mind with her bound eyes closed tightly, and in the darkness, she walks home blindfolded. She gets close to the edge of the clearing and stops. She pauses at the entrance of the tribe's home, turns back to the jungle, and, still with the blindfold in place, says, "Thank you for watching me tonight."

The witchdoctor replies, "I could never let anything happen to you, but I needed to let you change on your own."

Behind her blindfold, she could see her teacher's radiant purple soul connect to hers. She put her little hand on her eyes, taking off her eye's bindings, she opened them, and the purple spirit was replaced by the sight of the kahuna.

They took each other hand in hand and rejoined the tribe.

Huna and New Age Hawai'i

With that, I now need to talk about Huna. Huna is a neo-pagan tradition inspired by the old Hawaiian spirituality. When I was young, I read every book on Huna and studied as much Hawaiian spirituality in mythologies, dances, and stories that I could get my hands on. Since I wasn't being taught the Germanic ways from my mother (I had to just observe), and my Italian education had stopped with my Grandmother moving to Florida, I learned the Hawaiian ones.

Cancel culture is angry, and many Hawaiians want to eradicate "Huna" from existence. But hear me out. The Hawaiian ways inspired Max Freedom Long, the primary author and founder of Huna, in his limited worldview, to attempt to piece Hawaiian spirituality together with the comparative knowledge he had from psychology and a white-Christian-narrative. This was in 1945! Much of the Hawaiian language was illegal to be taught to others, expressed, or even thought about. As a white man, he did his best to keep it alive and named it after what he understood. Without Huna, we would have lost many old ways, even if much of it is taken out of context and misinterpreted. Newer books on Huna continue to mix and match from other cultures, using stones and crystals non-native to Hawai'i as healing tools, using

India's chakras as a road map to healing, and using Christian hierarchical religious themes to organize the faith.

The Hawaiian people didn't call it "Huna" because faith was a part of everything. You didn't name something that just *was*. A kahuna was an expert in a field, knowing information specific to that field that would be 'hidden' from others, basically because others were not experts and didn't need the jargon of detailed knowledge on their specific subject. Experts know hidden things about topics. Kahuna were experts. That means there were different kahuna for canoe building, healing, sorcery, charting the stars, leading, etc. Max Freedom Long misunderstood "huna" as hidden, equating it with "occult" as hidden. There are, of course, Kahuna of spiritual ways, for which we will discuss, but that isn't what "huna" meant.

> **Knowledge is power, folks. Teach, and people pass on the truth. Keep it hidden, and people make up information.**

This is what has happened with Hawaiian spirituality, and I hope to stop that. My culture, my people, my essence. We begin that journey with this book. What would it have been called if "Huna" did not come to fruition? The belief system would have probably been called Ho'omanamana (to make lots of spiritual energy and life force).

My understanding of the soul comes from Hawaiian spirituality, for which I will give you unedited and unfiltered. We will at times supplement with other religions, modalities, or words, which I specify such, and I only do so because what was there is now erased and lost to time and oppression. I will not use what is trendy (chakras and amethyst) because they don't blend and are not applicable. Instead, the aspects that are supplimented are from cultures that have similar belief, modality, and structure (Indian does not).

You will learn Hawaiian words and pronounce them correctly. Mispronouncing a word from what will now be your own language disrespects the people who fought to bring back the Hawaiian ways as best we could; so, you'll do your best, as well. Laziness and neglect is disrespectful. Your home accident and ignorance is not disrespectful. Do your best and always update your best.

Notice also that I do not italicize the Hawaiian words. The reasoning behind that is that by separating these words from the rest of the instruction teaches you and others that these belong segregated. Much like other forms of learning that have crept into witchcraft, healing, and psychic development, when they are part of our everyday use, they do not become separated. Furthermore, people are more likely to separate those things from BIPOC cultures than from European cultures.

> **We do not italicize "Persephone," and therefore, here, in my book, we will not italicize "mana."**

I will forever be thankful to Max Freedom Long for keeping some of this alive, even if he was looking through Jungian, Freudian, and Christian lenses (bless his heart).

The system of rules for Hawaiian spirituality is called kapu, which, over the years and through travel, turned into the word you know today as taboo. The kapu system is a set of rules and stories meant to keep people safe and create order within a society. However, this isn't the only section of spirituality. Huna is a Hawaiian-based spirituality, but it is not *the* Hawaiian spirituality. In reality, the totality of the old Hawaiian ways died a long time ago. There are a few of us who continue to try to piece things together as an attempt at resurrecting the old ways, the best we can.

Dear Mr. Long, even if you missed the mark in some of this, we thank you for using your privilege to keep some of this alive. I do not look your gift in the mouth but accept it graciously.

The First Kahuna

Characters
Pa'ao - Fisherman (the first Kahuna)
Lonopele - The chief of Kahiki (Tahiti), brother to Pa'ao
La'amaomao - Goddess of the Wind
Namaka'okaha'i (Namaka) - Goddess of the Ocean Waters
Kane - God of the Sky
Kanaloa - God of Magic and the Veil between the Ocean and the Underworld
Ku - God of War
Lono - God of Agriculture
Kanalo'a Mu'ia - The first kahuna canoe
Pele - Goddess of the Volcano and Fire

The sky voyeured the murder of Pa'ao's son. The sky just stood there. Watching. La'amaomao, the goddess of winds, and Kane, the god of the sky, just watched. They did nothing. They watched the child of a fisherman get gutted publicly for his reckless work.

You see, the king of Kahiki was Lonopele, and under his barbaric rule, his brother Pa'ao was a fisherman. That's right; you put those pieces together. Lonopele, the king of Kahiki, murdered his 10-year-old nephew.

Why?

La'amaomao's wind blessed this warm day of May with an easy breeze. The fisherman's nets cast into Namaka'okaha'i's ocean began to gather fish, but they knew they would have to release some back.

King Lonopele had a rule: His Lionfish was sacred and could not be hunted or killed. These delicious creatures were only to be enjoyed when a live Lionfish was brought before the king, killed, and stripped skillfully for the king to enjoy.

Lionfish are venomous. They are beautifully decorated, red, white, and black striped with lethal spines. Lonopele thought that their beauty equated to his own unique beauty, and the fish quills were as ruthless as his rule. He alone could consume the mana of these creatures. Anyone else who killed or enjoyed these fish was sentenced to death.

Pa'ao said, "Son, as you pull out the net, you'll need to hold it high above the water, like this." Pa'ao, leaning over his canoe, laced his fingers under one of the ropes skillfully knotted and lifted it high, forcing a cone collection of the net beneath.

"Father, it's easier if you do it like this," the boy said jovially and jumped into the water, gathering the edges.

"No!" Pa'ao yelled.

"Ouee!" The boy yelled. "I think I got stung!"

"Get out of the water," Pa'ao said, bracing the canoe.

No healing has been created yet. There were no uses of herbs, lore, or sight. When something happened, it just happened (as many, nowadays, still believe we exist). The child got into the canoe, and Pa'ao saw that the sting on the boy's leg was from the king's sacred red fish. The two quickly pulled in the net, with Pa'ao worried that his son may not be strong enough to withstand the venom.

Paddling back to shore with the catch for the tribe, Pa'ao worried about the visibility of the sting. "Son, I need you to hide behind me, and we need to conceal this wound as long as we can. If your uncle, the king, sees it, he will decide that your recklessness and the red fish's sting is an omen to have you killed."

"Yes, father," the boy said as his body began to fever.

Getting close to shore, Lonopele stepped out of the trees onto the beach, ready to see what his royal fisherman's catch brought in. Pa'ao's fear for his son conjured a sweat.

They pulled up to the water, and with natural habit, Pa'ao jumped out to one side of the canoe and the boy to the other. The boy winced as the salty life-force of the sea goddess stung the boy's leg. They pulled the canoe onto the sand. Once on land, as instructed in the canoe, the child stood behind his father.

"Let me see the catch," Lonopele said.

Pa'ao stepped aside, and the child stood behind him.

As they looked into the canoe, they saw that within the tuna, there lay a dead Rockfish. Pa'ao's heart raced. Lonopele's blood warmed. The child's fever swelled.

Lonopele spoke slowly, calmly: "You killed a royal fish, brother. Is your intent to overthrow me?"

"No, it was an accident!" Yelled the child. As he stepped out from his father, the boy fainted from the pervasive poison. As the boy fell, Pa'ao caught the child and smacked his face.

"Child! Son! Open your eyes!"

"He has the mark," Lonopele seethed through his teeth. Quickly, the king snatched the boy by the hair, pulled his shark-tooth serrated knife from his ankle, and thrust it into the boy's abdomen. He sawed. He forced the knife to chew through the boy, who gasped for breath, choking on his own blood. In the child's last blinking moments of life, he watched his uncle reach into his own torso and pull out his entrails, tossing his organs into the canoe like a disassociated task of tossing the remnants of decayed chum into the ocean. Pa'ao froze in horror, watching his king, his brother, mutilate and toss out all of the organs from his limp, dead child.

And the gods watched. Pa'ao could not move. Frozen and shaken in terror, his tears fell like the overflowing drips of a spring after a fresh tropical rain. With youth's blood coagulating in the sand, staining the king's hands, and draining down the legs of the lifeless form, all that stood out of place in this bloody horror was the mark on the child's leg from the rockfish. Pa'ao's freeze released into terrorized grief when his son's organs were piled on top of the fish in the canoe. Pa'ao screamed. His eyes jutted between the organs, his brother, and the tossing of the lifeless child onto the sand. Discarded.

Pa'ao fell to his knees, and to the villagers, it looked like reverence to the king. At Pa'ao's humanity breaking, the onlookers from the village also fell to their knees. If the brother of the king can bow in reverence through the murder of his own son, this king is all-powerful, like the rock fish.

The child must have kicked the fish when he got stung as a reflex, and it got stuck in the net. Tuna, one royal fish, and bloodied child organs filled the canoe like a cornucopia.

"Take his organs to sea and give them back to the ocean for your child's breaking of the laws," Lonopele said. With his blood-stained shark tooth knife in hand, he finished with, "he was chum, anyway," and he walked away.

None of the fish was any good. Pa'ao, on his knees, looked at his son's mutilated body, covered in sand. The boy's virgin face, stuck in horror, was coated with the pearly beach.

The day was still warm. The wind was still blessing the May afternoon. Nothing about the weather was ominous. This was life.

As Lonopele disappeared into the trees, Pa'ao jumped to his feet to rescue the body of his son. He held the limp child. He was so light. Squeezing his son, he pushed his canoe into the water, stepped inside, and let the ocean move him while he held his sweet boy.

And Kane, the god of the sky, knew it could be better. Life could be more than just accepting that inhumanity... that the inhumane... that the humans could live more like gods and carve out their destinies.

Kane arched his back, closed his eyes to look within, in order to look around. Namaka'okaha'i (of the ocean) is connected to his life force. Kanaloa, the god of the underworld and magic, connected through the womb of Namaka'okaha'i. Ku, the god of war, connected. Lono, the god of growth and agriculture connected. Pele did not connect because, frankly, she didn't care about anyone. Haha.

The gods communed.

"I'm disgusted," Kanaloa, the god of magic, said. "I don't know why you created such horrible creatures."

"They have potential," said Kane. Ku, god of war, just watched.

"They really are messy. They hunt and kill and eat each other," said Kanaloa. "My underworld is full of their violent deaths. They are worse than any other animal."

"They have potential," Kane said calmly, again.

"They are useless," Namaka'okaha'i said. "They only take up space. They don't give or provide."

"They have potential," Kane repeated.

"They take and take. They give no reverence for the beauty of our world," said Lono.

The god then spoke over each other, all complaining about how terrible humans are.

"La'amaomao," said Kane. All went quiet, for when Kane speaks, we listen. "La'amaomao, what do you think?"

The wind had watched, as it always does. She knows and speaks because she has the answers that no one else observes. She has seen everything. Heard all the words. The hate. The harm. The cruelty.

"They make hope," she said.

The gods looked at the wind, and Kane smiled.

"They have potential," Kane said with resolve.

"They what?" Kanaloa asked.

La'amaomao continued, "They don't make things grow. They only take what you grow, Lono, and repeat it. If we are being honest, they don't improve it either. Humans just take. And then they kill and eat and consume without respect or care. They steal from your oceans without replenishing, Namaka. They kill each other and flood your underworld, Kanaloa. They have nothing spiritual or godly. They fumble awkwardly, Ku, but you seem to benefit the most from their brutality. And Kane, they may have potential, but they don't build without destroying what they build on top of."

They all stared at her. The goddess affirmed how useless and barbaric humans were.

"But they make something we can't even make. They make hope."

"What is hope?" Namaka asked. Kane smiled knowingly.

"They know how horrible their own species is. Knowing how terrorizing these creatures are to our world and to each other, and in spite of it, they create a vision of an outcome that *isn't*. They use words and care to plan for the potential of something better. They cherish and give great love for a desire and anticipation that they, the worst creature of all, might do better," La'amaomao said.

"Hope is when you know things are dire and you create a reality within to strive for ease, peace, and solace." La'amaomao had such love for the human's ability to hope, she created *aloha*. "Hope is a gentle inward prayer of love and kindness and potential. We don't make that. They do," And on the gentle wind, her easy tears of love gently rained on Pa'ao. The gods looked down at the hopeless creature sobbing in the squishy organs of his child in his only possession, his canoe.

Pa'ao was curled on his side, covered in juvenile blood streaking down his body from the refreshing rain. In shock, Pa'ao didn't flinch at the cold rain beating at his isolated body. This man hoped that his evil brother would not harm his son. Pa'ao created hope by instructing his child to lie, to deceive. Hope was the prayer his heart sang so that they should not be punished. Hope said that the obvious breaking of a law could be forgiven, so the father and son could still relish in future memories instead of the inevitable demise.

"Hope..." Ku murmured.

"They have potential," Kane simply said.

"I love them," La'amaomao said. She continued to rain softly on her favorite creatures. "I know it doesn't make sense," she continued to cry on the poor grieving father, "but look at him. If they were so terrible, they'd move on and make another child like the boar or the fish. He had hopes for his child. And they laugh. A sound unlike any song a bird can sing. They tell stories about us and about the seasons, which are so much richer than our own conversations. They..." and La'amaomao, having no more to say, cried.

"Hope..." Ku finished.

Kane arched his back to connect to the mana of all the gods, and they knew that La'amaomao was right. In her aloha, they needed to help the humans, the people. They had potential but needed more.

Pa'ao found his way to a resolution. Releasing his lifeless child into the ocean, knowing he couldn't give him a proper burial at sea, all because of the royal law broken. The rain disguised his tears, and the sun set over the waters of Kane like a golden gate.

Pa'ao watched his son's body float away on the waves. Pa'ao lay down in his canoe, filled with blood, organs, fish, and one redfish. As it sailed onto the sea, he looked up at the stars, for La'amaomao had stopped crying and just watched as he sat on the waves. Namaka and Kanaloa came in close for a better look to see what La'amaomao had spoken of. The sky felt closer to Pa'ao as Kane moved closer to look at the precious human. Ku crept up around the boat, and the seaweed grew so Lono could hold the boat steady. The gods watched Pa'ao. Pa'ao collapsed into the boat, broken in spirit and weary in body. He cried, lying in the dead fish and the guts of his child.

"I hope," Pa'ao whispered. "I hope... that my baby will be safe with you, Kanaloa. I hope that he is held tight and loved like I loved him. I hope that he doesn't stop feeling love, even after such a loveless death. My baby... I love you," and Pa'ao turned his face into the lifeless, bloody fish, and cried until his body needed rest. The first kahuna, devoid of gifts soon to come, curled unconscious, so small, in a boat full of rot, a heart full of hope.

"Hope," Ku said again. The god of war and the way of things stirred.

"Hope..." Kanaloa agreed. The waves beneath billowed the boat. Pa'ao, curled in his canoe, didn't react to the shake beneath him, for his grief was tantamount to the human desire to expire. Kanaloa continued, "He should be able to do more."

Ku said, "Humans can be kind and can help and should be able to fight back against tyranny. This man should! Could! Can! Will!"

Thunder struck, and the winds blew to echo Ku's excitement.

"I will make the first human... changed in his grief, connected to the ocean, the wind, the life we make... I will make this human... magical," and Kanaloa rose high above the boat in a giant wave to spell Pa'ao.

Flies buzzed around the canoe, scoping out the available entrail snacks beneath Pa'ao's grief-stricken protection. Kanaloa's magic pulled the ocean's water into a pedestal, taking the canoe high into the night sky so it could be on display under the diamonds of stars. Those opportunistic flies followed the boat up into the sky, and in Kanaloa's disgust, he fused them into the canoe. The boat began to transform into something magical. It buzzed and vibrated, and gained the ability to cut through the roughest of waves. The boat became Kanalo'a Mu'ia (The Buzzing Flies). From the fish, Kanaloa grew a great mast, two outshoots, and a side connector, creating the first outrigger canoe.

Ku then stepped in, and holding Kanaloa's hand, they stepped into the dreams of Pa'ao, waking him.

Pa'ao awoke holding what was left of his son, and saw the gods floating around his levitating canoe. "Who are you? What's happening?" He said, frightened.

"We are here to give you skill," said Kanaloa.

"And to fight back," said Ku.

"I don't understand," said Pa'ao.

"There are ways that are hidden. The ways of experts. Knowledge. The ways of the gods. The way of my water," said Kane.

"Huna," said Namaka'okaha'i.

"What is Huna?" Pa'ao said.

"Huna is what is hidden. It's what is known but only to experts. Huna is well studied, and holding it helps others. The knowing... it brings more hope," said La'amaomao.

"What happened to my boat?" Pa'ao asked.

"I transformed it. I am Kanaloa and will gift you internal sight. Kane will gift you the Huna. You, in your knowledge of the ocean and with the guiding stars that surround you, will now be gifted as the first navigator. You will use your knowledge that Kane gives you with the gift of internal sight from me to move to a new land," Kanaloa said. His tentacles reached over the boat. One of the god's tentacles grabbed his wrist, and another grabbed his other, opening Pa'ao and forcing him to his feet. Kanaloa peered into Pa'ao's eyes deeply. A third tentacle touched the forehead of Pa'ao. In the instant of contact, Pa'ao's back arched and his muscles rippled in the surge of magic pulsing through his body.

"Stop! I'm just a fisherman," Pa'ao screeched through his transformation.

"You are more than a fisherman, and will forever be more than a fisherman," Kanaloa held Pa'ao tight so the other gods could gift the childless father.

Ku, still holding Kanaloa's hand, then spoke: "Your child's death is not in vain. I gift you the power of sacrifice. As you give up the things you need, other gifts will grow. Be it death, be it through reverence, or through the gifting to the gods, we will answer your requests through your sacrifices. And with the loss of your son, we give you the greatest gift we can. We give you the ability to change the world around you. Through Kanaloa's magic, you, too, will have magic. I am the god of war and of growth. You will no longer be oppressed. Learn these ways of mana, and you will always be able to fight back, in prayer, in lomi, in hilina'i. We believe in you, so you believe in you."

With this gift, Ku's magic moved through Kanaloa and into Pa'ao's body. Pa'ao's eyes rolled back in his head as he became stronger, fuller. His biceps grew, and his back broadened. His chest filled with muscle to contain the ability to believe in himself.

Ku and Kanaloa spoke as one: "Together we will give you the gift of the ana'ana, so that you may smite those who try to oppress, take more than they need, and control the vulnerable." And Pa'ao's fingers grew longer and stronger, giving him the ability to control the threads of life in the souls of people.

"But with this power," La'amaomao said, "I will step in." She separated Ku and Kanaloa's hands and replaced them with her own. "You will know the rules of kapu. The laws that are unspoken and steadfast. These rules will keep you safe and strong, and guide you. This is how you will make your choices as a man of Huna." In this gift, his strong and stiff body softened. The swollen muscles relaxed from the tension put on by the male gods.

Lono finally stepped in, taking the free hand of Kanaloa. When Lono connected to the god of magic, the tentacle connecting to Pa'ao glowed a fluorescent green, and the vines of magic then pulsed through the human's veins, making his veins glow green.

"I give you," Lono said, "the gift to heal. Use the plants, but ask them for permission. They ask only for a secret in return. In exchange for something held sacred by you, they will answer with the ability to heal. When those who harm cause pain or injury, you may use my life, the mana of my plants, and the life-force of animals to heal."

Kane took the free hands, completing the circle. The five gods, one of air, one of war, one of magic, one of growth, and one of truth, surrounded the outrigger canoe floating high above the resting ocean on a watery pedestal. Beneath, Namak'oka'ai swam, circling to hold the boat up.

Kane said, "May you create a place for the dead to rest. A heiau with high walls. The walls are to protect against mana of oppressors and to reach up to the gods for protection. May you be guided by Namaka'okaha'i. Although she has no gift to give in Huna, she will answer you. Pa'ao, you are the first Kahuna."

With that, Kanaloa released Pa'ao. Pa'ao fell to his knees onto his buzzing outrigger canoe. He looked up and then at his hands, and then at his transformed shape.

He was still Pa'ao, but different.

"I hurt so much," Pa'ao cried. "My heart hurts so much with my son's death. I thank you for these gifts, but... may I ask you... please... take this pain away from me?"

The gods let go of each other's hands and eyed one another without an answer.

"I..." Kane said, "I cannot take away your pain. But I can take the body of your child and make it into something else." The wind lifted the organs, and Kane turned them to dusk, spinning in swirls with the wind's fingers. Kanaloa found the lifeless body floating far away, and Kane lifted it into the sky. Ku vaporized the body into dust. The boy, as sand and dust danced in the sky.

"As the first Kahuna, you will pass your gifts onto others, through blood or through teaching. The curse is that the kahuna will hurt like you. This will remind you of your duty with these gifts. But I, through the wind, will remind you that you must continue to teach, and not hold these gifts tight. I will dance your son into your memory. Like a father to a son, you

must teach, and teach with the love and care you would give your child."
La'amaomao danced the dust of Pa'ao's son off into the wind's distance.

And with that, Pa'ao stood on the canoe alone, clean and a new man to start a new and uncharted journey.

"I feel so alone," Pa'ao said.

"If you call, I will answer. I will answer the Kahuna," Namaka'okaha'i said. "The water will always be there for you, as a companion and guide. Look for me, and I will answer." She lowered the canoe from its watery pedestal onto the calm ocean.

"Now," La'amaomao said, "travel and give hope with your gifts."

Pa'ao looked out into the night sky. Namaka helped get the first kahuna started by giving the Kanalo'a Mu'ia a shove, and it vibrated through the water, slicing it with ease. Pa'ao, the first Kahuna in the first outrigger canoe, looked at the stars and saw how they pulled his attention as a map. He looked deep within his green glow and felt his energy reach outwards searching for a new home. "That way," he knew. The wind listened. The ocean listened. The animals listened. And they guided Kanalo'a Mu'ia towards Hawai'i.

In Pa'ao's journey, he will find Pilika'aiea, whom he will take to the Hawaiian Islands. This new companion will, with Pa'ao as his vezir, overthrow a vicious monarch. Pa'ao's knowing to bring this man with him will begin the bloodline that gives birth to King Kamehameha, who unites the islands.

Pa'ao will give birth to the Kahunas, who, over time, vary in skill and expertise. Some will be his children, and some will become his children through the honor of adoption. Pa'ao will be the first, with the memory of his child on the wind, to begin the construct of hanai (honorable adoption), and it will be a foundation in Hawaiian culture.

From death and from hope, the first magical man was born to control the life of all things, guided by honor, the night-sky's stars, the wind, and the water. The Kahuna will grow hope.

The Hawaiian Tenets & Kapu

It is often easier to see the darker side of human nature in others because it is painful to face this in ourselves. For this reason, our work requires a certain kind of courage. When we go deep enough with our own lack of spiritual values, we discover the unsettling duality this exposes. The way that all humans are the same during birth to genuine humility, including taking accountability for our own taboos, is how we find solutions for spiritual unrest.

In Hawaiian culture, there are several foundational values or tenets that guide daily life, relationships, and interactions with the world. These values are deeply rooted in spirituality, respect, and the interconnectedness of all things. Here's an overview of some key Hawaiian tenets. In all of them, we need to find a sense of place, a sense of purpose, and a sense of power.

These values form the foundation of Hawaiian cultural identity and offer guidance on how to live a harmonious, meaningful, and respectful life. With every step in your healer journey, you should return to these tenets when deciding how to proceed in an event, in your journey, and in helping those heal themselves.

The Hawaiian Tenets

ʻAumakua

ʻAumakua are ancestral spirits who remain spiritually connected to their descendants. They often manifest in the physical world as animals such as sharks, owls, turtles, or birds. These appearances are not random. An ʻaumakua appearing is a sign, an omen from the spirit world into the animal world, affirming that we are on the right path, or gently warning us if we are not. Honoring them keeps the ancestral line strong.

ʻOhana (including Hanai)

ʻOhana means family, but it extends far beyond bloodline. It includes all those with whom we share reciprocal responsibility, care, and loyalty. In Hawaiian tradition, ʻohana includes adopted and chosen family, known as hanai. A hanai child is not seen as different from a birth child, and hanai parents carry the same kuleana (responsibility) to nurture, raise, and protect. ʻOhana is sacred, a structure of mutual dependence and collective identity. When I've tried to explain what hanai and ʻohana mean to mainlanders, they try to equate it to a *Friendsgiving*, where their "chosen family" is like family. Let me impose this: These people in your life are family (period!), not a novelty that you enjoy saying frivolously.

Aliʻi

An aliʻi is a chief or leader, but within the spiritual-cultural structure of Hawaiʻi, they are a parent to the people. Their role is to guide, protect, and uplift those under their care. The aliʻi carries kuleana for the well-being of their community, instead of power or dominance. The true aliʻi lives to serve. When the aliʻi do not follow the other tenants of Hawaiʻi, then they should be removed from the honor of a leader. Even parents need to be replaced, including the parents of state. Maybe we need a hanai aliʻi for a little bit...

Aloha

Aloha is the living expression of love. It is both a greeting and a farewell, but more than that, it is the purpose of life. To live aloha is to give love to oneself and others through responsibility. One gives love to the self by accepting kuleana for who you are (pa'ahana), what you do (pono), and how you do it (maika'i). Aloha is the foundation and the fulfillment of life. It's smiling to give love through your face when someone offers you safe passage across a road at a crosswalk. Yes, there may be an automatic responsibility to stop at a crosswalk for the person, but aloha is smiling and being thankful for the stop, anyway.

Ho'okipa

Ho'okipa is the value and practice of hospitality, but it is more than welcoming guests. It is the sacred offering of comfort, generosity, and protection to others, strangers, and family alike. It is making space for others in a way that honors their spirit and shows the strength of your aloha. How can you give hospitality to your co-workers, the person who is serving you at the bar, or to your neighbor? How can you welcome them into a fleeting interaction in your world?

Ho'okuku: Education

Traditional Hawaiian education taught children to listen deeply. They were trained to absorb without interruption, without commentary, without excessive movement. Children were expected to learn through presence and silence. Being niele (nosy, overly inquisitive without reason) was discouraged. Knowledge was gained through humility, observation, and discipline. At the same time, kumu (teacher) was responsible for the art of gifting information in a palatable way. This is why a kumu is the highest of respect in Hawaiian culture (which was a huge culture shock, teaching on the mainland, and being treated by parents as an indentured servant).

Hoʻoponopono

Hoʻoponopono is a sacred practice of restoration and reconciliation. It involves clearing resentment, correcting wrongs, and restoring harmony between individuals and the spiritual forces. It is not just about forgiveness; it is about returning to pono, the state of balance and righteousness. Through honest dialogue and prayer, families and individuals resolve conflicts at the soul level.

Inoa

Inoa means name, and in Hawaiian understanding, names carry magical prophecies. Your name is not arbitrary; it holds spiritual energy, ancestral memory, and often a prayer or prophecy. The words in your name affect your path and presence. Naming is an act of calling forth power and intention.

Kuleana

Kuleana means responsibility, but it is deeper than obligation. It is the sacred duty that arises from your place in the world; your role in family, community, nature, and spirit. Kuleana is what is yours to carry, yours to care for, yours to protect. It is both a privilege and a burden, but when accepted with aloha, kuleana becomes a source of strength and identity. In Hawaiian life, everyone has kuleana, to the land, to their ancestors, to each other, and to their own soul.

Lei

Leis are sacred adornments made from flowers, leaves, shells, or feathers. They are offerings of aloha, symbols of honor, beauty, and connection. Leis are worn draped gracefully, never slung or thrown. They are treated with reverence, and one does not wear a lei carelessly, especially a lei that has been gifted. A lei is worn halfway across the shoulders, where part of it drapes down the back. This is different from a necklace, which hugs the back of your neck. Lastly, I was always taught that if you are gifted a lei, you keep it on until you change clothes, no exceptions.

Lokahi

Lokahi means to obtain oneness, unity, and harmony. Think of this as the way you are complete within yourself and within your community. At its heart, lokahi expresses the idea of being "one together."

In practice, lokahi is about cultivating harmony in three primary relationships; with the divine and spirit world (honoring the gods, ancestors, and unseen forces that shape life), with nature and the land (maintaining balance with the ʻaina (land), kai (sea), and the natural world that sustains people), and with each other (fostering cooperation, compassion, and aloha within family and community).

To live with lokahi means to bring these relationships into alignment so that body, mind, and spirit are in balance, and people live in respectful connection with the world around them. It is both a guiding value and a lived practice in Hawaiian culture, often seen as essential for health, prosperity, and spiritual well-being.

Mahu and the Importance of Mahu in Society

In traditional Hawaiian culture, the mahu are individuals who embody both male and female spirits. They are neither solely Kane (man) nor solely wahine (woman), but a blending, a sacred in-between. The word mahu literally means "in the middle," and far from being marginalized:

> **Mahu were respected as healers, teachers, chanters, and carriers of deep ancestral knowledge. They were respected with such authority because they were divinely gifted with the ability to speak both male and female breath, being the perfect human for developing all other people.**

Mahu held roles of high importance in spiritual and social life. They were often chosen to be caretakers of sacred traditions such as hula, laʻau lapaʻau (plant medicine), lomilomi (healing touch), and hoʻoponopono (spiritual reconciliation). Their liminal nature, living between the binary, was seen as a spiritual gift. They could see what others could not. They could understand and hold the emotional and energetic complexities of others because they themselves walked between worlds.

In Hawaiian society, the existence of mahu was a reflection of the natural diversity of life. Just as there are many winds, many fish, many stars, there are many expressions of human beings. The mahu were a living reminder that spirit is more complex than the body alone, and that harmony includes all parts of the spectrum.

It was only with the arrival of Western missionaries that the status of mahu was diminished. Colonial and Christian influences brought rigid gender roles, binary thinking, and condemnation of anything outside their moral framework. Mahu, once honored, were suddenly shamed, hidden, or rejected. It makes sense (if you've read *Witchdoctor Exorcist*) that Christianity would again condemn anything that would challenge power, and there was no one with more influence than the mahu.

Today, there is a resurgence of respect for mahu, not only in Hawaiian communities but across the Pacific. In many modern Hawaiian ceremonies and classrooms, mahu again teach chant, dance, and healing arts. They are reclaiming their rightful place. The presence of mahu is a reminder that the health of a society is measured by how well it holds all its people, especially those who carry both shadow and light, both masculine and feminine, both the seen and the unseen.

To embrace the mahu is to remember the original aloha, that sacred love which welcomes each soul as it is, and honors its role in the great balance of the world.

Maika'i

Maika'i means excellence (in this case), but more than surface goodness. It is beauty in action, quality in behavior, kindness in spirit. Maika'i is how something is done, with care, with excellence, with refinement. It is one of the measures of living well: not just what you do, but how you do it. Be thoughtful, take your time, and be courteous. It's about being excellent in all things.

Makua and Kupuna

Makua are the parents whose kuleana is to model what life should look like: how to live with aloha, how to work with pa'ahana, how to behave with pono and maika'i. The parent lives these values in daily life so the child can see and embody them.

The kupuna (elders or grandparents) have the kuleana of raising the child. In traditional Hawaiian culture, grandparents are the primary teachers of spiritual, emotional, and cultural wisdom, ensuring the soul and story of the family are passed on.

Na 'Aina

Na 'Aina means "the lands," but in Hawaiian understanding, it is far more than physical terrain. 'Aina is the land that feeds, spiritually, physically, and emotionally. It includes mountains, oceans, forests, winds, rains, and all elements that sustain life. Na 'Aina are our elemental living relatives, ancestors in nature form, and sacred teachers. It isn't owned; it's cared for. To honor na 'aina is to remember that the land is not beneath us; it is part of us. Our kuleana is to protect, listen to, and live in the right relationship with na 'aina, because when the land thrives, the people thrive.

Pa'ahana

Pa'ahana means hard-working, but in a deeper sense, it is the spiritual practice of being in the right relationship with your labor. When one is aligned with their true calling, the work they were born to do, the work itself gives mana back to the self. Like Japan's ikigai, pa'ahana is where passion, skill, contribution, and purpose intersect. It is sacred to live from your pa'ahana.

Po and Milu
Po is the realm of darkness, the cosmic night where all life begins and returns. It is the divine mystery, the source of mana and knowledge. Milu is the underworld, often associated with where the souls of the dead go. Milu is a place of returning and reflection. Together, Po and Milu are essential in understanding life, death, and spiritual journeying.

Pono
Pono means righteousness, balance, and living in integrity. It is the condition of being spiritually and morally aligned with yourself, with others, with nature, and with the divine. To live pono is to make choices that restore harmony rather than create harm. It is not perfection, but the commitment to return to rightness whenever you stray. In Hawaiian culture, pono is the foundation of justice, leadership, healing, and daily life. When a person lives pono, their actions feed the well-being of the entire 'ohana, the land, and the future.

Pule
Pule is prayer, a constant communion with spirit. It is a way of being rather than an act alone. In Hawaiian culture, prayer is often woven into speech, chant, breath, and silence. One prays in gratitude, in seeking guidance, in alignment with ancestors and gods. To pray is to listen and speak with the unseen. Our words matter (as you will see with Inoa), so every affirmation or curse that comes from your lips are prayers for you and others.

Kapu: The Sacred Law of Balance in Hawaiian Culture
In ancient Hawai'i, there was no written code of law. There were no books of legislation, no jails, and no courtrooms. Yet, there was order, deep, spiritual, embodied order, governed by a system called kapu. The connection between the Hawaiian word kapu and the English word taboo is a fantastic study of deep linguistic and cultural curiosity, with their historical relationships tracing back through the earlier Polynesian voyages recorded by European explorers.

Origins of the Word "Kapu"

In Hawaiian, kapu is a sacred word. It means that which is set apart, forbidden, restricted, or protected by spiritual law. But this word is not uniquely Hawaiian; it exists across many Polynesian languages, because these languages share common ancestral roots.

In Tongan, the word is "tabu", and it carries the same meaning: sacred, restricted, holy. In Samoan, it is "tapu". In Maori, tapu also means spiritually restricted or set apart.

These words all come from the Proto-Polynesian root tapu, meaning "sacred, forbidden." The form "kapu" is specific to Hawaiian, where the k sound often replaces the t sound used in other Polynesian languages (a common phonetic shift in Hawaiian linguistic evolution).

So the root of the English word taboo is not Hawaiian kapu, but the older Polynesian "tapu/tabu". Hawaiian "kapu" is a sibling, not a parent. We know now that in some places throughout the Hawaiian islands, the "t" was still used in language, even if it wasn't documented like the "k" sound was.

Captain Cook and the Introduction of "Taboo" to Europe

The first known appearance of the word "taboo" in English came from the journals of Captain James Cook, during his third Pacific voyage in 1777. While visiting the Tongan islands, he encountered the word "tabu" and its sacred meaning.

Cook wrote: "Not one of us was allowed to touch what was taboo."

From his accounts, European readers learned that in Polynesian societies, certain people, objects, and practices were "taboo," prohibited or set apart due to spiritual significance. The word was immediately adopted by English speakers because there was no exact English equivalent for such a concept. It filled a gap in European language and worldview.

From Tonga, the word entered European languages (especially English and French) and was generalized to mean anything culturally forbidden or socially off-limits, whether or not it had spiritual significance. This began the long history of the English word taboo.

How "Taboo" Changed in English
When the word "taboo" was absorbed into English, it lost much of its sacred meaning. In the West, "taboo" came to mean simply something socially prohibited or culturally frowned upon, often associated with sexuality, superstition, or social impropriety. The deep spiritual, ecological, and cosmological dimensions of the original tapu or kapu were largely erased in translation.

In Hawaiian understanding, breaking a kapu might bring death, imbalance, or misfortune, because of violating a cosmic law of harmony. In English, "taboo" became closer to "awkward" or "forbidden topic," lacking the spiritual context.

The journey from kapu to taboo is more than linguistic. It is a tale of how Indigenous knowledge systems are translated, misunderstood, and reshaped in the process of colonization.

> **The sacred becomes social. The divine becomes awkward.**

The law of the ancestors becomes a curiosity of anthropology, but the root still speaks. In Hawaiian culture, kapu remains a living word. It reminds us that there is such a thing as sacred timing, sacred space, and sacred restraint. And it reminds us that words carry histories, of islands, of gods, and of the people who still remember.

The Meaning of Kapu
Kapu is best understood as that which is sacred, set apart, or restricted in honor of divine alignment. Kapu was the spiritual backbone of Hawaiian society, a living system of laws that governed human behavior, ecological balance, spiritual alignment, and social structure.

> *To understand kapu is to understand the foundation upon which Hawaiian culture was built, rooted in reverence for the gods, the land, and each other. It is to walk carefully and with awareness, knowing that every act touches the spiritual threads that hold life together.*

When something is made kapu, it is drawn out of ordinary use and held in sacred recognition. To violate kapu was to harm the harmony of all things! It could offend the gods, desecrate ancestral lineages, or disrupt the health of the land. But to live within kapu was to walk in pono, with the right balance with the universe.

Kapu can mean "forbidden," but more precisely, it means "protected by sacredness." A kapu was a law and a prayer in one. It was a recognition that the world was holy and that human behavior must bow to something higher.

The Spiritual Foundation of Kapu

In Hawaiian belief, everything is connected through mana. Mana must be respected and cultivated. Kapu exists to protect mana.

Gods such as Kane, Ku, Lono, Pele, and Kanaloa each had their own kapu, their own rituals, days, and offerings. The sacred heiau (temples) were surrounded by kapu, often so strict that entering them without permission could result in death. Certain foods, places, or even words were kapu on specific days or in specific contexts.

To violate a kapu was to invite imbalance. Illness, famine, or misfortune might follow. To live in alignment with kapu was to invite blessing, clarity, and generational strength.

The Ali'i and Kapu

In Hawaiian society, the ali'i (chiefs) were considered divine or semi-divine beings. They carried immense mana, and their bodies were often so sacred that their shadows were kapu. The people could not stand above the ali'i or look directly at them during sacred processions.

Please don't misunderstand me with colonizer or barbarian language; the ali'i were not tyrants. Their spiritual role was that of a channel. They were seen as the parents of the people, holding the responsibility of maintaining harmony between heaven, land, and community. Giving reverence to the ali'i was maika'i.

The ali'i enforced kapu, and they also lived under its highest obligations. They were responsible for leading rituals and timing for planting by the stars, managing food abundance, and keeping peace. If the ali'i violated kapu, the consequences were great. Some would step down voluntarily or offer ceremonial repentance (again, maybe mainland American Democracy could take a note here...). This is the essential difference between kapu and colonial law: kapu bound the leaders to the sacred just as much as the common people. No one stood outside of it.

Types of Kapu

There were many layers of kapu in ancient Hawai'i. Some were temporary and ceremonial; others were permanent and cultural. Some of the main categories included:

Wa Kane (Sacred Periods)

There were days dedicated to the worship of certain gods. During these days, fishing, bathing, or working the land might be kapu. People would instead fast, pray, and chant. The lunar calendar governed these sacred times, and breaking them was seen as a breach of protocol with the divine. Remember that the Hawaiian people were also seafarers and brilliant, innovative navigators. The weather was also an important aspect of kapu.

Gendered Kapu

Men and women had different roles and spaces, especially during ritual times. For example, women could not eat with men during ceremonial meals, and certain foods such as bananas, pig, and coconut were kapu to women during religious observances. This was part of a spiritual structure, reflecting balance, not inferiority.

The kapu system included gender distinctions, and some of them were severe, by today's standards, perhaps difficult to understand. During menstruation, women were considered to carry their own intense mana, and were therefore kapu from certain places or interactions. They were expected to stay in designated spaces during that time. While this has been interpreted as exclusion, within Hawaiian cosmology, it was also a protection. Women were carriers of generational mana, and their bodies were deeply connected to the movement of tides, moons, and creation itself.

That said, women also held powerful spiritual roles. Female kahuna existed. Goddesses like Pele, Haumea, and Hina were fierce and dominant forces in the Hawaiian pantheon. Women's kapu were not based on inferiority but on difference, sometimes misunderstood by outside observers.

Kapu on Place

Certain areas, like mountaintops, burial caves, and heiau, were kapu spaces. One could not enter them without permission or purification. These places were alive with mana, and even stepping foot there without ceremony could bring misfortune.

Kapu on People

High-ranking ali'i and spiritual leaders sometimes carried kapu moe, the sleeping kapu, meaning that if their presence approached, others had to prostrate themselves. This practice was rooted in the belief that their spiritual charge was so strong that standing upright in their presence could cause spiritual disturbance.

Seasonal Kapu

Certain fishing or harvesting activities were restricted at specific times to allow for regeneration. For example, taking fish during spawning season might be kapu. This was ecological wisdom wrapped in sacred law. What Western science now calls sustainability, Hawaiian culture upheld through kapu.

Kapu as Environmental Law

Perhaps one of the most brilliant aspects of kapu was its use in ecological balance. Hawaiian culture is rooted in a deep relationship with the land, sea, and sky. The people knew that their survival depended on living in harmony with these forces.

If a reef showed signs of being overfished, a kapu would be placed on it. No one would fish there until the ecosystem rebounded. Certain birds were kapu during nesting season. Forests could be closed off to harvesting. What's cool is that this was not enforced by a government; it was enforced by spiritual belief, social cohesion, and ancestral responsibility.

In this way, kapu was centuries ahead of modern environmental policy, and functioned without written law, fueled by mana and upheld through aloha 'aina, love of the land.

Kapu as Social Law

Kapu governed marriage, class, birth rites, and food distribution. It maintained order in a complex hierarchical society. But unlike colonial systems of control, kapu was inseparable from spiritual wellness. You did not follow kapu because you feared jail; you followed it because it honored your ancestors, your gods, your land, and your future children. Not fear, honor.

Children were taught kapu through story, example, chant, and ritual (as you are in this book, for example!). They learned by watching, by participating in ceremonies, by witnessing the natural consequences of imbalance. Education was spiritual, embodied, and generational.

Kapu and the Death Penalty

In some cases, violating a serious kapu could lead to death. This is one of the most controversial aspects of the system (as you will see in the next story). Yet within the cultural framework, such punishment was seen as necessary to prevent spiritual contagion. If a person desecrated a sacred site or defied a god's protocol, it was believed their actions could bring famine, illness, or war. Death was not vengeance, my love; it was the removal of imbalance.

The Fall of the Kapu System

In 1819, after the death of King Kamehameha I, the kapu system was publicly dismantled by Kamehameha II (Liholiho), Queen Kaʻahumanu, and High Priest Hewahewa. In an act called ʻAi Noa, they broke the kapu by having men and women eat together. Temples were destroyed, images of gods burned, and the old ways were ended (outwardly, at least), as an attempt to assimilate into colonized culture.

This was not done lightly. The aliʻi believed that a new way was needed to unify the islands, and that the kapu system, once so sacred, had become a tool for political abuse in some places. It is said that even the high priest Hewahewa saw the coming of Christianity and foreign change as inevitable, and that the gods of the old world had withdrawn their presence (but are back!).

Yet the spirit of kapu never left. Though the visible structures fell, the inner reverence remained. Many Hawaiian families continued to observe kapu in private. Certain places remained sacred, and the concept of kapu is still alive today in Hawaiian spirituality, land protection, and ritual.

Kapu in the Modern World

Today, the word kapu still appears (on signs, on beaches, in ceremonies). Modern Hawaiian practitioners invoke kapu when entering sacred places, when fasting, and when offering prayer. To say kapu is to create a boundary between the ordinary and the sacred.

> *In a world that often ignores sacredness, kapu reminds us that some things are not for taking, touching, or trespassing. Some spaces, times, and beings require silence, reverence, and restraint.*

We are once again remembering the value of spiritual law, for the sake of restoration, not control. The old ways knew what the modern world is forgetting: that harmony is upheld through respect instead of power.

Living Kapu

To live kapu today does not mean returning to ancient punishments. It means returning to ancient awareness. It means asking:

- What in my life is sacred?
- What behaviors disrupt the spiritual order of my home, my land, my body?
- What rhythms of rest, reverence, or restraint do I need to return to balance?

To live kapu is to protect what is holy: your soul, your ʻohana, your connection to na ʻaina. It is to listen before speaking. It is to honor your body as a vessel of mana. It is to refuse what harms the land and to choose what feeds the future.

> *Remember: Kapu is not about fear. Kapu is about honor.*

A Shark Boy Named Nanaue

Characters:
Kamohoʻaliʻi - The Shark God (Pele, Namaka, and Hiʻiaka's older brother)
Kalei - The beautiful woman that Kamohoaliʻi seduces to have his half-human child
Nanaue - The demi-god child of Kalei and the Shark God, Kamohoʻaliʻi
Laʻamaomao - Wind Goddess
Hiʻiakaʻakapoliʻopele (Hiʻiaka) - Goddess of Healing and Dance

    Waipiʻo is a valley that chooses whether or not to let you in. She is the most beautiful of all the island valleys, and that's saying a lot, being that I'm from the Valley Isle. But as beautiful as she is, Waipiʻo is the most dangerous. A sheer drop off of green cliffs over a thousand feet high guards her flanks, which dissuade invitation. In the old days, a narrow path clung to the cliff face, sharp as bone. Back then, this path was a test. Now, a broader trail winds down, just wide enough for a cautious traveler and one lover, and the valley still watches.
    At the uppermost end of Waipiʻo, a single silver ribbon drops from the precipice like a god's forgotten hair. Fifteen hundred feet of water throws itself into her basin, where waterfalls answer the call. Each one, a tongue of the mountain where streams spill downward, joining in the dark soil and emptying into the mouth of Waipiʻo's plains, lap at the rivers, and so go the prayers of the people.
    This place remembers greatness. Hiʻiakaʻakapoliʻople battled the great Moʻo here. The wind obeyed Laʻamaomao, who kept the storms in a calabash. Lift the lid a little and you were given a breeze. Pull it back fully,

and you were met with chaos. The birds spoke. The fish gave prophecy. The gods wandered in daylight and wore your brother's face.

And it was here that the valley gave birth to a monster.

Nanaue.

Before he was feared, he was just a child, and before he was a child, he was a secret.

Kamoho'ali'i was the king of sharks. He swam the deep water between islands and could wear human flesh when he pleased, always a chief and always majestic. When he emerged from the sea, he brought the weight of the ocean with him. He was striking, poised, powerful, and calm... you know... like how sharks are.

One day, just beneath the surface at the mouth of Waipi'o, he saw a woman. She stood in the surf with her arms high and skin wet with salt. Kamoho'ali'i forgot his own name in the sight of this bouquet of perfection. That night, black with sand and water, he crawled up the beach and changed into a man. His magic walked him into the Waipi'o valley as if he belonged.

The magic blessed the villagers with memories of the shark god being a part of this community without ever a day of absence. In their minds, he has always been there. He laughed with the people. Ate from their bowls. Listened to their songs. Always watching for her.

Her name was Kalei, and when he spoke, she answered. And when he reached for her, she did not pull away.

They married.

When Kalei swelled with child, he gave her serious instructions: Guard him. Cover his body. Let no one see his back, and never feed him meat.

The day that Kalei went from one and became two, he vanished, slipped back into the sea before she could ask him why. She never knew he was not a man throughout their marriage, throughout her pregnancy. The king of the sharks knew that once the baby was born, Kalei would know she had been deceived about his true identity. When the baby boy was born, he was right.

Her son was born with an opening between his shoulder blades. A wound that breathed. A mouth without a tongue. She waited for her husband, who never came. Alone, she named him Nanaue.

She kept him wrapped in fine kapa from the moment he entered the world. She fed him taro and bananas. No meat, not even fish.

But the child was hungry. Always. There was a weight to him... a pressure beneath his skin...

As he grew, she watched him with dread. Once when he was two years old, Kalei let him play in the pools beneath the falls, always alone, away from the other children, the other adults, and he would vanish beneath the surface... then rise again... the mouth on his back would gasp. Kalei gave her child a cape, as the son of someone royal, and forbade him from swimming.

Kalei told no one. She stayed close. Shielded him from questions. But a mother's reach can only go so far.

When he was of age, his grandfather took him to the men's house. There he ate meat for the first time. A single bite turned his body into fire. His appetite exploded.

The morning after his transformation from boy to man, he was muscular and stoic. His boyish play was transformed into stillness. A once lovely boy who played, now at thirteen, had the size and body of a virile twenty-five-year-old man. Instead of jumping and the frenetic play of children, Nanaue held his bursts of energy in a vault, hidden behind his ribcage, controlled.

No food was ever enough. His mother stared at her child in fear, while the rest of the village marveled at the resemblance this beautiful boy had to his exquisite father. During stories, Nanaue sat still, barely moving, only eyeing. Controlled.

And then... people began to disappear.

At first, it was those who swam in deeper water. Fishermen. Friends. Children. Then it was anyone. A man would go to the sea and never come back. A woman would bathe and vanish in the foam. A sudden fin would rise. A bite. Screaming. Then silence.

Kalei knew. She said nothing, for kapu would mean her son would be killed for his atrocities... This was her son's doing. And, technically, her silence made it so.

Nanaue was clever. He asked when his friends planned to swim. Then he would run to a different part of the beach. Take off his cape. Draped it on a nearby branch, and dove into the water. He disappeared beneath the waves. He became something else. And in the breeze, the cape waited.

Sometimes challenged folks to a race. In the water... he changed. He devoured them whole. He'd come back and ask, "Did he beat me to shore? Did he win?"

"He isn't back yet," the onlookers would say as Nanaue replaced his cape to hide the ravenous mouth on his back.

And the people began to whisper.

One day, the high chief summoned all the men to prepare the taro fields. Nanaue worked among them. The sun, high. The water, warm. The men, tired. One of them... joking maybe... curious perhaps... yanked the cape from Nanaue's shoulders.

The valley erupted.

Teeth. A gaping shark's mouth. Rows and rows of shining death across his back.

"Shark-man! Shark-man! Shark-man!" The people screamed.

Nanaue turned and snarled. Rage exploded in him. He bit down on a man's arm and tore it clean away. Another man's leg split open beneath his teeth. He thrashed side to side. Snap. Rip. Blood soaked the aina.

He ran for the sea. But the valley had already made up its mind. Men swarmed him. They threw him down. Bound him in a cord. He growled. They chanted. The mystery was over. Nanaue was the storm they had feared.

The high chief gave the order, "Prepare the imu. We burn the monster."

The people dug deep, laid the stones, and built the fire. The village was resolute. The beast had been caught. Justice would burn hot.

But Nanaue was his father's son.

He waited. He watched. Then... in a blink... he became a shark once more. The ropes fell. His body twisted. He rolled into the river.

The people chased. They threw stones. They prayed. They screamed. But no one dared dive in.

He reached the sea and vanished, and never returned to Waipi'o.

As much as we would love the story to end with the Ocean and his father embracing him for who he was, he wasn't only a carnivorous fish. He was also human. He couldn't belong in the embrace of Namaka'okaha'i or to the home of Kamoho'ali'i.

He swam to Maui, landed at Hana, took a new name, married a chiefess, and learned to smile sweetly.

But we all know that hunger does not sleep.

He began killing again, quietly at first. Then bolder.

One day, in full daylight, he took a young girl, carried her out into the deep water, changed into a shark, and tore her apart in full view of the people.

There was no pretending, now. The people launched their canoes, spears, and nets, and chased him from island to island. But he always slipped away.

He reached Moloka'i, hid again, and began feeding again. Naturally, more vanished.

The kahuna of Maui warned the kahuna of Moloka'i that in their waters was no ordinary shark. This was a man with teeth on his back. A god-child who honored his name.

One day, the local Moloka'i fishermen saw Nanaue when they saw a man dive off the cliff, hidden from (apparent) view, and become a beast. There was no more hiding.

They sneaked around the cliff out of view. They threw nets over him. They stabbed. Clubbed. Chanted prayers until the sea itself answered with blood-filled waves. Nanaue thrashed... weakened... failed. He could not escape.

They dragged him to shore. Hauled his great body up the hill called Pu'umano. There, they cut him to pieces and burned him in an open imu.

His ashes were scattered in the wind.

Waipi'o still remembers.

And sometimes... in the right moon... when the wind moves through the cliffs just so... you can hear teeth clack simultaneously in the wind and beneath the waves. Reminding you that even if it's someone's nature, there are laws to uphold. There are things we do not do. Even if they are the son of a king. Even if they are loved by a mother. Even if they take a chief's wife.

The Shamanic Transformation

You'll read about my shamanic transformation and that I have had another near-death experience since. On top of that, I live with an incurable chronic pain condition (that is thankfully under control). Believe it or not, this is the life of the shaman. Psycho-spiritual crises to connect us to that near-death reality of mortality are usually recreated in violent and frightening events or initiations.

They say that a shaman experiences many deaths, reminding them of their mortality so that they can stay connected to spirit and the cycles of life, so that they may heal others through their shadows. The kahuna who has been wounded and healed is capable of healing. The one who dies is capable of dealing with the dead. The one who is reminded of pain and suffering can remove pain and suffering. The one who has been thrown out of balance knows what it is to be balanced; to have real health.

In order for a witchdoctor to make this transition, their soul must invert. Picture your aura as the egg-shaped soul that engulfs your physical self, and it changes to have tendrils that reach away. Now, every soul has the tendrils.

When we interact with anything, our soul cords connect to those things, people, and places. It is through these cords that we receive or give life energy (mana). When we connect to forests, we receive mana; when we connect to a toxic boyfriend, we give mana; and when we connect to ourselves, we replenish mana. This is why most people need to go through cord-cutting.

Sometimes we continue to give away our energy to things where our attention remains:

"I miss that ex-girlfriend so much!"

"I was at my best when I played football in high school."

"I hate that bitch who stole my pen in third grade."

"That narcissist has ruined my life, and I can't move on. He stole those years."

"How come I never got that doll at Christmas?"

"My mom sucks all the life out of me."

"Living in Maryland was the worst eight years of my life."

When we are connected to things or people in the past that don't serve us, we give away our energy, making us feel lost and spiritless. A cord cutting stops the depletion of reckless draining of your energy to things you have no business connecting to.

The family of witchdoctors, which includes kahuna, shamans, and faith healers, undergoes the shamanic transformation, which inverts their souls. Instead of having an egg with tendrils that connect to a few things, their soul has a central point and only has tendrils, touching and letting go of many things. They can interact with tons of things, making them very psychic. Instead of their cords being used just for energy transfer like others, their tendrils are what sense energy, are read, and then interpreted by their nervous system as psychic information.

The Shamanic Transformation Happens In The Following Ways

- Enormous Fear

- Near-Death Experiences

- Death and Being Brought Back to Life

- Extreme Trauma

- Extended Torture

- Chronic Illness

- Deep Connection to the Spirit of the Natural World.

The little girl from the story already had a deep connection to the spirit of the natural world, and would probably transition naturally without the administration of Enormous Fear. My first transformation happened with the Near-Death Experience at Wai'anapanapa State Park, on Maui. My second one happened with the monster (the Pre-Chapter in *Witchdoctor Exorcist*). I was already a medium with the dark spirits who lurk in the shadows, but that in and of itself did not make me a witchdoctor; it only made me a medium. The practice of spell work did not make me a witchdoctor. And the training in dance and song did not make me a witchdoctor. My spirit had to die enough that it would transform, so that I may be able to heal.

With that being said, please don't create situations where you will have a chronic illness or chronic pain, die, or put yourself through unbearable situations of fear or torture. There is another way, which I will outline below.

Your spirit can grow and change into that of a kahuna healer through diligent connection to the Natural World. Although the other ways are one-and-done, including sitting out all night in the dangers of nature, this technique is just as viable. It just takes more time. Simply do these techniques repeatedly until the connection happens. For most, you'll need to do each of these a minimum of 25 times. A commitment to daily connection for a month or a moon cycle should do it, and it's worth it (and certainly better than the alternative).

Practice is the soil where aptitude grows. A single reading, or even a handful of attempts, rarely carries the weight required to transform knowledge into ability. When a person practices something more than twenty five times, they no longer encounter it as new. They begin to embody it. The body learns its rhythm. Repetition creates familiarity, and familiarity gives birth to skill.

In spiritual communities, there is a tendency for people to believe that a single exposure grants mastery. Someone reads an article, watches a video, or flips through a book and suddenly feels they are a healer, a teacher, or a guide. The hunger for mystery and power makes them eager to claim titles, but aptitude cannot be borrowed from a page. Reading once gives you awareness. Repeating the practice again and again, with humility and patience, gives you wisdom.

The twenty-sixth time you attempt a chant, you hear a vibration you missed before. The thirtieth time you hold silence in meditation, you notice the shape of your thoughts as they rise and dissolve. The fiftieth time you call upon spirit, you begin to recognize the difference between your own voice and the voice that answers. Each repetition strips away illusion and deepens your connection. Without that devotion, a person may know words, but they do not yet know the way.

Mastery is a harvest that comes after planting, watering, tending, and waiting. To claim mastery after one glance is like declaring yourself a farmer after holding a single seed. It is practice with hundreds of touches, breaths, and prayers that makes skill real. This is the difference between those who chase an identity and those who live in devotion. Aptitude requires repetition, because repetition is what changes the soul.

Sensory Deprivation

Another way to connect to (or invert) the spirit so it becomes shamanic is to do an evening of awake sensory deprivation. At the time of sunset, start an alarm for ten hours, and have something vibrate every hour to keep you awake. You are to sit, contemplate your traumas with noise-canceling headphones, and blackout eye coverings. No sound, no sight, for ten hours, and to also stay awake. This should trigger a kind of fear-based psychosis that should, hopefully, induce the transformation.

Outside Overnight

The most dangerous transformation is what was done with children in many tribes around the world in Neolithic societies. If the child seemed to be touched with the gift of spiritual communion, then they should have no difficulty surviving the night in the middle of a forest or jungle, or other dangerous wilderness, at the age of 13, as a right of passage, alone. Must not battle, but simply exist in the world of dangerous creatures, under the care of the protection of spirits.

Rituals for Deep Connection to the Natural World

With these connection exercises, your spirit should change over time, tugging and pulling your soul to reach and connect to all things in the world around you. As I've said, one practice with each will not be enough to transform your spirit, just as one class of Kung Fu does not make you a master.

Ritual of Land Connection

Find a location in nature where you don't feel or hear the awareness of the civilized world. This environment will need to be void of people, sounds from civilization, and free from the stamp of humanity. Once you find this place, you'll need to sit on the ground, making yourself as close to the actual earth as possible (in other words, no blanket).

Close your eyes and feel the ground underneath you; it's a tangible touch.

As you feel the earth, feel the hum of the energy of the earth. Feel it deepen the aspects of what makes the world thrive. Stay in this deep connection, reading and feeling its life force.

Be aware and only aware of the deep feeling of the earth's soul.

Once you can concentrate and lose yourself in her strength, focus on yours and how your hips, feet, calves, and thighs connect to her. Feel (don't imagine) how every part of you that touches her is fed by her and how you give back to her, a constant cycle of syphoning and gifting energy.

Feel and read how, through her, you are connected to everything that touches her, a conduit of feeding life energy, cleansing, and poisoning.

Feel how everything is connected through her. As you connect down into her, you can ride on her soul and feel the connection to any person, plant, rock, or life form on this planet. It's vast and wonderful.

This is the Deep Connection of Strength, Stability, Death, Resurrection, and Growth Potential.

Ritual of Sea Connection

Find a water source from nature: the sea, lake, river, ocean, waterfall, or stream. Sit near or in the water, being cautious of your physical safety. Connect. The spirit of the water around you. What does it feel like, the constant life and movement of the water? First, ride the energy of the water, allowing it to direct the speed at which you connect to it. As you passively connect to the energy and spirit of the water, ride and feel, and learn about the energy.

Once you've ridden the spirit of water, then force your own energy to keep up, racing and connecting with the ebb and flow of everything water. What does its spell feel like, what does its taste feel like, what does its texture feel like, and what does its spirit feel like? Keep up with the energy of water until you can feel (not imagine) the water in our air. The water in the rain that is yet to come.

This is the Deep Connection of Cleansing and Movement.

Ritual of Wind Connection

The wind will make the storm, which can destroy all life, and it can offer reprieve from the sun's heat. It can bite and it can kiss.

Find a location in nature where the sky opens up like a mouth to the sky above or under a long tree that reaches up to embrace the sky. In either case, you should be surrounded by some sort of obstacle to the ease of connecting to the wind.

Being aware of your own physical body and how the wind touches it, breathing on you, connecting to your skin, attempt to tune yourself to the quickest moving natural connection. As quickly as the moment of wind touches you, it leaves, and a new connection is made. Feel your body and what happens to it. Feel your breath and how you, in your life force, touch the air. You, yourself, affect the wind in the same way that the wind can affect you, albeit not with the same strength or vigor, but in connection, nonetheless. Feel how you and the wind flow around each other.

Match the wind's breath and then allow the wind to meet you and match yours.

This is a Deep Connection to Travel, Destruction, Comfort, Chaos, Fickle Adventure, and Vastness.

My Shamanic Death

Characters
Me
Namaka'okaha'i (Namaka) - Goddess of the Ocean Waters

    I was fourteen when I underwent my first shamanic transformation, and I was told that this would happen. When I was eight, my father's mother explained to me, in a vague and cryptic way, that I was destined to work in craft. When I met my power-animal, my spiritual self, I would need to teach my predecessors (whom, at the time, I thought would be my future children) to find their power-animal from the location of my own transformation. The clarity of her words came without her guidance in this story.

    As a witchdoctor, I was going to have a real-life transition. Somewhere in nature, someday, I was going to change. I would meet my power-animal, the animal of my lower self, and that location would be my sacred place forever. From my area of transformation, I would then need to guide others to meet their power-animals from my same location. I would spiritually guide them to my place of transformation and help them meet their spiritual selves.

    That meant that if I were to have my first death in a public park in New York City or the streets of Prague, then that is where I would guide my students to meet their power-animals. Each witchdoctor is different. The teacher will take you to the place of their first death. Mine was the bay of Wai'anapanapa State Park.

We were visiting our family in Keanae, Maui, at Christmas time. My family took us all the way to Hana, and we had a picnic lunch at my favorite place in the world, Wai'anapanapa State Park. This will be when I officially become that baby witchdoctor.

That warm midday, I played on the black sand beach, and I turned my back to the Ocean, something I had been told my whole life not to do. I figured I was deep enough in the Ocean that she wouldn't harm me, keeping me embraced in her somber body. I felt the pebbles under my feet and gazed towards the shore, letting my eyes land upon the high rock walls. I pondered the heiau (cemetery) that watched over the Ocean and its visitors. I bobbed up and down. My family was on the beach. My stepfather was under his umbrella in his camping chair. My mother was by his side, lower to the ground, feeling the sun on her skin, talking to my sister while they snacked on chip-and-dip. My brother was off in the brush with his action figures.

The pebbles seemed to give way, and I turned to face the Ocean's movement. A fun fact about me: I can't float. Because of that, I was always an excellent swimmer. My family made sure that I would survive if I should ever fall into water, since I had no natural buoyancy, by making sure I was a good swimmer. When the pebbles gave way, I started to swim in a small half circle to face the Ocean. It's time. I felt her whisper, and she jumped on me, pressing me down into the water.

Her hand hit me and took me down. I shouldered the pebbled floor and was pulled to the vastness of Mother Ocean. Above me, I could feel a push, keeping all those who would interfere away from us. I was hers alone. I didn't fight to swim. I intrinsically knew this was the time for something important.

In that moment, a thousand moments flowed through me. I was reminded that throughout my childhood, I had always been drawn to the water. I looked into bodies of water, trying to see her face (and will continue for that longing my whole life). I'm not sure why I was always looking for a woman's face. No one told me to. Whether I was fishing with my dad on a lake, playing with cattails by a brook, or swimming in the ocean, I was always longing to see her face.

With the current pulling me towards her and the waves rushing towards land above me, I was caught under the water. I felt my soul open. Where my soul's heart sat, my spirit unfolded, like a ball breaking open into a clam, inverting itself and transforming into a ball of tendrils.

I should have been afraid. I should have worried that my mortality was at stake. I knew the stories of victims of the under-toe. Why didn't I think a similar death would be the end of my story, too? Why just observe? Why didn't I feel my lungs harden with the pressure, my nervous system buckle in fear, and my life threaten to leave this plane? Instead, I observed my change, my transformation in her expert hands. I did not fight to survive.

At her Ocean floor, I felt my soul pull; death was upon me. As if a part of my spirit collected from deep within, hidden between the nerves, between the blood vessels, between the atoms within me. I felt my spirit-substance pull and pool together, leaking out of me from the inverted tendrils of my soul, and in the darkness, in the safety of Ocean Mother's womb, my soul, my spirit, pulled white like the foam of the Ocean break. Deep within the shadows of the Ocean, the white foam formed a great bear. A polar bear. It was me. He was my spirit. He was my power-animal, my totem.

Hello, it's nice to meet you, I thought. *But I'm afraid I'm dying.*

He warmly looked at me and said, *It's time for you to breathe, now.*

Not in the saltiest of waters was my 80-pound body going to float. But that day, I was lifted from the Ocean's floor by my bear and by Mother Ocean. I crested the top and took an easy breath. Not a gasp. Not a single feared sound escaped my body. I went down a child, and with my first breath, was born from Mother Ocean as a kahuna.

My family continued their lives; no one knew what had just transpired. I turned back to Namaka'oka'i. She was calm. There wasn't any inclination that she was tumultuous. I found the pebbles under my feet and stabilized myself, looking at her vastness. I said out loud to her, "So this is where I will take those who come to me? Like Grandma Maria said?" No one was near. My coming of age had happened in such silence, such isolation, and privacy. No ceremony. No one to witness or celebrate. Privacy. No living thing heard my question. It was for Namaka alone. Just a child asking for their mother's direction.

She calmed. No waves. At noon in Hawai'i, the idea of 'no waves' doesn't happen. This was her version of "yes." I'm sure of it.

"I couldn't be happier with your choice," I said. "Thank you."

A few years ago, I took my youngest daughter to Wai'anapanapa State Park. We sat on the black sand beach.

"It looks just like I thought it would," she said, moved. We sat in silence.

We had our picnic surrounded by tourists. Eating in the presence of spirit was also a divine part of my upbringing, so we enjoyed lunch in the presence of this great place. I said to my daughter, "I always wondered if I would have fought the transition... that death... that if I had fought the change... would I have drowned? Would I have died that day?"

"Probably!" She teased. My daughter was in so much awe from the energy of the Bay. "It's crazy, huh?" She said, "All these people who are playing on the beach, just wanting to be in Hawai'i, don't understand what this place is."

"Well, if you choose this path, you will have your own place of transformation. And then you will have to lead people to your place, helping them." I reminded.

"Yeah, I don't know about that." She said.

I try to come back to Wai'anapanapa State Park, to the black sand beach, every five years or so. This was my pilgrimage, my home, my religious transformation. The black sand beach and Mother Ocean were the first time I felt the gods.

I called Mother Ocean Namaka'okaha'i, and at times Yamoya (from my African roots). It never seemed to matter what I called her, as long as I respected her as a great Mother. I know she had always been waiting for that day, and halfway through my ninth-grade year (gosh, I was so young) was the time.

After that transition, I excelled in the arts of dance and storytelling. I was passing my fellow students exponentially and very suddenly. I had only started dancing at thirteen, and I don't think I demonstrated any talent or potential then. Dance was just fun. However, after that Christmas, the Ocean moved through me. And if you see me dance, I dance like she does. I'm strong, precise, and calm. She dances through me still, and my power-animal watches, in support and protection. At that moment of death, I became a prodigy child. I had my first professional dance job a year and a half later and continued on my way to New York, and danced throughout the country. I am forever grateful for the gift from the Ocean. A gift and transition from a god.

Only a few people knew about that place before I started teaching people about their power-animal. I now lead you with this book to The Bay, where you will meet with the energy of She of the Crossroads to the Otherworld. You may never see her, but she will let you through.

Spirit Walking: The Practice of Shamanic Journeying

To step out of the body and walk among spirits in astral projection, spirit walking, or shamanic journeying, your brain waves must enter a very particular rhythm, specifically, the theta brainwave state. This state rests between wakefulness and sleep; not fully conscious, not entirely unconscious. Theta waves are the frequency of visioning, dreaming, and deep psychic access.

Let's break this down. Alpha brainwaves dominate when you're focused or learning, taking in information, but are incompatible with stepping into the spirit world. Beta, though more relaxed, still keeps you too anchored in the physical. Gamma waves are the waves we give off when we are asleep. But theta… theta is the door. You touch it when you're drifting off naturally or surfacing gently from sleep without alarms or interruptions.

To reach this liminal space intentionally, sound becomes your most powerful ally. Repetitive drumming, particularly between 120 to 140 beats per minute, helps guide your brain into theta. The reason we relax with ease is that this rate reminds us of our own heartbeat, or the heartbeat of our mother when in the womb. The rhythm entrains the mind, drawing it inward while the steady volume helps keep your body slightly alert. Over time, your system learns to associate this cadence with the process of spirit separation, allowing you to slip more easily into journeying states.

> A quick note: songs with lyrics, especially if they are in the lyrics of the language you understand, will derail your focus. Your brain will want to engage, analyze, and follow along, pulling you right back to the physical. Instrumentals are best, but I still recommend traditional drumming tracks. Use noise-canceling headphones if you can. They cut out ambient interruptions that might tug your attention back into the room and keep your spirit rooted where you don't want it. I also recommend making it loud enough to hold you awake and drown out any environmental distractions.

Now, your body's position matters. We're aiming for relaxed but alert, not so comfortable you fall asleep. Personally, I sit on a meditation cushion cross-legged. You want to be in just enough discomfort to prevent you from slipping into unconsciousness, but not so much that your body is fighting you.

Christopher Penczak, in *The Temple of Shamanic Witchcraft*, lists several postures for journeying: lying down flat, sitting in a chair with palms up (Egyptian style), or even standing. What's important is to pick something that keeps you mindful of the moment but not distracted by your body. Any awareness of itching, barking dogs, or sore knees pulls your energy back to the physical plane. When you're truly journeying, the body vanishes. If it doesn't, you're likely just imagining rather than traveling.

This includes pain. I've battled kidney stones more times than I care to count. Chronic or acute pain can make journeying much harder; it anchors your awareness in the body. That's not a failure. It's simply your body doing what it's supposed to. Take care of your pain before attempting a journey. But be mindful: don't numb yourself to the point that your mental sharpness is compromised. Journeying requires presence, even in trance.

The Walk: A Step-by-Step Guide
1. *Choose a quiet space.* You need a dedicated area where you won't be interrupted, no phone buzzes, no pets, no background noise. This is sacred time.

2. *Set a clear intention.* Don't wander aimlessly. Ask yourself why you're entering the spirit world. Are you traveling for a client? Seeking your power-animal? Are you journeying for answers?

3. *Ground and center.* Take shallow, slow breaths. Drop tension from your body.

4. *Cue the drumbeat.* Use a recording with a tempo around 120 bpm. Avoid catchy songs or anything with lyrics. You want your brain to follow the rhythm into trance. A simple drumming track is best.

5. *Adjust your gaze.* With your eyes closed, lightly focus your vision upward toward your brow. Don't strain or lift your chin, just allow your attention to drift higher.

6. *Ignite the flame.* In the darkness behind your eyes, see a flickering flame. See it rise from the blackness. Let it lift above your head and light the space around you. When it's bright enough, it will reveal...

7. *The stairs.* See them clearly with ten steps, ascending, descending, or twisting in surreal spirals. With each breath, climb one step, and as you breathe out, stay on that step. This is the time to let the thoughts that distract you leave your mind. If you have a thought, don't control it. Follow it and let it bring you back to the steps. Inhale step. Exhale stay. Count down from ten. Let stray thoughts melt into the steps behind you. Your job is to empty the mental noise that keeps you tethered to the mundane.

8. *Enter the lobby of your mind.* Let yourself arrive in a place of spiritual resonance, your gateway. Your mind, the higher part of your soul, is the connector to understanding, rationalizing, and moving through different realms. In the lobby of your mind, we have three directions. To the left, you'll find a well. Straight ahead, you'll have a hallway full of doors, and to the right will take you out into nature. This direction is the mental plane, the path to other realms.

Your Power-Animal: The Psychic Avatar Within

Your power-animal isn't a guide you meet; it's you. Specifically, it's the psychic part of your spirit given animal form: instinctual, symbolic, and unfiltered by human complexity. It is not a separate entity. It's your psychic self revealed as something wild, pure, and wise.

When you engage in deep work, your power-animal will signal danger, offer direction, and show you how to move through spirit terrain. Its voice is direct, wordless, and unmistakable. It operates on instinct, not human reason.

Release your expectations of what this animal should be. Don't hope for a wolf or eagle just because they seem majestic. Whatever appears, no matter how odd, is right. Your psychic self is speaking clearly. Don't argue. Listen.

Let's be clear about a few things. No, your power-animal is not human. Never human. If a human shows up while you do this journey, it is a spirit who has a message for you. Kindly tell the spirit that now is not the time and that you will be willing to listen to messages from the spirit world or in the mental plane when you finish the task you have at hand.

Second, you may have heard of the trending term *aumakua*. There are two definitions of aumakua. First, an aumakua is an animal omen that your ancestors are letting you know you are on the right path. Many visitors come to the Hawaiian islands, fall in love with turtles, and say, "This is my aumakua." Unlikely, Becky. I doubt that turtles are showing up in your life in New York City to tell you that you are doing well on your path. Aumakua is not a spirit animal. It's not an animal you like. It's not an animal you wish you were. It's not an animal you dream about. And it is NOT your power-animal.

An aumakua is a sign. Think about an animal or bug that has shown up more than is normal for you. Also, this animal is generally the same animal for all generations. Your dad or your mom, for instance. Are there animals that show up in nature that tell you as a sign, "Hey, we see you and you're on the right path?" This is your aumakua. For me? It's a deer. When I or my daughter see deer, we know that we are doing well and our ancestors are letting us know we are on the right path.

The other definition of aumakua will be discussed later in the book, as it is relevant to how you heal people in psychic surgery.

Your power-animal should not be the same as your aumakua. This is you. Your psychic potential. And we generally have opinions (our mind's opinions) of what we are, and because of this, we are not objective. Don't guess who you are. Just do the journey and let it uncover.

A Different Path to Meet Your Power-Animal

This time, while sitting in the darkness with your eyes closed and breathing shallowly, feel your spirit. Let it expand around your body, your skin, your blood, your bones. Sense its color. Now, push a small piece of that energy outward. Let it take shape into a glowing orb, hovering in front of you. Watch it glow, then rise above your head.

Climb your staircase again. Ten breaths. Ten steps. At the top, find yourself in your lobby. You need to now turn right into nature, your nature. A forest, maybe. Take a path that curves through trees and around a massive stone wall until you arrive at a secret beach, a black sand beach surrounded by high walls and secluded. When you arrive there, notice that it is isolated and that you can look out into the vastness of the ocean.

Sit in the sand. The sun is setting. It's time to release.

Reach up, take the orb from above your head, and throw it into the ocean. Watch as it glows beneath the surface in your spirit's color. From that glowing seed, something changes and morphs. It's you, in your truest psychic form. Your power-animal rises from the waves.

Meet them. Don't name them. Just be. Stay open. Stay relaxed. Don't control the journey. From this point, we move away from visualization and into journeying, which means that the vision will fade. Allow it to be faded and meet your power-animal.

Power-Animal Rule: Keep the Name Sacred

Never speak your power-animal's name aloud. Not to your best friend. Not to your partner. Not to your teacher. This name is sacred.

Remember CATS? (Yes, I've performed in and directed that show.) There's a moment when they sing "The Naming of Cats," and you find out how each cat has three names. The third name... the true name... is secret. Sacred. If someone knows it, they hold power over that cat. Same here. Your power-animal's name is the vibration of your psychic self. If shared, it weakens your psychic boundary. Say it in the Spirit World if you must, but here? Never.

Walking the Spirit Current

When we speak of the Spirit World, we often divide it into three distinct landscapes: the Upper World, the Middle World, and the Lower World. These are the flowing paths of the Spirit Current. There are other concepts, like the Akashic Records or the Astral Realms, but for now, let's focus on these three.

Middle World

This is where you already live, but rarely see without the bumbling clumsiness of our physical senses. Journeying here allows you to see the spirit version of our physical world. This is where you check if there are spirits in a client's home... or help in locating a missing person. It's also where traditional witches often did their psychic battles. The Middle World is both here and it overlays our own with mystery.

When you see a shadow person, this is someone who is journeying out of the body into your space. In many cases, that person doesn't know they are spirit walking. In any case, to see different parts of our beautiful planet, you travel to the Middle World.

Lower World: Milu

Massive, dense, primal. The Lower World houses ancestors, cryptids, forgotten gods, and fragments of the soul. Some call it Milu or the Underworld, but it's not Hell. It's deep and vast. Much of the human dead reside here, though it's also filled with wild spirits, tricksters, and realms that echo Heaven, Hades, or Dante's visions. Never walk here without your power-animal. Think that all the versions of the afterlife are here. You have a country of Hell, a country of Nefilheim, a continent of a kind of Heaven, Milu, Duat...

Upper World: Po

The Upper World doesn't play by Earth's rules. For some, it appears bright and white like a cloud realm. For others, it's infinite black, dense with stars, or empty and still. It's not "Heaven" in the religious sense, though great beings dwell here: spirit guides, ascended ancestors, deities, cosmic beings, and Divine teachers.

You may meet Gandhi, Hekate, Harriet Tubman, or gods you never knew existed. There's also darkness here, strategic and intelligent. The Upper World holds the most advanced beings... and the deepest mirrors of self.

Let your body rest. Let your spirit rise.
You're ready. Enjoy the journey.

Hi'iaka's Epoch of Lohiau and Pele

Characters:
Pele - Goddess of the Volcano and Fire
Hi'iaka'akapoli'opele (Hi'iaka) - Goddess of Healing and Dance
Hopoe - Hi'iaka's consort and spirit of pono (righteous) messages
Lohiau - Prince of Kaua'i
Pili & Nolo - Lizard Dragons of Maui
Milu - The Underworld
Kukala Ohia - Hi'iaka's canoe to guide her home
The Mo'o - Giant Water Sex Lizard
Kane - The Sky God
Ohia - A man devoted to his love, Lehua - transformed into a tree
Lehua - A woman devoted to her love, Ohia - transformed into a flower

They say Pele does not sleep. The fires in her bones are endless. Yet there she lay, cradled by a grove of Ohia lehua trees, her body curled like molten stone cooled just long enough to rest.

The green twisted trees surround the sleeping goddess, protecting her from her rested vulnerability. Mist curled between her legs. Petals of red blossoms lay scattered across her chest and shoulders. It was the kind of stillness that ends before it begins. Stillness too deep to be simple rest.

Hi'iaka'akapoli'opele played nearby with her lover and best friend Hopoe. Hi'iaka is the goddess of life and healing. The keeper of forests. The sister who guards the fragile flame of Pele's slumber. There is no place safer than under the little sister's care, in the wooded shroud and protection of the forest.

Of all the voices in the world, the only ones near that grove were the quiet breaths of wind and the soft rustle of Hopoe's dance. Hopoe, the dancer of sacred vigil, part of the grove's heartbeat, was Hi'iaka's soulmate in body and spirit. The women's hands brushed as they wove ti leaves at Pele's feet. No one spoke. None needed to.

Pele lay wrapped in stillness so absolute that to look at her was to hold your breath. Hi'iaka tilted her head. A soft weight pressed into her eyes. She noticed the slight parting of Pele's lips. The barest tremor of exhale. Her sister's fire shimmered even in sleep, like embers beneath ashes.

They watched the grove pulse with Pele's absent breath. They felt the thread of her spirit extend outward like a starburst. It left. It soared above the ocean. The grove shivered.

At the edge of the world and spirit, Pele's spirit was not near her body. Pele journeyed as she did to find... men. Pele found herself on the island of Kaua'i. What pulled her there? What star called her away from that restless body? No one knew why the wind shifted and called from the north. Kaua'i did not with voice but with longing, a land of mist and green cliffs, a place where the heart could be found outside the chest, and a place where men have the power to love and devote.

Pele's spirit drifted across the sea, carried in silent chant, carried on heat that skipped along the waves. She traveled faster than any bird, and moved through the jungle and valley. Until her spirit found him.

Lohiau.

The mortal chief whose body had eyes like the red dirt. He wore the colors of sand and sun like a second skin on his rippled muscle. His flesh glowed with tan as though blessed by the earth. He was strong. His arms curved with the memory of paddles and pain. His chest rose and fell with quiet breath, like he held the whole world inside. His hands were calloused. His lips gently went, and they parted with an easy breath of security. His eyes were shy and clear, like looking into the molten soul of a cooling volcano. Lohiau, for being a chief, was young. His strong, virile body had only seen twenty migrations of the whales, but his hands and soul told a story of maturity and capability of devotional love and steady leadership.

In the morning, Pele arrived at the rise of the bay. Lohiau stood on shore, wet from the ocean, laughing with other inconsequential men. Pele appeared on the beach, freezing the men with the sudden apparition. Her body was dressed all in white. A maiden in pure light. Her hair blazed with the reddened kisses of ehu, giving a fiery glow to her waist-length hair, matching the height of Lohiau's eyes. Pele walked into Lohiau's presence as though she belonged there. She moved toward him until she could feel the breath from his parted lips. The men would have moved out of the way if they could have removed their feet frozen in the sand. Before she spoke, her glow made his heart thunder.

He opened his mouth. Words died. He stood still. The air thickened. Beads of sweat trembled on his skin. His breath went shallow. The pulse in his throat was like a drum. Feeling the tremble in Lohiau's warm breath was the only place Pele wanted to be. She vowed to always remain close enough to those parted lips. If she could not feel his breath, he would be too far from her grasp.

"Who are you?" he asked.

She called herself a traveler. A stranger come to find new skies. He offered her fruit. Twenty days sewed their souls together, like the cosmic weaver forced Pele into reason and calm with the gentle stability of a sexual youth. Consecutive nights, she bathed beside him. Each sunrise, she touched the breadfruit with care to gift his waking form. Then she'd touch his body. He could feel the warmth of the sun when they made love. She felt his breath on her chest.

They talked over the surfaces of rivers, under palms, and beneath stars. Their words were not always words. Sometimes they were a touch, a smile, a silence shared at midnight while the bay shimmered.

One dawn, she cried without tears. He watched as the white of her dress absorbed the red light of sunrise. He said her name at that moment. Pele. It was a word made of longing. She opened her mouth. The first sound was fire and ash and unmentionable memory. He stared into her eyes and really saw her. His eyes of fire saw the love that was meant to be. He drew her in to kiss her, as if to kiss the goddess for the first time. And she vanished.

Back in the grove beneath the Ohia lehua trees, Hiʻiaka sensed the shift. A movement through spirit. The wind spoke to her. Hopoe paused in the braid of ti leaves. Hiʻiaka placed a gentle palm on Hopoe's arm.

She whispered, "Take heart." Hopoe nodded.

The forest breathed softly around them, rich with the scent of lehua and damp earth. Ohia trees rose like elders watching over the dance of two young women, their red blossoms heavy with morning rain. Hiʻiaka ran barefoot through the undergrowth, laughter caught in her throat like birdsong, her hair wild with mist. Behind her came Hopoe, quick and radiant, feet brushing the ferns without sound, her hips swaying like wind through tall grass.

"Catch me then," Hopoe called, teasing, her voice rising above the rustle of leaves. "Or are you as slow as the lava that sleeps?"

Hiʻiaka turned her head and grinned, "I could catch you with three words."

"Then don't speak," Hopoe said, leaping lightly over a mossy log.

"I love you," Hiʻiaka said. Hopoe stilled. She turned back, breathing hard from the jaunt.

"Dance instead," Hopoe said.

So Hiʻiaka did. She slowed, then began to move through the understory, her body singing the rhythm of the land, arms rippling like ocean swell, knees bending low, hips swirling like smoke. Hopoe circled her, laughing, their two bodies weaving a pattern in the ferns. The forest seemed to lean closer, lulled by the song their movements created.

They danced until they dropped into the soft earth, breathless, tangled together in the lehua petals that carpeted the grove.

Hiʻiaka brushed a leaf from Hopoe's shoulder. "I should check on her."

Hopoe's smile faded. She turned her face toward the distant hill where the grove thinned and the earth steamed gently under Pele's still body.

"Why?" she asked.

"It's been twenty days," Hiʻiaka said softly. "It's too long."

Hopoe sat up, knees tucked to her chest. "But it's been peaceful. There are no earthquakes. No ash. No heat in the wind. No competitions where men die. No tests or trials. She's gone, and the world is quiet."

Hi'iaka said nothing.

Hopoe turned to her, voice softer. "Every time she wakes, something breaks. A canoe sinks. A family dies. The gardens are flooded with war with another sister. She doesn't mean to, maybe, but she doesn't stop either. And you..." she reached out and touched Hi'iaka's hand, "you are always the one who cleans up the burning."

"I know," Hi'iaka said, eyes distant. "But she is my sister."

"You owe her nothing."

"I owe her everything," Hi'iaka replied. "She gave me life. She gave me body. Gave me voice. Gave me a name. You would have no love sitting before you if it weren't for her."

Hopoe's eyes softened, but her jaw stayed tight. "But what has she taken?"

Hi'iaka blinked.

"I am not saying this to wound you," Hopoe whispered. "Only that I wish she would sleep a little longer. Long enough for the land to grow thick with peace. Long enough for you to dance only for joy."

Hi'iaka reached out and touched Hopoe's face. "If she never wakes, then what am I for?"

"For this," Hopoe said. "For us. For this grove. For laughter. You can have purpose when the world is not on fire."

Hi'iaka looked toward the east, where the sky was reddening. She felt the thrum of her sister's dreaming, distant but flickering, like a torch left too close to oil. Pele was stirring.

"She will wake," Hi'iaka said at last. "She needs me by her side. She will be weak."

Hopoe closed her eyes, rested her forehead on Hi'iaka's.

"Then go," she said. "But come back."

Hi'iaka pressed her lips to Hopoe's brow.

"I will always return," she said. "The grove is sacred because you are here."

And with that, she stood and walked toward the sleeping flame.

Hiʻiaka touched Pele's shoulder. Her chest rose. She breathed in and exhaled. Then she did it again. The grove hushed around them. No bird called. No petals fell. The world held its breath.

Hiʻiaka remembered the last eruption. She remembered the heat. The torn sky. The fire that licked at the gardens of her spirit. Her groves. Her companion's home. She remembered dancing barefoot in the smoke just to save a single sapling, to cool a stream with her breath so that it would not boil. She had always known her sister would burn it all.

Hiʻiaka reached up and brushed shadows from her sister's lashes. She pressed her hand to Pele's cheek. She whispered, "Pele... Pele wake."

Her body shuddered. Earth thrummed beneath her.

"Pele," she whispered. "You must return."

The body of Pele shuddered. Her back arched as if a wave had passed through her spine. Her body awakened, warming red as fresh lava, her breath dragging through her mouth like wind pulling through a deep tunnel. Her throat was dry, and her lips cracked as she moved them.

Pele's eyes opened quickly, grasping for a body not there. Pele's eyes, black as freshly cooled lava, stared at Hiʻiaka. Her gaze held both fire and emptiness. Her lips parted. A spark of flame lurched in her belly. When her eyes focused, they searched not for her sisters but for something else.

Hiʻiaka swallowed.

Pele's hair glowed molten in the dawn light. Her shoulders were bare. The petals of the grove clung to her like moss. Her voice was soft but struck the grove like lightning.

"Why did you call me?" Pele bit.

Hiʻiaka lowered her head. Behind her, Hopoe had joined the sisters and bowed.

"We thought you needed to return," Hiʻiaka said.

Pele breathed, then closed her eyes, "I sleep. I travel. I don't die like a woman of flesh," she opened those black eyes to pierce Hopoe. "I've died so that I may live and give life with the fire of fertility and growth. I died so that passions may exist. You woke me for what? Childish fears, my naive sister? Does the mortality of your plaything cloud your memory of who I am?"

Hiʻiaka felt Hopoe press her arm.

"We know. We held the grove. We cared for your form. We stayed vigilant. It was out of vigilance that I needed to wake you."

Pele sat up. The grove responded. Vines seemed to recoil. Flames flickered beneath her skin like stars waiting to ignite. She looked north. She closed her eyes.

"It is done," Pele spoke as though tasting an ancient wound. "I went there. I found him."

Hiʻiaka and Hopoe looked at each other.

"Where is he?" she said. The voice sounded like branches burning. "Where is Lohiau?"

Hiʻiaka blinked. "Lohiau?"

Pele's voice was furling to play with the sound on her solid tongue, "Lohiau... I have tasted his tongue and slept in his arms for twenty days," Pele said, rising to sit. Her hair fell around her in coils of cooled lava, glistening with embers. "He is mine. I gave myself to him, far away on Kauaʻi. He is a chief. His skin is brown like roasted kukui, his hair black like the ocean at night. I was with him in spirit. I touched every part of him. His body called me. I need him here."

"You've been gone for twenty days!" Hiʻiaka said.

Silence. The grove filled with the slow swell of Pele's words. "It has been twenty days and nights. I carried my spirit on the wind. I became a maiden of light. He held me, and I felt something beyond fire. Beyond vengeance. I felt longing." In Pele's grief, the wood beneath her cracked and began to smolder.

Hiʻiaka swallowed. She thought, *Let me help you. Do not let him be the undoing of everything*, but she only said, "Yes, sister."

Pele looked at her then. Fire in her eyes like molten rock. "Bring him to me. Bring him to me, now. Bring him back whole and in flesh. I will feed on him with my eyes. With my blood. I will taste him again and become whole. He calms my fire. But if you fail..."

She paused. Lava licked her voice.

"You will burn. Hopoe will burn. My fire will make your precious love garden ash."

Hiʻiaka's blood froze. The grove trembled. Petals dropped with a cacophonous thud to the ground.

Hiʻiaka's brows drew together. "I would go without asking. But why do you hesitate? There is more."

Pele rose to her feet. Fire trailed down her thighs. Her body was strength and threat and allure, the kind of beauty that devours. She stepped close. Too close. "If you touch him, if you let your beauty move him, if you lie with him, if you take from me what I have named mine..." Pele's hand raised, and her fingers curled in the air as if crushing something unseen. "I will burn Hopoe."

The forest went still.

"I will burn her where she stands," Pele whispered. "I will crack the earth beneath your grove and melt it into the sea. She is your heart. I know this. And I will turn her to stone."

Hiʻiaka's chest rose with a long breath. "You did not need to threaten me."

"No. But I remember your magic. I remember what your body does when it moves."

Hiʻiaka looked down. "She will remain here?"

"She will be safe. As long as you return."

Hiʻiaka turned her head and stared at her sister.

"I will go," she said. "But not because of your threats. I go because you are my sister. And because you have no patience to retrieve your own heart."

Pele smiled.

"You speak with fire. Good. You will need it."

"Why can't you get him yourself if you love him so much?" Hopoe challenged.

"You won't *help*, sister. You'll obey. You must get him. You're the only one I trust," Pele said. And with a wave of her hand, Hopoe's ankles solidified to the ground. "Your precious dancer will be my collateral."

Hiʻiaka didn't stir at the theatrical threat, "I must go now. I can hear the song of the winds. It will carry me."

Pele's gaze pierced her. "Do not take his flesh into your arms. Do not let his body be yours. If you hold him beyond your duty, I will murder your precious Hopoe."

Hiʻiaka nodded, though her heart cracked.

Pele said, "She stays here with me, and if you bring back my Lohiau safely and whole, you'll live out her mortal days together with peace."

"Give me the night, sister? One more night? Just one like you got with Lohiau?"

Pele nodded and released Hopoe. Hopoe stumbled, but marked around her ankles were rings of burn marks, making it impossible for the dancer to run away.

They journeyed through the night holding each other. Hopoe rested her forehead against Hiʻiaka's shoulder. The fire in the grove pulsed slowly as they did. Pele watched in silence until her lids dropped. She slept again. Hiʻiaka stroked the tendrils from Hopoe's hair.

Hopoe looked at the two arms now cupped around her. Hiʻiaka whispered, "Thank you." The grove sighed like a story ending.

Dawn came slowly. The sky was molten gold. Hiʻiaka gathered herself. Pele did not wake. No song. No prayer. Only the echo of destiny.

She walked toward the ocean, toward the rising sun, toward the beginning of the journey that would burn sisters apart.

The journey was long, but not unfamiliar. Hiʻiaka had walked the cliff faces and sea trails many times. She moved lightly and with grace, her footsteps pressing into ash and moss and old lava flows. She slept beneath tree canopies and in caves cooled by the breath of her ʻaumakua. She did not linger, not even when birds sang her name.

On the second day, the wind brought her to rest on the next island. Maui was in chaos because of the wind. Something had awakened and was torturing the island.

When Hiʻiaka arrived at the chief's house on Maui, the people greeted her with eyes full of ancient prayers. They had heard of her battles. Her name was a chant in the dark.

"The dragons Pili and Nolo," the chief said, "they come with no form. They haunt the mountain paths. They ride the dreams of children and leave their eyes white. They ruin the crops and steal the fish. And when we fight or challenge them, our people are found dead in their sleep."

Hi'iaka nodded. "I will slay your dragons and bring you peace, but we must be fast. I am on a journey for my sister, Pele, the great goddess of the volcano. I need you to prepare a place for my body. Make me a bed of ti leaves so that my form may be safe while I journey to battle these dragons. Keep the fire burning so I do not grow cold without the heat of my spirit. You will not see what I do, but when the wind shifts, you will know."

The preparations were swift. Her body lay wrapped in ti and smoke. Her spirit stepped out free.

In that form, Hi'iaka moved through the unseen parts of our world, much like how Pele walked among the living in Kaua'i. Her skirt flickered with sacred patterns. She danced. Each step echoed. The dragons came, invisible to mortals, but not to her. They hissed. She answered with movement, arms slicing the air.

The dance summoned lightning. Wrapped in her delicate fingers, she pulled the mana of lightning and directed it at the dragon. Pili was struck down. As the lighting grew through his veins, he burned from the inside, charring and making him solid, his spirit frozen, turned into stone.

Before the villagers' eyes, half of a mountain ridge grew, west of Wailuku. This first giant dragon was frozen into stone, with its coils and length creating hidden and treacherous valleys.

Nolo coiled, lunged, fangs of spirit aimed at her chest. Hi'iaka reached deep into the earth. Haleakala responded. A river of lava answered her call low beneath the volcano's core. She danced the mana of the volcano upward, wrapped in her chant. Once within her spirit, Hi'iaka cast it onto Nolo.

He froze mid-scream, carved into the cliffside, wrapped around his brother.

She returned to her body, breathless but whole. The people wept with joy and wonder. The dragons were so great that they created the West

Maui Mountains. Much like the dangers that the dragons created in life, their frozen mountain forms will continue to take life should anyone dare, with too much bravery, walk within the dragons' resting place.

The chief offered gifts, but Hi'iaka asked for only one thing: "Safe passage for me and the woman I love. A resting place in your valleys, always."

"It is yours," the chief said. "You will be remembered." And we will celebrate in your dance and in your honor within the Valleys that you created to keep us safe.

She bowed and continued her journey.

Dancing on the wind, her path ahead led to Kaua'i.

But what waited there was not life.

Not yet.

The sun had not yet touched the ridges of Kaua'i when Hi'iaka descended to the coast of the small island. She walked with the stillness of one who carried the world's breath in her chest. With the silence was the promise of a peaceful life with Hopoe on Maui, and beneath that held an ache she couldn't name.

Hi'iaka remembered Pele's orders. Lohiau's beauty haunted the older sister's sleep and stirred the roots of jealousy. Pele did not like to want. She liked to have. To possess. That was why she demanded loyalty. That was why she left Hopoe's life hanging like a ripe 'ulu above a flame. If Hi'iaka dared not bring a healthy and thriving Lohiau to Pele, her beloved garden, her beloved Hopoe, would be devoured by fire.

But Hi'iaka had no time for rest. When she reached Kaua'i, she followed the wind's voice inland. The forest was damp and trembling. A sorrow hung like mist. She walked into a clearing, and Lohiau lay there.

Alone.

Still.

Dead.

His body had not rotted, yet, but his skin had lost its color. His chest was silent. And yet... she knelt beside him. Her fingers touched his cheek. A memory struck her like surf slapping black rock:

Rain falling, heavy and thick.
Night falls.
Lohiau, seated on the ground of a stone lookout.
Arms loose at his sides, face turned to the sea-soaked sky.
He was weak.
No food, no water.
A self-made punishment for being under the spell of a goddess.
He was giving his life. His spirit had fallen in love with a spirit.
The only way to let his spirit meet hers was to be in spirit himself.
So he starved himself.
"I would give everything to taste her again," he murmured to the clouds.
"Even if I must meet her in the shadows of Milu."
He wept. Quietly.
Then let go.
Falling limp onto the ground.
The supple muscle, like an offering served in the rain to the gods.

Hiʻiaka drew back. Her hands shook. She must have only been a day late. He must have just died.

If she had not taken the challenge to secure a sanctuary for her and Hopoe, she might have found him in time.

Pele will kill Hopoe, now. Hiʻiaka can't deliver a living chief.

She knelt on the rain-covered ground. It was morning. How could she have been so selfish to take on the extra time for her love...

No.

Pele had done this.

This was the cost of her desire. She had enchanted him with longing, and then left his body starving without the source of his love. His soul had wandered out of its own despair.

But Hiʻiaka would not leave him like this.

She cleared the forest. She swept vines into a circle. She cleaned his body with water and fern, and at the peak of the sun, she danced.

Not the dance of celebration. Not the gentle sway of lovers. This was the dance of breath and bone. The dance that calls back the shadow.

Day one, she chanted until her lips bled and her voice became sharp like ʻaʻa. The spirits stirred. The trees leaned in.

Day two, her feet bled. She swayed and spun until her skin glistened with power.

Day three, she screamed. She reached with her hula into the threads of Milu. She sang to his soul, calling it back from the edges of the underworld. She was raw now. The string of her own body was nearly snapped. Her body withered and aged with the dance of time. Each day of dance made the most beautiful goddess look ten years older than the previous day.

Day four, the goddess's skin hung, and her bones bent into curves. With a final push as the sun crested its peak, the wind stopped. The earth paused. She cast her paʻu like a net and searched the shadows for his spirit threads in Milu. She pulled the soul through his feet, anchoring it with chant. Her body trembled. The moment his breath returned, she collapsed. Lohiau's foot twitched.

He awoke.

He opened his eyes and gasped like a newborn pulled from saltwater. She lay beside him, one hand still pressed to his chest.

"Who are you?" he asked.

"I am the one who called you home," she said. With her stillness, her aged body, from the four days of magic, siftly returned to her youthful appearance.

Their eyes met. As his ruddy eyes blinked, the old woman whose hand lay on his chest transformed into a beautiful young woman. His body remembered the dream of Pele, his spirit leaned toward the woman whose breath had caught his soul.

"Pele?" She looked like Pele, but her hair was not kissed with the fire of the sun. The young woman didn't give the same powerful matriarchal essence of fire and destruction. She gave a different kind of power. This powerful woman, who looked like Pele, was of something nurturing.

He did not reach for her.

She did not remove her hand.

"I am Hiʻiakaʻakapoliʻopele. I'm here to take you to my sister."

Hi'iaka laid her palm upon the great koa trunk and whispered the prayer of shaping. The spirit of the tree woke from its nap and answered. There was a warmth in her hand; the breath of the living koa lingered beneath its bark. It cracked and sang, transforming into a marvelous canoe. The men of Kaua'i had already begun the work by the time her magical food had returned Lohiau from the threshold of Milu, and now the hull was nearly finished, long and sleek as a waterline between two worlds.

She named the canoe Kukala Ohia, for it was Hi'iaka's will to call out to the grove of her homeland with every glide upon the sea. Lohiau stood beside her as his men worked. The two observed, and they moved around each other with the strange, quiet rhythm of those who have died and come back with the scent of the other world still clinging to their skin.

At night, they did not touch. Lohiau was deeply grateful to her. She had stitched his soul back into his flesh with the power of hula and chant, and she had not asked for anything in return. There was a trembling between them. An unspoken current. But Hi'iaka's hands had held the dead, and her mouth still tasted of sacred words.

Still, the sea was their companion now, instead of the wind. Hi'iaka had to travel with someone else, so dancing on the wind would not work for the return home.

It was on the fifth night of their voyage when the winds betrayed them. A current pulled the canoe away from the path to Hawai'i. Clouds churned thick over O'ahu, and dark water slapped against the side of Kukala Ohia. Lightning flickered deep within the clouds, but no thunder followed. There was a silence in the storm that made Hi'iaka's skin tighten. Her voice was still healing from the chant that brought Lohiau back to life. They had to survive with skill instead of magic.

They fought the storm, and as the cliffs of Oahu towered over them, they lost to the storm and crashed.

They found shelter behind a great curtain of water in Waipi'o. A waterfall poured from the mouth of the mountain and offered them a dry alcove in its rocky belly. The cave was narrow, but held the scent of ferns and black earth. The boat was dragged onto a flat shelf of stone. It would need mending in the morning.

They lit a fire, but the heat never touched the chill in Hi'iaka's chest. She had seen the signs. This place was not empty. Something ancient lived behind the falls. She heard it breathing in the pulse of the stream, in the hiss of mist on stone. She was too tired to care, and slept.

The next morning, the storm had passed, the breeze was welcoming, and Lohiau had already risen. When she opened her calabash of awa, Hi'iaka stretched and felt that the sleep was enough to mend her voice and body from its recent trials. She went down to the canoe to mend it, hoping to find Lohiau there.

He wasn't.

Lohiau was at the edge of the pool and kissed the waterfall, looking into the swirling water as if it spoke his name. Hi'iaka found him staring into the water. She felt something ominous here.

Hi'iaka called to him softly, but his head did not turn. His body leaned forward, pulled not by his will, but by something more primal. Something smelled his morning sexual urges on him. His skin glistened. The hairs on his arms raised. He stepped into the water.

"Lohiau," she said again, but he was already waist-deep, already reaching.

The Moʻo rose.

She didn't have a human form at first. She was all shimmer and lizard shadow, water folding around water. Then, as Lohiau reached her, she took the shape of a woman with skin like wet lava rock and long, green-black hair coiling like eels. Her eyes were rivers. Her mouth, a whirlpool.

She clung to Lohiau like a vine. He gasped and collapsed into her embrace. Their bodies moved together in the current of the stream as she pulled him beneath the surface and dragged him across the rough floor of the pool until his clothes tore away, exposing him. She drew him toward her lair beneath the waterfall and pinned him there.

The Moʻo's power was ancient and raw. Her thighs locked around his hips with the pressure of the current. The friction of rushing water and stone sent waves of ecstasy through Lohiau's body. He tried to cry out, but the water was in his throat, and her water was wrapped around his groin. His resistance pulsed through his veins. His body writhed, and his crotch got thicker and stronger with the pulsating water and the succubus-lizard's writhing hips. He fought, pinned to the waterfall. His muscles shook as he cried out, leaking. The Mo'o muscled his mouth with her lizard tongue, sliding it in and out of the cold water's noise. Lohiau's abs tightened, and his legs quivered as he was out of losing control over his arousal. Overtaken, his seed shot in a shudder of violent pleasure beneath her slick weight.

Hi'iaka stood at the edge of the pool, chanting low and furious. She did not look away. There was no shame. Only fury. The Mo'o had broken the kapu. This was not a seduction. This was a theft.

The vines that hung from the cliffside writhed at her call. She reached up and pulled Lono's name through them, binding the god's breath to their curling lengths. The vines thickened, green to bronze to black.

Hi'iaka stepped into the water, her body glowing with the 'aina's mana. She did not fight the water. She moved with it, danced with it, called it to coil around her wrists and ankles. The Mo'o turned, too late. Hi'iaka's hands had already found her throat.

The vines lashed like snakes. One wrapped around the Mo'o's neck, another her hips, another her ankle. Hi'iaka chanted as she strangled her, with divine law, and justice for her sister's lover. The Mo'o writhed, hissed, screamed with the voice of the stream. Lohiau floated to the edge of the pool, half-conscious, sated.

When the water went still, the Mo'o was bound. The vines held her to the wall of the waterfall. Hi'iaka couldn't kill the primordial creature, but she could curse the creature to never leave the waterfall. We still warn boys today of the power of the Mo'o in the waterfall, for she will steal your ecstasy with her seduction of her friction.

Hi'iaka lifted Lohiau from the water. He was shaking, teeth clenched, eyes glassy. She carried him to the cave and wrapped him in banana leaves.

"You are safe," she whispered, placing her hand on his chest.

He wept, silently. She did not comfort him with lies. Only warmth.

The night came slowly. Mist clung to the leaves like ghosts. Hiʻiaka stepped from the cave and watched the light fall through the trees. She knew Pele had felt it. The pulse of Lohiau's climax on the wind. Pele would have tasted it in the air like a bitter fruit.

Thirty-one days had passed.

The canoe would be mended. The sea would open once more. But something else had broken, and Hiʻiaka hoped there was time left.

She walked to the water's edge and prayed, not for strength, but for clarity. The journey had changed her. Lohiau's body had touched the Moʻo, and Pele's flames were surely already rising. Still, Hiʻiaka stood tall in the setting sun, her skin steaming where the water's cold still clung.

She would not stop. She would carry Lohiau to Pele. She would face whatever came next.

Even if it meant walking into fire.

The wind shifted.

It carried the smell of salt and wet bark, but beneath it all was a scent that did not belong to the sea. It was musky. Male. Alive. Pele turned her face toward it, her eyes still half-lidded from impatience, and inhaled deeply.

It was the scent of Lohiau's ecstasy. Betrayal!

She knew it. She had consumed it herself. As if her tongue remembered his mouth, her nose remembered his groin, the fever of him beneath her long ghostly limbs in the dreamscape of Kauaʻi. But this... this scent was not from her journey. It was from the world of flesh.

She rose from her home within Kilauea of cooled pahoehoe, strands of her molten hair coiling and uncurling like fiery serpents. Her skin hissed as mist from the groves met her heat. She stood in the center of the garden Hiʻiaka and Hopoe had planted with song and sweat. The garden was damp from morning rain, the leaves still trembling.

Hopoe was dancing.

She danced barefoot in the soft mud beneath the trees, her arms painting love into the air. Her skin was slick with dew. Her mouth opened slightly in the rhythm of breath that came from joy and ritual. Her skirt, layered in red lehua, flared with every turn.

Pele watched her with a gaze that held revenge and hunger. Dancing in a grove made of love, of devotion. The Ohia lehua trees.

She remembered when she had first wanted the boy, Ohia. He had stood tall, beautiful, but unwilling. She had reached for him, demanded that he love her. The man, Ohia, loved some wispy girl. This towering muscle of a man was a prize to win for Pele. This prize refused her out of loyalty to someone inconsequential. Puny. A nothing. How could he have refused a goddess?

When he refused, she had turned him into gnarled wood. She took away his beauty and twisted his bones into a deformed tree without anything remarkable. If she couldn't have him, she would make sure no one would. No one could even look upon his beauty again. Pele would be the last one to see the beautiful man. The only thing she could claim from him.

Sometimes you can still hear his screams of pain when the wind whips through his branches.

Later, Pele found the Lehua girl, weeping under the twisted tree. She had wept at the roots, praying to be with her love. Pele had softened. The girl was kind of pretty. Probably still stupid, but devoted nonetheless. Even in Ohia's ugly form, the Lehua girl still loved him. So, Pele transformed her as well. She made Lehua into a flower that could grow only from the tree's branches, so they would never again be parted. It would also be kapu that only a woman could pick Lehua from the tree. No man should pull a woman from the man she loves.

But today, the smell on the wind soured her kindness. It reminded her that love is not loyalty. Not always. It reminded her of what she feared most, being replaced.

Hiʻiaka had not returned. And now the wind gossiped of Lohiau's climax, to tease and torment Pele. Alone. Again. As if to whisper, "He didn't choose you, again."

Pele felt her body heat with betrayal. Her lips cracked with flame. Her hair lifted like cinders dancing upward into the sky. She moved without thought, without mercy.

Fire bloomed in her footprints.

She walked into the Ohia grove and raised her arms. The flames leapt from her fingertips like spears. They pierced the bark. They split the earth. The ferns curled into ash with a single breath.

Hopoe turned mid-dance. She saw the rage in the way Pele's body cracked open like a faultline. Lava spilled from her chest in glowing ropes. Her eyes were two black pits swimming in fire.

Hopoe only stood silently. Her feet rooted in the same soil she had tended with Hiʻiaka. Her arms lowered to her sides, open. She looked at Pele the way a flower looks at the sun, trusting even as it burns.

"I kept your sister safe," she said softly. "I danced in prayer for her every night, so you may have your love. I kept my love safe so your lonely, vile ways could finally end."

But Pele wouldn't hear her sister's words. She saw only the imagined betrayal in the curve of Hopoe's smile. The way her skin held the same sweetness Hiʻiaka had once laid her head against.

Flames swallowed Hopoe in a single breath.

Her body twisted once, arms lifted in a final shape of hula. Then she was stone. Her mouth opens. Her lei of lehua frozen mid-sway. She stood forever captured in dance, coated in black glass, red fissures glowing across her chest.

The Ohia grove blackened and collapsed in on itself. Roots hissed. Leaves curled into skeletons. The songbirds that once nested in the canopies fled for the safety of the snow goddess Poliʻahu's domain.

Only the scent of fire remained.

On the sea, one day from shore, Hiʻiaka lifted her head from tending the waters.

She smelled the smoke before she saw the plume. It clawed into the sky above Hawaiʻi like a spear hurled from the gods. She felt her throat close. Her hands went numb. Lohiau, still traumatized, naked, wrapped in banana leaves, still recovering from the moʻo's violence, noticed her change but did not speak.

He had no words.

Hiʻiaka stared at the faraway horizon, the captain of the Kukala Ohia, the sorceress of life, the kumu hula of the web of story... She could feel Hopoe's dance had stopped. Not ended. Not finished. Just... stopped.

There was no pulse in the Ohia trees.

She said nothing. Her arms moved like branches in a storm to propel the Kukala Ohia to split through the waves and fly with the winds. Relentless. Silent. Lohiau followed her lead, though his body ached with confusion. Guilt curled in his belly like a sleeping eel.

When they made landfall, the earth was still hot.

Hiʻiaka stepped barefoot onto the scorched trail that once led into her grove. Her feet did not burn. The fire recognized her. It licked at her skin but did not consume her. She walked through ash. Through smoke. Through the ghost of what she had loved.

The garden was gone.

And in its place, a statue of stone, locked mid-dance. The smooth curve of Hopoe's exposed dancing thigh was frozen. Hiʻiaka traced Hopoe's cheek, mouth soft and still. Her arms open as if asking for an embrace from the Po that never came.

Hiʻiaka knelt.

She placed her hands on the blackened earth.

She did not cry. Her grief was too sacred for tears. Her voice cracked with chant, but not the chant of healing. Slow. Low. The chant of unweaving. The chant of unraveling. ʻAnaʻana.

Lohiau stepped forward.

Hiʻiaka stood, turned, and faced him. Her eyes were empty. The growled out the pule of death. She no longer pitied herself, this prized pig, or her endless and pointless devotion to her violent sister. Empty.

"You were the reason," she said.

Lohiau bowed his head. "I never asked..."

"You did not have to," she said. "Your body chose. And my sister burned my beloved to prove a point. I've learned one thing. Things that are beautiful can't stay beautiful forever. They wilt. Even love.... Even your beauty, Lohiau."

He did not resist when she raised her hands, continued the chant, and danced the violent hula to destroy the aka that kept his soul attached to his ridiculously fragile and beautiful form.

The hula she danced was the violent cutting of what she danced for four days to bring him back to life. The sways of her hips and the violence in her hands were for ending.

She drew the power of the ana'ana into her limbs, pulled the threads of life from the space around Lohiau, and teased them loose with slow movements. Every sway of her hip unraveled a breath. Every arc of her arms thinned the light in his eyes.

He gasped.

She danced on.

She called to the gods with her feet that a new soul was coming to Milu, and death was in the hands of the goddess, who only knew growth. Her dance created a circle of mist around her. Lohiau lost sight of the goddess in her tunnel of fog. Terrified, he watched the flashes of fingers and flesh within the encircled mist. And when she stepped across the circle and touched her fingers to his chest, his heart untied and lost its beat.

Lohiau fell.

The air went still, and the mist cleared.

From atop the mountain, as the mist disappeared, revealing Hi'iaka and the dead Lohiau, with only the dismembered Ohia groves and the frozen Hopoe as audience, Pele, for the first time in her life, cried.

Pele stepped down from her mountain, her skin still glowing with the fury of eruption. She saw the body. She saw her sister, hands trembling, mouth set in the stillness of grief. She moved to strike. To scream. To tear Hi'iaka apart for defying her. Roaring down the hill until she was face-to-face with Hi'iaka.

The sisters stood there, breathing on each other.

Stone and ash stood where once there had been laughter.

Hiʻiaka looked down at the ash-covered ground, and then deep into Pele's black eyes. "One for one," she said.

Pele stepped back, looked to Hopoe, and looked to Lohiau.

And for the first time in a hundred lifetimes, Pele had no answer.

The wind died.

The trees that once danced with Hopoe stood still in their charred silence. No birds sang. No insects stirred. The ʻaina held its breath beneath the stare of two sisters.

Pele stood before the corpse of Lohiau, her arms molten at the edges, her hair still simmering with the glow of lava. Hiʻiaka stood across from her, the ash of her lover's garden clinging to her bare feet, her chest rising with fury and grief in equal measure.

Smoke curled around them like a lei of ghosts.

"You said you would not touch him," Pele said, voice low like lava sliding beneath the surface of the earth.

"I did not," Hiʻiaka answered.

"I could smell his..." Pele's rage regrew.

"The Moʻo of Oahu," Hiʻiaka interrupted. "I kept my vow to you, and you..." Hiʻiaka broke into tears. She fell to her knees and buried her face, which mirrored Pele's, into the ash. Hiʻiaka, in all her trials, finally broke.

Pele's face twisted with the bruised pride of a deity whose power could not undo the ache in her chest. She looked at Lohiau's lifeless body. She looked at the stone that was once Hopoe, one arm frozen in a forever hula, her lehua lei now veined with obsidian.

"One for one," Hiʻiaka repeated. "Your fire took my love. My chant took yours."

Pele blinked slowly. The air around her shimmered with heat, with regret, and with shame. A wound only a sister could carve. Pele turned her eyes to the horizon, where the ocean roared far off and the clouds held back their tears. "What do you want from me?" she asked.

Hiʻiaka walked to Lohiau's body. She crouched beside him and placed a hand on his chest. His skin was still warm from her hula. His soul was gone, but the vessel had not cooled. She traced her fingers over his face. A high priestess preparing an altar.

"I want justice," she said.

"You already took it," Pele whispered.

"No," Hi'iaka replied. "Justice is not pain. It is balanced."

Pele narrowed her eyes. "Then speak it."

Hi'iaka stood. "Bring Hopoe back. I will return your man to you."

Pele flinched, her heat curling upward again. "You will what?"

"You heard me," Hi'iaka said. "We cannot remain in this war forever. Not as sisters. Not as goddesses of this land."

Pele laughed once, sharp and bitter. "You would give him back now that he has chosen you?"

Hi'iaka said nothing.

Pele looked at her. "You think I cannot smell him on your body? Even if your hips never met, your spirits tangled. He belonged to me, and you knew it. You waited too long. You let him die twice. You want me to believe he wouldn't choose you."

"I did not choose him," Hi'iaka said.

"Then why did he choose you?" Pele asked.

"He hasn't chosen anything!" That silenced Pele.

The silence between them deepened until it cracked with power. Pele lifted her hand and called the gods.

"Kane!" she shouted.

The earth rumbled. The trees groaned. A warm wind moved through the dead grove.

Hi'iaka joined the chant, but did not need to shout. She sang.

The voices flowed into the cracks between lava rocks. It threaded into the veins of the Ohia trees. It coiled around the stone body of Hopoe like water returning to dry land.

A white mist gathered.

From that mist, Kane appeared, as the stillness that comes before the first drop of rain.

He asked no questions.

He only placed one hand on Lohiau's chest, and one on Hopoe's shoulder.

Light poured from his palms.

Hopoe gasped first.

The stone cracked and flaked from her skin like shedding bark. Her chest rose and fell, eyes fluttering open as if from a long dream. She fell out of her broken form, looking around in wonder, her gaze finding Hi'iaka.

She smiled.

Then Lohiau stirred.

His hand twitched. His jaw clenched. He opened his eyes and saw Pele standing above him. Her glow softened. She knelt beside him, gently brushing his damp hair from his face.

"Do you remember me?" she whispered.

His lips parted.

His voice came slowly. "I do."

"And do you still love me?"

He hesitated.

Hi'iaka looked away.

Hopoe jumped up to grab Hi'iaka's hand, fingers tightened around her own.

Lohiau sat up, his breath shallow. "I dreamed of you," he said. "But in the dream, you were not kind. As I died again for your love, I floated on the wind heading for Milu. I saw what you had done in my name."

Pele's mouth trembled. "And now?"

"She made me live. She gave me life. She fought for me. Hi'iaka, born from Pele. Maybe you gave away your love in order to give birth to such a sister. But that means all you want is control. I chose the one who loves," he said.

Hi'iaka gasped.

His eyes moved to Hi'iaka, then to Hopoe. He looked at the grove, scorched and quiet. "You burned what she loved. To own me."

Pele stood. Her heat returned, but it was quieter now. Like embers.

"So you choose her?" she asked, voice hollow.

Lohiau met her gaze. "I just can't choose you."

Hi'iaka turned to Hopoe and kissed her deeply, in a panic. "I love you. I am tied to her. I will dance your dances and you'll always be with me…"

Hopoe kissed her again and gave breath to, "... but one for one."

Pele turned away from the crowd, looking up to her mountain, and said, "Will you still love me?"

Hi'iaka looked deeply into Hopoe's eyes and answered them both, she said. "I always have."

Hopoe returned the look into Hi'iaka's eyes. The woman who planted Ohia seeds in her footprints. Who danced beneath moonlight and waited by the sea. Who stood in the fire and never once turned away.

Pele stepped back.

The sisters looked back at Kane together, bound to each other.

"One for one," said Kane. He swiftly touched Lohiau on the chest, and his body fell, dying a third time. He gathered Lohiau's spirit in one arm, cradling the weak soul.

Hopoe hummed and began to dance. As Kane touched Hopoe, she was once again transformed into stone. He reached inside and pulled Hopoe's soul from the stone statue. As Hopoe's spirit joined Kane, the flecks of embers that danced on the lava impression of her solid form went out.

Pele let her heat fade. Her feet cooled. Her arms lowered. She turned and began to walk back to her crater.

As the sun rose, the Ohia trees bloomed once more. But the bark remained black. The petals always looked as if they had been dipped in flame. A memory scorched into beauty. A garden that would never forget.

Hi'iaka stood at its center.

And she danced.

Traveling in Spirit

Traveling to the Middle World

Remember that the middle world is here on Earth. Look around. It's right here. Imagine how a ghost walks. They traipse through this world, able to see and experience the aspects of life and energy that we, in our numb senses, cannot experience. Before the ghost passes on to the world of the dead, they are still here, navigating this world in spirit form.

When you navigate the middle world, you are doing it similarly to the recently deceased.

In order to travel this world in spirit form, you're going to follow the steps similar to meeting your power-animal. It is vastly important that you travel with your power-animal, because that psychic part of you will make sure that you don't end up in precarious situations. That psychic part of you (your power-animal) can anticipate dangers, help you find the locations you're looking for without the slowness of the analytical mind, and they will constantly remind you of your spiritual potential.

Once you get to the bay, there are a couple of ways to journey to the middle world. Remember that the bay is part of the mental plane. The mental plane is where all thoughts, creativity, and energies intermix. This place is how a psychic connects from one person to another. So, we have to be able to step out of our minds in order to release our physical form.

The first way is when you are at the bay, sit in the sand, or lie in the sand, the same way that your physical body is before you started your journey. What is the pose your body is in now? In your mind, you will sit/lie/be in the sand the same way. Once your mental self is relaxed and in the same form as your physical self, have your power-animal take you by the hand and step out of your "mental form" and into the spirit location you are trying to reach on earth.

Another way, which I find to be the most successful, is this: With your power-animal, tell them where you want to go, as if it doesn't already know, and leap over the rock wall, flying in spirit to the location on earth that you are trying to visit. This technique tends to yield the highest results.

A third technique is simply to walk over to the rock wall. Find in the rock wall a handle or stone that you can push. Once you find it, push on that rock or use that handle to reveal a door. The door will be an entryway into darkness. Step into the darkness. As you become accustomed to the darkness, your eyes will adjust, and you will arrive in the location that your totem needed to take you. Your focus fades out into darkness, along with separating from your body fully, and fades into the new location.

These are three really great techniques for you to journey in the middle world, here on earth.

Traveling to the Lower World: Milu

Remember that the lower world is the place of the deceased, many different kinds of spirits and entities, and is a strange spirit reality. If you enjoy the books of *Alice in Wonderland*, you'll have an idea of the different forms of landscapes that you may encounter. Again, you should not travel without your power-animal so that you can remain safe from certain kinds of spirits that may want to trap your soul, leaving your body in an unfortunate coma.

The best way to get to the lower world is to simply step into the water. Remember that in most mythos, the deity that is associated with the ocean is also associated with the journey to the place of the dead. For this book, the low world is called Milu.

One way to journey to Milu is to step into the ocean. The ocean is made up of Kanaloa himself. This god is the god of magic and is the veil. Traveling through him, and not through the actual waves on our real Ocean of Namaka'okaha'i, his essence transports you into the lower world. Let me clarify that again. Namaka'okaha'i is the mother of the Ocean. Kanaloa is the Spirit of the Ocean, the Magic of Water, and the God of the Passages (which includes death).

When you travel through the essence of Kanaloa, the water then becomes the sky. You'll notice that you are in the lower world when you look around, and the sky doesn't look blue anymore. It almost has a pinkish haze. The laws of physics and those "existence rules" of our solid world are no longer chains that bind us here. The space within space is vast. The spirit world is the essence of the moisture in our atmosphere. The space within space. The spirit world isn't actually down. It's around and within.

We as humans are not capable of understanding all of the possible landscapes that are in the spirit world. I like to think that all of the cultures that documented the different parts of the spirit world are all correct and only got tiny slivers of the story right. Stepping through the ocean at the bay is one easy and productive way to travel to the world of Milu. In some mythos, Milu or Lua'o'milu is ruled by a god of the same name, but this may have been a restructuring based on two Colonial ancestral narratives (like that of Hades of the Underworld and Hel of Hell). Because it's a possibility that Milu was created as part of a white retelling of a brown story, we will leave Milu (the god) out, and maintain that it is Kanaloa's realm.

Another way is to climb up onto the rock wall at the bay. You'll find a giant tree. Hopefully, this is a breadfruit tree, but if not, just climb onto this tree of transition. You'll find a branch that is long and hanging over the cliff, dangling above the ocean.

You and your power-animal will sit on this branch. You, again, will talk to your power-animal about where you plan on going. Once you decide, either the branch will break, dropping you, and that sensation of falling will transport you, like a teleportation, to the lower world. As if to fall and show up where you're supposed to be. Some people fall into the Ocean, and in that splash, they arrive where they are supposed to be.

Traveling to Upper World: Po

The Upper World is the world of the gods. As I've talked about in the previous chapters, the upper world is a world of the mind. It's some sort of shadow of our third dimension. We can't comprehend it, being that we are three-dimensional creatures, and the only way we can talk about it is in three-dimensional structures. So how do we connect to a world that is above our comprehension? How do we commune with entities that are as smart or smarter than we are? Those who are more elevated, regardless of their prescribed ethics? And how do we find it? In Egyptian mythos, you look within. It is within that you can travel without. As within so without. As below, so above, and this is how they travel to Duat. In Hawaiian mythos, this is called Po. Po isn't of actual darkness, but it is the realm of the gods, obscurity, and the primordial darkness of the universe. How do we reach the cosmos of primordial darkness where the gods reside?

Well, we go up.

I will again give you two different options. The first, which again I have found to be most successful, is to simply fly out of the atmosphere in your mind into space itself. I don't mean the visualization of outer space. Those visualizations are taught to us. At the bay, just travel upwards. For some of us, it will appear like blackness. For some, it will be all white, like you see in some of the movies where it's a divine space of white without walls. For me, everything is black. Devoid of the impressions that we learn or present in our reality. Remember that this holy place does not mean it is devoid of danger. There are incredible demons, gods of war, mischief, and masters of human turmoil that also reside in this plane. Again, journeying without your power-animal is not recommended.

The other way to journey upwards is to find that same tree that is used in order to drop down into Milu. But instead of climbing it and getting on a branch, you're going to get inside. Once you're inside this tree, you're going to climb upwards into the darkness until you are in Po.

Trance

Trance is a form of psychic experience where you have one foot out of the body, and the other foot in the solid. You can feel your body and move your head from side to side, while also viewing the worlds that I talk about. Unfortunately, unless you are actually out of your body, which means that you are not moving your body while observing or traveling, you are unable to affect these other worlds or be affected. That means that you cannot heal remotely without certain tools if you are in trance. I will give you those tools later on in the book, as you will need to heal, in most cases, in trance. Although if you are able to journey to a client, healing them while in spirit form is better and less cumbersome than having to do it in trance.

Communing with spirits is sometimes just as effective in trance as it is in spirit walking. However, remember that trance is simply a viewing. You aren't able to open and close the veil, you're not able to touch or be touched by a spirit. The limitations of trance have their benefits for safety. The limitations of trance also prevent full spiritual interventions.

A Father Travels to Milu

Characters:
Kane - God of the Sky
Kanaloa - God of Magic and the Veil between the Ocean and the Underworld
Maluae - a farmer
Ka'ali'i - the son of Maluae
Milu - The underworld

The rains at the back of Manoa fall heavy and kind. They soften the stone and give breath to the roots. And it was here, beneath the weeping mountains of Oahu, that Maluae worked the land like a sacred task. With bare feet in the streams and dirt packed beneath his fingernails, he fed his people.

Bananas bowed heavy with fruit, dripping yellow sweetness by the brook's edge. Taro leaves wide as shields tremble in the shallows of his handmade pools.

Maluae also fed the altars to Kane and Kanaloa with his food. A portion of every harvest he laid on the stone altar, a gift for the sky and the deep. Bananas first, still humming with sunlight. Taro pulled dripping from the water, peeled with care. Sweet potato sliced with a shark tooth, cleaned with coconut water. The gods feasted beside him.

Maluae had a son, Ka'ali'i. Ten summers old and reckless, he was wild with joy and lazy in love. A child who threw stones to chase spirits off the path, who talked to dogs as if they were uncles, and splashed through riverbeds as if they were made of fire is the purpose behind this story.

One day, the boy passed the altar. He had not eaten. The bananas there shone golden. He took one. Then another. Then all. His small mouth was full of fruit meant for gods.

The altar watched. The wind stopped. The gods waited for the moment to pass. It did not. So they descended. Kane in the air. Kanaloa from the root. They found him behind the grove with banana on his teeth and laughter in his eyes. And they killed him.

They tore the spirit out of his chest. It screamed, and they cast it into Milu... the underworld... not just a place of rest, into the lowest pit, a pot of hunger... the wettest dark. The Ka'ali'i's new home was the echoing belly where ghosts do not forget and shadows rot instead of vanish.

Maluae came home with food in his arms and a smile on his lips. He went to deliver the food to the altar and found it was barren. He found his son's body beneath the trees. Bananas still stuffed in the small mouth, now stiff and open.

Maluae did not fall to his knees, as you would expect, nor did he scream. He walked forward. He wrapped the boy in kapa cloth as one would wrap a blessing. He carried him home and laid him on the mat where they once told stories to the fire. Then Maluae lay beside him. He refused food. Refused drink. Refused speech.

The gods stood at his mat. They told him what had happened. They were simply unmoved.

"Your son stole from us. His death was justice. His spirit is in Milu."

Maluae sat unmoving for a day. Then another. The gods waited. But no prayers came. The altar stayed empty. No awa brewed. No chant rose into the mist.

Kanaloa watched. Kane frowned.

"We killed a faithful man's only child. He fed us every season. He sang to us as though we were his elders. And now he prepares no food. He lifts no offering. His love was clean, and we answered it with wrath," said Kanaloa

They visited him again. His body, weak. His soul curled inward like a fist.

Kane knelt beside him and whispered, "Do you love your child?"

Maluae blinked once. Then again. "Yes... my love is endless," as he petted the kapa cloth.

"Would you go down and bring him back?" Kanaloa asked.

Maluae's voice was dust in his mouth, "I am no kahuna. I am no warrior. I am a father."

"That is enough," Kanaloa said.

They gave him a hollow cane filled with things of power: Food that would not rot. Weapons forged from coral and shadow. A fistful of lava that could make anything burn. They gave him the path to Milu and told him to walk. Was Maluae so weak that he stepped out of his body? Did he, full form, make the way, weak and tired, with the only sustenance propelling him forward, the perseverance to acquire the soul of his son? We only know he walked. He did.

In the night, he walked to the ghost tree called Leiwalo, which stands near the shore at Moanalua. The place where the dead leap. Where souls climb into the branches of the breadfruit tree, hoping to find a landing soft enough to fall through the descent to Milu.

He climbed up the tree, and found the branch that reached out over the ocean. He took a deep breath and shook his magical staff.

The branch cracked under his weight. He dropped through the mist and into the black throat of Milu. He fell through absence. He fell past grief. He fell until falling was floating.

When he landed, the air was thick with smoke. No sun. No fire. Just endless forest where the trees screamed without mouths and the ground pulsed with the hunger of things never named. The ghosts of chiefs walked naked, some wailed, some stared... And some chased him.

He opened the cane. He tasted food that did not exist in the world of the dead, and it gave him power. Within his hollow staff, he pulled out his spear, and he raised his coral club. The dead attacked. They remembered the joy of violence, but with the magic of the gods, Maluae struck them again and again. And they stayed dead.

He walked until the forest turned to bones. He passed through the valleys of teeth. Caves full of crying. Rivers made of spit and regret.

He found Ka'ali'i deep in the lowlands of stolen pride, at the edge of Milu's stomach where no light ever touches. The boy's ghost sat choking on the ghost bananas shoved into his throat by unseen hands. He was gagging and blind, eating forever what had damned him, his face frozen in screams, and his arms bound by sharpened bones of those who died from malnutrition.

Maluae, horrified at the sight of his son, whose eyes were forced wide, tears streaming down his youthful face, pinned to a rock wall with the sharpened bones stabbing through his dainty blood-gushing wrists, choking on the endless yellow pus of banana guts, screamed.

Maluae struck the ground with Kane's staff, which shook the boy loose from his bondage. He struck the darkness with the firelight from within the magic lava rock. He wrapped his arms around his son's spirit and held him close. The ghosts came. So many. Too many. They dragged at his arms. They reached for the boy.

Maluae took the last bite of god food. It burned in his veins. He screamed again. He dropped the lava from the cane, and Milu burned.

The ground cracked open. Flames burst through the bones. Trees of screaming faces exploded. Ghosts fled. The dark grew brighter. This was fire for war, not warmth.

He forced Ka'ali'i's choking spirit into the cane and ran. He ran through heat, through shrieks, through things that had no legs but still chased, up through the mouth of Milu, through the roots, through the tree, through the mountain, and crested up into the world.

When he emerged from within the Leiwalo breadfruit tree, all of the world was untouched. His altar still waited.

He laid his son's body out again. Pulled the spirit from the cane. Pushed it through the feet. Into the chest.

Ka'ali'i breathed. Once. Twice. He opened his eyes and screamed and cried and clung to his father.

They wept together.

Forever after, Maluae never forgot the feel of death beneath his feet. Ka'ali'i never forgot the taste of bananas. The gods never again demanded perfection from those who loved them honestly.

And deep beneath the world, Milu still burns. Still waiting. Still hungry.
Then they fed the gods.
It's quiet... for now.

Part 2

The Biology and Parts of the Soul

Maui and The Quest for Fire, The Quest for Life

Characters:
Maui - Demi-god of Pure Will
Hinenuitepo - Primordial Womb Goddess of the Underworld

    This is an allegory. In this story, Maui journeys to Milu to find fire. He isn't bringing back actual fire. The Hawaiian people know how to make fire, but what they don't know, and can't explain, and use the story of Maui to help teach is... where does our spirit come from, the fire within? Why do some people burn brighter than others? Our light, our internal fire... it must come from somewhere. Maui finds the light within us by stealing from the walls of Milu by journeying through Hinenuitepo.

    The morning breathed soft and slow. The sky stretched pale pink fingers across the mountains. Maui sat among the people. He spoke with the certainty of one who has touched the edge of existence and returned with a sacred gift.

    Maui said, "Fire is the breath that stirs within us. It is the pulse of our bones, the light of our spirit, and the song that calls us forward when the night is deepest."

    The people gathered close, their faces eager and open, thirsty for the secret that had been hidden beyond the reaches of sun and stars. Maui showed them how to coax the ember and how to whisper to dry wood until it sang with heat. He taught them that with their breath, they could inspire life into the smallest spark until it became a blaze that chased away the cold and shadow.

They watched as the first flames danced, flickering like the laughter of children in the firelight. They felt the heat spread, creeping through their fingers and toes, wrapping their bodies in strength and safety.

Maui spoke directly to the beating hearts around him: "The fire lives in you. It is the fire that wakes when you laugh, when you cry, when you hold someone in love. It is the light that burns bright when your soul chooses to shine."

The people felt the ember stir that Maui had carried back from the edge of death itself. The fire was a gift that could grow, heal, or become more than the sum of its fears and shadows.

"We each carry this fire," he said. "But it must be tended. It must be fed with courage, with aloha, with dance, and with community." The fire was a flame that burned beneath the skin, unseen but always felt. It was the spark that made the blood rush, the breath catch, the spirit rise. Some held it quiet, some let it blaze, but all carried its light.

Before that morning, before the ember warmed palms and hearts, the world lay quiet beneath a heavy veil. The people knew warmth from the sun, but only in its light. Maui, restless and searching, would not accept the silence. He asked questions that rattled the stars. "Where is the fire that burns inside us? What breath feeds the light in the bones? Who holds the flame that makes us whole?"

His answers came in whispers from the winds, carried in dreams beneath the moon's gaze. The path led downward, into the place where life folds into death, where breath slips into stillness. The land of Milu, the realm beneath the earth, could be accessed through the waters of Kanaloa, or through the original womb, the tunneling caverns between the gargantuan stone legs of the first woman.

Maui prepared for the journey. He knew the path would demand more than strength. It would demand courage, humility, and a spirit willing to dance with darkness.

As the two mountainous walls came to a secret public enclosure, Maui braced himself with the reminder that he was clever, jovial, and durable. The mouth of the cave waited for him, sharp with ancient teeth, breathing a slow pulse like a great beast in slumber. Maui stepped forward. The earth swallowed the light as he passed the lips of the entrance. The air thickened, moist, warm, and sticky against the skin. He moved deeper, feeling the heat of Hinenuitepo, the great goddess whose body formed the threshold between worlds.

A voice curled through the chamber, low and knowing. "Who dares to enter my body?"

Maui answered, "I am Maui, the seeker of light. I come to carry fire to those who live in the shadows."

From the darkness emerged Hinenuitepo, her skin shimmering like wet stone, eyes deep pools that held the weight of night. She moved so quickly as if her stone overwhelming presence just appeared feet before Maui. She stepped closer. Maui's breath hitched.

"The fire you seek burns beneath the sun," Hinenuitepo said. "But here, fire is spirit, breath, life. You seek to take from the place where life ends."

"I am Maui, who slowed the sun. I know heat, and I can prove that I can warm your caverns better than any man," Maui said.

She smiled, slow and wide. "Then dance for me," she said. "Dance a fire into my bones."

Maui moved, his body weaving between shadow and light. Each step was a prayer. Each breath was a wave breaking on the shore of being. The dance was as ancient as the earth, as the stars, as the heartbeat of creation itself. In the light from the flames on the walls of Milu, Maui's muscles showed in his strong arms and thighs. His hips oscillating made his abs flex from the power and grace of sudden bursts of authority, and then the slow and controlled undulations of his story. He finished, glistening in sweat from his incredible masculine performance.

Hinenuitepo's hands rose, fingertips glowing with ember light. She pointed one single finger, and it glowed bright with fire. She plucked a tiny flame from her fingernail. Her lava-rock eyes met Maui's. He stared into her unblinking, charred soul, and maintaining eye contact, Hinenuitepo pressed her burning ember fingernail into Maui's waiting palms.

"Take this fire," she said, "the breath of Milu, the pulse of life."

Maui held the ember close, its warmth a gentle sun in his hands. But as he moved to leave, the ember slipped through his fingers, vanishing into the dark.

He returned to her side, voice humble. "I lost the fire. May I have another?"

Her eyes glimmered. "Again, the dance."

The dance repeated. Each time, she gifted him a flame, each time it slipped away into the shadows, a fumble, a slip, a trip over a rock...

Maui bowed his head and whispered, "May I have another?"

Hands like the slow turning of tides reached for him. Fingernail by fingernail, she gave fire, and Maui lost it. He returned, steady in spirit, ready to receive again, after giving his masculinity to her as an offering.

At last, the flames from her hands were gone. The room grew colder, the air heavier. Hinenuitepo's voice held a note of warning: "The fire from my hands is spent. The final flame lives in the walls of Milu. To take it is to steal from the bones of the earth. Leave, you clumsy human. You are not worthy, after all. You're just as much of an oaf as any other man. Leave me."

Maui didn't. He remained silent. His gaze did not waver. He watched the flickering shadows on the stone, the faint pulse of light resting just beneath the surface.

Hinenuitepo's eyes blazed with anger. "You come here to steal, reckless mortal? This place is sacred." She laughed and turned her back away from him, dismissing his uselessness. "You will join the dead inside me forever, locked in darkness. You'll never leave here with the fire of the original woman. You'll never leave here more than you are."

She moved toward him, the cave tightening like a great mouth ready to close. "There is no leaving once you cross this threshold."

Maui stepped back. His breath slowed. His body began to move... a different dance, one soft and slow, weaving warmth into the cold air, pulling at the edges of shadow with fingers of light. Hinenuitepo stopped her ascent on Maui and was taken aback by this new dance.

He danced for her, a dance of seduction, a song without sound. The air around them shimmered, no drum beat, silent heels. The cave softened as the audience of the underworld listened to Maui's breathing. The teeth of the cave retreated.

Hinenuitepo, eyes wide, cooling, said, "What is this dance that stirs the cold from my bones?"

Maui tried to hide his smirk, his sweat flowing like water over rocks. "It is the dance of life," he huffed as he continued. "The dance of soul and fire. It is how we call each other from the shadows."

The cave seemed to breathe with him. The firelight returned to her fingertips, brighter, softer. She offered the flames once more.

But Maui's eyes were fixed on the walls, dancing closer and closer to the firelight encasing the womb of the underworld. The ancient stone glowed faintly with hidden light. His fingers brushed the wall. Maui grabbed the ember, and instead of trying to escape with it in his hands, he swallowed it whole. The warmth burst through his chest, a rising sun inside him, wild and free. The fire changed, burning steadily and slowly, the fire became mana, the fire of the soul.

Hinenuitepo roared with rage, the cave trembling as she lunged forward to catch the thief of fire. Her shadow stretched long and sharp, teeth like 'a'a lava, claws like lightning. "You steal from me, you defile the sacred. You will burn in the dark with those who cannot dance."

Maui leapt, the fire within him flaring bright. He twisted and turned, moving through the narrowing cave with the agility of the honeycreeper and the cunning of the eel. His breath was fire. His heartbeat thundered.

Behind him, the shadows writhed, the walls reaching to trap him, to swallow him. He called upon the winds, his voice a fierce chant: "Bring me strength. Spirit of the four winds, carry me home."

The cave shuddered as the breath of La'amaomao swept in, tearing through the earth. Rain and wind battled the fire and shadow, shaking the gates of Milu. Maui burst out from the cave, gasping, the sun blinding and warm upon his face. Behind him, the angry roar of Hinenuitepo faded into the deep earth.

He fell to his knees as he escaped, and when he fell, the fire jumped out of his mouth and onto the ground. The 'alae bird saw the fire and gobbled it up and flew away.

The 'alae bird had stolen it! Red-legged and cunning, the moorhen swallowed it whole and flew across the cliffs. Maui, chest still glowing from the echo of his own theft, had been burgled himself!

Maui chased the bird through the forest and stones. The bird cackled, hopping from branch to branch, refusing to give up the secret. Maui's patience thinned, and he pushed his demi-god speed through the thicket.

He caught the bird in his strong hands, eyes locked on its small dark pupils. "Give it back," he said, low and certain.

The bird clucked and tilted its head, pretending not to know. Maui pressed the bird close to his lips and growled. The bird trembled.

"It's gone," said the 'alae. Its feathers smoked.

"Tell me," Maui growled, his fingers tightening around the bird's body. "How do I bring fire back?"

The bird screeched. Smoke hissed from its wings. In its cry was the sound of surrender. It opened its beak and sang how to make fire: "Rub the hau against 'alaa, and with your breath, your mana will ignite the wood into flame."

"That's not what I mean!" Maui yelled.

But the bird persisted with its story. Repeating again that if you rub the hau against the 'ala'a and use your breath, it will ignite fire. As the bird sang, its feathers turned black. The heat of the truth scorched its plumage. Its red legs burned deeper. The darkness clung to it, marking it forever.

This is why the 'alae is black.

This is why it walks close to water, head low, never laughing again. The bird paid a price for its secret. Maui did too.

As he watched the bird turn black, he thought about the bird's riddle. The hau is about softness, flexibility, and forgiveness, and the 'ala'a represents endurance, spiritual wisdom, and truth. When you rub them together... when you put softness with wisdom, flexibility with endurance, truth with forgiveness… and if you use what makes you live… your breath…

In that moment, Maui learned that fire could be made, not just stolen. That fire could be called up from within if one knew the rhythm, if one dared to breathe life into lifelessness.

He sat staring at the blackened bird, his chest still rising with the heat that had lived in the underworld. He rubbed the sacred woods together. Hau and 'alaa. He then moved with breath. The ember came slowly, a glow from nothing, a heartbeat from wood and soul. Maui smiled. And that was the lesson. Fire lives inside us when we make it with purpose, when we call it with breath, when we hold it in the rhythm of our being.

The people gathered.

Maui rose, fire alive in every fiber of his being.

"This fire," he said, voice trembling with awe, "is the pulse of life itself. It is the breath we carry when we laugh, when we love, when we dance beneath the stars. It is the fire of our souls, the light that will never dim."

When I stole the fire from the womb of Milu, from Hinenuitepo and swallowed it whole, my knowledge was what gave me way, my body gave me a vessel… my soul burns brighter, but I can make it grow with *who* I am."

He reached out, hands steady. "I pass this fire onto you. And you can stoke this fire with what lives within us all. Stir and grow your fire, your mana, with the song of ancestors, the dance of the living, and the promise of those who walk beyond the edge."

He touched them all, and as he tapped each person, he gave them fire. And as we touch each other, we give them fire. The fire inside them stirred, a quiet ember growing bright. But we have to stoke the fire.

This fire, the breath that moves in us, is the pulse of ancestors who dared to step beyond the edge. The fire that Maui brought through the shadow is the light we carry in every breath, in every heartbeat. Mana is the dance of life itself… fierce, tender, and eternal.

Mana Check

In Hawaiian faith, mana is a concept that refers to a spiritual energy or power that is present in all things. It is the life force that flows through everything. Mana is seen as a sacred and powerful energy that can influence and impact various aspects of life. It is believed that individuals can cultivate and strengthen their mana through spiritual practices, connection with the land, and living in harmony with the natural world. Mana is also associated with leadership, strength, and divine presence. But you'll also find the energy life force in plants, in rocks... heck, even your computer. Everything has a kind of energy. Maybe today, we call it electromagnetic energy, or during the 1930s, it was ectoplasm. Man is energy, but not the kind of energy that gives a home life or a car drive; it's the energy that gives will.

Whether it's plants, animals, the landscape, or even ourselves, there is an essential energy that sustains us all. If you're struggling to connect with the spiritual realm or have difficulty with astral travel, it could be a sign of weak or deficient mana. It's important to acknowledge that blaming oneself for not trying hard enough is not constructive. Our spirit, body, and mind are intrinsically linked, and if any aspect of our being is unhealthy, it can hinder our ability to travel or connect spiritually. Just as physical pain can distract us from focusing elsewhere, a weak spirit due to mana loss or poor health may naturally prefer to stay rooted and heal, preventing us from exploring other realms.

To assess the state of your mana, you can perform a simple check. Close your eyes and visualize a bowl deep within your chest. Examine its appearance, its material, whether it has any cracks, and its thickness. Inside the bowl, imagine water and a tree, with the tree's roots reaching through the water and over the bowl. Assess the roots, their length, quantity, thickness, and strength. Examine the water's behavior: is it still or turbulent, clear or murky? Does it spill through the cracks or overflow? How much water is present, and is there anything else in the water aside from the tree's roots? Consider the tree's health, its fullness, height, strength, and flexibility. Lastly, observe the sky around the tree, noting the weather, whether it's sunny, windy, or if other elements such as bugs or birds are present.

After opening your eyes, reflect on the results of this meditation:

The bowl represents your connection to community, family, and nature. If it's weak or cracked, consider the need to strengthen your community bonds and deepen your connection to nature.

The water symbolizes your emotional state, with turbulence signifying turbulent emotions, overflowing indicating an abundance of emotions affecting others, stillness representing emotional stability, and depth indicating emotional depth.

The roots represent what you feed your mind, so consider whether you prioritize a diverse range of interests or spend excessive time on social media.

The tree reflects your life's purpose and path, so assess the state of your connection to your life's journey and whether you need to make adjustments to fulfill your destiny.

The sky represents external factors that may influence you, such as opinions from others, news, or encounters with people in daily life.

This meditation allows you to dive into the different aspects of your soul, gaining insight into yourself. However, some aspects may require external assistance for healing. No amount of personal effort can fix certain soul components, which may necessitate seeking help from others.

In terms of mana loss, it's crucial to manage your energy on a daily basis, especially if you fully dedicate yourself to your craft. While it is possible for one practitioner to transfer their mana to another, emptying themselves, this practice should be approached with caution due to the negative consequences. To cultivate new energy, one must already possess energy. Managing your own mana involves various practices such as faith, connection with the land, venerating spirits, engaging in self-care activities, maintaining a healthy diet, and fostering positive relationships (all of the things listed in the Hawaiian tenets). Practicing for praise will lead to misalignment and eventual depletion of mana.

Your mana is your energy, your spiritual essence. How is your energy today? When it comes to your mana, you manage it every day in every way when you practice the craft full-time. One kahuna can pour their mana into another person, emptying themselves. With their practice, they can refill themselves, but this isn't without negative consequences. You need energy to cultivate energy. My faith, the land around me, the spirits I venerate, self-care activities, food, and healthy relationships are some ways I manage my own mana. I have only had to empty myself once and did so into May (in the next story).

If this is part of your practice, you are naturally healthy. If the root belief is praise and gain, you are practicing for the wrong reasons, and your mana is not in alignment and will empty. In other words, if you fix cars but don't focus and pay attention to fixing cars, and brag about how great you are at fixing cars, don't try to continue to be the best at fixing cars, but only boast about your skills, bring down others who fix cars, and focus on the intake of funds. You are bringing in money by destroying others, not fixing cars.

You can lose your mana by misusing your skills. In the worst-case scenario, if someone loses their mana, a spirit can move into one of the three areas of their spirit. If there is a hole in their soul, a parasitic spirit can move in.

> If boasting is not your problem, there are other reasons for mana loss.
> - Is there something in your life that should be celebrated for which you are not celebrating?
> - What is in the way or holding you back from your goals, relationships, connections, and a thriving life?
> - What does your heart really want?
> - When was the last time you were your most authentic self?
> - If your power-animal could give you a lesson, what would it be?

We will also be addressing getting cursed or cursing yourself later on in the book. In any case, your mana changes. It becomes thinner, or changes color, or changes in vitality. When we are cursed, hexed, or jinxed, it is our mana that is affected, which then affects the rest of us.

Furthermore, if you are given something, and energetically you don't give back, your mana will deplete. Give for being given.

Some items care mana in them (electromagnetic energy) from the person or event that touched or interacted with it last. These are usually touched, worn, or handled during the lifetime of the person, unavoidably washed with the person's personal mana. This is why items that were once used by someone else should be cleansed of the mana residue from the previous person, which may also mean any cords (aka) still attaching the previous user to the item.

Mana can also be purposefully moved into objects. Magical tools, ropes to help with sailing, fish hooks for hunting, and other objects were infused with mana (talismans as well) in order to benefit the user. This can also be done in a baneful way.

Creation Story and Pele's Hawai'i Home

Characters:
Po - The Upper World of the Gods
Papa - Earth Mother
Wakea - Sky Father
Kane - God of the Sky
Lono - God of Agriculture
Ku - God of War
Kanaloa - God of Magic and the veil of the ocean to the underworld
Hina - Goddess of the Moon
Haumea - Goddess of Birth
Kamoho'ali'i - Shark God (oldest brother of Pele and Namaka)
Pele - Goddess of the volcano and fire
Namaka'okaha'i (Namaka) - Goddess of the Ocean Waters
Hi'iaka'akapoli'opele (Hi'iaka) - Youngest Sister of Pele, Goddess of Healing and Dance

Before reef met tide, before root met stone, before flame knew her name, there was the darkness that curled, vast and alive, like a great womb with no edge: Po, a place of unshaped sound, a silence so full, no one could lean close to hear it.

From that great depth stirred a thought, and the thought was motion. The motion became rhythm. The rhythm became a call, and from that call came the first becoming. It was Earth Mother, Papa. It was Sky Father Wakea. It was the union of the Above and the Below. The Sky and the Earth. The One who stretched wide, and the One who rooted deep. They embraced, and they pulled into being that which would become all things.

He Kumulipo (The Creation) translated by Queen Liliuokalani in 1897 while imprisoned in her Palace under house arrest at Iolani Palace.

FIRST VERSE.

At the time that turned the heat of the earth,
At the time when the heavens turned and changed,
At the time when the light of the sun was subdued
To cause light to break forth,
At the time of the night of Makali'i (winter)
Then began the slime which established the earth,
The source of deepest darkness.
Of the depth of darkness, of the depth of darkness,
Of the darkness of the sun, in the depth of night,
It is night, So was night born.

SECOND VERSE.

Kumulipo was born in the night, a male.
Poele was born in the night, a female.
A coral insect was born, from which was born perforated coral.
The earthworm was born, which gathered earth into mounds,
From it were born worms full of holes.
The starfish was born, whose children were born starry.
The phosphorus was born, whose children were born phosphorescent.
The Ina was born Ina (sea egg).
The Halula was born Halula (sea urchin).
The Hawae was born, the Wana-ku was its offspring.
The Ha'uke'uke was born, the Uhalula was its offspring.
The Pioe was born, the Pipi was its offspring (clam oyster).
The Papa'ua was born, the Olepe was its offspring (pearl and oyster).
The Nahawele was born, the 'Una'una was its offspring (muscle and crab in a shell).
The Makaia'ulu was born, the Opihi was its offspring.
The Leho was born, the Puleholeho was its offspring (cowry).
The Naka was born, its offspring was Kupekala (rock oysters).

The Makaloa was born, the Pupuawa was its offspring.
The Ole was born, the Ole'ole was its offspring (conch).
The Pipipi was born, the Kupe'e was its offspring (limpets).
Kane was born to Wai'ololi, a female to Wai'olola.
The Wi was born, the Kiki was its offspring.
The Akaha's home was the sea;
Guarded by the Ekahakaha that grew in the forest.
A night of flight by noises
Through a channel; water is life to trees;
So the gods may enter, but not man.

THIRD VERSE.

Man by Wai'ololi, woman by Wai'olola,
The Aki'aki was born and lived in the sea;
Guarded by the Manienie Aki'aki that grew in the forest.
A night of flight by noises
Through a channel; water is life to trees;
So the gods may enter, but not man.

FOURTH VERSE.

Man by Wai'ololi, woman by Wai'olola,
The A'alaula was born and lived in the sea;
Guarded by the Ala'alawainui that grew in the forest.
A night of flight by noises
Through a channel; water is life to trees;
So the gods may enter, but not man.

FIFTH VERSE.

Man by Wai'ololi, woman by Wai'olola,
The Manauea was born and lived in the sea;
Guarded by the Kalo Manauea that grew in the forest.
A night of flight by noises
Through a channel; water is life to trees;
So the gods may enter, but not man.

SIXTH VERSE.

Man by Wai'ololi, woman by Wai'olola,
The Koele'ele was born and lived in the sea;
Guarded by the Ko punapuna Koele'ele that grew in the forest.
A night of flight by noises
Through a channel; water is life to trees;
So the gods may enter, but not man.

SEVENTH VERSE.

Man by Wai'ololi, woman by Wai'olola,
The Pua'iki was born and lived in the sea;
Guarded by the Lauaki that grew in the forest.
A night of flight by noises
Through a channel; water is life to trees;
So the gods may enter, but not man.

EIGHTH VERSE.

Man by Wai'ololi, woman by Wai'olola,
The Kikalamoa was born and lived in the sea;
Guarded by the Moamoa that grew in the forest.
A night of flight by noises
Through a channel; water is life to trees;
So the gods may enter, but not man.

NINTH VERSE.

Man by Wai'ololi, woman by Wai'olola,
The Limukele was born and lived in the sea;
Guarded by the Ekele that grew in the forest.
A night of flight by noises
Through a channel; water is life to trees;
So the gods may enter, but not man.

TENTH VERSE.

Man by Wai'ololi, woman by Wai'olola,
The Limukala was born and lived in the sea;
Guarded by the Akala that grew in the forest.
A night of flight by noises
Through a channel; water is life to trees;
So the gods may enter, but not man.

ELEVENTH VERSE.

Man by Wai'ololi, woman by Wai'olola,
The Lipu'upu'u was born and lived in the sea;
Guarded by the Lipu'u that grew in the forest.
A night of flight by noises
Through a channel; water is life to trees;
So the gods may enter but not man.

TWELFTH VERSE.

Man by Wai'ololi, woman by Wai'olola,
The Loloa was born and lived in the sea;
Guarded by the Kalamaloloa that grew in the forest.
A night of flight by noises
Through a channel; water is life to trees;
So the gods may enter, but not man.

THIRTEENTH VERSE.

Man by Wai'ololi, woman by Wai'olola,
The Ne was born and lived in the sea;
Guarded by the Neneleau that grew in the forest.
A night of flight by noises
Through a channel; water is life to trees;
So the gods may enter, but not man.

FOURTEENTH VERSE.

Man by Wai'ololi, woman by Wai'olola,
The Hulu-waena was born and lived in the sea;
Guarded by the Huluhulu Ieie that grew in the forest.
A night of flight by noises
Through a channel; water is life to trees;
So the gods may enter, but not man.

FIFTEENTH VERSE.

A husband of gourd, and yet a god,
A tendril strengthened by water and grew
A being, produced by earth and spread,
Made deafening by the swiftness of Time
Of the He'e that lengthened through the night,
That filled and kept on filling
Of filling, until, filled
To filling, 'tis full,
And supported the earth, which held the heaven
On the wing of Time, the night is for Kumulipo (creation),
'Tis night.

THE STORY

From Papa and Wakea came the gods. Kane first, whose breath lit the sky and filled it with sunrise. Lono, whose rains softened the land and made way for the seed. Ku, whose stillness held strength and steadied the wild. Kanaloa, deep and coiling, who ruled the secrets of the underworld and the currents that know no shore. And there too came Hina, who wore the light of the moon in her bones, and Haumea, mother of birth and blood, who would carry the goddesses into form.

The gods breathed into dust. They spoke into the coral. They sang into skin, and the people came. The ali'i and the maka'ainana. The fisherman, the farmer, the mother with salt on her shoulders. They came, each one holding in their chest a little of that first unshaped silence.

But the gods were not finished. The stories never end at the first birth.

Haumea, red-handed and wild-haired, labored again. She bore many daughters, each with her own fate etched in her mana. One of these children was Pele. She came wrapped in heat and quiet, already burning. Pele opened her eyes, and the land trembled. Haumea knew. This one would not be easy. Fire never is.

The day she was born, the sea hissed in fear. Lightning shattered coral groves before she could open her eyes. Her mother wrapped her in kapa woven from the clouds above. Still, Pele radiated like coal in the night. The village of her birth could not contain her. Rocks split. Breadfruit trees wilted. Water refused to flow near her cradle. Her sisters, beautiful and unshaken, gathered in a circle and whispered.

"She will consume us all," they murmured.

"She is meant to remake," said Haumea. "Even the destroyers must be birthed."

Pele walked before she could crawl. Her small feet blistered the floors of her father's house. Her laughter filled the forest with smoke. When she touched a stone, it melted. Her fiery gaze never lingered. Even as a child, she moved as if following something distant. Something older than time. A pull from below the earth, or beyond it.

But it was the dreams that frightened them.

At night, Pele dreamed of flame. She saw islands rising from the sea, then being swallowed again. She saw trees with blossoms the color of blood. She saw a man she had never met. His face was always turned away. She would wake with ash on her tongue, a foreboding of the future.

By the time Pele reached her maiden years, her power could no longer be hidden. She scorched the grass behind her when she walked. Her shadow grew long even at noon. The men of the village began to tremble when she passed.

Pele's name whispered through the bamboo forests. Her footprints boiled the earth. Her glance woke lava beneath stone. She had the face of a girl and the soul of pure, forceful play. Her siblings watched her with awe, some with fear, some with hunger.

But there was another sister. Older. Water-born. Wave-blooded. Namaka'okaha'i watched as Pele danced through the sand, as men gathered around her glow, and something ancient stirred in her chest. Water remembers, and her blood remembered betrayal before it even came.

Pele did not mean harm. She only moved where her fire led. Pele's nights grew louder. In the earliest days of her wandering, Pele did not yet know the hunger of her own flame. She walked softly across the islands of Tahiti, her feet still cool, her body still human. When she came upon the sacred grove of Namakaokaha'i, sister of the deep and mistress of the hidden currents, she was drawn by its shimmering beauty.

Water pooled in crystal basins, vines wept with dew, and fish leapt through roots like silver prayers. Pele sat beneath the hau trees, her heart aching with silence, and exhaled a single breath of warmth into the cool air. But her breath caught fire. The grass hissed. Steam curled. The bark cracked. And before she could whisper an apology, the grove wept itself to ash.

Namakaokaha'i arrived too late to save what she had tended for centuries. The waters had boiled, the trees had collapsed into themselves, and the sacred fish had turned belly to sky. When she saw Pele, young, wide-eyed, trembling with the heat she did not yet know how to hold, her grief became fury.

"You have taken what you did not understand," Namakaokaha'i said. "You are not nurturing like the water. You are not of the breath of life. All you create is destruction, and pain. I will show you, teach you as a pained sister goddess can, that you need to feel pain, you reckless, horrible child!"

And so, sister turned against sister. One bore tide. One bore flame. From that moment, Pele was no longer welcome in the realm of waves. Her exile began because of an accident. Fire had entered the world, and it would never again leave softly. Namaka'okaha'i brought the sea into the house. She flooded the night. She threw water against bone. She screamed until even the trees bent away from her wrath.

Haumea, worn from births and tired of war, turned to Pele. Her hands were firm. Her voice was stone. "You will go. Take the canoe. You will search for a home where your sister cannot drown."

Her brother Kamoho'ali'i gave her a canoe carved from the bones of whales. Its hull shimmered with sharkskin, and it obeyed her thoughts more than the paddle. He gave her a gourd filled with sacred fire from the stars. And before she left, her mother gave her a lock of her own hair, braided into a lei, bound with chants to protect her from forgetting who she was.

"You are still our child," Haumea whispered, "even when you are alone. I'm gifting you the egg of your sister. You have to know, once, what it is to create, my child. I will not birth your sister; instead, you will when the time is right. Take your sister's egg and go, knowing love from a mother, a sister, and a child."

So Pele left, and so the journey began.

She crossed the deep waters, guided by stars that bowed in respect. The canoe carved a trail of heat across the ocean that even the winds dared not cross. Islands rose to greet her and fell as she touched them. She first found Kaua'i, a small atoll, and built there with her long staff.

Namaka, in her vengeance and in her oath to teach Pele pain, hunted Pele. Pele found Kaua'i, then a small atoll. Pele built that small island, but while she built it, Namaka, who traveled as fast as a tsunami, found Pele to squelch her fire. Pele fled and found O'ahu, trying to build higher and bigger. Namaka fought Pele, and they tortured each other with fire and salt, water, and soot.

Kamoho'ali'i stole Pele away, and as they drifted on the canoe, Pele, in her maiden play, created Kaho'olawe, Moloka'i, Lana'i, and Molokini. The next morning, Pele told her brother to leave her.

"I am *the* woman of fire. I can do this myself with my staff!" Pele said.

Her brother agreed, abandoning Pele on the first parts of Maui. Pele built and built and built. She created the house of the sun. With her staff, she created a volcano so high that Namaka could not reach her with her waves.

For now, Pele stood upon a land that welcomed her. Her hair was wild as she stood there silently. Her heart was burning with something too large to name. She felt the man again in her dreams. The one who would love her, the one who would betray her, the one she had never met.

"I am alone," she said aloud.

No one answered but the cinders.

Hiʻiaka stirred within her egg. Still sleeping. Still unborn. But near.

Pele pressed her palm to the earth. Felt its ache. It's waiting. It's hunger. "What else must I give?" she whispered. The wind circled her, like a prayer unanswered.

Then came the visions.

They clawed through her sleep. Faces she did not know. Lovers who had not yet touched her. Islands she had not made. Eyes full of grief. Arms reaching. Dying. Pleading.

She woke with lava on her lips.

She screamed. The mountain split. The sea boiled.

Her sisters came to her in dreams. Haumea, with her thousand wombs, whispered of balance. Grandmother Papa wept cool stones into her ears.

When she fully woke, Pele's soul returned to Haleakala, torn and flickering. She coughed up smoke. Her skin cracked. Her eyes bled. She screamed again, but this time it was not lava. It was sorrowful.

Hiʻiaka's egg pulsed.

Pele crawled to the edge of the crater. She vomited flame. Her legs gave out. The land trembled.

"I have given it all," she cried.

No voice answered.

Her body broke.

First her ribs. Then her spine. The heat inside her escaped. She shook with pain beyond naming. Her fingers burned from within. Her teeth turned to obsidian.

Then the egg broke as Pele held it against her bosom.

Hiʻiakaʻakapoliʻopele (Hiʻiaka in the bosom of Pele) was born from smoke and salt, and sorrow. She rose, untouched by flame, wreathed in wind. Her feet stepped lightly upon the scorched stone. Her eyes held the sea and the forest and the stars. She knelt beside Pele and touched her face.

And Pele wept.

"I cannot hold myself," she said.

Hiʻiaka cradled her head in her lap and sang, "You are held. I will carry what you cannot."

The body of Pele smoldered. The bones cracked. The spirit fled to the wind.

But the ember remained.

It glowed in the cave of Hiʻiaka's heart.

Pele danced with joy. She was no longer alone, and she created crater after crater at the top of the glorious desert mountain home.

As Pele struck with celebrations of cinder cones and lava tubes, she hit so hard that her staff drove all the way to the ocean floor.

Namakaʻokahaʻi now knew where Pele was hiding, and in her built-up fury, Namaka roared up the tunnel, grabbing Pele by the throat, and instantly drowning Pele. Pele was killed on Maui.

And so the body broke.

The land was still. As the water washed away from Pele's body, the remnants of the great fire woman were blackened stone, for what remains when fire is extinguished? Her limbs were buried beneath crusted rivers of her own grief. Her mouth, once the song of thunder, was silent. Only the steam vents whispered now, and the brittle hissing of earth cooling in sorrow.

Hiʻiaka stood beside her sister's bones. She pressed her bare feet into the hardened lava and listened.

Deep inside, the ember still lived.

It flickered below her, faint but refusing to vanish. The kind of fire that remembers itself. This time it wasn't a flame that destroys. The fire inside was a flame that *remembers*.

Hiʻiaka closed her eyes and called upon the womb of her mother, Haumea. She called upon the winds of Laʻamaomao. She called to Papa, to Wakea, to the ancient stones beneath all living things.

"Let her rise again," Hiiakaʻakapoliʻopele said.

The birds came first. Then came the mist. Then the vines. Ferns split the ash. Hiʻiaka laid her hands upon the black rock and sang a chant of return. A chant of pathfinding. Of breath after silence.

From within the stone, the ember pulsed.

The soul of Pele had not been lost; it had only shed its skin. Her unihipili had entered the veil, wandering through the bone-halls of the dead. Her ʻuhane had remained here, clinging to the land. But from beyond, Pele's pure soul turned back.

The body does not reincarnate. The spirit does.

So the fire that once wore the form of a woman began to stir again, not in flesh, but in form, not in bone, but in presence.

From an explosion on Haleakala emerged the full goddess, Pele.

Pele, immortal and impenetrable, swept up her sister-child Hiʻiaka and created a new home. Maui could not be her home, as it was now a heiau for her bones, and her life ruled by running, fear, and loneliness. Pele created Mauna Kea, Mauna Loa, and Kilauea.

Pele built a place where she could have what she wants, never fear, and love whom she wants. Kilauea is the home of that which destroys. What's funny is this: even in all that Pele takes and destroys, one thing continues to reincarnate and become something new from her fire and murder: the stories.

The Three Parts of the Soul

This area of belief regarding the soul and how it can be healed is called hilina'i (he - as in the pronoun, lee - as in the name, na - as in not, ee). Hilina'i translates to belief. Then why is the name for the soul, the healing modality, and belief named the same thing? Simple, in much of the Hawaiian language, what you feel, its context, and its essence are the same word. We exist because we believe we exist. I think, therefore, I am. We are ill because we are taught what illness is. Or we are ill because others impose their learning of what disease is onto us. Belief is a connection to the spiritual, to understanding, to existing. Belief is how the soul fractions and how it can be healed through knowledge, lessons, and planning (and not necessarily empty-headed pipe-dreams). It is in our belief, our believing, and our beliefs that shapes us, and therefore also shapes the shadow we cast on the land. As we change, grow, and mold, based on our beliefs, so does our shadow, and so does how we affect others (and the land).

Remember that hilina'i is not the Hawaiian belief system, nor is it the totality of any part of it. This part is only associated with the soul and how to heal it.

Before we continue, we will move away from the idea that certain parts of the soul are located in specific parts of the body. We need to move beyond the concepts you've learned in other modalities and the fashionable healing ideas that are currently popular. It's time to wipe your mind clear of conceptions of the zodiac, chakras, and Reiki for the remainder of this book, with no comparative analysis to other religions or famous areas. Wipe clean.

We move into thinking that the pieces of the soul are made up of a web, a liquid, amorphous web, ever-changing and adjusting. Your soul is a net, holding in, protecting, reaching out, exploring, changing, and adjusting. Your soul is like a net.

One kind of rope in your spiritual net is called **aumakua** (au - like ouch, ma - like mama, coo, ahh).

The second kind of element in your soul-net is called **uhane** (oo, ha - like haha!, and ne - like the sound a horse makes. Not oohawnee. NEY. In English, we don't have the sound 'eh' without adding a sweetening to the end. We can tolerate you saying uhanei over uhani, but work toward pronouncing it correctly: uhane.).

The third kind is called **unihipili**. (oo, knee, he - like the pronoun, pea, lee. You really shouldn't get this wrong. We have these words in English, so just mush them together.)

Each part of your soul is just one thread-type in the makeup of who you are.

Aumakua: The outer layer strings that reach inwards and outwards. This is our "mind" part of the soul. This is our intellect and ability to understand the spiritual, physical, and instinctual phenomena.

Uhane: This is connected to your physical space. Your actual body. This is the spiritual expression of your bones, body, blood, and physical health.

Unihipili: This is your "spirit," connected to your instinct, psychic abilities, sorcery, and primal nature. This is the animal part of you, the instinct.

or

Aumakua - Mind Soul Pieces, Threads, and Mass
Uhane - Body Soul Pieces, Threads, and Mass
Unihipili - Spirit Soul Pieces, Threads, and Mass

- Aumakua's health and substance are influenced by belief, what we learn and experience.

- Uhane's health and substance are influenced by what our body does and genetics.

- Unihipili's health and substance are influenced by past life and spiritual evolution.

These threads make up your soul, and together, they influence the spiritual aspects of yourself. Before we continue, I want to point out that one area affects the others. If we believe that we can only feel safe and validated by eating cake, then our physical body is affected by the change in our blood, bones, and physical way of accepting food, including the nervous system response to affection or nutrients. Unlike other systems, we accept that although disease or strength may come from one area, our spirit is a web, and each affects the other.

Everything has soul. We respect the spirit of all things because everything has a soul.

Does an animal have intellect? No. Therefore, they have little to no aumakua in their soul. This is why we did not reincarnate from animals. But it does have body and instinct.

In the Hawaiian language and spirituality, we use words for many different things. Your aumakua is the mental part of yourself (in some toxic belief systems, we call this your 'higher self,' but again, all parts of you have equal value and importance, as well as can be injured or sick).

Because one word can have different meanings based on context, there are also aumakua spirits. When we talk about your aumakua, we could mean the mental part of your soul or your ancestors who are showing themselves as a specific animal in nature. Popular new age Huna will tell you that your aumakua is probably a turtle or an owl, but this is not necessarily the case. The ancestors, the aumakua, are a sign specific to you or your family line. Your lineage gives you omens by offering the presence of real animals in your life as a means to communicate.

Aumakua are ancestors who show themselves to you in everyday life by giving you the sign of an animal. My ancestral aumakua are deer. The ancestors who want to steer my life will provide me with guidance by bringing deer into my life as a sign. Some non-Hawaiians interpret aumakua to mean their spirit animal. That is false. We use the term power-animal or totem, and we handle that part of ourselves differently. For me, my power animal (connected to my unihipili) is a polar bear, and my aumakua ancestors are shown when they put a deer in my life. This is the aumakua outside of ourselves. Higher spirits are your ancestors because we respect our elders.

Your aumakua, when we talk about your soul, is the mental, spiritual health, and expression spiritually. Your aumakua ancestors are real animals that wander around the land to say, "Pay attention!" Just pay attention to context (the good news is we are going to talk about your soul here, not your ancestors, but you need to know the difference in language). So, although your ancestors will give your aumakua a visual sign of an animal to let you know they are there, that animal is not part of your soul. It's a sign for your aumakua, as "Hey, family is here."

Back to Your Soul

Aumakua connects the easiest to the Upper World. The Hawaiian god Kane is an expression of your aumakua, and this is the mind's way of comprehending spirituality, science, learning, and more. Much of the philosophy of the spirit is part of this area. Most of what Max Freedom Long wrote about would fit into this part only, ignoring two-thirds of soul-healing.

Uhane is where a lot of the worldly delineation of the self takes place. Suppose you were to apply the chakra system into the hilina'i system, or yin and yang. It would go here. It's the physical expression of the body. This is connected to the bones when we die and therefore also goes with the bones. This is why it is so terrible to move someone's bones at rest. You are moving part of the soul! This is why this disruption of a heiau, or other burial grounds, is just terrible. The spirit of the bones doesn't have the energy of the mind or soul to prevent damage from them. We, in the living, need to defend the resting areas of our ancestors until their bones are absorbed by the aina (land). Meanwhile, for us living, the expression of how spiritual illness takes place in the body will be found in this area.

Unihipili is the psychic, spirit, instinct part of your soul. This is the part that animals also have.

I must disagree when people talk about what is best for their 'highest self.' I would argue that when someone is trying to figure out what is best for themselves, they should be looking to connect their hidden self (instinct) to their higher self so their physical self can thrive. "What is best for me to be my most complete self?" Look to your hidden self. Your unihipili intrinsically knows what is best for you; it is psychic after all.

All three parts make up the human soul.

Why is this important? You will need to understand where a spirit is connected, and after removal, where to heal so future attachments are prevented. Furthermore, you may need to heal a spirit who is injured (yeah, that's right!).

Past life healing - the area of the unihipili attaches injuries from a past life, which include phobias, habits, toxic non-learned traits, and psychic blocks or gifts. This is also the channel of how we connect to our land, each other, and the craft.

Psychic attacks hurt the body, so we heal the uhane, including the spiritual expression of physical illness. We also treat with medicine, life balance, massage, and healthy lifestyle interventions.

Soul retrieval is done when pieces of our aumakua break off and die from trauma that has affected our intellect. When we feel depressed, lethargic, anxious, or need to heal spiritually from cognitive trauma, we heal from this direction.

Instead of treating the spirit's health as one item, you need to be able to treat the diseased part with the correct form of healing. Don't give blood pressure medicine for a broken bone. Don't attempt to do Reiki on the aumakua.
This means that you have to be able to tell the difference between the three and see/experience the three parts of the soul.

Animals only have uhane (body) and unihipili (spirit), and there are exceptions. Do animals have a soul? Yes, of course. But not like ours.

Rocks only have uhane. Places, mountains, rivers, oceans, and homes have the soul of the body, of substance, uhane. They have no mind, no instinct, only a body. That means they still have soul.
And if a house seems to be alive, that kind of 'soul' comes from something else and should be attended to, like remnants of a human's energy in a religious site or war zone. Is there a soul in the mountains? Yes, of course. Is it evil? Then it was attached by something else and is not the mountain's authentic self.

Spirits have aumakua (at least spirits that can 'think' and believe) and unihipili. They usually have no physical body. Does that make them any less real than the mountain? Of course not.

When places like houses, mountains, or battlegrounds have pieces of someone's aumakua or unihipili, their energy is left in a place and now sits there, absorbed by the location. This is when electromagnetic energy or spirit is left or broken in an area, expressed as thought or spirit. Think about homes that feel like they can think. This is because of the people whose spirits have 'leaked' all over the place and absorbed into the uhane of the house.

Biology of the Three Parts of the Soul

"Isn't it odd. We can only see the outside, but nearly everything happens on the inside."
<u>The Boy, the mole, the fox, and the horse</u> by Charlie Mackesy

Let's look at the biology of each part of the soul. We have three different components that make up the soul. Each area is divided into three parts: mana (ma - as in mama, na - as in not), keawe (ke - as in ok, awe, vey - as in oy vey), and aka (awe, kah).

Mana is the life force. Mana is the energy that pulses through us. Everything has mana. This is the magic or spirit of something. It's energy. (see Mana Check chapter)

Aka is the shadow of the mana. It's the cord that connects us to each other, our thoughts, and our places. Aka is the energy cord/tendrils that move mana and space. This is what we look for in cord-cutting. Although it's what we look at when it comes to moving mana, we do call it the shadow. Why? We all cast a shadow. Everything casts a shadow. And in the dark, all of our shadows connect. It is through the understanding of aka that you can connect to anything, through its darkness, its hidden-ness, its expression from choices, in the dark. And it is in this dark that we find the life that pulses through us all.

Keawe is everything; the space between you cannot contain. It is the space, the IS, the substance. What is the space between? What is dark matter? How do we find the veil in a space of solids? This is it. The space in between is keawe. If we were to talk about the veil itself, it would probably be pure keawe, the substance in-between. Not the substance itself, but in between. Keawe is space.

> *All of these parts of the soul can get sick or can be well:*
> Aumakua mana (mind energy)
> Aumakua aka (mind connections)
> Aumakua keawe (mind space)
> Uhane mana (body energy)
> Uhane aka (body connections)
> Uhane keawe (body space)
> Unihipili mana (spirit energy)
> Unihipili aka (spirit connections)
> Unihipili keawe (spirit space)

Examples of Soul Sicknesses

Aumakua Mana Sickness: sick energy of the mind, difficulty concentrating, loss of focus with life purpose or direction, paranoia, and other cognitive disorders.

Aumakua Aka Sickness: sick mind connections like negative beliefs, toxic people, social media addiction, poisonous political or religious influence. Remember that this is the connection to negative things regarding what you connect to your mind soul.

Aumakua Keawe Sickness: Thought-forms and habits that are negative. Beliefs and behaviors that continue to cause illness.

Uhane Mana Sickness: Illness of the energy of the body. This is where we can insert a subset of rules, like the chakra or yin/yang system. I feel the balance of male and female attributes matches better with the hilina'i system, but I know others who place the Chinese elemental system here. Unfortunately, this area is maintained with herbs and chants only. I say, unfortunately, because the spiritual words and ideas associated with the body are gone. We only read the spirit body of something and understand its health overall, then dig specifically. If we had had the old ways of determination, we would insert it here. I hope similar cultures, like that of the Philippines, may be able to sublet their system here for us to use. In the meantime, Uhane Mana Sickness is the illness of the energy of the body, as determined by an overall health check. This is also our physical energy.

Uhane Aka Sickness: This is what we connect to physically. Sexual partners, food, water, drugs, movement, etc, and how we affect the world around us.

Uhane Keawe Sickness: This is the actual illness of the physical body. Aka is what we do to it; mana is the physical body's energy, and keawe is the authentic expression of physical illness.

> ***Note:** At this point, I want you to see how everything is interconnected, like a web. One part affects another, from the mind to the physical, the space to connect to expression. They feed, take, and affect each other.

Unihipili Mana Sickness: Soul loss or deterioration of connection to your psychic abilities or magical influence. This is the energy and expression of your psychic self. If this is sick, you aren't connecting to your psychic self. Many will say, "I am not connecting to my higher self," and what they mean is their spiritual self, this part. Or maybe someone's psychic abilities are off.

Unihipili Aka Sickness: What we connect to spiritually or psychically is draining us. We have no desire to connect to others or the world around us. When this is sick, our magic doesn't work. Remember that magic is using the energy around you to cause change. If you can't connect to the energy of the world around you magically with this part, you can't get your magic to work. I value this area the most as my way to communicate as a psychic medium and protect it at all costs.

Unihipili Keawe Sickness: This is the bleed-over of your spirit. The muck or spiritual sludge that fills up your auric body, your soul. The in-between of your psychic-ness? Probably the hardest to define, right? I like to think of this as what your full spiritual expression looks like.

To incorporate all of this knowledge, you must:
1) Be able to identify the sickness from the nine parts of the soul
2) Interact with those parts
3) Mend, remove, replace

Let's experience yours first.

Setting A Demon Free

(Republished from Witchdoctor Exorcist Book 1)
    Characters
    Me
    My sister-friend
    Her son
    The possessed brown-haired woman in the hospital
    Caym - The demon of language and truth

"He's this way," my friend was guiding me down a sterilized corridor of the mental health wing at Maui Memorial Hospital toward her son's room. That April evening was the second time her son had tried to take his life. I paused for a moment before we walked into his room. "How can I help?" I asked.

"Just be there for me," She said.

"OK, I'm here. Whatever you need," I said. Although I was only twenty-three at the time, I had already experienced the fragility of life and the severity of how it feels when mortality is eminently delicate. Death itself didn't faze me, especially since I had already come close to it multiple times by then. Hospitals, however, were a different story. I looked around wearily. Hospitals had the spirits of death looking to escort those who have died from the physical plane to one of the spirits, the actual disembodied humans who have recently vacated their living organisms, and the entities who can easily prey upon the weak of constitution.

My friend noticed me looking around and asked, "Can you do this?"

She was one of the few people who knew about my sensitivity to spirits and the spirit of people. I was very secretive regarding my psychic self and inherited practices.

"Yeah, let's see him."

"I know hospitals are hard for you."

"It's not about me right now. I'm here for you so you can be here for him."

"Thank you," she always looked deep into anyone's eyes when she thanked them.

I could feel the energy strings spinning and twisting inside the hospital. Some were stale, some were infected, and others searched for something to connect to.

We were let into his room through a metal door, which was self-locked and had a handle on only one side. Her son was staring at the floor. The room only housed a bed, bolted to the ground, with nowhere for us to sit. My friend didn't know what to do. She felt lost. Neither did I. He was suffering from bipolar disorder, had run away from home a few times, and had a history of violence. She was alone, a single mom, and struggled with figuring out the right thing to do. I scanned him. Maybe there was a spirit involved? A parasite. But no, there was only one energy when looking at this poor, sick pre-teen. Just him.

I heard a screech coming from the hall. I looked at my present company, and since they did not react to the loud, bird-like scream, I realized it must have been supernatural. I didn't know then that I was only clairaudient with spirits, or how to identify what was a psychic experience versus a tangible one. "I'm going to step into the hall," I said. My friend was afraid.

"Is it ok for me to be here alone? I mean, I'm not af..." she trailed off. She was embarrassed by her words, accidentally villainizing her child, but at a loss for how to ask how things were best for him, for her, and appropriate.

"Of course. The doctor will be in shortly. It will be good for you two to have alone time together for a few minutes. I'm not leaving. I just need a minute. I'm on the other side of the door."

"Ok." She said. I knocked. Someone let me out into the hall, closing the door behind me. I stood there watching the nurses and workers in their blue scrubs move quickly and with purpose from place to place. They didn't seem to actually be doing anything constructive, but were still busy. It was about 11pm, but without windows and the energy of a summer hive, you'd think it was the prime morning hour for productivity.

I closed my eyes to see a little more clearly. I needed to know what spirit was trapped here. Like an overlay of the room, I could see the energy tendrils, the connections we have to each other and our environment. This kind of trance was a way for me to look at the Middle World clearly. My sight of the Middle World was already pretty good because "the filter" most living people experience broke with all of the near-death experiences I have had, especially after the one with the monster (see the Pre-Chapter of *Witchdoctor Exorcist Book 1*). But every once and a while, I need to see the Middle World a little clearer, so I close my eyes, preventing my physical sight from dominating my psychic input.

The energy cords all looked like a cool aqua in the black background of my closed eyelids. Just then, I heard the screech again. I searched with my sight for the creature in need. Room by room, scanning quickly.

Finally, I found in a room a young woman, probably in her mid-twenties. Her hair was down, and she was rocking. Her spirit's soul was a salmon-colored net reaching away from her body. Attached to her soul was a bird-like entity. He thrashed and pulled, and as he did, she thrashed on the bed.

Hey, I whispered in my head. *Stop pulling; I can help.* He stopped. *Hello.* I thought.

Where are you, witch?! He demanded.

I'm just outside your door. How did this happen? How did you get tangled like this? What's happened to you two? I asked.

This idiot child summoned me for possession. She has pulled and conjured with a weak fettle and lazy practice. Can you see that she cannot handle the strength of Caym? He boasted. From what I could see with my clairvoyance, which wasn't my strongest of psychic senses, the creature's head was a sunken skull of a bird. He had wings like a large crow, a humanoid torso, four legs all wrapped and tangled in the web of the woman's soul, and a lion-like tail. Her body was in pain on the hospital bed, with the soul stretched out and spread like a human net, knitted around and through this creature, keeping him caught in her soul.

Why would she try to be possessed by you? I asked.

You said you could help. If you can, you should give fruit to your words or take leave. It demanded.

Alright, but I have to understand something in order to help. I haven't done this before, but I think I can untangle you two. My family comes from two different lines of witches, and I can see the energy cables and how they intertwine. I think I can unhook you both, but I need to know if you are also inside of her or just affecting her from the outside. Are you literally possessing or just tethered? I asked.

He calmed. He perched on her chest. Her soul-net lowered and rested around the spirit. She was exhausted. In her hospital gown, she rested now. He studied her, looking her body up and down. She whispered to herself, "Stop, Caym, please stop. I'm sorry. I don't want this. I take it back." She whimpered.

Perched on her chest, he looked down at her. *I wish I could,* he said. His talons adjusted on her body, picking up one foot at a time and replacing it down on her. He opened his wings and tried to fly. Her soul kept him close, and her back arched on the bed. He landed, adjusted his talons, and lowered his head again. He continued to study.

He turned his head to me and thought, *I don't know the answer to your question.*

I clarified, *Alright, Caym, can you tell me who you are? I don't want to put myself in any harm, but I am happy to help you get free.*

I am Caym, seer of the future, voice for animals. I have it within my powers to allow one any animal, including a human, to hear another's language. I speak all that will be, from all that lives or has lived.

Well, that's cool! I thought. *But are you going to tell the truth if I ask if you will hurt me?*

The truth of the future can drive someone mad. Look at this child, Caym said.

His riddles were confusing. I thought, *I think it actually physically hurts for you two to be connected like this. Let me set you two free. Just please don't hurt me once I do.*

One by one, I moved the aka, the energy chords that her spirit had wrapped around his soul. It appeared that with someone so powerful, he could do this himself. Maybe from the inside, it wasn't doable? Like attempting surgery on your own organs? This young woman did not have a backup plan if she changed her mind.

"Sir, you can't sleep here!" I was jolted back to the hallway. A male nurse was standing over me.

"I'm sorry, uncle. I was just trying to calm myself. My nephew is inside here," I pointed at the door. He looked at the door and changed his tone.

"You can't stay out here," he said. "I will come back in a few minutes. Calm yourself, and then go back inside."

Why did you stop? The voice of Caym was in my head.

"Ok, ok. No problem," I said, and the nurse went about his business down the hallway.

At that moment, I remembered my sister telling me not to get involved in this dark stuff. But my instinct, my animal nature, was telling me to go through with helping this creature and the woman with the brown hair.

I closed my eyes again and went back to work. Moving, untangling, and setting the spirit free. *Is she possessed by you?* I asked while I worked.

No. She possesses me, he said. He started to flap about, pulling on the energy cords. Yanking. With every yank, the computer beeped, and the woman screamed. Nurses came into the room, but I just kept moving the cords.

"What is this patient's diagnosis?" One nurse asked the other as they tied her down to the bed.

"She thinks she is possessed by a demon. The doctor suspects paranoid schizophrenia," the other nurse said. "Now, help me restrain her."

Set me free! Caym screeched.

"Hey!" Coming from the hall, probably directed at me. Everything was so distracting, but I was almost done. Just a few more.

"She's coding!" The nurse shouted.

Stop pulling, stay calm; I'm almost done, I said to the creature.

As I moved the last few cords, I heard "Clear!" An electric shock went through my body, shocking the male nurse who grabbed me by the arms to pull me out of my trance.

"Ouch!" said the nurse who held me.

I looked at him as he looked at his hands. The spirit was free, and I needed to get out of the hallway. "Sorry," and I opened the door and went into the room with my friend and her son.

"We will keep him for two weeks," the doctor was mid-speech. "Your son will be under twenty-four-hour monitoring, and we will hopefully find a medication to help with his depressive episodes." My friend, an amazing mother, felt helpless and in shock. "Is this?" The doctor trailed off.

"My brother," she said. The hospital makes it less complicated if you're related. Support is support.

"What does visitation look like, doctor?" I asked. My friend could not handle this right now; she needed help asking the questions that we are all supposed to somehow know and then remember the answers in times of tumultuous trauma. I tagged in to take over so her constitution could rest.

"She can visit him twice a day if she likes. The hours will be given to you at the front desk. She will need to see a caseworker with him tomorrow. Is the phone number on file the right one to call?"

"Yes," I answered for her. "What happens right now?"

"We will take him to be examined and then get him to the Molokini ward. He will be taken care of there until you meet with the social worker tomorrow."

"And you will call to set up that appointment?"

"Yes, the social worker will."

"Is there anything else we need to do tonight?" I asked. My friend and her son were both staring at the floor. I felt shame, guilt, confusion, anger, mistrust… and those feelings were coming from both of them.

"No, there is nothing left to do tonight. You should go home and get some rest. He is safe now, and we will take care of him."

"Thank you, doctor," I said.

"Thank you," my friend said to the doctor. "Can I hug him?"

"Yes," said the doctor. She grabbed her son and held him close. "I love you." He said nothing.

Leaving the hospital room, I looked around to see if the spirit was wandering about. I couldn't close my eyes to look around since I needed to keep my eyes open to not bump into things in the hospital. I couldn't feel him. I couldn't feel his shadow or the cords. And I didn't know if the woman with the brown hair was ok.

We walked out of the car. "Do you want to smoke?" I asked.

"Fuck," she exhaled. She opened her purse and took out a cigarette. "Thank you," she whispered.

"No worries," and grabbed her and hung on to her tightly. We stood in the parking lot for a while, hugging, letting our cigarettes burn down and ash on the other person's back.

"You ok?" I asked.

"Yeah, I think so," She said. "He's safe. Nothing to do until tomorrow."

"Do you want company? I can stay with you as long as you need," I said.

"No. Let's finish up and head home. Let's end this day," she said.

We finished up our cigarettes and got in our cars.

On my drive home, I felt a presence in my car, in the back seat. I knew better than to look in the rearview mirror.

"Hello," I said aloud, knowing that the response would be in my head.

Thank you. It was Caym.

"You're welcome," I said in a kind of sing-songy way.

I can give the gift of knowing the future for your kindness. A payment. My gift will tell the truth of what is to come. But be warned that the truth can drive a person crazy. Do you want this gift?

"Um, no thanks. I think I'm sensitive enough without having to know the future. I'm just happy to help you two." I was almost home. What a crazy night...

Then allow me to assist with your current gifts. It seems that your 'sight' is weak.

"Yes. I am more of a physical medium than a clairvoyant."

I will gift you a sight for truth. As a voice speaks to you, you can see only if they tell the truth. Your visions will be clear. I must insist on repayment for my freedom.

"What kinds of complications am I going to have? My current sensitivities can be exhausting."

When someone talks to you, you will see what they share up until and only until they start to lie. When the lie begins, the vision will cease. You will share in my knowledge of how people fabricate.

"So, if someone isn't telling the truth, I won't see what they are sharing?"

Yes. My gift to you is a clear sight of truth. Goodbye.

He was gone. Nothing happened. No razzle, no dazzle, no feeling, nothing, but this gift he gave me will come in handy throughout my life, including now speaking my truth: I would like to start by stating that I, at that moment, did my first exorcism.

How Reincarnation Works With The Parts Of The Soul

Our mental spirit, unihipili, is connected to the veil. This part crosses, like invisible pollination, waiting for the aumakua to arrive. Our uhane stays with the body and goes dormant unless used to call the other pieces back or if it is disrupted.

When we die, we become ghosts. A ghost acts like a zombie, missing its unihipili. It wonders as only thought-forms from its life, like zombies, devoid of humanity and the interactive part. The ghost needs to cross the veil so the aumakua and the unihipili can magnetically come together and become a human spirit.

Now, the human spirit's aumakua is only as intellectual, learned, and opinionated as they were when they were alive. As they leave this Earthly form, they may know of the other Earthly lessons they have had from previous incarnations, but that's it. Spirits are still not all-knowing. Asking a spirit, like your grandma, what will happen next at your job through divination is probably only going to result in what they think will happen. Not a prophecy, not all-knowing. Asking for your father's guidance on what to do next should be considered advice, not all-knowing.

When a spirit is no longer needed, either by memory or through invocation by the living, they will probably reincarnate. This means that the aumakua goes to rest, recycled back to everything, a second death, the unihipili will be pulled (past-life), and a new soul will be created.

Wait, what what?

We die.

Got it.

Our uhane stays with the bones.

Got it.

Our unihipili becomes part of the veil.

Got it.

Our aumakua wanders until it crosses the veil.

Got it.

Once it crosses, aumakua absorbs its unihipili, and the ghost becomes a spirit.

Got it.

When it is time to reincarnate, does our aumakua die?

I guess. I don't know. I like to think it gets refurbished, recycled. I know that we don't take that with us. Those lessons learned and such become part of the akashic records, or the area of all things learned and experienced. Maybe it heads there? Perhaps there is a spirit recycling center that mashes up forgotten aumakua and makes new ones? But in some grand design, some deity or spirit makes a new higher self from something/someplace, slaps it into a soul, and sends it down to be born, and the genetic code, that spiritual part, is handed down from your biological parents.

Boom. You understand (ish) all the parts of the soul.

Reread if necessary.

You are combined with the physical soul of your genetic parents, your past lives, and your new, thoughtful life.

Scolding From An Oni

Characters:
Me
Naomi - Coven sister
Oni - Japanese ogre demon
My youngest daughter
My ex-husband
The woman I did a reading for on Twitch

    I was sitting at the veil, waiting. I was doing a reading for a woman who had asked me to talk to her late father. She said that she had had signs of him, that he showed himself to her; however, when she spoke to him, he didn't seem to understand what she wanted.
    I was streaming late one night, and this was my last live client of the night. I loved streaming because I had no way of knowing anything about the person being read besides what they told me. I can't see them or verify anything about their identity. All I have is a screen name.
    I connected to this viewer's spirit and went from there. Once I connected to her, I reached out to the veil, calling to have the father answer my reply. The other side of the veil was dark. While wearing this woman's energy should have been enough for the spirit to recognize her and come forward, especially if her father had been around so often, there was only darkness. Nothing. I opened the veil further and looked through, and still, no one was there. I opened it wider, feeling the vastness of the otherworld blending with my office.

A huge red figure with horns appeared at the veil. I knew him.... He was an Oni, and not just any Oni, my dear friend, Naomi's spirit guide.

You see, I taught classes for psychics and mediums to help them understand who they are and why their experiences happen to them. In my first psychic medium development class, I did a guided trance to help these potential mediums meet their spirit guides. I watched the eight students like layers of an overexposed TV. Everyone was a little faint, but I could see them all, making sure that no funny business happened.

Each student waited at a table in the Upper World, and in this darkness, there was a light coming from nowhere, a few chairs, and more darkness. Anything from the Upper World could approach, so my job was to watch, to ensure only their guides did (well, that their spirit guides got there first). The idea behind such a dangerous spirit-walk is that their guide will sense them on the other side of the veil and quickly show up. This usually prevented other problematic creatures from the Upper World from joining the table. To make things even safer, I required the students to light a candle. When they started their breathing exercise before the spirit-walk, I linked my flame to theirs. If something went wrong, I planned to ask them to open their eyes and blow out their candles. I would then blow mine out and close their veil for them. This process would give me a 10-second head start before whatever nasty joins them in their room.

The students waited at their respective tables, each a little different. They had anxiety, nervousness, and anticipation. *Who will show up? Is this all in my head? What's going to happen?* Then, from the darkness, the guides started to appear.

One student had a wolf spirit who had been following her. Another's grandmother was there showing her appreciation. Another student had a glowing tree, who wouldn't talk, but could drop information into her head as a means of communication. Then there is my new sister, Naomi.

Naomi was very much like me. Her abilities were very similar to mine, but her strengths differed slightly. I've always felt so linked to her since her first day taking one of my free classes. Later, I will call her one of my soul-sisters. We are connected through our own two-person coven, and she will always be someone I hold dear to my heart, like the twin sister I should have had.

She sat at her table, tracing the edge of the table to help with focus. In the darkness, I saw a huge shadow moving within the shadow of the upper world. A colossal creature came from the dark. He was red, muscled, gigantic, and had horns. He sat at the table. He looked like a demon. My mind raced: *I can't believe this is happening in the first class!* I thought to tell her to open her eyes, and we could begin the shutdown procedure. But wait... I had one rule. Their guides were not allowed to touch them. You see, our guides are not going to push our boundaries. They are respectful, and they are there to protect or guide us through life's difficulties. He sat there with his hand close to hers, but would not touch her. Their hands closed at the table, but he waited.

I attached myself to his energy to feel what he was feeling. I understood his motives if I read the spirit psychically instead of my student. To him, she felt familiar. As in, he wasn't new to her. They weren't just meeting. This giant creature, who sat in a small chair, looked over her in appreciation, in loving protective adoration. He appeared to be happy that they could sit and gaze upon each other, really seeing each other for the first time. As horrified as my Hollywood-based bias was, it diminished when I learned that they were linked, and this meeting was actually quite beautiful. To be totally honest, I was even jealous of so much love.

I said to the class, "You can touch him." In my mind's eye, I watched her reach for his hand. While they spoke, I could not hear their conversation. It was hushed and intimate, like two close friends meeting after a long time of sharing secrets. The two of them leaned in, whispering, and connecting. He was stoic, and she was enthralled. Seeing Naomi and the Oni was beautiful, kind, and powerful. I never did get his name.

Fast forward to my live-stream reading. While waiting in the openness of the otherworld, Naomi's Oni appeared quickly and stood in front of me, blocking my view and my access through the veil of the otherworld: "Um," I said into the camera, "Can someone see if Naomi can come on stream or call me? Her guide is here." My thoughts were racing. *Why was he here? Why not one of mine? Was Naomi in trouble?*

The veil is too open! The Oni dropped into my head. *This is reckless!*

"Seriously, can someone call or text, or dm Naomi? Anyone on stream who knows her?" The chat was crazy after my plea. I said out loud to the Oni so all could hear me, "I am looking for this human's dad. He has been visiting her, so I reached out to see if I...."

He is not here, said the Oni.

"No, he has to be there," I insisted. "He is visiting her."

That's not possible. He has reincarnated.

"I thought reincarnation happens when the living no longer mentions the deceased," I said. The chat was lighting up. They were only hearing my side of the conversation, but most of them are getting the gist. The camera filming me for the world to see was showing one part of a phone call to the other world.

The woman typed that what the Oni was saying wasn't possible. She then wrote:

> He is here now.

"She says that her father is there now, so he can't be reincarnated. Do you have the right person?" I asked the Oni.

See for yourself, said the Oni:

>   a child playing on a video game
>   early in the morning, just before sunrise
> the child was a ten-year-old boy, either South Asian, Indian, or Middle
>   Eastern.
>   too dark to tell
>   sitting on his bed with the covers kicked to the floor
>   covers were pale blue
>   twin-size mattress was low to the floor
> I couldn't see if the mattress was raised or not because the vision was from
>   above

the room was small
a door next to his head
his small bed was pushed up against the wall
no pillow on the bed
maybe it had fallen
in a plain shirt and tied pajama pants
objects on the floor...

And I was back. *Close this veil!* And the Oni shut the veil so quickly the candles on my desk flickered, as if a breeze had come through my computer across my face. I have never seen the veil shut so quickly, so perfectly. It was shut tight.

I told the group what I had seen. The woman confirmed that her father had been dead for just over ten years. Time to try a different tactic.

I connected to the woman instead of the veil and dug deep. Who was she seeing if her father had reincarnated? While digging into her spirit, her space, and reading her situation, I explained that most spirits reincarnate when the living no longer mention the dead. However, I don't know all of the rules of spirit, the gods, and how things work. I only know what I've interacted with. There must be exceptions, and his spirit must have been needed.

I was able to connect with the unknown woman. I could see her and only feel one energy, but as if it had been replicated. Were there two of her? No. There he was, her father, made of her spirit, her energy. There was a glowing snake-like cable moving from her to the specter.

Since streaming was relatively new for me, my husband and daughter had come in to check on me. They sat on the bed watching me talk to the chat screen and reading and explaining to the woman what was going on. She had created, in her grief, an artificial elemental of her father. An effigy, a living spirit-shrine dedicated to her most beloved, and he stood in this room. I explained what was there, how this is a beautiful way to remember someone, but that it was time to let it go. The artificial only stayed alive because it was being charged with her energy. Keeping the artificial spirit going was depleting her energy. Long-term effects could be depression, leaving her open to possession, lethargy, or chronic pain conditions.

She didn't respond. The chat was showing so much sympathy, but she wasn't responding. I asked the chat if anyone knew her and could check on her. That all of this was probably devastating. Her father wasn't there, well, not the real one, and she had manifested a replicated version with her own energy (which I thought was a beautiful, albeit unhealthy, way of honoring her father).

Just then, another chatter came online. This chatter said that she was the woman's therapist and that this was a perfect opportunity to address the grief around her father. When the woman reached out to me to talk to her late father, she had also called her therapist to watch the stream. The therapist typed:

> Thank you. You are truly amazing, and this will help her begin healing her grief. I can't believe the candles moved the way they did. This was amazing. Thank you.

I unplugged my spirit from the woman. I hadn't realized how my energy in doing all that work depleted me. I was empty. I couldn't get up from the chair. I quickly ended the stream, and my husband ran over to me.

"What's wrong? You were ok, and now you aren't. What's going on?" He said quickly.

"So, while I was connected to the woman, I was so deep that I confused her energy with my own. I thought I was ok. Being connected to her made me think I had plenty of energy left to keep going. I guess I thought her amount of energy was mine. When I disconnected, I realized I had been in too long," I said.

"What's going to happen?" My daughter said.

"Nothing. Give me a few minutes," my head lulled back, and I closed my eyes in my office chair.

"Oh my god, are you ok?" My husband was frantic.

"Yeah," I said, "I just need to rest. Can you make me a grilled-cheese sandwich?"

Part 3

The Healing Process of Hilina'i: Psychic Surgery & Belief

Hilina'i, Belief, and Medicine

Belief: Hilina'i

Hilina'i is a Hawaiian term that refers to a form of psychic surgery and healing rooted in the rooted in Hawaiian spiritual traditions of Hawaiian culture. It is based on the foundation of spiritual and energetic principles unique to Hawaiian traditions and worldview. In hilina'i, the healer utilizes their intuitive abilities, connection with spiritual forces, and deep understanding of the energy systems of the body to facilitate healing and restoration. The practice involves working with the mana to address physical, emotional, and spiritual imbalances. Hilina'i emphasizes the importance of faith, trust, and belief in the healing process, as it recognizes the interconnectedness of the mind, body, spirit, and the healing power of the individual's own beliefs.

The power of belief cannot be underestimated when it comes to healing and overall well-being. Our beliefs have a profound influence on how we perceive and experience our health, and they can play a crucial role in both the healing process and our ability to stay sick. Belief forms the foundation of our health journey, as it shapes our thoughts, emotions, behaviors, and physiological responses. In this essay, we will explore how belief influences how we heal, how we stay sick, and why it is the foundation for healing anything.

Belief is a fundamental aspect of the mind-body connection, which recognizes the intricate interplay between our psychological state and our physical health. Our beliefs about our health, the efficacy of treatments, and the possibility of recovery can significantly impact our well-being. Numerous studies have highlighted the importance of belief in influencing various aspects of healing, including pain management, recovery from illness, and even the course of chronic diseases.

When we believe in our ability to heal, our thoughts and emotions align with positive expectations. This positive mindset can create a cascade of biochemical changes in our body, including the release of feel-good neurotransmitters, reduced stress hormones, and enhanced immune system function. Research has shown that individuals with a positive outlook on their health and recovery tend to experience better outcomes, including faster healing, reduced pain, and improved overall well-being.

Furthermore, belief can shape our behaviors and actions, which play a vital role in healing. When we have faith in the effectiveness of our chosen treatments or approaches, we are more likely to adhere to them diligently, make necessary lifestyle changes, and engage in self-care practices. This active participation in our healing journey enhances the effectiveness of interventions and contributes to improved outcomes. In contrast, a lack of belief or skepticism can hinder our motivation to take necessary steps for healing, potentially impeding progress.

To build a foundation for healing, it is crucial to explore and challenge any limiting or negative beliefs we may hold. This involves examining the stories we tell ourselves about our health, questioning assumptions about our abilities, and reframing any self-defeating narratives. Engaging in practices such as affirmations, visualization, and mindfulness can help us cultivate positive beliefs, reduce stress, and promote overall well-being.

The Blocked Imbalanced Energy

In Chinese medicine, the understanding is rooted in the belief that any form of treatment is better than not treating an illness at all. This perspective is based on thousands of years of study, practice, and documented cases, which have consistently shown the value of proactive intervention in promoting health and well-being.

Chinese medicine places great emphasis on the concept of Qi (pronounced "chee"), which is the vital energy that flows through our bodies (sounds like mana, hu?). It is believed that when this energy is blocked or imbalanced, it can lead to physical and emotional disharmony, ultimately manifesting as illness. By addressing these imbalances and restoring the flow of Qi (mana), Chinese medicine seeks to restore the body's balance and support its innate healing capabilities.

However, Chinese medicine does not rely solely on one particular treatment modality or approach. Instead, it incorporates a range of therapeutic techniques, including acupuncture, herbal medicine, dietary interventions, lifestyle modifications, and mind-body practices like Qi Gong or Tai Chi. The specific treatment approach is determined by the individual's unique constitution, symptoms, and overall health condition. This is the same in Hawai'i.

One of the key principles is the belief that early intervention is preferable to waiting until an illness becomes more severe or chronic. By recognizing the signs of disharmony and addressing them at an early stage, we aim to prevent the progression of disease and promote optimal health.

Even if the exact cause of an illness is not fully understood, supporting the body's natural healing processes can still bring about positive outcomes. This recognition stems from the belief that our bodies possess an inherent wisdom and ability to heal, and by providing gentle and supportive interventions, we can help facilitate that healing process.

By incorporating lifestyle modifications, such as dietary changes, stress-reduction techniques, a sense of community, and regular physical activity, people can actively participate in their own health and help prevent the onset of illness.

The Placebo Effect

The placebo effect remains one of medicine's most revealing phenomena. It refers to the beneficial effects experienced by a patient, even when they are given an inactive substance, such as a sugar pill, instead of an actual medication. This effect highlights the power of belief and the mind-body connection when it comes to healing. In this essay, we will explore why the placebo effect works and how being an active participant in belief can affect how our bodies heal.

At its core, the placebo effect demonstrates the significant role that our beliefs, expectations, and perceptions play in influencing our physical well-being. When a person believes that a treatment or intervention will work, their mind and body respond accordingly, triggering a series of physiological and psychological responses that lead to healing. This response is not imaginary or illusory but has been proven to have measurable effects on the body.

One explanation for the placebo effect is related to the brain's release of natural chemicals and neurotransmitters that promote healing. When a person **believes** that they are receiving a treatment that will alleviate their symptoms, the brain interprets this information and activates the release of endorphins, dopamine, and other pain-relieving or mood-enhancing substances. These neurochemicals can have powerful effects on the body, providing pain relief, reducing anxiety, and even boosting the immune system.

The placebo effect is also linked to the body's innate ability to heal itself. Our bodies have a remarkable capacity for self-regulation and homeostasis. When we believe in a treatment's efficacy, this belief can trigger a cascade of biochemical changes that facilitate the body's healing mechanisms. Whether it is the release of natural painkillers or the activation of the immune system, the placebo effect can harness our body's natural healing processes to bring about real physiological changes.

Another critical aspect of the placebo effect is the role of expectation and conditioning. Past experiences, cultural influences, and the therapeutic ritual surrounding a treatment can all shape our expectations of its effectiveness. The belief that a specific intervention will work can create a psychological framework that primes our minds and bodies to respond positively. For example, the act of taking a pill, undergoing an acupuncture session, or receiving a therapeutic touch can create a sense of hope, comfort, and relaxation, all of which contribute to the healing process.

Nocebo Effect

However, belief is not limited only to positive expectations of healing. It can also influence our ability to stay sick, often through concepts such as the nocebo effect. Like the placebo effect, the nocebo effect is the negative counterpart, where negative beliefs and expectations can actually worsen our health. For example, if we firmly believe that a certain treatment will not work, our mind and body can respond accordingly by limiting its effectiveness or even causing harmful side effects.

Beliefs can also influence the development and progression of chronic diseases. For instance, chronic stress and negative beliefs about one's ability to manage their condition have been linked to exacerbated symptoms, increased disability, and poorer quality of life. This suggests that negative beliefs can also perpetuate a cycle of illness and suffering.

Understanding that belief is the foundation of healing is essential. Our beliefs form the framework through which we interpret and respond to our experiences, including our health challenges. If our belief system is rooted in negativity, fear, or a sense of powerlessness, it can create barriers to healing and limit our potential for recovery. On the other hand, cultivating positive, empowering beliefs can foster resilience, encourage proactive actions, and mobilize our body's innate healing mechanisms.

Ritual and Including the Patient

Being an active participant in belief can influence how our bodies heal. Research has shown that the more involved and engaged a person is in their treatment, the greater the likelihood of experiencing positive outcomes. This concept, known as the active placebo effect, suggests that when we actively engage in our healing journey, we are more likely to experience improvements in our health. This participation can involve actively adhering to treatment protocols, making lifestyle changes, and adopting a positive mindset towards the healing process.

When we actively engage in our belief in healing, we become more receptive to the positive suggestions and messages we receive from healthcare providers and our own thoughts. This receptivity enables our mind and body to work in synergy, restoring balance and well-being. By actively participating in our belief in healing, we empower ourselves to take control of our health and contribute to our own recovery.

It is essential to recognize that the placebo effect does not discount the effectiveness of proven medical treatments or suggest that all treatments can be replaced by sugar pills or placebos. Instead, it sheds light on the complexity of the mind-body connection and the need to integrate both the biological and psychological aspects of healing.

The placebo effect works because our beliefs, expectations, and active participation play a significant role in influencing how our bodies heal. The power of belief, conditioned responses, and the mind-body connection can activate physiological and psychological changes that contribute to real improvements in health.

May's Misuse

May had misused her gifts as a practitioner. She was extremely talented. She did Theta-Wave Healing, an energy-based healing modality where she goes into a trance and heals by taking bad energy waves and absorbing them, then flushing them out. With her great success and full docket, she developed such a strong sense of accomplishment and self-worth that her process was rooted in her sense of bragging and ego.

May went to galas where rich clients would spoil her, and although there is nothing wrong with accepting these gifts, she came to expect them. Her identity was focused on what she was rather than what she was doing. Her ego and high opinion of herself were depleting her mana. After working on clients, May bragged about being the best in the field and being meticulous about her financial worth. May *was* a healer, but *wasn't* anymore. May had become an icon instead, and May was now empty.

Even though May was a fantastic healer, Theta-Wave Healing is a very different modality from the Hawaiian "psychic surgeries." In Hawai'i, we are taught that all things have mana, life force, spirit. In psychic surgery, we can take the mana from other things and transplant it into the person, especially when someone isn't regenerating their own mana.

She couldn't heal herself with her own modality because she didn't have anything to "pull out."

I told her that the gods were probably mad...

The healer had lost her mana. When this happens, I wait patiently for Kane to connect to me. He doesn't need to answer my prayer, and I could sit there quietly, learning if he will or won't help in the process of filling someone with mana loss. I waited in front of his idol. He answered. The sky felt like it opened, and through me, his white cloth filled me like a channel filled with a broken dam.

I poured myself into May by dancing and asking the gods for help to transfer from me to her. Fortunately for her, it worked. However, I was now empty. In my emptiness, I did not know if the gods (or nature) would reward me with mana to continue my work. Would they fill me back up, or did I trade my life force for the practice of another?

I warned May to change her ways because I would not do this a second time. I didn't know if I would ever be able to work on another person again. The necessity to heal a healer is one of the highest forms of duty in the field of healing.

This sacrifice would put a healer back into the world, and many will benefit from this sacrifice. I knelt in front of my altar. I didn't ask. I didn't pray. I just said thank you. Thank you for allowing me the ability to help a healer, and if they felt me worthy, to grant me the seeds within to regenerate my mana. My spirit felt weak, and with a small spark in my mind's eye, like the flame Maui stole from Milu, I knew I would be fine. With rest and care, I would regenerate.

SPIRITUAL ILLNESS TEST

> Figure out below what area of the soul is affected by the following diseases. Remember that your choices are Aumakua, Unihipili, and Uhane:

Genetic Trauma, like slavery?

It has to do with genetics...

Uhane!

Generational Trauma, like fear of finances?

Has to do with belief...

Aumakua

Phobias?

Ok, trick question. Let's specify with Rational Phobias?

These are based on things we learn...

Aumakua

Irrational Phobias?

Hint: Theory has to do with past lives....

Unihipili

Insecurities?

Aumakua - learned from what we think others judge us for having or not having.

Lethargic response to stay unmotivated?

Physical response to something cognitive

Aumakua connected to uhane

Why is this Important?

If a spirit is attached to a person, it is connected to a hole or missing piece, or tangled in parts of someone's soul. Is the spirit inside their uhane? Has it replaced a part of their aumakua? Is it tethered to their unihipili? Is the spirit trapped in the web of someone, affecting many areas? Understanding where the spirit is attached helps with its removal. Furthermore, once you remove the spirit, you will need to heal the hole or torn area of the person so another spirit does not move in.

Lastly, the spirit itself may need healing interventions. Understanding how the spirit is will allow you to help in its healing. Happy spirits mean less hostile spiritual activity.

Ego and D'artanian's Damage

Characters:
Me
D'artanian - Client of mine, butchered by healers
KC - YouTube self-proclaimed prophet and healer
Heather - Self-proclaimed akashic healer
Bella - A psychic

I have a client who has an opioidal brain injury. He is a lovely man. He hired me to work on him with Hilina'i. When I went in to work on him, the brain part of his aumakua and uhane were shredded. I opened my eyes and told him such. He was relieved that he wasn't "crazy," and that he knew this to be true. I worked on his uhane mind for an hour, periodically stopping to do a cognitive check with him. No change. After the hour was completed, he felt different, better, as in an easier time concentrating.

I then worked on his aumakua, trying to mend the missing pieces. What he needed was a soul retrieval. Grandmother Spider handed me the spirit of a swallow and the spirit of a cardinal to place into his aumakua. There wasn't enough in his soul to mend, as it was thrashed.

I was then given some soul of moss to patch another hole; however, this would make him more complete, but not completely him. He needed a soul retrieval.

"D'artanian," I said, "you need a soul retrieval. There is only so much I can do this way."

"Aly, what is a soul retrieval?" I found it interesting that he said my name as often as he did.

"Well, the parts of your soul that have been broken off because of the trauma you've been through are in the spirit world. I go there, get those pieces, and integrate them back into your soul. There is a side effect that we need to talk through, though."

"What's that?" He asked.

"Well, the first six to eight days of a soul retrieval, the highs can be really high, but the lows can be really low. I'm concerned about the lows…"

"I can't." He cut me off.

"Ok," I said.

"Aly, I won't make it through. I've been hospitalized for suicide twice. I'm barely hanging on. I'm not a danger to myself now, but I don't know if I could make it through lower. Even for six days," he said.

"Then we don't do it," I agreed.

"I wouldn't make it," he repeated.

"Alright. Don't worry about it. I will do what I can here, but there are limitations. I am transplanting the soul from other things with the direction of Grandmother Spider. They will complete you, but it isn't completely you. You'll integrate them just fine. You'll be a full soul. It won't change your personality or cause any kind of distress. You'll have an easier time thinking, but not as good as a soul retrieval would do. We've already successfully worked on several parts of you. I do have to say," I took a sip of my coffee, "that I will not be able to fully fix your brain. It's really damaged. I can mend it some, but there will likely always be hardened scar tissue that I can't break up. The amazing thing about the brain is that over time, it figures out new pathways. My hope is to mend you enough that you can create new pathways and function fully again. It will just take me some time."

"Wow," he said, "you are the real deal."

"I sure hope so," I giggled.

"I've never had a healer tell me their limitations. Ok, tell me what to do."

"Just lie down. I can work for another hour, and then we will have to schedule another session in over a month. I want to see how everything works on its own without messing with it. How about a check-in in about six weeks?"

"That sounds perfect," he said.

"And of course, you can email me in between," I finished.

I went to work.

I hadn't heard from D'artanian for a few months. I don't tend to check up on my clients because it feels predatory. I figure if they need me, they will come to me. D'artanian said he was being attacked by beings. He said they were reptilian, but he determined that based on watching YouTube videos where the craze of star-seeds, higher self, and reptilian aliens is all the craze.

What is my philosophy on reptilian spirits in outer space? If they are a thing, why haven't they been documented by cultures for the last 10,000 years? Are people regurgitating what one guy has said, creating a populous of incestual information? I think so. In any case, if you've read Witchdoctor *Exorcist*, I don't take much weight in the classification of spirits from a client. I just listen to symptoms and descriptions.

"D'artanian, let me take a look," I said on our Zoom call. "Are there any other people in the house?"

"No. Dad is out." D'artanian lived with his father because he was unable to hold a job after he got off opioids. D'artanian was about thirty-eight. Handsome, smart, fit, clean-cut guy. You'd never know he was so tormented by looking at him.

"Ok." I played the drum track. "Just sit still and don't do anything while I look around. Can you light a candle for me so I can find you quicker?"

"Yes, sure." He said.

"Tell me when you light it so I can light mine at the same time," I said.

"Let me get one from the bathroom. I will be right back."

I closed my eyes and listened to the drums, relaxing my pulse.

"Ok, I have it, Aly," D'artanian said.

"Light it," I said. He did. I closed my eyes and let everything go black.

It was easy for me to feel the pull of his flame, so moving from the darkness, through my mind, out of my body, over the ocean and rock wall, and into his Southern California home was relatively effortless.

I saw him sitting with the candle in his hands. In his back, there was a hole in his spirit. As if he were a basket and the weaving was shredded by some kind of vermin. I looked inside his soul, and there was a small elf-like entity trapped in the webbing.

How'd you get in here? I said to the brownie.

He thrashed about trying to get free.

I won't hurt you. Let me move you. Be still, little fella. I reached in, untangled a bit of D'artanian's aka, and offered my hand. Its eyes jutted from me to the entrance out of D'artanian's soul. Back and forth. Back and forth.

If you run, you won't have a home to go to. I can take you home. I tried to use the calmest, most nurturing voice I could. And if you've met me, that is my basic state.

He put his hand in mine.

I brought him close, and we stepped out of D'artanian's soul. I held him close to me, and we took off, as spirits can, back to the middle world of my town outside of Austin, Texas. I knew there were brownies in the wooded nature around the San Gabriel River, so it seemed like the perfect place for him to find others like him.

We settled down, and I unwrapped him from my spirit, gently placing him into the grassland. I took a step back. He looked around. He looked at me. He pointed at the tall grass by the water. He put his hand down and looked at me again. Then he took off running into the tall grass, making it bend as if a strong breeze had tickled the blades.

I focused on my physical body, the darkness behind my eyes, opened them, back in my body, and said, "D'artanian, there was a spirit inside you. It was a brownie. Harmless, but it didn't want to be there and was probably causing a ruckus trying to get out. I let it out, and it's gone, but I need to do some repairs so something else doesn't take its spot. How did you end up with a spirit? I put you together only a few months ago."

"Aly," D'artanian started, "I've been working with a few people. I knew I had a spirit in me."

"Well, it's gone," I said. "What people?"

"I found this guy, KC, on YouTube, and he is a higher self light worker. He said he opened up a portal so my spirit guides could talk to me. He connected my soul to the higher plane and connected it. He said he opened up the spirit world to have access to me."

Oh my gods, I thought.

"He said I have a reptilian spirit possessing me," D'artanian said.

"Well, you didn't. You had a brownie that he probably put there."

"What?!" D'artanian said.

"You said he tied you to a portal or something. Well, he cut open your soul somehow, a wretched job, and tried to tie you to something, and this little guy got in."

"He tormented me. He was trying to torture me," D'artanian said.

"I'm sure you were tormented. But if you put a raccoon in a sack, it will try to get out, tormenting the sack in the process. That was this. It wasn't trying to harm you. It wanted to get out. It was not a personal malefic attack. You were a sack it wanted to get free from."

"Oh," D'artanian said. "Why would he do that?"

"Because this guy doesn't know what he's doing and is messing with stuff he has no training in. Don't get me wrong, when I first started, I made mistakes, but this is a big one. Made from ego and overconfidence," I said.

"Aly, fix this?" D'artanian said.

"Ok," I paused. "Well, what is his background? What are his credentials?"

"He has a following on YouTube, and he practices back and forth between here and Hawai'i."

"Celebrities have followings, D'artanian. What are his cultural, spiritual, or contextual credentials? Is he self-naming? And if so, based on what or who? Did a deity pick him? Is it back with any other information?"

"I don't know. I don't think so?" D'artanian said.

"Cult leaders have followings. Healers work. Send me his information? He just opened portals to spirits so they can have access to you? No mediation between spirits and you? No..." I stopped my temper from getting out of control.

"I have some work to do on you," I said. "He cut you up somehow, and some brownie got in. I'm not sure how. I don't think this guy knows what he's doing. If a brownie is walking around, what else could be? You send me that information, and I'll go back and look around in your place. When I'm back, I will tell you what I find and then patch you up. I have to work quickly because I have... no, let me text the other client to see if they can move an hour."

D'artanian said, "You shouldn't do that."

"I have to. You're too vulnerable. I can't just leave you like this," I said.

"I will compensate you," D'artanian said.

"Thank you. Send me his information; I want to look him up. Then lay down," I said. I sent a quick text to my client, explaining that I had a client emergency and needed to either reschedule our reading or move it back. She answered immediately, saying it was ok. Most of my clients know the array of work I have to do, so they are flexible if I hit exhaustion or have someone with an emergency; they would want me to do the same for them.

I closed my eyes, focused on the black, felt the candle flame, and, moving through its connection, spirit-walked to his house.

Looking up and around this place, there were holes in the veil, vortexes, everywhere. One by one, I closed them.

After I got to the 43rd hole in the veil, I stopped counting. Most of them were really small. Like an amateur cutting and slicing to the upper world without focus or sight, trying to connect to something higher but not really knowing how, doing so with flippant disregard for possible effects.

When I finished, I told D'artanian what I had done. He was furious that KC had forced him into vulnerability with promises of an outcome he didn't have the qualifications or know-how to do. We wondered how many other people lay prey to his neglectful ways. In any case, D'artanian was back to being patched and taken care of, again.

A few months after that, I heard from D'artanian again. Keep in mind that because of D'artanian's brain injury, I take everything he says with a grain of salt. I need to listen and discern. His injury could be playing tricks on him. He told me he went to a psychic, Bella, who told him that he was being attacked by spirits. D'artanian naturally believed this because it confirmed his disdain for KC. Reading D'artanian, I could find no such thing. He said he felt like it wasn't in his home, and that I had done a great job of closing up the veil. He said he felt like it was an attack coming from a higher plane, through the veil, like how spirit guides talk to us through the veil. He felt like this attack was being coerced by KC.

At that, I defended KC with his own ineptitude. There is no way this person was capable of contacting a spirit of this magnitude, if this were the case, because of his obvious incompetence in the mystical. He listened and agreed that, based on the previous evidence of KC, it was likely not him.

Needless to say, he felt like he was being attacked and wanted to hire me for an exorcism. He paid me, and we started the process.

During the week leading up to the exorcism, he sought out religious counsel from a deacon at his local church. He was also seeing Bella, the psychic, twice a week, and a new healer, Heather. I told him he needed to stop. If I were going to run an exorcism, I needed full control of the process, as I knew he was flailing and felt desperate, and that he wanted to have control over a situation for which he felt he had none.

He called: "Aly, I understand. So, walk me through what will happen."

"Ok," I said, "I've already done the intake. I will do a reading the night before so that I can tell you what exactly is going on and how it will be handled. After the disconnection, you will need a soul retrieval or psychic surgery to patch up or remove whatever has been done. I really recommend a soul retrieval, but I understand."

"I can't do one," he interrupted.

"I know."

"The deacon is giving me some great prayers, but it hates them," D'artanian said.

"How?"

"How do I pray?"

"No," I clarified. "How do you know it doesn't like them?"

"I feel worse."

"Are you still Catholic?" I asked.

"Yes."

"Do you have a problem with me interacting with a demon to help stop whatever is going on?" I asked.

"What do you mean?"

"I work with a demon. She is really scary. So scary, other demons and entities run. By her showing up, I can stop everything, cut you free, get rid of anything there because she will scare it, and lock down the area."

"You are the kindest person I have ever met, Aly. And if anyone were to be labeled the most Christ-like healer, with compassion and care and giving of your energy and skills, it would be you. And yet, I'm not surprised that even an arch-demon would be willing to help you. I'd help you. Who wouldn't want to help you? This scares the fuck out of me. You'd be inviting a demon to stop an attack… And yet, I trust you… I don't think this is very Christian…."

"It's not," I said. "I'm not Christian."

"I mean, to invite demons is everything the Church has said to not do, and yet, I feel that you are doing the most Christ-like thing."

"If you need to tell yourself that for me to get the work done. I just want you to be better. But you need to let me do my work, like a head surgeon. You can't have multiple hospitals all performing the same surgery simultaneously. Pick one. Either fully me, or not. I need guaranteed control for guaranteed care. Does that make sense?"

"Yes."

The night before the exorcism, D'artanian cancelled. He said he couldn't do the healing afterwards, and that he wanted to go another direction.

He went to Heather, and she did "work."

A month later, I got another email from D'artanian, and all it said was to call him, and it was urgent.

Because I had had over a year relationship with him, I called.

"When you did the psychic surgery, and you put the souls of birds in me, does it change my opinions, things I like, or my personality?"

"No, it doesn't."

"I want to be sure," D'artanian said. "So, what does it do?"

"Well, the part of your spirit that holds opinions, values, and likes is part of the mental part of you. This part of you needs to be repaired with a Soul Retrieval. The threads and sections of it, since I couldn't bring back those pieces that have been broken off from trauma, were patched in with something that doesn't have opinions or values, right? So, it isn't going to be taken away; we are just filling in space so you don't have a hole. This is done with all three soul bodies. It works best with the psychic part of you because animals are intrinsically psychic. The spiritual part of you accepts psychic surgery the best. The body, or physical part of your soul, also does well because, generally, what I'm given is also from something that was once physical."

"Aly, I'm not going to live long," D'artanian said.

"I'm listening." I tried to hide my shock. I need to just listen and stay calm. Do I need to report him? I am not a mandated reporter, but I care about this client of mine.

"I'm not going to harm myself, but I don't know how long I will be able to hold," he said.

"Tell me what happened."

"I went to Heather. I should have listened to Bella. I asked Bella if she would do the work, and she said it was out of her abilities and said I should use you. She mentioned that she had read about you and believed the best option was for me to use you to stop the attacks. I told her about the healing and the Soul Retrieval, and she said that she still thought I should work with you to figure it out. I said I wouldn't survive the integration process. The deacon also thought that, although it was unconventional in his beliefs, God said it was the right decision. To use you. I told him the same thing. He prayed with me. Heather said she could do it by cutting me free and making me into my higher self, thereby connecting me to it. I should have listened."

"She did some kind of cord cutting and..." D'artanian started to cry.

"What happened?" I said.

"Aly, I love shopping. I love looking at things, walking through malls, stores... I like shopping online. I don't usually buy anything, but I like it. I love it. I don't love it anymore. I also don't have any opinions about politics. They are gone. I didn't vote. I didn't care. I used to really care. I don't care. I don't care about anything."

"Are you taking ashwagandha?" I asked.

"No, why?"

"Taking too much ashwagandha has sometimes led to anhedonia. That's the inability to experience joy or pleasure. A numbness. It can be a condition of your brain injury," I said.

"Would it show up out of nowhere? And after her work?" D'artanian asked.

"Hmm," I pondered. "I don't think so, but I don't know. Sorry for interrupting. Tell me what she did."

"So, it wasn't you."

"Well, if it were from psychic surgery, which doesn't work like that, it would have shown up a year ago," I said.

"That's what I figured. So, Aly, when I went to Heather, she said she cut me free from what was attacking me. But then I felt this way, so then I asked her what she did. She said she cut me free from the spirit connection and attack. All connections. And she cut me free from worldly possessions because she believes that they cause pain and suffering. That was the one thing I had joy from. She took from me..."

"Oh my gods," I whispered, covering my mouth.

"What did she do?" D'artanian asked.

"She..." My mind raced. "D'artanian, when you do a soul retrieval, you bring parts of the opinions, mind, values, direction... the parts of the mental soul back that break from trauma. She took more of them off. She cut parts of our soul off. She cut off the parts of your aumakua. What did she do with them?"

"She said she gave them to 'source.'"

"What the fuck does that mean?!" I lost my temper. "This idiot decides to mutilate a soul because she decides personally what a human in the human condition should and should not feel or connect to? She thinks she is some sort of god? She thinks she has the authority to decide what should be part of human happiness or pain. What the fuck! D'artanian, I... I don't know if I can fix this! I don't think she 'gave them back to source,' but the only way I can put you back, to really put you back, is a Soul Retrieval."

"I really won't survive it," D'artanian said.

I paused. I sat in my thoughts, my diagnosis, my planning, and remembered that D'artanian is a person. A loving person.

"What can I do for you, D'artanian? Tell me how I can help."

"I don't know. I got clarity. I know what she did was not ok."

"It was not ok. She mutilated you. I can reconnect you upwards. I can reconnect you to spirit or to God. I... You know what I need to do. What if you checked yourself into a place during the six days after a Soul Retrieval? Do you have a place to take care of yourself? It's only a week. One week of your life to have a better rest of your life."

"Thank you for always being honest with me. I know you don't work with the Christian God, but he must love you. How could he not?" And D'artanian hung up.

Many practitioners acted out of ego, rather than serving others. Which kind of practitioner are you going to be?

Psychic Surgery

No witchdoctor should be so removed from the pain, the smells, the sounds of a client's suffering. In this compassion, the care of our patients, we can really see through the dark shadows of the patient what is really hurt, out of ease.

Good things happen and bring a strong constitution, and when terrible things happen, misery joins. The sounds of suffering that may lead to death are some of the most horrific we face as a species, greatly fearing the transition to the other world and how that affects our souls.

With the urgency of healing because of death, we sometimes dismiss the need for healing for lesser sufferings because "everyone goes through them, so suck it up." Depriving the acknowledgment of suffering can cause extreme damage, resulting in a deterioration of the aumakua because the patient is learning that they are not worthy of compassion. The art behind healing involves understanding the individual's suffering and addressing it through customized care.

With that, I am also going to point out that 80% of the world is using "alternative medicine," while only 20% is using western (hmmm... sounds like demonization, again), and although it is easy to recognize a western medical professional with degrees and certifications, it's impossible to figure out the validity of faith healers, medicine men, shamans, priests, and other cultural healers.

And if physical, emotional, or mental anguish can harm the soul, why can we not then go in through the shadowy substances of our soul and repair or heal the soul to then affect the physical, the emotional, and the mental? If our soul becomes sick because of a disease, why can we not use the soul to affect the physical (as best we can)?

Psychic Surgery: Hilina'i - Healing Energetically Through the Shadows of Belief's Energy

Hilina'i is the ability to heal the spirit parts of anything through psychic surgery. I will give you a set of exercises to practice before going to people, but you may also be able to help heal an injured spirit. Remember that this is pronounced Hee-lee-nah-eeee (not heeleenae). Psychic surgery causes no pain to the patient during the session, and has two very polarizing opinions:

1) miraculous gift of healing
2) fake show for charlatans to gain money.

My answer is this: Although we cannot all comprehend the phenomena of psychic surgery and other forms of energy healing, we can't deny its efficacy when continued use with outcomes has been practiced by 80% of the world for hundreds of years, in some form or another. No matter the thought pattern of reality, we still can regard this form of healing as ethically sound, possible, and tangible. Just because we can't see radar with our eyes, doesn't mean it doesn't exist. With this, the healer must be concerned with the three soul bodies: physical (our form), spiritual (totem), and mental (astral body).

I want you to sit or stand comfortably. I want you to close your eyes and put your hands out in front of you, like radar. I want you to feel the energy around you, and you're going to read it with your mind. Like holding a book, your mind reads the words, but your hands find the pages.

You will just find energies with your hands and allow your mind to see the changes. This is the preliminary step to reading energy. You will be using your hands, your mind, and your psychic spirit simultaneously when healing others with this modality.

> Note: Remember that this can heal any part of the damaged soul, not the missing soul. If parts are missing, you'll need to do a soul retrieval. You can't heal something missing, but you can heal something that's damaged. Also, never pull something out without filling it back in.

Exercise 1: Since you have already done mana checks, this is a deeper dive. Mana check is the visual interpretation of your spirit and how it is doing in the various areas of your life. Here, we will look at the micro-level of your spirit. Let's start with something simpler than the complex human spirit: a crystal. A crystal only has a body, uhane. I want you to feel the spirit of the crystal. How is the spirit? Intense? Weak? With your eyes closed, how is the intensity of what you're seeing of its energy? Then I want you to dive further, look so far into the spirit of the crystal that you can see the space between the aka. You can feel the mana flowing on the aka and the keawe between them. Are there any spots of the crystal's energy that need to be repaired? Don't worry about repairing it yet. This is just discovery. You will have time for repair work.

Exercise 2: Now, apply your skills to read your computer. What is the spirit of your computer? It, too, only has uhane, right? It is inanimate. It has no instinct and no capacity to wonder or comprehend. Every physical item has uhane: a box, cup, microwave, and other inanimate objects. Feel the cords: how is the strength of the spirit? Feel and see the energy within the threads: how is the vitality of the mana? Feel and see the airy space between: how is the health of the keawe?

Exercise 3 Self-care: Where do you get your energy from? How do you rebuild your energy? Sleep? Possibly food? What activities refill your cup? Make a list of these things; you will need them later, and you are not allowed just to answer "source" because that is the trendy, vague answer. Realistically, how do you refill your energy? Is it watching scary movies?

Is it in prayer? Is it taking walks in the forest? Is it an intimate connection with your boyfriend? Is it playing the banjo? How do you fill yourself?

Exercise 4: It's time to add another layer to what you have read so far. Wildlife: look at plants and see more than their bodies. You'll find another part of its spirit. This part isn't a majority or even half. This is the life, the psychic aspect of the plant, and the soul energy. In plants, this part of their spirit will be small compared to the body, but you should still be able to detect the unihipili. Trees will be much larger, but still not even half the size.

Exercise 5: When you get to animals, you'll see the balance shift from half to higher than half. You will see both parts. In some animals, like octopi, dolphins, and gorillas, you'll find that they even have traces of aumakua (the analytical part of the soul, the part that questions). Feel the energy of animals. I like to practice this at the zoo or the aquarium. Recently, I went to the zoo in Waco, TX, and that elephant had the happiest, healthiest spirit of any elephant I have ever seen in captivity. Reading the spirit of creatures will tell you how they are and should be in the various areas of their health. You are still not healing them, just reading.

Exercise 6: Your aka is connected to those things that fill you up and those things and people who drain your energy. Please keep in mind that a drain of energy is not a negative thing. Parenting can be draining and rewarding, but parents must find ways to refill their cup. I want you to feel your aka, and when you read an inanimate object, I want you to now see the cord of connection to the object. Just by reading it, you are connected to it. Notice the interaction between you and the object. Which way does the mana move? Toward you, toward the object, or is it at a standstill? Can you absorb the energy of the object into yourself? Can you use the object like a battery? Probably not, but try? What you are more likely to be able to do is pour yourself into the object. Can you pour some of your energy into the object by interacting with it? You do that when you parent or care for a pet: you are putting your energy into the care of what you are interacting with. Can you do it from only an energetic level? Without the interaction? Try. Try to care or send (abs & intercostal muscles) only.

Exercise 7: It's time to try to pour your energy into a plant or animal. Use your personal power, rooted in your soul, to heal the holes or parts that need recovery. But Stop! Are you a healthy vessel? Or will you be spreading an infected spirit to an innocent cat? Remember how I brought up self-care? You must be spiritually fit to use yourself as a resource to heal others. This exercise is for contemplation of your own spiritual health. Ha, I tricked you!

Exercise 8: Clean up time. You are going to look into your spirit and push out the ick in the keawe, cut cords that are attached to things or people that don't serve you, patch up broken cables to yourself and others, and when you are done, you are going to replenish your mana with activities that fill your soul back up. In order to do this, I would like you to use these tricks:

Bamboo Pipe/Straw: With your eyes closed, pull your ick keawe from areas of your soul into your mouth, blow it out of yourself into a rock. Then set the rock in the sun or give it to the Earth.

Sewing: Lomi uses touch to move energy, connecting through the uhane to heal. Lomi Lomi is to be done more, with more pressure and the power of the aina. In hilina'i, you will not touch, but pull and move from above the surface. Float your hands above the surface of your body, and only touch and find the ak, and use the aka to move the mana around. Keeping your eyes closed, sense with your hands, touch the aka, find the broken pieces, then sew them to connect and heal. If there are holes, use the broken pieces of your own energy to sew them back together (you are not "visualizing;" you are clairvoyantly seeing).

Dance: When you dance, you move your energy around and purge your ugly or ill keawe. Dance to and with the music. The music heals because it is the seamstress who sews, and your movement is the sewing, back into healing. Dancing without music is no longer an indigenous practice. You must allow the music to do the healing while you move to it.

Exercise 9: Try another plant or animal. Now that you know how to mend yourself (sew, breathe, dance) and fill yourself back up (self-care), you will do this only when you've done your mana check and found you are healthy and looked at your mana, aka, keawe, and found that you are good to go. You will not be the vessel that heals. Please take out the infectious parts of their soul and blow them into the Earth. When you blow it out, make sure that you get all of the "ick" out of you. When what you are working on is clean, patch it up with parts of your own mana: I pull out with a bamboo pipe and sew up to mend. I will pull strands from my own aka, depending on the parts, and use them as the thread to mend someone else's. I use my hands as an instrument to sew myself into them. I take parts from myself and sew those parts into the plant or pet. If they need more, and you are healthy, you will pull from a healthy part of yourself and transplant it into your client. Yep, use up some of your soul and put it into your client (you will repair yourself with self-care).

The test to see if what you did worked or if it was imagination. You will need to observe the outcome. If it doesn't get better, then use more energy and push harder. Less visualization and more actualization. You are reading them and responding. Not imagining what you "think" they will look like. You are not using deductive reasoning. You read and respond. If you can't read them, then there is nothing you yourself can do.

Exercise 10: Find a relationship with a spirit willing to give to you, filling you up in exchange for an offering, gift, sacrifice, or time in prayer. Time to research and reach out. You will connect to them, their unihipili to yours or aumakua to yours or their aumakua to your uhane, connecting the aka and them, gifting their mana to you in exchange for self-care they require (gift?).

Exercise 11: Eating animals and plants. If you remember, the energy of one thing, if consumed by another, becomes part of that other. In the case of the Blemmya, if you get eaten by one in the Spirit World, you don't 'die '; you get absorbed. Please think about this when you feed yourself. The energy of animals and plants is vital to our existence, providing essential nutrients. And the energy from the herbs we eat, the tea we drink, the alcohol or drugs we consume, and the coffee that I pour into my body is my primary source of nutrition. The energy of food is something you should now consider. When you pick herbs or fruit at the grocery store, are you picking based on how you read the food energetically or by the label? Make a pointed effort to feel the energy of what you consume before you consume it. Your exercise is to grocery shop and feel the spirit of all things you purchase. Everything you put in your body over the course of a week needs to be monitored and read energetically. How are their spirits before consumption?

Exercise 12: Find a partner or friend willing to work on. You will not be allowed to mix hilina'i with Reiki, so keep the Reiki hand motions and symbols away. Do not mix modalities, please. You will read your partner and only read them. After reading their energy, including all its components, you will then give an account of what you find. This is *the* essential skill of a witchdoctor. Then find another willing volunteer. Do not do readings on people who don't ask for them. That is like a doctor walking through the mall and diagnosing everyone they encounter. It's inappropriate. Find volunteers, and read the nine parts of their energy. You may need to bring this book with you and reference the different areas to be completed.

Exercise 13: Finally, time to do a healing. Hopefully, your friends or volunteers from the previous exercise will be willing to help you try to mend an area you see as injured. You will need to pull out of them (I use a bamboo straw and blow it into a pile of Lomi stones that I then cleanse in the Sun), all of the ick. Make sure you don't ingest any of their ick. Once the three keawe are good, then it's time to sew or refill mana. You will need to sew up their aka. Yes, all three elements. Find where the attachments are not suitable.

Once you've done these steps, then back up, look at all of it as a single aura. I like to spin it. There should be no darkness when you've finished and it should spin and move easily with the vibrant color aura of the person's soul.

What if they have an unhealthy attachment to their ex-boyfriend? Shouldn't you cut it first? Honestly, it isn't up to you to decide if they have an unhealthy attachment. If you do a cord-cutting, they will just reconnect it unless they address the underlying foundational beliefs. They need to want to break unhealthy attachments, and then you can do a cord-cutting.

In the meantime, just repair the cords. Yep, cut yours off and sew them onto theirs. I'm not kidding. A witchdoctor makes this sacrifice. We use our own, from deep within, as a transplant for others to thrive. You will take a piece out, then put your piece into them. After you have done keawe and aka, you will feel your natural connection to them and pour your mana into them, filling up what needs to be filled up in the three different areas. After you are done, you will need to mend yourself, like you did in Exercise 8 and Exercise 3.

After doing this, you will replenish yourself with rest, activity, food, stress relievers, exercise, and joy. Many of us refrain from doing many healings in a single day. Because we use ourselves, we have to make sure we are also healthy so we have something to give.

Remember to disconnect.

Exercise 14: How long does it take you to recover from healing hilina'i? If you are 'bouncing back' quickly, you are not doing it right (or the patient didn't need a lot). The contemplation of knowing how far you can go and how far you can heal is essential. If you go too far, your value is gone for everyone. If you're just going through the motions, you are a con artist. You must know your limits, and if you push too hard, know how long it takes you to recover.

Doing The Steps

Do you know how many people just jump right into pulling out the ick of others without understanding all of the parts of the soul, where to put that energy, and how to repair and replace it? You need to start with stones, plants, animals, and complex people! And even then, you keep practicing with plants and animals. I spend time in my garden just reading the plants. Trees have been my favorite to read ever since my twenties. Just know that when a tree gets cut down, you may feel it scream. Help it transition. Help its spirit.

I work on many Reiki practitioners and light-workers who need someone who 'plays in the mud,' as some of them call me. We aren't afraid of the darkness in others and don't have a problem mending others' darknesses. If you repair a darkness, you might be mending their self-control or patching up a warrior.

Hilina'i is not "light work." You need to heal the darkness in people, too. We also don't believe in consent in healing. Aka will grow back if they want attachments regardless of what you do, so don't bother, but you don't need consent to heal someone this way. We do what we must to make the world a better and thriving place. You heal the thistle and the flower. You mend the murderer and the doctor. Witchdoctors are not justice warriors. We are teachers, we are healers, we strive for a world that is even. Balance.

You might need a patient's focus, but you don't require approval. I have been hired by many people who have had me mend someone they love in secret. I have also restored spirits that some of you would say are evil. Witchdoctors believe in balance. Without the dark or the destructive, the light has nothing to shine on. I am proud to say that this energy work is my pride and joy, and I am pleased to play in the mud in order to get you all healed. I think if you've picked up this book, you would be, too.

Ana'ana, The Death Spell & Ho'ouna'una, The Killing Spirit Conjurer
I'm sure I'm eventually going to get the question about ana 'ana, which is the "sorcery" used by indigenous Hawaiian healers to reverse the flow of healing. Pouring yourself into someone and using yourself to heal is much easier than taking or pouring out of someone. The kahuna ana'ana 'prays' (at least that's what the observing colonizer thought) their victims to death. However, with how difficult and highly trained one needs to be in order to accomplish the reverse direction of hilina'i in order to commit ana'ana, you'll probably be more affective at kahuna ho'ouna'una, which is the conjure and send spirits on errands of death, especially since you're already a spirit walker (at this point), and in the next section, you'll learn elements of conjuring. Naturally, these kahuna were called necromancers and *only* conjured *evil* spirits (see demonization), but in actuality, kahuna ho'ouna'una were simply the priests of the Milu.

Milu is a deity or spirit of the underworld in Hawaiian mythology. He is associated with death and is believed to rule over the spirits of the dead. Some stories portray him as a fearsome figure who tests the souls of the deceased, while others depict him as a compassionate guide who helps the departed navigate the afterlife. Milu is often invoked in chants and rituals to honor and appease the ancestors. These priests, in actuality, were in an order of healing (see Healer Spirit chapter).

In either case, knowing how to cause illness and death, with spirit or by harming the spirit, also gave great knowledge to repair and the skill to exorcise.

Because of this, a specific chant is performed, which essentially loosens the parts of a victim's soul. Then the witchdoctor or kahuna (arguably not the correct term, but for this, we will use the term as an expert in healing and destruction) can reverse the flow and kill someone or something. Saying the words alone isn't enough, unfortunately. Even if I could put the words here, you would have to learn "how" to chant and master all the exercises above in reverse, and to create the fire made out of uhaloa wood as an anchor. Ana'ana and other death curses are only effective because of these things:

1. An understanding of the parts of the soul

2. Ability to manipulate and heal the soul

3. Understanding the ability to pull and sacrifice parts of the self

4. Applying additional concepts to:

    - Specific words

    - Specific burned herbs

    - Specific way of pronouncing the words

    - Specific cadence of the words

    - Specific use of voice for the words

Even if you could mimic the way someone says an ana'ana chant, you would still need knowledge and aptitude for the rest of the list. And in order to train, you would do all of the exercises again, but with the purpose of emptying the energy into someone or something else: starting with a rock and pulling the energy out of it, then a plant, an animal, etc.

Please note that doing this draws a lot of attention to the spirits who protect those things, and you will be a target for death or disease as payment for your actions. The only way to do this without spirits' revenge is to build a relationship with the spirits who protect your victims, give offerings, and exchange for the opportunity to practice.

That's a lot of time and energy put into relationship building, which is why Hilina'i is a profession you study and invest in. You can't accomplish it in a weekend. The relationship you hold with spirits, their guardians, those wandering, the study of energy and healing, and food and care is a lifetime's worth of work.

Master healing first.

Psychic Surgery and Cancer

Characters:
Me
Wendy - a client

Before I tell this story, which I will do quickly without any flourishments, please know that this outcome isn't common.

Wendy came to me for a witchdoctor diagnosis. She wasn't feeling like she was connected to her body and wanted me to do psychic surgery. Before starting the process, we conducted an intake that covered her social circles, job, diet, sleep patterns, medical history, spirituality, and sense of self. Overall, she seemed relatively healthy from the intake, so we started the process.

I set up my space while she lay down.

As I went into trance and looked at the aumakua, I saw that her spirit was pliable, healthy, and moved like the ocean. When I got to the uhane, I saw a huge dark mass in the keawe of her abdomen. With the help of Grandmother Spider, we pulled out this darkness, heavy with infection, and placed it into my basket of lava rocks.

We patched up the area with the soul energy of rainwater.

Moving onto the unihipili, there was nothing to mend.

When I came out of trance, I told her what I had found.

"Oh, I had ovarian cancer," Wendy said.

"What?!" I was shocked.

"Yeah, you must have found any soul infections left over from the cancer," she said.

"There isn't usually 'left overs,'" I said. "When do you see your oncologist again? When did you have the cancer?"

"I'm actually going back for my six-month check-in tomorrow," Wendy said.

"Can you let me know what he says?" I asked.

"Of course."

Wendy didn't reach out. After a month, I got an email from Wendy.

> Dearest Aly,
> My sweet kahuna! I did have a mass. Small, but a mass nonetheless. They took it out, and guess what? It was benign! The doctor said it didn't make sense to have a new mass and that it be benign, but I'm convinced that you found the mass and took away its malignancy, making it easy for them to take it out. The surgery was relatively simple, and I'm on the mend.
> Thank you. Thank you. Thank you.
> With much love,
> Wendy

Cord Cutting and the Flow of Mana

There is a part of your soul that stretches. Like mist, or like the glisten of a spiderweb catching the first light of morning. This part of you is called *aka* (ah-kah), and it is how we are connected to all things we have touched, spoken to, loved, feared, hated, fought with, danced beside, passed by, or even dreamed of.

Think about that for a moment. Every conversation, every heartbreak, every glance across a classroom. Your aka connects you to everything: the places you walk, the people you remember, the memories that pull at your gut, the conversations you replay in your head, the emotions that live behind your ribs.

Aka is the invisible sticky net that surrounds and threads through your soul, holding memory, belief, connection, and your energy. Every time you interact with someone, even briefly, your aka reaches out. If the interaction is meaningful, repeated, or emotionally charged, the thread connects and becomes a cord.

These cords are how your mana flows. They are the pathways through which life force travels. If you have cords to people, places, or events that are uplifting, your mana flows in a healthy circuit. There is give and receive. There is life. But if your cords are tied to someone who harms you, to a place that keeps you small, to a memory that siphons your strength, your mana will flow out of you and into that. You get tired. You feel anxious for no reason. You snap at things that do not matter. You dream of people you have tried to forget. This is your mana being pulled or given out of your aka.

Aka Cords Can Bind You To:
- People: exes, mentors, abusers, ancestors, children

- Places: your childhood home, a hospital, a battlefield

- Experiences: trauma, illness, love, ceremony

- Patterns: addiction, abuse cycles, generational habits

We do not control *whether* we make cords. We are relational beings. It is natural. What we can control is which cords remain.

When Mana Leaks Through a Cord
You might be tired all the time. You might have certain people you think of obsessively, even when you don't want to. You might dream of an old house or feel waves of emotion that belong to another time. You might hear someone's name and feel your stomach turn. That is *mana* moving and getting depleted. If you still have an aka cord to a person or event that no longer serves your highest good, it means your mana is still flowing toward it. You are feeding a past that gives you nothing back. Energetically, this looks like a cord with no return loop. The mana just... drains. You give. It takes. That is how people end up depleted, haunted, obsessed, or stuck.

Cutting cords is an act of healing and protection, a way to stop the leak. By cutting a cord, you are ending the flow of mana into something that does not feed you.

To cut cords, we must step back, spiritually, as if you're looking at the whole spiritual body (the aura, if you want to give it a modern term). You're going to cut from the field around them. Some people see this as threads of light. Some feel them as tingles, or heaviness, or the sudden memory of someone who has not crossed your mind in months.

When you are ready, you name the cord. You find it. You feel it. You cut it.

Cord Cutting: How to Do It, and Why It Matters

When we cut cords, you aren't erasing the memory; you're severing the energetic pipeline. This is sacred soulwork and must be done with care.

To Cut Cords
1. *Access the Aka Layer:* You step back, pulling your awareness out of the mental storytelling and into the aura, or outer soul-body. You enter a trance or meditative state where you can *see* or *feel* the aka connections.(Sometimes they look like ropes. Sometimes, like threads. Sometimes, like glowing vines or wires. Trust what you perceive.)

2. *Identify the Cord That Needs Release:* Feel it. Name it. Acknowledge. Thank it.

3. *Cut It Cleanly:* This can be done with a knife, flame, chant, hand motion, or breath.

4. *Reconnect the Loose End:* This is the step most people miss. Aka that has nowhere to flow will find something familiar.

That is only the beginning, so don't stop there.

A cord that is cut becomes loose. The thread flails and will want to connect again. If you do not choose something new for that cord to attach to, it will return to what it feels familiar, even if that connection hurt you or drained you.

This is why, after a cord is cut, there must be a new bond, a healthy one. If someone cuts the cord between you and your abusive step-mother, your soul will need a new place to receive connection, like a loving aunt, a teacher, or a friend. The new connection could even be divine. It just has to be someone or something that offers nourishment. Otherwise, the aka floats, and it will try to reattach.

So, part of healing is choosing new connections. You choose. You decide what your spirit wants to touch next.

Reconnect to:
- A community that loves without condition
- Ancestors who uplift
- A deity or deity-like force that reflects your wholeness
- A practice (chant, hula, music, prayer) that feeds your soul
- Yourself—your highest self, your aumakua
- Call in a connection where mana can flow both ways.

The Aftermath

Cutting cords doesn't leave you empty if you're worried. It leaves you whole. You may cry. You may feel strangely free. You may feel wobbly at first, like a toddler learning to walk without the weight they got used to carrying. That is okay. This is soul reconfiguration. This is remembering what you felt like before the cord was ever there. You are allowed to cut the rope. You are allowed to stop bleeding for something that no longer lives. You are allowed to change the patterns. You are allowed to reclaim your mana.

Namaka'okaha'i and Kanaloa: Guardians of the Flow

Characters:
Namaka'okaha'i (Namaka) - Goddess of the Ocean Waters
Kanaloa - God of Magic and the Veil between the Ocean and the Underworld
Kanekua'ana - Sleeping Water Lizard Dragon (a mo'o)

In that sea lived Namaka'okaha'i. Her limbs were long and glistened blue-green. Her voice was the crash of the surf. Her eyes, white as seafoam. She moved across the surface of the water and beneath it, and wherever she moved, the tides listened. The waves obeyed.

Deep below her domain, where the light had never touched, where coral turned to bone and silence sat heavy, Kanaloa listened to a different rhythm. He moved slowly. He moved with the old current. His arms held the pull of moons. His voice hummed inside whales. His eyes carried stars. The water was his breath. The stillness was his temple. Navigation, dreaming, change, decay, rebirth... all belonged to him.

They never clashed. They never merged. They circled, as the sea circles the shore.

But there came a morning when the ocean was still. The fish scattered in circles. The whales sang without direction. The tides paused. The voyagers sat on still water. No current, no drift, only waiting.

Kanaloa opened his eyes beneath the deep. The stillness was not his stillness, so he rose.

When he broke the surface, Namaka'okaha'i was already there. Namaka'okaha'i came with salt in her step and foam in her voice. Her hair whipped in strands like eel tails.

"The sea grows sick," she said.

"It does."

"And this sickness did not come from me."

"Nor from me."

She turned her head toward the horizon. "Something old has moved."

Kanaloa nodded. "I felt it too."

Together, they dove. Down past the reef. Down past the bone fields. Down where the water folds into itself and memory swims sideways. Together, they reached the trench.

And there they saw it.

Kanekua'ana.

Longer than any whale. Broader than any canoe. Kanekua'ana was a giant mo'o. His scales carried the shape of mountains. His claws carved canyons into the floor of the sea. He slept, coiled and unmoving. In his sleep, though, he blocked the flow itself. His body filled the trench. His breath disturbed the current. His tail pressed against the flow. The water around him thickened with confusion.

Namaka'okaha'i narrowed her eyes. "If he wakes wrongly, he will thrash."

Kanaloa said nothing. He placed his hand on the sea floor. He felt the pulse of ancient restlessness. He knew this dragon. The mo'o belonged as part of the balance of all things. He had turned in his slumber and lodged himself in the arteries of the world.

"He is not angry," Kanaloa said.

"But he blocks the waters! All waters!"

"He does."

"Then we must move him."

"We must ask him."

Namaka'okaha'i frowned. "Ask?"

Kanaloa turned to her. "Even a stone listens better when you speak with care."

She looked at the dragon. She looked at the still sea. She looked at Kanaloa.

In her humility, and against her will, she agreed.

Together they sang a song that moved with the water. The waves rolled against him, and their lullaby current stirred like a sigh in a sleeping child.

The mo'o twitched.

Namaka'okaha'i summoned her waves gently, so they wouldn't crash but would cradle. Kanaloa brought his deep current to guide the loving massage to the giant sea lizard. They spiraled together around the dragon's shape. They whispered welcome into the walls of water.

The mo'o opened one eye. He blinked.

Kanaloa floated near his brow.

"You slept well."

The mo'o groaned. His voice was stone-breaking under pressure.

"Too long."

"Too deep," Kanaloa added.

"I forgot the way."

"Then let us help."

The mo'o looked at Namakaokaha'i. She did not speak because she dared not offer an angering demand. Only space.

He uncoiled.

Slowly. Very slowly. His body slipped from the trench. The pressure lightened. The sea floor sighed. The currents began to stretch and flow. The color returned to the coral. The whales sang direction. The fish realigned.

He turned his head once more toward Kanaloa.

"You remembered me?" the mo'o asked.

"I never forgot," Kanaloa smiled.

The mo'o swam to the far places, past the edge, past where sound is heard, and past where knowing knows. The dragon left without any anger in his heart, just a rested body and a lot of size.

Namaka'okaha'i turned to Kanaloa.

"We could have fought."

"And broken more."

"We could have trapped him."

"And sealed the wrong flow."

"Instead, we asked."

"And he moved."

She lifted her chin. "A garden grows when water moves."

He nodded. "And water moves when we make space."

Together, they rose. The sea pulsed around them. The tides danced, and the voyagers felt a pull again. The life of the ocean stretched out, wide and sure.

The people felt the return of the waves, in the path of the fish and in the stirring of the seed beneath the sand.

The story spread about how the sea had stopped and how it moved again.

Because two gods remembered that even the old ones need help.

Let's not use force when we don't need to. Let's simply ask. It's in the asking and in stifling our ego that the water flows.

Hands that Hold the Soul

The hands do more than simply finish the wrist. They are an extension of the soul, an expressive channel for the energy that flows within us and through the world around us. Across cultures and healing traditions, the hands play a pivotal role in moving, shaping, and sharing energy. They are the translators of our inner essence, the tools that can connect to the unseen. In the sacred work of healing, the hands become more than anatomy; they become instruments of transformation. Because many of the hand motions of healing have died (except in lomi and lomilomi), we turn to supplements from other traditions:

Tai Chi: Shaping the Flow of Qi
In the practice of Tai Chi, the hands move like whispers on water, guiding the unseen currents of qi, or life energy, with precision and purpose. Watch a master of this art, and you'll see how their hands draw circles in the air, seemingly carving pathways for the energy to flow. The movements are deliberate acts of alignment.

In one of the foundational forms, "Grasping the Sparrow's Tail," the hands sweep outward and fold inward in a fluid motion that mirrors the balance of giving and receiving energy. The practitioner is interacting with the world around them, harmonizing with the invisible forces that sustain life. In Tai Chi, the hands are seen as gateways, connecting the personal reservoir of qi to the universal flow. By mastering the hands, one learns to master the self and the energies of the universe.

Ballet: Energy in Elegance

Ballet, though often regarded as purely an art form, is another example of the hands moving energy in profound ways. A ballerina's hands are active participants in the storytelling of the body. The energy flows from the core, spiraling through the arms and culminating in the fingertips.

In the iconic "Swan Lake," the swan's grace is in the arch of the back or the pointe of the foot, of course, but the magic is in the fluid undulations of the hands. They mimic the flutter of wings, the yearning of a soul in flight, pulling energy outward to captivate the audience. Each flick of the wrist and extension of the fingers communicates something intangible, reaching into the hearts of those who watch. Ballet teaches us that the hands are bearers of emotion, intention, and energy that originates deep within.

Japanese Reiki: The Hands That Heal

In traditional Japanese Reiki, the hands are revered as channels for universal healing energy. The practice of Reiki is simple in its approach yet profound in its impact: the healer places their hands either directly on or above the recipient, allowing ki to flow through them into the person in need. This energy is invited and directed with humility and focus.

The position of the hands is vital in Reiki. Whether cradling the crown of the head, resting over the heart, or hovering above the abdomen, each placement is intentional. The hands are vessels of compassion, opening the pathways for balance and harmony. What's remarkable about Japanese Reiki is the absence of physical manipulation; the hands don't need to touch to transfer energy. This underscores a profound truth: the hands reach into the energetic layers of our being, facilitating healing where words or medicine cannot.

Hula: The Hands Tell Stories

In Hawaiian Hula, the hands do more than move; they speak. Each gesture tells a story, embodying the history, myths, and spirit of the Hawaiian people. A dancer's hands become waves, mountains, stars, or rain, bringing the natural and spiritual worlds into the present moment.

The art of Hula is a living example of how the hands connect to the soul. Take, for instance, the motion of the hands forming a downward sweep; it could symbolize falling rain, bringing nourishment and healing to the earth. These motions are acts of invocation, pulling energy from the universe and weaving it into a story that heals and inspires.

In the sacred spaces where Hula is performed, the hands hold the power to connect the dancer, the audience, and the ancestors in a shared experience. It is a reminder that energy flows from the histories and spirits that surround us.

The hands are more than flesh, bones, and tendons. They are extensions of the soul, the conduits for energy, emotion, and intention. Whether guiding qi in Tai Chi, painting emotion in Ballet, channeling healing in Reiki, or storytelling in Hula, the hands hold a power that transcends the physical.

To heal with the hands is to understand this truth: They are the tools of our inner light, the translators of our deepest intentions, and the bridges between the seen and unseen.

When we move energy with our hands, we touch the spirit.

Kapua Accepts Kanaloa's Healing Waters

Characters:
Kualana - A young male loving chief
Kapua - Kualana's sister
Kanaloa - The God of Magic and the Veil between the Ocean and the Underworld
Milu - The underworld
Hei'au - religious resting place

Kapua Accepts Kanaloa's Healing Waters in Milu

They speak his name softly, for he is no simple spirit of waves or storm. Kanaloa, the god of the Ocean veil between the living and Milu, is the healer who remains unflinching in the face of death, serving as the hand that opens the doorway to both healing and the ultimate end. Where salt and stone meet in silence, and the caves echo with a sound that is older than language, Kanaloa owns the place where the sea breathes inward.

In a time remembered by bones but forgotten by words, there lived a young chief named Kaulana. He had eyes like rain and laughter that could calm a tide, which is why his people trusted him. The land grew strong under his care.

One day, his body faltered, a fire beneath his skin forced him into submission, where no herb could cool. No kahuna could ascertain the root of his pained limbs as they withered. Kaulana's voice failed, and in the long absence of his sweet laughter, the village waited in the geometry of fear.

They lit the torches. They made offerings. They called to Kane, the god of life. They sang to Lono for mercy. They offered fish, awa, chants, and tears. Still, the sickness deepened. The young chief slipped toward the veil.

And in the quiet of the last page of Kaulana's life story, when the stars were smeared like salt across the sky, his sister Kapua bowed her body down beside the sea. She pressed her cheek to the cold stones. She called the name of Kanaloa.

He came to her in the place between breath and sleep. His voice moved like water inside her.

"If you would save him," Kanaloa said, "you must follow me. There is a spring that lies beneath the world. It's water heals, and current runs through death and back again. But you must walk the path yourself. And you must pay its price."

Kapua woke with the taste of salt on her lips. She rose.

She gathered awa, pounded by her own hands. Kapua also caught a red fish and wrapped it in banana leaves, then placed the offerings at the edge of the sea and prayed for Kanaloa, for her brother, and for the strength to descend. She took a finely crafted ipu (a guard, strong and solid in case she needs to carry something from the land of Kanaloa).

As the wind blew, we knew the offering was accepted because behind a veil of vines, the cave appeared. No one had walked it for generations, not since the story of Maui and the fire.

Kapua bowed her head to Kanaloa's hei'au, the stone-cold black stones of the beach at dusk. She turned her back on the ocean, adjusted the guard on her back, and walked towards the cave opening.

Kapua pressed through stone and darkness. The air thickened. Salt clung to her. Her footsteps no longer echoed. The silence closed like water. In the magic of the gods, Kapua felt as though she was at one point walking through land, but as the salt in the air clung to her long hair, the air became water. In a moment's memory of her brother's laughter, Kapua suddenly knew she was no longer traveling through a cavern in Hawaii Nei; she was traveling through Milu.

Then light. A dim, unearthly glow rising from below. She stood before a pool that stretched farther than sight. The surface shimmered and pulsed with something old. From the center, a voice stirred the water.

"This is the spring," Kanaloa said in the echoes of the hidden valley of life. "Do not take from it freely. The guardians watch, and they do not love the living."

She stepped forward.

The water began to move.

From beneath the pool's skin, shadows rose… figures… eyes that remembered death. As they stepped out of the pool, Kapua kept her stillness. The guardians surrounded her in silence, and with the magic of the pool, they began to show her visions.

She saw Kaulana dead. Saw his bones scattered. Saw herself returning to the village empty-handed. She saw the world turn cold and dry, for without the soft rain of Kaulana's jovial leadership, the village would be barren of aloha. Her hands trembled.

Kapua closed her eyes tight, and a single tear escaped her eye and fell into the pool.

She began to chant, first in whispers. Then louder. Words her grandmother had taught her. Words for Kane. Words for Kanaloa. Words that reminded the dark of who she was, the sister of a chief of light. It was the chant, He Mele No Kane, asking the riddle, "Where is the water of life?"

Her voice was a light. The shadow guardians receded into the walls of the ocean's tunnel. She finished. What's incredible is this: She did not ask for Kanaloa or Kane to save her brother's life. She saw that one day he would die, which is true and will happen no matter what. Kapua sang only of the mysteries of life, giving gratitude for life, hers and her brother's.

Kanaloa spoke once more.

"You have remembered. The healing spirit of the water will be your healing spirit. You may collect her and take her with you."

She stepped to the spring and bent low. The quiver in her hands calmed, and she filled the gourd. The water in the ipu wasn't magical water. It wasn't a fountain of European youth. Inside the ipu she carried was the life of water itself. The spirit of water was to be her healing spirit.

Kapua turned back toward the mouth of the cave, and humbly she walked.

Above, in the land of the living, the sky had not changed, the stars still watched, and the sea still breathed. But inside her, something was different. She had carried her brother's name through the underworld. She had returned with... a friend, a companion, and together, they would see if the prophecy in the pools of Milu was to come true as the sun sets over the Kanaloa.

Kapua walked straight out of the cave, past the vines that covered it, and without looking back, continued to the village without pause, until her continuous movement halted with the reuniting of her brother.

Kapua gently swung the ipu around, dipped her finger into the mystical waters, and touched her dainty finger to Kaulana's brow. When she did, a song came to her lips... one she wasn't taught... that no one knew. Kapua sang the chant Kanaloa had placed in her heart, and when she did, his breath deepened. Her eyes stayed closed, but the village watched his eyes open, and then watched him rise.

When Kapua finished the song, her finger still moist with the water of life, she opened her eyes to see that her brother was no longer lying next to her kneeling frame; instead, he was standing over her with his brilliant smile of light.

The village wept, and then they danced.

The chief danced with them, and they shared in fish and bananas, and awa. The dawn that turned to night now filled the space between the stars with the echoes of Chief Kaulana's laughter.

But Kapua did not dance. She went alone to the sea. She walked into the water waist-deep and placed one hand upon the waves and whispered, "mahalo."

Kanaloa does not heal through ease. He heals through the willingness to descend. To walk into the dark. To face what others cannot. Healing is a journey through shadow. Through death. Through courage.

Kanaloa is the god who waits beyond the tide, and does not ask for praise, nor a temple, because he won't exchange one gift for another. For those who come with truth in their chest, he opens the spring.

Heal It and Let it Go

If you haven't figured it out so far, I want to encourage you towards the philosophy of treating spirits as equals to humans. Naturally, whoever your client is should have your priority, so if the spirit seeks your help, then the spirit is your client. If a human seeks your help, then the human is your client. However, if you can choose a path that can benefit both, please choose that path.

In turn, I would like you to now take this exercise as a means to heal spirits based on the hilina'i modality:

Exercise 15: I want you to find a building that gives you a bad feeling. Like, there might be something there that is angry. Spirits don't have the uhane part, and depending on what it is, you may find that it leans more aumakua (Upper World spirits) or more unihipili (Lower World spirits). The theory that the parts of our soul are connected to a Holy Trinity comes from this: Kane of the mind, Lono of the body, and Ku of the spirit. Father, Son, and Holy Ghost. Crone, Mother, Maiden. Although we don't necessarily need to go into the correlation of all of these things, we can recognize that spirits (who are not elementals) will not have the uhane part. This means they will be similar to animals in healing because you're only looking at six areas instead of nine. I'm not kidding. You can heal an angel or a demon more easily than a human or a goblin (have or use physical form).

From Upper World and Lower World Entities, you are looking for these parts that may have illness (and the amount of each area will vary based on the entity itself):

Aumakua mana
Aumakua aka
Aumakua keawe
Unihipili mana
Unihipili aka
Unihipili keawe

From Elementals, you will need to look for the uhane parts as well. Your homework is to go find injured spirits and offer help. Be cautious not to get hurt or attacked in the process. An angry, hurt lion will probably lash out before it allows you to help it. Take the same EXACT caution with spirits. Stuff your ego or your magician archetype and ground yourself.

Once you find a haunted place or encounter an entity or spirit, your job is to heal it. You will do it the same way. Good luck.

Please do go find some spirits to mend. They need us, too.

Skeletal Gazelle Bird

If you take a look at me, you'll not think of me as an exorcist. I'm not brooding or dark and mysterious. I don't wear a lot of black, smoke cigarettes, nor am I darkly bitter at the world with a face worn with marks that say "life is hard and so are demons."

I look friendly. I have an intimidating gaze and strong posture, but I believe in being accessible and friendly-looking. I love fashion, being presentable, and keeping friendly and open body language. I'm also a dad, so I keep myself available for nurturing and caring for those around me. Students have said that I'm everyone's mom and a fashionable elf on a shelf. I'm a small person, so my stature does not give the impression of demanding that anyone or anything bend at my will. In fact, I present so friendly and with poise that everyone is shocked when I tell them that I'm an exorcist.

However, because I'm non-threatening, humans and spirits know that they can ask for help, whether it's to lend an ear for the broken heart, to give some needed energy in hugs and attention for the broken spirit, or to give guidance or direct healing to the many aspects of things that can break. My father used to say, "Make it happen, Aly. If anyone can, you can." He didn't mean it as a I-believe-in-you kind of thing. Dad meant that if someone was broken, I could fix it. If a spirit was hurt or scared or angry, I could fix it, and if a group of people or spirits needed help to find resolution, I could see how, even if that meant severing the cords so they can go their own ways towards health and thriving.

One late night, I was driving home from my friend's house, and I could sense something out in the fields keeping up with my car. It was probably a deer, right? So, I slowed down, hoping that it would veer off back into the field, but as I slowed, so did it.

I blinked my eyes slowly, so I could see a little clearer with my mind's eye. It was naturally too dangerous to close my eyes while driving to sense if what was keeping up in the field was something living or non-corporeal. I found it best to simply pull over. I put the car in park, closed my eyes for a moment, and felt something large come up to the car.

She had an arched back like a gazelle, six legs, with thick feathered growths sprouting down the back of her legs. She was tan and white, like she was tie-dyed and dropped into swirled paint. Her tail was wide and full of feathers like a pheasant. She looked like her body was complemented with fine downy feathers and soft fur. Her face was a mix of bird and mammal, with a pale mocha fur-covered beak, ears that lifted like a deer, with white on the inside, and bright green eyes. She was about the height of a short elephant, so she was a bit taller than my Mini Cooper.

I opened the car door, knowing that she was seeking help. Much like people, monsters were drawn to me. They want to come up to me with ease, usually seeking care, compassion, love, companionship, or company. Our Gazelle-fowl was seeking healing. I could sense desperation in the dark of night. I looked out on the country road to see if I was being watched. From the naked, filtered eyes of normal humans, I was outside my car and probably appeared to need assistance with my car, not that I was there to help a spirit in need. Since the hour drew close to midnight, I thought it was unlikely that another car would drive by and be curious enough to stop. I walked over into the brush, hoping there wouldn't be a snake or feral animal for me to disturb while I took care of this injured spirit.

She followed me. Our unspoken understanding. She bent her front four legs in, onto her shins, and then tucked her back legs underneath. When she settled, she looked like a meadow of wheat. As she lowered her head and wrapped her neck around her back, she lifted a hidden wing. Under the wing was a gash. This hole, looking in, was black, like a rift in the universe could be found within this beautiful animal. If you could look into the injury of a spirit and see darkness, total blackness that leads to nothing in the universe, you would understand. It was a portal to the space in between space, and that's what this injury looked like.

Where does emptiness, nothingness, in our universe reside? Within the injuries of the spirits.

I sat next to this feathered soft creature of wheat, crossed my legs, and closed my eyes. I dug into my own spirit. I pulled at my unihipili aka and sewed in my tendrils to patch the hole. When the hole was patched, I pushed some of my mana into the spirit, giving her strength to integrate the transplant, and as that completed, I could feel her space fill in with her own essence. She didn't appear to glow; she just felt like something glowing. I opened my eyes. She wasn't there.

I felt silly, sitting on the ground on the passenger side of my car in the dirt in the middle of the night. I looked up into the sky. I loved the moon and how she was something always there, looking over us. The breeze blew warm, and I looked out into the field of grass. As the wind blew across the meadow, I thought I could see her shadow leaving a trace of her departure.

Borrowing From Taoism: Li (Why Are You So Pretty?)

In Taoism, Li refers to the underlying natural pattern in all things. Li is the principle of harmony in Taoism and can be understood as the subtle, organic patterns that naturally show up when things align. These patterns arise spontaneously when beings and actions flow in accordance with the fundamental nature of the universe. Think of Li as the space between actions. It's the Yin, the transition, the movement of how you get from one thing to another.

The best way to describe Li is to compare it to the grain in wood. It represents the way things naturally unfold when left to follow their inherent tendencies. Each line is an action. But the lines aren't what make the wood grain beautiful. It's the relationship of all the lines to each other. And there is no relationship to the lines without acknowledging the Li, the natural space between the lines, which allows them to exist together. Li is the interconnected web of relationships that binds all things. It highlights the interdependence of all aspects of the universe.

This is the effortless harmony, leading to wu wei (effortless action). This is about allowing actions to harmonize with the natural rhythms of life. In order for the natural rhythms in life to unfold, we have to also accept that everything holds infinite potential for pathways from where you are to infinite options of what could be next. Just find the most graceful, complete, simplest path from where you are to what is coming next.

I do Tai Chi, but before that, I was an expert in eighteen styles of dance. While I was in class, a black sash student (not the Elder Master, of course, because he doesn't over simply for his ego) said to me, "Oh, I believe you're so pretty to watch because of all your dance background."

Hmmm. No. If that were the case, every dancer would be graceful. What makes a dancer graceful? Or powerful? It's Li.

Let's take one movement, or one pose. And from there, how do we move from one to the other in the most effortless way? What is the path of most harmonious sense? Do that. Not more, not less.

By doing more, you are making space between the grains of the wood that are not natural, which takes away its beauty. By moving too much, your ego about how you move is taking precedence over the authenticity of the movement itself.

By not finishing the movement, the lines aren't faded and weak, making it an amorphous space, which also doesn't offer the authentic beauty in nature we crave.

Lastly, but finishing a movement and then smoothly moving onto the next movement by way of natural harmony (which sometimes takes strength, awareness, and practice), then you have the beauty of the thin line. If you are bold and hold the end of a movement, you give the line thickness.

The last piece of Li, in beauty of movement, is those moments of bold randomness. You know how, when you see a knot in the center of a log of wood and the space and other lines move around it, incorporating these big events into life with care and inclusion? This is also Li.

Why am I going into Chinese philosophy in a Hawaiian healing book? Awesome question, but before I go into that, I am going to quote *The Next Right Thing* from my favorite movie, *Frozen 2*:

I've seen dark before
But not like this
This is cold
This is empty
This is numb
The life I knew is over
The lights are out
Hello, darkness
I'm ready to succumb...
But a tiny voice whispers in my mind
"You are lost, hope is gone
But you must go on
And do the next right thing"...
Take a step, step again
It is all that I can to do
The next right thing
I won't look too far ahead
It's too much for me to take
But break it down to this next breath
This next step
This next choice is one that I can make

Remember that the concepts of Hawaiian healing were annihilated. We have to substitute concepts. The ease from one movement to another is apparent in Hula, but the concept of how or why isn't there. I offer you Li.

And what does this have to do with healing? A few things.

First, understanding the life of someone coming to see you. I hate that the healing has turned into trying to go back in time instead of accepting life's changes and moments. I have had forty-five injuries as a professional dancer. One tear in my shoulder so badly that it will probably pop until the day I die. I am missing half the cartilage in both of my knees from repeated impact, and I broke both wrists when I was nineteen. These injuries affect my life. Medicine tells us to try to have it back, instead of accepting the smoothest route, promoting a denial of the grief and acceptance of life moments. If I were to remove those moments, I would remove the impact of how they have made me who I am, and the people who got to have moments of entertainment, escape, if you will, that which they needed at that time.

I have no desire to change my injuries. I do have a desire to live with them. Some things mend and can return someone to the way they were. Some things do not. And sometimes, some healing agents can give us ease by repairing something. As a healer, you have to accept that some things in life are meant to be there to continue with, instead of being repaired. An asymmetrical tree is still a tree. What if the best direction of life is to move from an injury, whatever it is, into the next thing, accepting the scars of the injury?

A student of mine was recently certified in tuning fork healing. She asked if she could do a healing to repair the energy fields that connect someone's aura (soul). I said, "No, thank you."

Here is why: There are parts of my soul that are scarred, open, holy, and warped because of the work I've done, and those spaces and movements make me good at what I do. I don't desire to go back to what I was before a healing. In my book *Witchdoctor Exorcist*, I open with the near-death experience of the attempted homicide by my fiancé. I call him "the monster," and in the book, I try to illustrate that the real monsters are usually humans, not spirits. This moment in my life broke the filter most people have when they go through puberty between them and the veil of the spirit world. If that were repaired, I would no longer be able to do what I can do! If someone were to patch me up to go back to "normal," you wouldn't have this book. The ego's desire to stay in the past without accepting the need to build more "wood rings" or knots can prevent you from achieving something truly incredible. A better life. An asymmetrical tree is a more beautiful tree.

Second, understanding your life. You will go through chapters in your life. If you accept those moments and move gracefully from moment to moment, regardless of what they are. Your hands will get older, your bones might creak. The love of your life might die. You might find the care and healing from a neighbor's cat. You may finally build a community from unlikely misfit toys who all take Tai Chi together. How you get from moment to moment, the space between, is up to your acceptance of each moment. Get out of the space between by finishing it (get the thickness of the line down) and move into the next right thing.

Third, when healing, take the simplest route, not the shiniest. Humans need so much validation. If you learn to heal. Is the next step to heal, or is the next step to brag about what you're doing so you can get validation? Humans really want the shiniest way of doing things, with pomp and circumstance, so that they get noticed. Everyone wants to be seen, valued, and welcomed in. But what are you doing? Are you healing or are you shining? What if you took the simplest route and just did the work?

When I go to work, be it a psychic reading, an exorcism, or a healing, I am not dressed in gauze-clothes with five strings of stone beads, bathed in essential oils. They are not necessary. That's a costume, and I don't need to dress up for this job. My hands and my knowledge are necessary. I get up, put on a cute sweater (I love fashion), probably some stretchy jeans, put on deodorant, wear some cologne, and show up as authentically me, not some shiny version of what people are supposed to accept someone like me to look like. Again, what is my motivation? Is it about putting on a show (which I know show business is) or doing the work? Do you want to "be famous," or heal? If you're meant to be famous, because that is the natural movement from one ring to another, then it will be where your tree grows.

Fourth, conserve your energy. There is a guy in my Tai Chi class who moves way too big in each movement. He believes that the bigger and stronger, and more aggressive he presents himself, the better he is at being a warrior. When he moves, I can see a few things in his Li. I can see his vulnerability in that he is susceptible to being hit. I can see that he is not in alignment and can fall over because he is making such grand gesticulations; he isn't moving in the most efficient way. He is exhausting himself, wasting his energy.

Now, he can spend his energy any way he wants. But, if his purpose is to be a Tai Chi warrior (haha), he would exhaust himself, leave himself vulnerable to getting hit, and would not be grounded, easy to knock over. His overly masculine posturing is indicative of his purpose: to present himself as a warrior instead of warring. To get to the next right thing, you will need to use energy (don't be lazy or overly conserve). Like the last lesson, don't perform, just do. Use as much energy as you need to be efficient and complete, and then stop.

Fifth, if you have a difficult time, it could still be Li. Li doesn't mean without pressure or strength, and you may need to apply those tactics. Complete the movement in healing, in life, and in the story that we weave. A moment in life may require you to use everything you have, and the same in healing a client. A river applies pressure to make the best path for her to flow.

Strong Woman Doesn't Need Healing

Characters:
Me
Alice - a client

"My daughter told me to come to you," said Alice.

"Oh?" I asked. "Who is your daughter?"

"You are currently treating her for spirit problems. She just had an exorcism with you," she said. I could feel that she couldn't believe that she was saying that out loud.

"Oh my! You're Laura's mom! It's so nice to meet you!" I said. Laura was a difficult client. I liked meeting her mom, though. "Why does Laura think you need a soul retrieval?"

"I don't know. I just want things to be better between us. She is distant, so in order to keep a relationship with her, I just do what she says." Alice's truth broke my heart. I related to this truth.

"That's painful to hear, Alice. I'm so sorry. Do you know what a soul retrieval is?"

"Not really," she said.

"Ah, ok. Do you believe in spiritual healing?" I asked.

"I guess. I know that Laura is getting better, so I will take that as proof that you're doing something right. And if my life can be better, too, why not do it, too? I don't think it could go wrong and hurt me..." she trailed off. "Wait! Could it?"

"No, no." I laughed. "A soul retrieval is a healing modality where I get the pieces of your spirit that fractured off or died off during times of trauma in your life. I bring them back from the world of the dead and put them back in your spirit."

"Wait, so do I have to go through the traumas again?" She protested.

"No. It's not a regression. You don't interact with your traumas at all. Your trauma is like the knife that created spirit loss. I will interact with the events in your life that were traumatic, the knives, and bring back the pieces cut off, and place them back into your spirit. It is painless for you. It's like taking a half-nap or meditating," I reassured her.

"Ok," she said.

"All that I need you to do is put on your headphones and listen to the same drumming that I am listening to. You'll hear some singing. These are power songs to help me get going. Just close your eyes and relax. I don't want you to try to help me or to interact in any way. You just relax. If you go to sleep, I will wake you up when I'm finished. Make sure you aren't going to be disturbed by a pet or a husband, though." I said.

She laughed, "Let me put the dog out, then." She got up from the screen. I do all of my soul retrievals remotely, using video messenger. I still need to feel connected to the person and know (for my peace of mind) that they are lying still and doing what they are supposed to be doing.

Alice came back from moving the family dog, "Ok, ready."

"Go ahead and lie down. Close your eyes. I'm going to mute you. Just listen to the drumming, and I will let you know when I'm back." I started my drumming track. I lit my appropriate candles and incense, closed my eyes, and began.

When I got to the bay, I sat with my power-animal. He told me *Alice doesn't need to be healed. Look at her. She is whole.*

I came back into my consciousness and opened my eyes. Instead of continuing with the retrieval, I read Alice's soul. It was full, healthy, complete.

"Alice, I'm back," I said.

"How is that possible? That was so fast!" She said.

"It's because you didn't need one," I said.

"Really?" she asked.

I replied, "Really. There is nothing for me to go get. Remember how you said, 'It couldn't hurt?' Well, it's not that it couldn't hurt. If you don't need one, there is nothing to go get; the retrieval just doesn't happen. There is nothing for me to retrieve in the retrieval." I laughed.

"Oh," she said.

"You're a strong woman. Psychically, I can see that you've been through some difficult times, traumatic even, and yet it never fractured you. Does that resonate?"

"Yes, it does, actually," she said.

"So, we can sit and do something else instead, with the time you've hired me for. You have me for the hour, and we have determined that you're a strong warrior of a person. Let's pause and take the armor off. Want to do some spiritual counseling instead? Want to just talk?"

We talked.

Thoughts on Reiki

Reiki is a form of energy-based therapy that aims to promote healing and relaxation. It is based on the idea that a life force energy flows through every living being. This energy can be harnessed and channeled by a practitioner to help with a variety of physical and emotional issues. During a Reiki session, the practitioner will place their hands on or near the body in a series of hand positions to balance the energy and promote healing. Reiki has been used to help with a variety of issues, including stress, chronic pain, anxiety, and depression.

A Little About Reiki & Mastery

Dr. Mikao Usui officially developed Reiki in 1922 in Tokyo, following a lifetime of studying healing and spirituality, including Chi Kung and Sanskrit. In his practice, he taught a few people, who then passed it to 22 people. The lineage we have in the West goes from Dr. Usui to Dr. Chujiro Kayashi to Mrs. Hawayo Takata, who then brought it to the USA. These founders and master teachers breathed this healing modality. They didn't study or master it in a weekend. They studied and applied, becoming masters.

Short sidebar: I was a ballet dancer. Do you know how many hours it takes to master ballet? Yeah, never. You never master it because the human body isn't supposed to do any of those things naturally. You have to balance the perfection of the modality with the human imperfections needed for a beautiful, relatable performance. Impossible, but you keep trying. After hundreds of thousands of hours, people still don't consider themselves masters. I was fortunate to one day call myself a ballet master, and at the exceptionally early age of twenty-five, and even then, I still watched and studied and continued upgrading my mastery. After that, I was one of five master choreographers in the United States by thirty five, actually mastering eighteen styles of dance, which meant that I was not able to spend my hours on movies, bars, dating, friends, scrolling, tv shows... to this day, people ask me if I have seen a certain movie and my answer is usually "no," because I spent my time mastering.

Someone who takes a weekend Advanced Reiki Master Certification is not a master. They have learned about Reiki, but they haven't mastered anything yet. The throwing around of awards dilutes the validity of those who are actually Reiki masters, which makes me sad. According to Maxwell Gladwell, mastery should have 10,000 hours associated with it. 15 hours of video instruction serve as an introduction (not a mastery), with little to no practicum to demonstrate results and aptitude.

And even then, massive amounts of time learning doesn't automatically give you high levels of achievement. Practice does not make perfect. Perfect practice makes perfect, my loves. It would be best if you were doing proficient work with repeatable results.

This kind of mastery comes from learning with or from someone, getting the experience, having a mentor, and making mistakes where you can get feedback to help improve. Try to manage any ego response to feedback. Constructive criticism is phrased to give you something to improve upon without judgment or character. Someone who attacks your character is a troll. Trolls on the internet who tell you "nobody wants you here, you idiot" aren't giving your criticism; they're just trolls.

I was hoping you could apply your knowledge to something practical and use it to fulfill your hours. Volunteer at a cancer hospital and put your learning to work. Ask if you can practice and if any patients would like to try your work. Ask if they felt change, and that you need to know the truth to become a master in your craft.

Does this sound unappealing to you? Find another way to put in the hours and get the feedback to become better, because you need to do that before you call yourself a master at anything, and more than a piece of paper from a weekend class.

Mastery

I am not as eloquent as Dr. Ralph Crawshaw in his book *Compassion's Way: A Doctor's Quest into the Soul of Medicine*, so I quote him in what mastery looks like:

> *"Look carefully at the phenomenon of presence personified in the prima ballerina. The prima ballerina has supreme presence as she gathers up her audience. They become hers in spirit, breathlessly alive as she inspires... She suspends all motion and awaits expectantly with all her body poised as the music announces her next step. In that moment, with the lift of her neck, with the position of her feet, with the relaxed tenseness of her slender frame she strips away the history, the freedom, the identity of the audience... with instantaneous awareness of anticipated joy all submit willingly and entirely to what she chooses to do... she chooses where to look without a flicker of hesitation. Her posture proclaims an uncompromising acceptance of self-imposed discipline."*

I implore you to find such mastery in your practice, with practice, and masterful practice, to have such grace as a healer. There is no shortcut to greatness.

Advanced Certification Weekend

"I just finished my Advanced Reiki Master Certification this weekend, and I'm still having problems." I hate this statement. Listen, I am all for people learning healing techniques. Still, anything worth doing is worth spending time training, and you aren't acquiring complete training on an entire healing modality from a pyramid Americanized healing technique.

"mmhmm," I replied, trying to keep my face blank.

"And I keep having issues with my back. I feel lethargic. And I swear I'm dumping out everything I work with," the healer said.

"OK. Dumping out? That means that you are absorbing it first? In Reiki, aren't you supposed to push out the energy, and you're not supposed to absorb any of it? " I pressed.

"No, but I know what I'm doing," she defended.

"Right. So, if absorbing isn't part of your training, how do you really know what you're doing?"

"I'm an empath," she said emphatically.

"Right."

"I'm using my intuition," she said.

"And we still have pain… Neither your intuition nor your training is working, empath. You should be using the healing technique as intended. Ok, let me take a look at you."

As I closed my eyes to see her energy cables, I could see something inside her throat, down her back, and blackness in her hip. Her aka were reaching out around her like hungry snail antennae. I opened my eyes. "How do you remove the energy you take in from your clients?"

Proudly, she said, "I visualize a blue tornado and flush it down the drain." I wanted to come unglued.

"Visualization?" I asked.

"Yes." Reader, you know how I feel about that. "Ok, that isn't enough to get it out. Do you engage in any exercises or movements to help release energy from others? Tai Chi is a great way to move energy out of you after working on others and becoming aware of your energy." She was not open to that; I could tell. "Ok, let's get you healed. I will put on some music, and we will mend you. But do me a favor and relearn the basics of Reiki, do it the way you're supposed to do it, stop visualizing, and learn some self-care energy techniques. I don't want you back in here for the same thing."

Healing Spirits

Healer helpers are spirits equipped to heal and help you heal. This may be the spirit of a medicine woman, a deity who has shown themselves to you (which makes you fortunate), or the spirit of specific plants that comes to your aid. Shamans, medicine men, and witchdoctors all work in tandem with spirits. Working alone is just not done, and any shaman who does should be questioned about their techniques and efficacy. Not to say that a shaman can't work alone, which I do on many occasions; witchdoctory is simply not a solo practice. You have co-workers and a spiritual support system for various needs. Exorcisms don't work for priests (just them and Jesus), so why would they work for a shaman? I bring in a team of experts to help me out based on the case, if I can't do it alone. Sometimes an exorcism only takes one spirit to help me, and sometimes it takes a whole team.

This is where I need to quote Hank Wesselman in his book *Spirit Medicine:*

> *"In spirit medicine, illness is caused by intrusions - by something that comes into us from without. It could be a virus, a bacterium, an arrow, or a negative thought-form. However, from the shaman's perspective, the illness intrusion is not the primary issue. The real problem lies in the diminishment of our personal power, stemming from the holes torn in the fabric of our soul that allowed the intrusion to enter in the first place. Negative thoughts, feelings, and intentions can be directed toward us like spiritual poisons by those who hold us in disregard - an old love or spouse who just can't let go, a hostile neighbor who spews forth profanity at us, in-laws who find us unworthy, or a jealous sibling or co-worker who simply despises us. When this is done with outright malice, it forms the modus operandi of negative witchcraft and sorcery."*

A spirit to help you break down the hold illnesses or entities have on a victim, to repair broken parts of a person where a spirit could enter, or to point out the self-sabotaging behaviors that keep a person ill is most valuable to you in your work. They can also help you determine if the person is connected (aka) to someone who is harming them energetically, for which they will need a cord-cutting.

Finding a Healing Spirit
BUT I WANT A HEALING SPIRIT! Whoa, take a breath. Only healers have healing spirits. Seriously. You aren't a healer if you aren't healing. Remember, you are based on what you do, not on what your potential is. You must take action. If you are not a doctor, you cannot prescribe medication even if you want to. We don't all get what we want just because we think we are entitled. So, as I give you this meditation, remember that you only access the spirit of healing if you are a healer. Otherwise, the spirit that will show up in the area of consciousness will simply leave you after there is no use, no working together. This

is not a spirit guide, nor a companion. This spirit is a co-worker and a master teacher. The Healing Spirit is meant to instruct you with expert knowledge and help you in the healing.

Follow the process of spirit-walking to the bay. From there, go back where you came from, into the forest where you usually let your mind dump out all of those unnecessary thoughts. Stop on the trail. You need to walk inland, away from the bay, but off the path and into the forest. There you will find the spirit circle. Sit in the grass, put your hands into the grass, and tell the grass that you would like to meet a healing spirit who will work with you in your endeavors.

Lift your hands off the grass and let the rest happen. This is where we stop the visualization and allow the spirit-walk to take place. Allow it to happen to you.

1. Do shamanic breathing

2. Close your eyes and focus on the blacks of your eyes.

3. Empty your mind with the stair visualization.

4. Once you are in your mind, go right into the area of consciousness, into the woods.

5. Once you are on this path, stay on the path and call for your healing spirit. This co-worker. You will find that the spirit will show.

Don't Look a Gift(ed) Spirit in the Mouth

Horses were valued by their mouths. Did you know that? That's why you don't look a gift horse in the mouth. It's a horse! Don't look at its teeth to see its value. You're still ahead one gifted horse. The same goes for healing spirits.

I know one shamanic practitioner who met a fox along her track and ignored the fox. "This isn't my power-animal, so why is it here?" She said to me.

"Because it wants to work with you," I told her.

"But foxes aren't known for healing or helping. Aren't they independent?" She said.

"And yet, here it is," I said.

Another student had the spirit of alfalfa. "It was like a gummy weed," she said.

"Don't look at the size of this spirit as a detriment. A virus is small and can kill." She looked at me with surprise. Of course, my point was for her to: "Allow the alfalfa spirit to help you in your healing. You are better with it than without. I'm sure it has some great things to share with you, and I hope you may share your stories."

You may want a healing goddess or a dolphin spirit, but you shouldn't let the power or potency go unnoticed by any healing spirit. Please accept the help in whatever form it comes. One is not better than another. This is not a spiritual contest as to who is more special because of the spirit that came to help. The spirit who comes is the one best for you.

Arianrhod Grandmother Spider Teotihuacan Yevabog

Characters:
Me
Grandmother Spider

This story feels the most far-fetched out of all of my experiences, and yet, I am reminded daily of my connection to this spirit.

A while ago, one of my service agencies asked me to do a soul retrieval on the owner, healing his trauma from a vehicular accident. I agreed, although I was nervous. What if I failed?

I began the soul retrieval. I did my breathing, went into my mind, through the area of consciousness, and started to head down to the lower world to begin the search for his missing pieces.

Just then, I felt a pullback into my body. *I must be distracted*, I thought. *Focus, Aly!*

And a sudden change happened. I was in the middle world, looking at myself in my office. *I am not supposed to be here*, I said to myself. *I need to be in the lower world looking for his soul pieces.*

Standing behind my body was a giant woman spider. Her eyes had so much age that they looked like they were closed. She had four arms and four legs. Her body was hunched over as if she had been carrying the world on her back for thousands of years. I stood there in awe. Layers of red, blue, and tan burlap woven fabric sat upon her hunch and draped across and around her limbs. Through her hands were golden threads that she weaved back and forth, then glowing electric blue, one string at a time. She looked as if she would begin making a cat's cradle, but restarted. Gold. Blue. Gold.

Who are you? I asked the ancient spirit.

Her gaze stayed fixed on my empty body, downwards. She outstretched one of her left hands, and I knew I could trust this old spider woman. I stepped forward, presenting my right hand to her. As I approached, I knew that this creature in front of me was not a cryptid itself. She wasn't one of many creatures in a classification. She was one of a kind. She was a deity, a lone spirit.

I put my hand in hers, and we stepped into my body together. I felt my muscles ache with the change of having something large and foreign inside me. At that moment, I knew for sure I was a channeler. I had always suspected, but was too afraid to let anything in me. I could feel my soul adjust and move to make space for her energy. My bones creaked and tried to make space, and my muscles adjusted to try to mold around her spirit. If I could see auras, I imagine mine would have expanded to make space for her to be a part of my spirit.

I could feel extra arms reaching from under my sides, and my arms were light as a feather. My face hurt as the muscles fought to use themselves, being forced to do things they were not accustomed to. My back ached with the pain of age, and my stomach felt full.

I still don't know what to call you. Although my bones and muscles were not used to having this spirit drive my body, I felt safe. Pained and yet safe with her driving. She searched my mind for a word that would work.

Yevabog. She chose from my mind. Yevabog is the spider character from Brom's *Lost Gods*. I had just read it.

I mean, ok, but can I call you something else? This seems so fictional, I protested.

She searched in silence, patiently. I had learned of Teotehuacan, a spider spirit from South America who healed like the Grandmother Spider.

Arianrhod was her second choice. Another spider healer, mender. On my mother's side, the German side, who introduced me to the Hawaiian ways, I was given a spirit who was Celtic. It made sense that a goddess from Druid ways would come through since my mother was a Druid witch, and it made sense while I was doing a Hawaiian healing technique. I had always hoped for a Hawaiian healing spirit, but this did make sense. Anyway, it doesn't seem to matter what I call her. I think this was some audition, anyway.

I relaxed, and we started to work. Using my mana, we reached into my client and pulled out the poisoned keawe in his head. We mended aka, and we filled him back up with the spirit in water.

She played me like a well-crafted puppeteer, and I felt like a beautiful violin. My energy was moved around in ways I can't even describe. I complied, and we sewed, pulling from elemental sources of the earth to supply mana into his spirit, and mended. I followed directions, being the tool she needed as a witchdoctor and as her assistant.

She stepped backward out of me gently when she finished. I sat up, regaining my body. I felt her disappear into the veil of the upper world, and she was gone. I opened my eyes, and I was freezing. My body had dropped incredibly in temperature, not being entirely worn by a human soul. Was I partly dead if I wasn't fully alive? I was thirsty, and my lips were dry and cracked. I felt like I had been in the freezing desert in meditation for an entire night, waking to find my body suddenly needing care.

I woke up the client and explained what I... we... had done. He was surprised. "Grandmother Spider channeled through you?"

"I guess?" I said timidly.

"You are very lucky, son. Thank her for me when you see her again?"

"If I see her again," I said. "I don't know that she will be back. Maybe it was a one-and-done kind of thing? Maybe she was only here for you."

He looked at me and said, "Brother, she will be back."

She has helped me ever since. Yevabog, Grandmother Spider, Teotihuacan, Arianrhod... Names are things we humans require when interacting, but many animals don't, right? They just know. I know it's her, my teacher, my guide, a master, and my friend. We rarely talk (I'm the chatty one), and we just get to work. She has rescued me numerous times from difficult healing situations and has helped so many clients through me.

At first, I wondered why me? Then I remembered that day that she first stepped into my body. She couldn't heal without a channeler, and I know I couldn't do the fantastic job (I thought I was so good before meeting her, too!) without her teachings or her running the show.

I now call her Grandmother Spider to others, but address her directly as Arianrhod. I reach for her help, and she shows, not because I use an arbitrary name, but because she and I are now connected. Woven.

Part 4

Aumakua & Soul Retrievals

Lucifer's Forgiveness

Characters:
Me
George - a young client
Lucifer - Christian god of condemned souls

George hired me for a soul retrieval. A soul retrieval is a healing process where a shaman, kahuna, or witchdoctor travels to the spirit world or land of the dead to retrieve parts of a soul that have mistakenly died off, usually from trauma, and brings them back to incorporate them into the living person for a full and productive life.

George was young, like early twenties or maybe even nineteen. He had said that he had been harassed by demons and that they were trying to get inside him. He was keeping them away, but was becoming weary from the work. George wanted them to stop, and he felt my help was the only way.

I listened to this and took it lightly. I didn't sense anything around him, but I did a watchtower protection ritual, anyway. After I had finished asking the gods to protect us, lighting candles at the cardinal directions, and settling back down, I told him to put his headphones on, close his eyes, lie down, and relax, and that this would be very easy for him. I told him that I would bring back the shards of his soul that had broken off during past traumas, and then we began the integration process of healing and becoming whole again. I had done over a hundred soul retrievals at this point, but this would be the first time I was at the mercy of an all-powerful being.

I began the spirit-walk, allowing my mind to wash away any muck that was troubling me. Suddenly, everything went black, and in the blackness, in the nighttime shadows, I saw fire. The vision was a wooden floor in a basement. There were a few young men, George, candles, and junk which had been stacked high on the side basement walls. George was brought to the middle of the room, and stripped of his shirt. He was told to kneel on a pentagram etched into the floor. The men set candles around him on the wooden floor.

As the vision adjusted to nighttime, the small lit candles in a circle surrounded George, still shirtless but now on his hands and knees, looking at the floor, keeping his gaze away from the men. The candlelight was the only light in the room now, with mostly shadows dancing as company. George was maybe sixteen years old, cold, shaking, trying to be brave, holding his gaze at the feet of the leading teenager.

Standing outside the circle in front of George was an older teenage boy or young man, reading from a book. He looked fuzzy to me, but he wore a brown monk's robe. I couldn't get a description since the hood's shadow shrouded his face, and earlier, I could only see him from behind, bullying George to comply. I guessed his age from the sound of his maturing voice at about eighteen. Behind George, also outside of the circle, was another young man dressed the same. He had his arms crossed and was waiting. The shelves behind the second boy were disorganized with junk piled high; clothes, bicycle parts, books, and cardboard peaking out when the moments of shadows no longer hid their presence. Off to the side, there was more junk, piled out of the way to make enough space for the circle encasing George.

"George!" I yelled. But his past self couldn't hear me. "George!" Nothing. I honestly couldn't tell if we were in a memory haunting our world or if we were in the Lower World, where his spirit fled in fear from the ritual taking place. My power animal finally arrived, my wonderful polar bear. I walked up to the candles to touch George and ask his past self to come with me, but I was locked out. The candles and ritual had protected him from me like a ritual forcefield, much like how the watchtower ritual of protection keeps anything out when I am working.

"I can't get through the candles!" I said in a panic. My power-animal lifted his paw and stomped on the floor. I walked over to him, and his greatness lifted to full height on his haunches. He put his paws on my shoulders and pushed me down into the floor. My spirit descended into the floorboards beneath the ritual. "What is happening?" I asked my power-animal.

"Satanic ritual," he told me. Above, I heard the clank of something metal being thrown to George. The second boy laughed, and I heard some kind of order barked at him.

I walked a few steps under the boards until I thought I was directly under George. I reached up through the boards and pulled my spirit up through the boards, joining George from the inside of the circle. Now George and I were both inside the enclosure of candles. As I pulled myself up, George cut his hand, lifted it above his head, and blood dripped down his arm, across his naked chest, and onto the floor.

The boys continued reading in a strained, ominous performance, and honestly, I was afraid. There was a parchment written into some kind of contract. In this environment, the contract seemed so relaxed, as if it didn't care what the children were doing. I didn't see it there earlier, unless it was thrown there with the knife.

"No!" I yelled. But George's memory did not hear me. He took his bleeding hand from above his head, and with his blood, he signed his name to be the property of Lucifer. I grabbed that poor, cold, shirtless boy, trying to pull this soul fragment from this place, but he wouldn't move. It wouldn't budge.

Was I trapped there with him? I looked past the candles, and as George finished signing his name, the breath of the basement left. I held this thin blood blood-covered body, with my soul satchel still swinging by my hip, looking out over the candles. I couldn't feel the softness of the skin. He felt completely solid, and cold, like a marbled statue, devoid of life.

Everything froze. The candle flames stopped moving. Solid and still. The flames solidified like wax. My power-animal was still, peering into the circle with concern, but also frozen. The young men with their delighted faces were statued into place, and George's bloody hand was still against the uncompromising parchment.

From within the circle, all of the environment seemed to fade away until we were surrounded by blackness, leaving George, the parchment, me, a knife, and the frozen candles. Everything was replaced by blackness, darkness, emptiness. Everything faded to black. I sat there, frantically looking around, the only life in this vignette of terror. The blackness seemed to go on forever. No boys, no totem, no junk… just blackness walled around the frozen painting of candles, a stone child, and me.

After what seemed like more than a collection of moments, the floor seemed to move. Like a flying carpet, the ritual circle levitated in the darkness. We floated like a disc through space, floating around, up, and down until we jolted to a stop. I was scared, terrified. The scene froze around me, nothing visible but darkness. My power-animal was gone, and I felt trapped. I wondered if I had died attempting this soul retrieval, but nothing like that had ever been documented (probably because if this had happened to someone, they died and couldn't document it!).

The sound was a vacuum of inverted silence, and the darkness, ominous. Soon, I could see a small light moving quickly towards us. I could barely make out that this was a person coming. A man appeared, glowing white. He glowed so brightly I could not make out his face. His featherless wings were also white, bright, and shining. He gave off more heat than I have ever felt in my life, like someone leaving the oven door open. He was warm and bright like the sun and white like the hottest flame. He was like an angel, but his featherless wings and the context of what had just taken place told me I was in the presence of only one possible entity.

Lucifer.

"Thank you for seeing me," I stumbled in my own fear, managing to say something and to stay on task. "I am here on behalf of this boy." My voice shook. Was I actually doing this? Was I attempting to save a soul given to… the Devil? Did I have any other activity options provided to me?

Does the Christian Devil actually exist? Was I in the presence of ultimate greatness and autonomy or in merciless danger? Am I about to bargain with Lucifer, the great star child, and without a fiddle? Looks like this was what we were doing today.

He looked down at me and didn't speak. Not that I could see his face because of the brightness that came from him. I assumed he was looking at me because his head tilted down toward the ground where I was clutching this child. "He is not here of his own free will. George was deceived and pressured by those older than him. They took advantage of this child. I thought I had learned that you accepted souls who pledged to you willingly through contract or actions in life. Is this incorrect, your greatness?" I calmed and slowed my case down: "This child did not give of himself, nor was he offered by his family. This was bullying and coercion. I am here as his... his..." when you're at a loss for words... "His advocate."

I waited. George's skin was cold and lifeless.

"Most gracious and exalted Dark Lord, Lucifer, master of the underworld and arbiter of souls," I reminded myself of formality. "I approach you with a heavy heart, burdened by the weight of an unjust tale. I implore you to consider granting mercy to a young soul. This soul, a child still, was forced into a vortex of malice and treachery, his innocence tainted by brutal coercion. Robbed of agency and entrapped in cruel circumstances, this tender spirit was coerced into the ritual dance of darkness. How can one hold this soul accountable for sins not brought on by his own accord?"

At that, I let go of the youth, and placed myself on my knees with my hands outstretched, keeping my gaze respectfully at Lucifer's feet: "I beseech you, Great Lucifer, the Morning Star, whose wisdom and fair judgment are renowned, to consider the merits of leniency. This child, who has felt the cruel bite of fate, deserves the chance to forge a path untarnished by the malevolent machinations of others. It is not in my place to question your divine judgment, but I entreat you to recall the fleeting essence of childhood."

At that, I stood, placing my palms upwards and keeping my gaze down, showing my lifeblood as a traveler who should not be in the world of the dead. "Grant this soul another opportunity to bask in life, a chance to reclaim the purity that was once their birthright, and to purge the false vestiges of darkness that have sullied his existence. I beseech you, Lord Lucifer, let mercy temper justice this day, for the soul of a child hangs in the balance of fairness. If he chooses to follow you, let it be of his own honest and free will, for you are great and should have the honor of greatness who willingly honor you."

I waited.

There was movement under my feet. I lowered my hands and looked down at the contract under George's bloody hand. The contract floated from under George's blood-stained hand into the air. In this horrifying moment, that vile piece of deceitful paper was the only life in this place of darkness. "He did sign it, yes," I continued, "and that is his blood, but I ask you to give this child a chance to pledge to you or another with his free will."

I knelt, "Please allow me to take this broken soul back to his living body. Allow him to choose for himself, willingly, not from the pressures and insecurity of adolescence. Please consider my request." He lowered the contract back to the ground, letting it sit in front of us. His wings pulsed, and his arms moved to consider, resting one on his face and the other across his body.

I stopped. I was talking too much. Why would such a great spirit consider what a small, insignificant kahuna requests? I needed to stop and let this great figure ponder my appeal. I didn't have anything else to present, so if I continued, I would probably annoy him. I lowered my head in reverence and respect as he made his decision. I put my hand on the hand of the lifeless stone child. I had resigned to the fact that I was not going to succeed in this retrieval, and I would probably perish in the process.

Suddenly, I felt a breeze. The lifeless room gave air, and the candles resumed their flicker. They reached upwards in a stretched relief from their imprisoned stillness. The wax started to slink to the floor, and the boy's blood continued to drip from his hand. I grabbed the boy around the shoulders as if I were going to begin a wrestling match.

Holding onto George's frame, I looked back at the great white spirit and studied his albino gargoyle-like wings. As Lucifer breathed, his wings pulsed and flexed slightly. He stretched out his three-fingered hand. Was Lucifer missing a finger from a typical human hand? The contract levitated above his outstretched hand and, gracefully, all at once, sizzled out into a flame. Lucifer lowered his arm and turned to leave. As he turned, the floor flew away, again flying into darkness. The god of firelight shrank to nothingness in the distance before I could thank him for granting my request.

George, the memory of George, breathed and felt my locked embrace. I squeezed the child as if I were clinging to a cliff's edge to prevent my demise. And with his constitution came his awareness of me. In fear, he pulled away from me, from my grip, and backed against the wall of candles, distancing himself from me within the circle.

"George," I breathed desperately, "your current self needs you. My name is Aly, and I'm a witchdoctor. You want to be healed in the present, but this terrible event has broken you into pieces. Your current self hired me to heal you? Will you go with me?" I was all over the place. I was usually better spoken.

George looked into my eyes. He cried. Instead of tears, blood ran down his face in droplets. He was still afraid, searching for trust in my gaze. He studied me, crying blood. I believe it was my desperation that made him trust me. He lunged at me with the tightest, trusting hug. His bloody hands smeared across my back, his bloody tears in my collar, I held him. In his embrace, I came back to my body and gasped. I looked for the blood that should have stained my clothes, but it wasn't there. I reached for my ritual sticks, and with several claps of the wood, I released him to rejoin his living soul, catching my breath.

I managed a bunch of huge steadying breaths before waking him, staring at the older George in front of me. His eyes were closed. Looking at his resting form, I noticed that he had aged so much in those last four years. That night had forced his young body to wear the lines and age of someone in their fifties. George's young, twenty-year-old face had bags under his eyes and stress marks on his forehead. His face had a green tone, and I could see his bony clavicle protruding under his t-shirt. How did I miss how spiritually he had been so worn down to the point that it affected his physical body into quickened deterioration?

"George, I'm back." While George stirred, I sipped my cold coffee and shook my head, figuring out how I would tell George about this retrieval.

"George…" I trailed off, still hoping for divine intervention to give me the words to say what had happened.

"Yes? Was it that bad?" He asked. Looking at his face, knowing he would be ok, I started to cry. "Am I going to die?!" He reacted to my tears.

"No, no!" I said. "I'm sorry. You're… er… pardoned?"

"What?" George asked.

"I… When you were about fifteen or sixteen, did you… Did you…. Were you part of a ritual where those men convinced you to sell your soul to the devil? Lucifer?"

He was still shocked. I sensed his fear coming back, replicating the moment he cut his hand and touched the parchment. His past was exposed. "Yes."

"I met Lucifer," I blurted out.

We stared at each other. I heard birds outside my window. I heard a bug throwing itself against the window pane, trying to get into my house. I heard the stirring of life in my home. I pondered all of these lives, not knowing how fragile they were. My own family could, under a series of unfortunate events, find itself in the same situation as George. I pictured this happening to my daughter, fragmented and kept by a divine spirit as payment, because of a ritual found in a book, because sadistic deceivers pressured her into a game of dominance and fear. I imagined a situation where my daughter believed that terrible people were the only family she could trust, and how they, in my imagination, convinced her to be in a ritual where she would be spiritually wounded forever.

George was someone's child. I wanted to stop the session, run away from George, and hug my daughter. She and George were about the same age, too. I wanted to yell into her face, his face, never to trust anyone ever, and that I was always there for her, for him. Someone to protect this child. This grown child.

George stared into my eyes the same way his fragmented self did, searching for honesty, for someone whom he could trust.

I tentatively continued, "I can't believe I'm saying this, and I can't believe Lucifer himself would take the trouble to see me, but I saw what those boys were doing, that you were in too deep, too afraid to turn back, and that it was against your free will." George was frozen. Although my instructions were clear, a tear fell from my eye, "He gave you back."

George gasped... and in his breath, he lost control of his stone face and sobbed.

"George, you're... you're you, again. No one is coming for you. The contract burned up. It is gone, over. I think he agreed that if you wanted to give your soul to him, that *you* should do so, but understanding what you are doing."

George studied me. "Wait," he caught his breath. "Lucifer..."

"Yeah?" I encouraged.

"Lucifer said I could choose him or not?"

I thought about how Lucifer didn't actually speak to me, "basically."

"Is it weird to think that my captor, Lucifer, was also who saved me?" George said. Those wise words will stay with me forever. "Those men, they were the ones who broke me, who stole my soul that night. Even if it was for the Devil, Lucifer didn't take it. It's almost like he kept it safe until someone looked for it. Those bullies took my soul. Lucifer held onto it so you could find it, again."

"I guess we can look at it that way, yes. Lucifer was understanding and fair. You have choices, sweetheart. That includes who you spend your time with."

"Thank you, Aly."

"You're welcome, but you may want to thank Lucifer, too," I surmised. George's eyes filled with terror as he looked at me, untrusting again. Then he took a steadying breath.

"The spirits will leave you alone," I said. He was whole. He was safe. He was now in control of the choices of his soul, of his life.

"Would you do it for me?" George asked, pained with fear.

"I would be honored."

I learned so much that day. I did hug my daughter, and I yelled at her not to trust anyone ever, and she laughed at me and told me to get my craziness off of her.

George wrote a few weeks later:

> Aly, I just wanna let you know, ever since the soul retrieval, I've felt so much better, and also we are moving into a new home that is in a great neighborhood. I can't wait! August 1st! Thanks for everything once again… also thanks to Lucifer for coming to an agreement. It's not like I'm on his side, but I understand his side.

Two years later, George reached out via Instagram. I had never told my husband about the day I met Lucifer, because I didn't feel like he would believe me. Hearing from George triggered high emotions for me:

> Thanks, Aly, again. I'm making progress slowly, but I've come a long way.

> One day, George, I really want to hug you.

> Oh, wow appreciate that. I've been through a lot I know.

> I just… the day of your soul retrieval is an important day in my story. In saving a piece of you, it saved a piece of me. So one day, I just want to hug you.

> I wanna be like you tbh. Helping ppl

> Well, one day, I will get to see you in person and I will probably cry.

> What why cry?

> Just out of happiness. That day really changed me.

> What how?

> What you went through, those terrible boys… ugh… I'm just blessed to have been able to help.

> The people who led to the temptation? Idk what happened but meeting Lucifer is not something to take lightly. That's a heavy commitment toward the help you provide.

> Yeah. That. It was terrifying. Thanks for reaching out. You mean the world to me.

Evil is a matter of perspective. When you are working, you need to be aware of what is actually danger (the boys of the ritual) and what you're primed to believe is danger (Lucifer).

Cursing the Self (Yes, the Problem is You), Thought Implantation, and Psychic Attack: Ho'upu'upu, Ho'opi'opi'o

Ho'upu'upu

Thought implantation is when a *sorcerer* victimizes a person with unpleasant, impending prophecies or determinations. Thought implantation is ho'upu'upu.

Now, I have italicized the word *sorcerers* because in many cases, this is not literal. This can be any person with the pointed action of harm. All in all, this is the implantation of negative beliefs or energy into the aumakua. Like a seed, we are most effective at extracting such a poison the sooner we catch it. If we don't remove these kinds of psychic attacks, they fester and grow, imposing themselves on the belief structure of the victim.

For example, if my mother were to tell me as a child, "You'll never be a beautiful boy, Aly. You'll always be a little rough-looking." If no one were to tell me that I was beautiful, I would let that seed settle and grow into my foundation. As an adult, with this foundational belief, I may make choices in destructive partners, settling for people who tend and encourage that seed.

Now, let's talk about how you **Hex Yourself**!

Let's do it with this little side quest: I had a client who needed an ancestral healing. In her family, she had drug addiction, phobias, abuse, choosing spouses who hurt each other, fear around money, and compulsive habits, including hoarding and other kinds of resource guarding. The side effects are, of course, that once you've had the ancestral trauma within your genes removed from the ancestral healing, that your body, mind, and spirit need to reactively change and transform because of the procedure. During that time, the client will go through some discomfort, but, for the most part, the changes are relieving.

This client, after the session and after I told her about what had happened in her family history, obsessed over the history of her family. "I can't believe all of this pain happened! I'm at my grandmother's cottage, and I'm just so sad. Is this normal?"

My response? No. Here's why: She is taking what she heard from my findings in the healing and deciding it is much worse. She is creating a large new issue in her mind with things that didn't affect her before. She didn't know they were even there!

I fix the actual problem in her DNA. She then, creates a new problem with her beliefs from what she heard.

Here is another one from the same client. She hired me to do spell work for her condo to sell. From my spell work, she got buyers. The busiest showings she had ever had. Tons of people had interest and were excited about her condo. Everyone was very excited, and it looked like she was about to get competing offers. But then...

She told me that she felt that she was cursed because of ancestral problems and that she had a cord attachment to the condo. Guess what happened? No one, not a single person I pulled to her, bought. She created Ho'upu'pu against what she hired me to do. A client working against me (this actually happens often, by the way).

In my first book, *Witchdoctor Exorcist*, the Hawaiian rules following a healing after an exorcism include to only think and speak positively. The reason is exactly ho'upu'upu. If you say or think you're possessed, then you are inviting it in and creating the manifestation of it to happen. If you believe that you are cursed and can't sell your condo: Ho'upu'upu! Dorothy Morrison in *Utterly Wicked* calls it a memorex (or that you are self-hexing yourself). In ancient Hawai'i? Ho'upu'upu!

One more example: In spell-work, one of the tenets and rules is *secrecy*. There are a few reasons why, but the biggest one has to do with "intention." If you talk about how great your spell is that you're doing on somebody, then the intention isn't to do a great spell. It's to get validation and attention from the person whom you told. So, if you tell someone that you cursed them with a poppet and have their feet bound and that they are deteriorating into nothing with disease and isolation, the intention of the spell changes from actually doing those things to "getting attention."

It's the listener's fault then, for creating a spell on themselves based on the words they heard and what they believe (hilina'i), for making those things happen, not the supposed spell that was done.

Stop cursing yourself. Your beliefs matter.

Ho'opi'opi'o

Ho'opi'opi'o is a psychic attack. Psychic attack is the implantation of thoughts without the use of words, by the influence of spiritual power, a negative person, or from the spells of *sorcerers*.

Let's say that you belong to a burlesque company, one that has terrible luck. This luck is so terrible that a tsunami literally hits the island, loss of power, global disease, or strife with performance locations every single time your company goes to perform. Turns out, one of the performers is attacked by such hatred from a family member, in thought, that she brings bad luck to the entire company.

Both situations are hexes, spiritual attacks. Without tending and healing, these aspects can bleed over into our uhane, making us physically sick. Without attention, these poisons can harm our hidden selves, forcing us to lose connection to our spirituality, community, and sense of purpose.

These nasty words and spells can disconnect us from our spirit guides, making us deaf to their company, compassion, or help. Their poison infiltrates the line of communication and connection to the spiritual world that keeps us safe. Loss of spirit guides and guardians is a terrible spiritual illness not to be taken with very real seriousness.

In both cases, healing spells, psychic surgery (like hilina'i), or a soul retrieval are necessary to help heal. Now, if the victim has the implantation of harm, and a part of their spirit did not break (they're just poisoned), a soul retrieval is not a good choice. Talking story with a witchdoctor (or other spiritual counselor), where the healer can help to break down those foundational beliefs and help to implant new ones through conversation (words harm, words heal) and the addition of healing spell work or hilina'i are the prescriptions. Be mindful of the life balance as well (under the uhane section), so that their environment can support the healing benefits you are initiating.

Assist in pointing out what harm was created, and refute those 'truths' with new truths. Help to build self-esteem, reframing (was the mother jealous of the looks of the child, and therefore didn't want the child to thrive in a life better than hers?), and assertiveness training. This all needs to be done omnistically, or rather, from the point of view that is culturally inclusive to the victim's spirituality.

Being Sick Is How I Experience Love

Jessica was ill. She was suffering from fibromyalgia and had severe pain in her leg down to her foot. In her spiritual counseling session, she told me that she felt neglected in her marriage and that her children were distant from her. She didn't have close friends, and she felt lost in her life.

I had her do a crystal grid throughout her whole house. "Let's change the home completely. Take a ton of smoky quartz and place them on every corner of the home. Make sure that the quartz can see each other. You only need to do one floor, but you need to do the biggest floor to cover the most square footage. You want the quartz to hit every corner. All of you will then interact through and around the house within the grid. Put a piece on every table, ledge, corner, etc. Little pieces will do. The size doesn't matter. If you have any Himalayan salt, you can mix that in, but just those two things. Leave it up for at least one week."

After a week, she returned and said that when she completed the grid, her boyfriend felt weak and dizzy. "It took a day for him to regain his balance again. But I don't feel better. I feel the same," Jessica said.

"That's interesting," I said. "How do you feel about sick people?"

Jessica replied, "What do you mean?"

"What is something that sick people get that no one else gets... in your opinion?" I asked.

"Care," she said. Oof.

"What do you mean?" I needed to clarify and double-check my theory before understanding her pain.

"They get someone to care for them, so they get better," Jessica said. She could have said medicine, that they get better, or about their discomfort. But she associated being sick with getting cared for and with getting attention.

"Ok. I'm going to do an energy healing on you. It's called hilina'i. I'm going to pull out the illnesses. You will need to heal afterward, so you will need to take care of yourself and be patient. Like surgery, you need to be mindful of your care and progress. This will not be an immediate fix, but you will feel relief when I'm done. Watch your gate, as in how you walk. Go through physical therapy, make sure you are eating right, and manage your sleep and water intake. Do you understand?"

"Yes, Aly."

I pulled out energetic muck in her hip, down the back of her right leg, and through her foot. I put them into lava stones so they could sit in the sun and go back to the land. In her head and neck, there were oil-slicked tendrils of poison leaking into the rest of her. I pulled that out, too. After I was finished, she said, "Oh, wow! I feel so much better! Thank you."

She emailed me two weeks later, needing my attention. Jessica hadn't done anything herself to help her healing process. She continued her bad habits, complaining about being sick, and forcing her family away by only complaining about them being distant. She didn't actively do anything to bring the family closer together or to mend any of her relationships. Jessica didn't go to her appointments and continued obsessing over the sickness. This was like giving someone suffering from cirrhosis of the liver, giving them a new liver, and then having them behave in the same ways that caused the cirrhosis of the first liver.

Jessica was holding on to needing care and not living as a healthy person. "Jessica, I can't help you until you change your focus," I told her.

"What? Why?" she wrote.

"Your focus is on being sick. The neglect you felt as a child is being expressed right now. Your belief that the only way you will receive love from others is if you are a burden to them, and you get care for being sick. You don't honestly believe that someone will care for you unless you're not well. If you are well, take care of yourself, and there is nothing that needs fixing, you might think they will have no reason to stay. They need a reason to care for you; otherwise, no one will care about you, in your belief. I want you to pause and think about that. It's a deep belief that needs to be addressed." She went to argue with me, but hesitated, so I continued.

"I'm not your band-aid. I can't continue to patch you up when you aren't taking the time to mend yourself, Jessica. I need you to work on your foundational beliefs around neglect and care. I recommend *Mind Over Mood* for some Cognitive Behavioral Therapy, or for you to do the shadow work around this, break it down, accept, and start mending. Then I will heal you again so that you can have a healthy life. But you have to decide you want a healthy life. You don't get to have my attention just because you need attention. I can give you the option of spiritual counseling to help with the foundational beliefs, but I won't do the healing again until you've done the work."

"You don't understand what it's like to be forced to pay attention to my pain all the time." She refuted.

"I do." I said, "I have a rare pain disorder that I manage. The difference is I know my family will care for me even if I don't have this disorder because I trust that they won't neglect my basic needs, and in turn, I make a conscious effort to make sure their basic needs are also met. I can take care of my pain and allow their help when they can offer it. Your situation is unhealthy. You are using your boyfriend and family, and still don't feel it is enough. If you are healthy, you believe that they will leave because they have no purpose. People don't need a purpose in order to love and care for each other. You have to break down that foundational belief because it is very unhealthy. You have an attachment to being sick. Allow them to help, but you have to help yourself. Until then, I can't help you. I won't help you. Start to take care of yourself, and I will then help as well." I could tell she wasn't hearing me. It made me sad. "If you need guidance," I finished, "I am here."

Spiritual Bypassing and How to Deal With Failure

Authentic spirituality doesn't rush and isn't romantic. Dabbling here and there may bring a sense of achievement and a feeling of knowingness, but many end up loudly expressing immaturity from their high of novelty and the need to feel superior. These individuals get caught up in the allure of unconditional love and the promises of spirituality, leading to spiritual bypassing. This is a common tendency to expedite spiritual growth with a belief in enlightenment without engaging in the actual practices of spiritual systems.

Spiritual bypassing involves using spiritual ideas or activities to sidestep or suppress emotional or psychological issues that require attention. It entails utilizing spiritual practices, such as meditation or positive affirmations, to avoid the challenging or uncomfortable emotions and situations that arise in life, rather than fully addressing and healing them. This behavior can give a false impression of spiritual progress or enlightenment while leaving underlying problems unresolved and unattended. To achieve genuine healing and development, it's essential to strike a balance between spiritual practices and emotional and psychological work.

In spiritual bypassing, individuals employ spiritual practices or beliefs to rationalize or evade real-life concerns. For instance, someone might turn to substance abuse to cope with emotional pain, stress, or anxiety, and then utilize their spiritual convictions to justify their substance use. They may convince themselves that drugs help them reach a higher state of consciousness, enrich their spiritual experiences, or serve as a form of therapy. However, this reasoning is merely a way to avoid facing their addiction and actual issues, impeding their recovery and preventing them from seeking necessary help.

Spiritual bypassing within the spiritual community can manifest in various ways, such as avoiding confronting emotions and challenges, ignoring systemic issues, engaging in exclusionary behavior, prioritizing superficial positivity, denying reality through magical thinking, and discriminating against scientific and medical knowledge. It's important to recognize that these behaviors can arise in any spiritual or religious group and often stem from individuals who are not prepared to address their challenges or lack the emotional tools to do so.

Confirmation Bias

Confirmation bias is the inclination to favor information that supports one's existing beliefs, while dismissing contradicting information. It leads people to seek out and interpret data in a way that aligns with their current convictions rather than objectively assessing all available evidence. This bias can result in closed-mindedness, misunderstandings, and errors in judgment. Spiritual bypassing can further fuel confirmation bias by promoting a black-and-white perspective on spirituality, prompting individuals to selectively seek or interpret information that validates their views and ignore evidence that challenges their worldview. Additionally, spiritual bypassing may encourage emotional detachment, leading individuals to discount conflicting information that may challenge their beliefs.

Superiority

Spiritual bypassing can lead to a false sense of superiority, detachment from the world, and an inflated sense of personal power. When spiritual practitioners engage in spiritual bypassing, they may place an excessive emphasis on their spiritual abilities, supernatural skills, and mystical experiences, leading to a sense of megalomania. This can manifest as a belief that they are above the laws of nature, that they are invincible, and that they can control their environment through sheer force of will.

Furthermore, the idea of being impervious or invulnerable can lead to a sense of detachment from humanity, a sense of being above the fray. This can lead to a lack of empathy and a tendency to minimize or dismiss the emotional struggles of others.

Spiritual bypassing can lead to an overemphasis on individual power and a sense of superiority that can ultimately lead to negative behaviors and attitudes. It is important to engage in spiritual practice in a way that is balanced, grounded, and connected to the realities of daily life and the struggles of others.

There is nothing virtuous about expansion and being a 'higher being.' Some examples are cancer cells, colonization, and imperialism. In spiritual bypassing, we are encouraged to look down on those who are less than us, giving us a false sense of feeling special and better than, without the actual earned accomplishment.

When Spirituality is Uncomfortable

Facing our shadows, negativity, mortality, and pain allows spirituality to provide genuine support through these challenges rather than denying them. Embracing discomfort can lead to a deeper sense of self, vulnerability, and authenticity. The journey towards enlightenment may involve struggles and practice, akin to how shamans often undergo near-death experiences. The repetition and effort required for healing practices contrast with the spiritual bypassing seen in practices like Reiki, which may avoid discomfort and the learning process. The most insidious aspect of spiritual bypassing involves attributing non-spiritual events to spiritual reasons in order to seek validation or evade uncomfortable truths.

How Does A Healer Avoid Spiritual Bypassing, Especially When This Work Is So Massive?

Healers can navigate a delicate balance between acknowledging their limitations, accepting failures, and avoiding spiritual bypassing by following these steps:

1. Recognize their boundaries: Healers must acknowledge that they are not infallible and know when to seek help or refer patients to other professionals.

2. Embrace setbacks: By accepting that failures may occur, healers can learn and improve their skills from mistakes.

3. Avoid spiritual bypass: Healers should be mindful of using spiritual practices to evade uncomfortable feelings and strive to find a balance between spirituality and practicality.

4. Prioritize self-care: Taking care of their physical, emotional, and spiritual well-being allows healers to provide quality care for their patients.

5. Maintain skepticism: Remaining objective and open-minded helps healers approach healing from various angles, ensuring effective and holistic care for their clients.

It is natural for healers to experience a range of emotions when unable to heal as expected, but it is essential to perceive healing as a process with varying outcomes. Understanding both the positive and negative results can enhance their practice and help them aid others effectively. Healing is about mental, emotional, and spiritual transformation, guiding individuals towards wholeness even amid permanent changes.

Toxic Positivity and Victim Blaming

Toxic positivity, spiritual bypassing, and victim blaming are interconnected behaviors that involve denying negative emotions or responsibilities in favor of a positive mindset. Spiritual bypassing promotes the idea of finding a silver lining in every situation, potentially minimizing genuine pain and suffering. Toxic positivity pressures individuals to maintain an overly positive outlook, leading to the suppression of negative feelings and potential shame if they struggle with mental health issues. Both toxic positivity and spiritual bypassing can hinder emotional processing, potentially causing repressed trauma and mental health challenges. These behaviors can also lead to victim blaming, where individuals use spiritual beliefs to justify harmful actions or dismiss the experiences of others, shifting responsibility onto victims and overlooking systemic injustices. These harmful patterns prevent meaningful acknowledgment and resolution of complex issues.

La'ieikawai, La'ielohelohe, The Rainbow, and The Song

Characters:
La'ieikawai - The twin of beauty and grace
La'ielohelohe - The twin on nobility and word
Waka - The twin girls' grandmother
The mo'o - The magic dragon lizard protector

High above the sacred cliffs of La'ie, where the mist rises from the sea like breath, a prophecy took shape in song and shadow. A chief's wife lay belly full with twins, a union of rare lineage, children meant to bind islands and dream gods into one peaceful reign. Yet the kahuna chanted a warning: such twins would shatter the balance among the ali'i. Two flames born together in one hearth promised too much power, too much light, too much longing. In fear, the mother made a vow she would later regret: one child would remain. The other must vanish.

By night, under moonlit palms, she carried the infants to the liminal edge of the village. La'ieikawai and La'ielohelohe lay in the same arms. She chose by whisper and breath. La'ieikawai was placed into a carved basket of hala and sank into a hidden water cave, where cool shadows swept and the world held its breath. She hid there, wrapped in her mother's kapa, beneath the water's surface and the rainbow's glow. The rainbow appeared only to those of sacred birth, and it arched low to shelter her place, to mark her as a daughter of rain and sky, hidden yet honored by nature itself.

The other sister, Laʻielohelohe, remained behind, raised in secret under the care of the chief's sister on Oʻahu. She learned the arts of the aliʻi, to speak with chiefs, to weave the cloak of wisdom. But she grew with a gap in her chest, a yearning for the sister she could not remember but whose presence hummed beneath her flesh like a distant drum.

Inside the cave, Laʻieikawai grew in silence and song. Waka, her grandmother, guarded her with a magical moʻo, scales glinting in the torchlight, eyes ancient as the bones of the earth. Night after night, she whispered to Laʻieikawai in dreams and taught her the names of the winds and the tides. The cave walls echoed with chants and dripping water, teaching the child the voice of the ocean and the rhythm of breath. She did not know she was a princess or a twin. She only knew at dawn that the rainbow stretched across the sky, and it was hers.

Time rippled. A chief from Kauaʻi came to visit the royal court seeking a bride of mana. Laʻielohelohe stepped forth, her voice like moonlight on still water, commanding respect. The chief admired her. Yet he sensed something more, something waiting beyond.

One night, he sang down the coast, and the winds carried the message into the cave. When Laʻieikawai heard a song and steps above her hidden home, the moʻo submerged her deeper, coiling around her like smoke around fire, protecting her. The visitors saw nothing but water. They whispered of ghosts and left.

The sun passed. Seasons turned. Laʻieikawai emerged once, gliding through the shallows in a robe of white, face masked by shadow and rainbow. A suitor approached. He could not see who she was, but felt a song in her eyes and asked her to marry him. She answered only with a song, and when he reached out, he grasped air. She vanished like mist.

On Oʻahu, Laʻielohelohe sat by the ocean and sang, remembering the child she had never met. She stepped into the water and reached for the reflection of the rainbow. The reflection wavered, and she realized her twin lived, a legend and rope of gossip that was true.

By then, the chief's council began plotting. Jealous advisors said one bride would not be enough. They spoke of politics, of alliance. The chief hesitated. He yearned for both wisdom and mystery. He demanded to see the child beneath the water, the one whose face still haunted his dreams. They brought him to Laʻie and to the cave. The moʻo rose from the water, gliding forward. The chief saw the girl within the cave through the mist. He saw the rainbow over her. He entered the water with reverence, and she stepped into his arms.

It was Laʻieikawai.

Laʻielohelohe also arrived that night, walking beneath the moon with the voice of her choir, arriving at the cave's edge. The sisters saw each other for the first time. Their eyes held the memory of womb and separation, of half a soul trembling in two hearts. They ran and embraced. The rainbow flared above, brighter than ever, a bridge of color connecting their bodies.

The chiefs were stunned. Jealousy flared. But the sisters stood together. The chief saw not one but two streams of mana. He stated that he would marry them both in separate ceremonies, pledging land and peace between islands, ensuring the balance the prophecy had feared. The jealous advisors argued, no one paying attention to the transformation of the sisters, happening before them.

One sister had learned the language of water and hidden power. The other had learned the government of the court and counsel. Together they carried the soul of their people, the unihipili of a twin light fused. Their mana became like water that heals and sky that touches. They became both hidden cave and open court, guardian and ruler, echo and song.

Their unihipili moved beyond one realm into the light of ascension. Laʻieikawai became the rainbow itself, bridging Earth and Sky whenever rain and sun met. Her shape passed into mist, into spray, into the breath of travelers. Laʻielohelohe became the song of governance, echoing in chiefs' decisions and the counsel of women in the courts of islands.

The people arguing over trying to possess the perfection of the twins lost them both. To this day, our souls are touched by the rainbow and by the song. Both things we crave but can't own or grasp. Pure soul.

La'ieikawai and La'ielohelohe did not vanish. They abide in the rainbow's light and in the voice of wisdom. They teach that our unihipili persists, even when our bodies change. That transformation is not a loss. It is becoming.

Healing Aumakua: Soul Retrieval Diagnosis

Soul Loss & Fragmentation

Soul loss happens when something traumatic happens to a person, and a piece of their soul, usually part of the aumakua, breaks off. This part of them dies and drifts through the veil. Traumas can cause a part of your soul to fragment off, leave, and it may never return. To make the soul whole again, a client must undergo a soul retrieval for a kahuna or shaman to retrieve the missing pieces and integrate them back into their spirit.

Soul loss can happen from physical abuse, sexual trauma, a car accident, getting shocking news, surgery, and even heartbreak. Some people lose part of their soul from putting up with terrible jobs, friendships, and family relationships (and on that note, stop telling people to mend things with toxic family!). Soul fragmentation can even happen through consistent immoral behavior. The patients' guilt, personal shame, or thrill-seeking behavior can continue to shock and break up someone's soul. Finally, being put through a society of not being accepted (racism, xenophobia, homophobia, political upheaval, shaming from income, class, or origin) can cause soul fragmentation.

When soul loss happens, symptoms of disease, lack of willpower, depression, bodily pains, memory loss, or even addictions can arise. Have you met people who were no longer whole? Are you not a whole person? What happened? You or they may need a soul retrieval.

Trauma looks like a lot of things. One of my clients had a trauma in the hospital nursery only a few hours after being born. Another client was bullied terribly. One survived a fire set by her father and was rescued by the next-door neighbor. Another client was raped by a group of men in the forest. Another person was forced to stay in a marriage due to circumstances. Another was frightened so severely from a car accident that it changed him forever, even though no one was hurt. Another had to retire from a job that was the prime identifier for who he was as a person. Another lost his sister to cancer, and the grief traumatized him. Trauma looks different from person to person.

Nowadays, should someone have a soul retrieval done? I would just say yes. I lived on the same street when Jaycee Lee Dugard was kidnapped, was in school during the Columbine shootings and 9/11, and watched the world implode into a self-serving cacophony of entitled "social justice" warriors, only interested in the attack so they could feel fulfilled. There are lots of traumatized people walking around in this world.

Here are some symptoms that someone might need a soul retrieval:
* Inability to make decisions
* Lack of initiative
* Difficulty finding joy or enthusiasm
* Having feelings of not being fully here
* Blocked memory or inability to remember parts of life
* Feeling emotionally remote
* Having moments of apathy
* Failure to thrive
* Inability to run their life
* Unable to feel love or receive love or help
* Feeling stuck in your life

* Impulse control in order to fill a void, but not knowing what the void is
* Unable to get out of feeling like a victim
* Unable to get out of feeling like a martyr
* Feeling disconnected from people
* Feeling like others don't listen

The Perks

The actual process is painless. It's like a calm pseudo-nap. After a month of integration, they will feel connected with the world and themselves. They will recognize direction in mind, body, and spirit. They will be able to manage things in their life that cause them stress, anxiety, or depression, and have the motivation to remove those things or create change. They get their soul back. They are fully themselves again.

The best perk of all is that if the soul is whole, there is no space for a parasitic spirit to enter.

The Downside

When the soul fragments are reunited with the body, the integration process begins. During the integration process, which takes about a moon cycle, there are steps of healing that happen. Remember that healing is painful. Cleaning out a wound hurts, and the healing process is painful while the injury is recovering. If you break a leg, the beginning part of healing is quite painful. There is an unfortunate side effect to soul retrievals. The first six days of the integration process have significant ups and downs, especially downs.

On the day of a soul retrieval, the client will be instructed to abstain from alcohol and recreational drugs. No exceptions, and this is for the entire day, including after the retrieval is complete. After the client has had a full sleep, they can return to their recreations. The integration may not take if they consume something that prevents them from fully controlling their constitution.

The following six days can be an emotional rollercoaster. For some unfortunate clients, this first part of the process can last up to three weeks, but that is rare. Almost everyone undergoes the rough patch for exactly six days. Your client will probably be part of the 'most' group. Remind them before the soul retrieval that this will happen. A really great reminder is that if they can get through the trauma that caused the break, they can get through the six days of discomfort. It's only six days. They can get through the six rough days. Count it down on a calendar if they need to, but it will be rough. Their low emotions will be noticeable, but they can conquer them.

During these six days, the spirit is getting reacquainted with how it expresses itself, with emotions. The soul itself expresses through emotions. This is why we don't consider there to be 'an emotional body' or an 'emotional part of the soul.' Emotions are how the soul expresses, not as a part of it. Emotion is action. The way we feel is an expression of our spirit for all the parts of our spirit. And if we have part of our spirit missing, our emotions are not expressed fully. Guess what naturally happens when every part of the soul is back in its place: a full range of emotional expression. The soul has to get used to its full range of expressive movement, which is uncomfortable. The good news is that it only lasts six days. Please make yourself available via email to your client at any time that is especially low, and have resources to help a client with any mental health obstacles that they may encounter during those six days.

The second week of integration is when the cloudy mind starts to lift, and focus gets better. Clarity about life direction may begin to occur, and a desire to reorganize life so that life is better. Sometimes clients become upset with the choices they made because the clarity of purpose takes hold.

The last two weeks of the integration process are less noticeable. The integration is complete after all four weeks have passed.

The transition and healing continue for about six months to two years after a soul retrieval, continuing to feel better and better and more fulfilled.

What If I Need More Than One Soul Retrieval? I've Been Through a lot!

I have had a total of three people ever need two soul retrievals, and the reasoning is at the hands of the practitioner. I, myself, have been through terrible trauma, so I feel equipped to hold a lot when bringing those trauma-filled pieces back. However, if a client has been through more than someone should have been able to survive with, or if there are just too many for me to hold, I will need to do a second one to finish the job. A second soul retrieval must happen about a month later, giving the first pieces a chance to integrate. Remember that the first soul retrieval takes four weeks to integrate the lost pieces? Allow them to integrate. After the first integration, you can do the second soul retrieval. There should never be more than two. If someone says they need to do more than two, they are trying to rip you off.

Now, everyone feels that their trauma is the worst, and that the shaman will have to make an exception for them, but that is not the case. With my private practice, I have done over a hundred soul retrievals, and I have only ever had to do a second one three times. Don't get me wrong: I have seen some terrible things that have happened to people in the visions of the retrieval, and bringing back the traumatized soul fragments can be difficult. Those of us who are appropriately trained attempt to get it done in one shot so the patient will feel better as soon as possible.

If a second one is necessary, it happens (usually) after a whole moon cycle has gone by. That way, the current pieces have fully integrated. If someone says they need to do a third, find another witchdoctor and get it done properly. That practitioner obviously needs more training, or they are ripping you off.

I Had A Soul Retrieval, and I Underwent A New Trauma

You might need another retrieval if you undergo a new trauma. Have a kahuna look at your spirit to see if there are holes. A new trauma could require a new soul retrieval.

I Had a Soul Retrieval and My Life Is Still Hard

There are other identifiers of illness. A soul retrieval does not fix all spiritual problems and dis-ease. Simply put, if you have an infection in your ear, the antibiotics are not going to fix your broken bone, too. The spiritual body is made up of nine areas, if you remember. This is why you may have to turn to other forms of healing to help with other illnesses.

Sure, the outcome of the soul retrieval feels beneficial, even euphoric after that first month; however, if your life is still out of balance, if you have psychic attacks from co-workers or live in a socio-toxic environment, mistreat your body, have no spirituality, suffer from addiction, or don't recover from risky behaviors, then a soul retrieval will not be the fix-all.

Soul Retrieval Diagnosis

In many indigenous and shamanic healing traditions, including Hawaiian, Native American, and other spiritual systems, a soul retrieval is believed to be necessary when someone experiences soul loss—a disconnection from parts of their soul or essence due to trauma, emotional pain, or life-altering events. The symptoms of soul loss are often subtle but can manifest in emotional, physical, mental, and spiritual ways. Here are common signs that someone may benefit from a soul retrieval:

Physical Symptoms

1. Fatigue or Low Energy: Chronic tiredness or a feeling of being "drained" without a clear physical cause.

2. Chronic Illness or Ailments: Recurring physical issues that seem resistant to medical treatment or explanation.

3. Sleep Disturbances: Insomnia, vivid nightmares, or an inability to feel rested even after sleeping.

Emotional Symptoms

1. Feeling "Empty" or Incomplete: A sense of hollowness or a feeling that something important is missing from within.

2. Emotional Numbness: Difficulty feeling emotions, such as joy, sadness, or anger, even during significant events.

3. Chronic Sadness or Depression: Persistent feelings of sadness or despair that seem unconnected to current circumstances.

4. Difficulty Letting Go of Trauma: Feeling stuck in the past or unable to move forward after a traumatic event.

5. Disconnection from Others: Struggling to form meaningful relationships, feeling isolated, even in the presence of loved ones.

Behavioral Symptoms

1. Addiction or Escapism: Turning to substances, overeating, or excessive distractions to avoid inner pain or emptiness.

2. Over- or Under-Reaction: Intense overreactions to small situations or, conversely, a lack of reaction to significant events.

3. Lack of Boundaries: Difficulty maintaining healthy emotional, physical, or spiritual boundaries, often resulting in codependency or burnout.

Mental Symptoms

1. Lack of Focus or Concentration: Difficulty staying present or persistent forgetfulness.

2. Self-Sabotaging Patterns: Repeating destructive behaviors or making choices that harm your well-being.

3. Chronic Anxiety or Fear: Feeling unsafe or on edge without a clear external reason.

Spiritual Symptoms
1. Disconnection from Purpose: Feeling aimless or lacking direction in life.

2. Loss of Passion or Creativity: A diminished sense of inspiration or enthusiasm for things that once brought joy.

3. Feeling Spiritually Blocked: A sense of separation from spiritual practices, intuition, or the divine.

4. Recurring Unresolved Patterns: Repeated life challenges or themes, such as toxic relationships or financial struggles, that feel beyond your control

Causes of Soul Loss
Soul loss is often linked to life events or circumstances that cause deep emotional, physical, or spiritual wounding. Common causes include:
- Trauma: Abuse, violence, or witnessing a traumatic event.

- Loss: Death of a loved one, a miscarriage, or a major breakup.

- Sudden Shock: Accidents, surgeries, or unexpected disasters.

- Prolonged Stress: Living in a toxic environment, chronic illness, or extreme hardship.

How Soul Retrieval Helps

Soul retrieval is a spiritual healing practice in which a healer or practitioner journeys to recover the lost pieces of a person's soul and reintegrates them into the individual. This process is believed to:

- Restore a sense of wholeness and vitality.

- Reconnect the individual with their passions and purpose.

- Help release lingering emotional or energetic blocks tied to past trauma.

- Strengthen emotional and spiritual resilience.

If someone resonates with these symptoms, a soul retrieval can be an opportunity to explore deeper healing, but it's important to seek guidance from a skilled and trusted healer familiar with this practice.

The Death of Souls of 2020

May 2020. The people of the world were trapped in their homes, and we were all afraid. Some people were anxious to go back to the abusive life they had at their in-person jobs, some people had no money and were literally starving, and some were thriving with the realization that they were doing everything wrong. The global pandemic caused trauma for everyone, and my practice was busy because of this global trauma.

We all had a moment, at least one week, where we had to sit and think about our lives. Many people posted on social media ways for us to self-care and handle being at home together, me included. I offered free videos of dance instruction and concerts to keep people occupied while they were all stuck at home. And in the activities for folks to distract themselves from the very probable imminent illness (or mortality), we watched the tragedy of death sweep the world. Some handled this with blatant denial, while our health professionals risked their traumatized lives every day to save the thousands of people dying. Some handled it with sorrow, realizing their impermanence. Some were distracted, and some had to face being ill themselves.

My practice was busy. People realized from this trauma that they had other traumas as well. These people saved money on gas and other frivolous things and decided to turn to healing themselves. I was hired to do soul retrievals. From April 2020 through November 2021, Soul Retrievals were my most hired service.

However, during this time, I also learned that I needed to address my own healing. A healer is uniquely in tune with their energy and the energies of others. A healer who brings in their own personal issues and energetic sicknesses to a healing session is irresponsible and ineffective.

I learned to reprioritize love and affection, updating my hobbies, physical exercise I enjoy, and no longer tolerating volatile interactions at the top of my actions so that I could be more effective at healing others.

This purging went on through the pandemic and then afterwards. I continue in the spirit of the virus to attack and remove those things that infect my life. No more friends, family, or partners of any kind may be as poisonous, infectious, or debilitating as the coronavirus in my life.

I encourage you to hold onto that lesson, as well.

Remember where your money should go.

Remember where your time should go.

Remember not to get an infection.

Keep a distance from strangers until you know who they spend their time with.

And know your inner bubble.

Oh, and wash your hands.

Soul Retrieval Process

A soul retrieval is used to heal aumakua. Traumas that have happened to us, which have affected our brains, need to be put back together and repaired. The mind part of our soul, when missing pieces, can leave someone vulnerable to spiritual attack.

Tools You Will Need:
Stand-up mirror: This will be your portal to find your client's flame if you have difficulty connecting with your client while on the other side.

A *tea-light candle*: This will be the flame of your client. It sits in front of your stand-up mirror. It should be white.

Boat: This boat is a symbol of a journey. Your boat can be a candy dish or a bowl. Mine is an outrigger canoe. When you get up into the lobby of your mind, the energy from your symbolic boat will transform into a bag of some kind. When I travel, I usually carry a blue Santa bag, but many people have a side satchel or something like that. It will just happen; don't worry too much about it.

Statue: Have an effigy of some kind that connects you to spirit. I have a figure of Kane. Yours can be the cross, Yamoya, Jesus, Lucifer, or whatever grounds you to your faith.

Grey Candle, Orange Candle: Let me walk you through a pinch of candle theory. Everyone wants blue for healing, which, yes, it does, through relaxation and calming the system. We, however, are going to use orange to invigorate the system during rest to accept the pieces of the soul. With a grey candle, the black parts of the color are almost nullified. This is particularly beneficial for the dead, as it pertains to the natural aspects of good and evil. Because trauma may be the fault of the victim, or there may be guilt, or worse, something polarizing happened, the grey candle will help to keep you neutral and objective while receiving the pieces.

Sending Tool: I will clarify this, but you will need a way to send the pieces back to your client. I will give you a multitude of ways (Mirror with breath, ritual sticks, or a stone to give the client).

Noise-Canceling Headphones: You can't get distracted while handling someone's traumatic experiences.

> **NOTE ON TOOLS: Do not skip this part. Doing a soul retrieval without your tools is like performing surgery with your fingernails.**

Set-up:
Prepare the room as a sacred space, performing a Watchtower Ritual of Protection, making the space full of soft light and soft fabrics, and making it look peaceful and healing. Environment matters to you. I will tell you that doing a soul retrieval in the middle of a busy hospital emergency room is quite difficult because the environment is not created for such an event (let's say that it is spiritually not sterile), or perhaps to perform a soul retrieval in an abandoned haunted mental institution. Clean your space and make it spiritually ready for healing.

We put you in the center. However you lie or sit, that is the center point. In front of you, directly, is your mirror with your candle in front of it. To your right are your sending tools. On your left is the boat, the grey candle, and the statue. Behind you, a bit away so it doesn't get knocked over, is the orange candle. I keep my notebook (book of mirrors), my sticks, my lighter, my headphones, and my rattle on my right. If done remotely, have your computer and camera in front of you, but quite a bit away. You don't want the electromagnetic energy of the computer to keep you from traveling. In any case, your client should be about five feet in front of you, behind the mirror.

The Process of a Soul Retrieval:

1. *Why Do You Need A Soul Retrieval?* Talk to the client to find out why they believe they need a soul retrieval. Ask them about their life symptoms. Generally speaking, I do not ask about their traumas, so it doesn't affect my travel. Remember that your travel needs to happen to you, so any of that information could influence what happens in your imagination, taking the reins.

2. *Explain how the process will go:* They will need headphones and will listen to the same drums that you listen to (if done over a video call). They will lie there with their eyes closed, listening to the drums. If they go to sleep, they don't need to worry because you will just wake them when you are done. They are not allowed to try to help. They just rest and relax. The process of the soul retrieval is easy for them during this part. Enjoy the rest time. While you are gone, they may see your aura (like a color) in their eyes with their eyes closed. This is normal, but it's also normal not to see or experience anything. They just need to relax and not participate while you work. You will connect with them, their energy, and their brainwaves at theta. You will be able to sync up and find their fragmented pieces.

Remind them that soul fragments happen when people have trauma in their lives and that parts of their soul break off and die during those times of trauma, going to various locations of the Spirit World, usually the Lower World. You will find those pieces with the help of your power-animal and other spirits and bring them back. Explain that a soul retrieval is usually "one and done" unless a new trauma happens after they've been healed, and new pieces of the soul are fractured. In rare cases, they would need a second retrieval. This depends intensely on what the shaman or kahuna can handle.

In most cases, you should be fine with doing it in one shot. If they need a second one, you will need to do it a month after the first integration to ensure that the pieces you brought back the first time are fully integrated.

3. *Go over aftercare instructions*: On the day of the retrieval, it is very, very, very important (yeah, three very-s) that they do not drink alcohol or have any recreational drugs until after they have had a full night's sleep. After that first night, they can go back to their recreational activities. The first six days are the worst part of the integration process. During the integration process, they will experience both highs and lows, likely to be in extremes. All of this is normal. For those who partake in recreational drugs or alcohol during the first six days, the six days will probably last 2-3 weeks. It doesn't mean that integrating their soul isn't working; it's just taking a little longer to heal. Most people get through the rough part of the integration process in six to eight days, but this turbulent period can last up to three weeks. I have noticed that clients who use marijuana based interventions (even regularly or prescribed) fall into this category. It doesn't mean that they won't be healed. Use just means that it will take a few weeks longer.

Please make yourself available to them via messenger or email for this section of their healing. They may feel crazed or depressed or like they are emotionally spinning. Tell them, "It's only six days, and I know you can make it through six days, considering you've made it through terrible trauma." That statement is true and gives them back their power.

4. *Ask if they have questions.*

5. *It's time for the retrieval*. Ask them to lie down and listen to the drums with their eyes closed. Put on your drum music. Do your Watchtower Protection while they settle in. Check your tools to make sure they are all there. Take one look at your boat and then the statue. Light your grey and orange candles. Then, light your tea candle, focusing on connecting your client's energy to the flame and have them settle down. Remember that lighting this candle represents your client. You will feel them connect to this candle as you burn it. Suppose you don't feel that connection; have them light a candle as well at the same time. Ensure both candles are at a safe distance from you both so as not to get knocked over while you are spirit-walking (and away from pets and children).

Put on your noise-canceling headphones (mute them if they are on video). Settle in.

A. Breathe

B. Stairs and Mind Dump

C. Feel for your "bag"; this will be how you collect the pieces.

D. And now it's time to travel. Once you decide if you are jumping the hedge, The Bay, or another way, tell your power-animal that you two are retrieving so-and-so's missing soul pieces and that you will need guidance to take you to the traumas. Believe me, you will just go.

E. Do not interpret the traumas. Just go and watch what you see. Sometimes the soul fragments will be in the Middle World, stuck like a ghost in a location, and sometimes the fragments will be lost in the Upper World, but most of the time, they will be in the Lower World. Remember the *Alice in Wonderland* metaphor? Yeah, it's about to get weird.

F. As you come across a trauma, watch it play out in how it is presented to you. You will probably see your client at a different age. When there is a pause, approach the client kindly from that memory replay and ask if you can take them with you. That their current self needs them and wants to be whole again, you may need to hug them, embrace them, or, in some off-handed cases, take them by brute force. Put them in your bag, then get the next fragment. Again, allow what happens to happen (see Lucifer's story for an example of an odd soul retrieval. He only had one piece to bring back, but your clients may need many brought back.).

G. When you come across a fragment, you will ask the segment to go with you. You will collect that fragment and be ready to release it. You are temporarily holding their trauma until you can give that piece of them back.

As you do the retrieval, you will find that some of this trauma is hard to experience or carry. Remember that you can do it and that this is temporary. Be as resilient as you can. Every once in a while, someone has been through more trauma than the witchdoctor can carry in one go. Some of what you see/experience will be delivered in metaphor. During the retrieval, don't try to interpret, just experience. You may see some strange things, and you may see some very real things. Each event/fragment is individual, meaning that just because the first seems like a metaphor, it doesn't mean that all of the fragments you are gathering will be metaphors. Experience, collect, leave.

H. When you have all the pieces, you will go back to your body.

I have found that I usually get a message on my way back from one of the gods or a spirit, either for my client or for me. Don't rush back; journey and allow the Spirit Current to feel your presence.

6. **Send back:** Through one of the techniques listed below, send back the pieces from the spirit-walk. Bad things will happen to you both if you do not do this part.

If I could make this part blink with red and white flashing lights, I would. If you don't give the soul pieces back, you will have parts of someone else's soul, the parts that split from trauma, stuck inside you, becoming a part of you, and you will need an exorcism from the soul pieces that will fuse with your soul, after they are cut out. These scared parts, which were replaying their trauma in the Other World, will replay in you. When they incorporate back with their soul body, they find comfort and heal back together, fusing beautifully. When in someone else, they are tormented and confused, tormenting and confusing the retriever. You must release the pieces.

Here are your choices:

Blow: In many cultures, the shaman will blow the pieces out into the person's forehead, chest, or through the feet. You may use a bamboo pipe or cup your hands into a tunnel. You will blow until all of their pieces are out of you and in them. Some of my students blow out their fragments into the candle and the mirror. They will continue to blow at the candle/mirror until they know the pieces are out of them, even though the candle's flame is already out. You just know.

Press Into a Stone: You can press the pieces out through your hands into a stone or crystal for which you give them. Your client will then carry or wear that crystal. This takes a bit longer to work because their soul pieces have to move from the crystal to them.

Hit Two Large Sticks: This is the technique I use. I have two large sticks that were once a staff I used in my craft. The spirits told me to lean into my African roots and do it this way. I used to do the stone method for years until one of the spirits I work with told me to switch. I rock and shake the sticks in my hands above my head, moving their fragments into my arms and then to my hands. I then hit the sticks together, releasing them into the sky, allowing the air we all breathe to carry them to the client within minutes. I keep rocking and hitting until I feel the pieces are out of me.

Make Sure To Send The Pieces Back!

You can do a final step, which I recommend, of sealing the soul into place. After you send, take a rattle and rattle over the body/mirror. I like this part in case you feel the soul fragments were disagreeable or squirrelly.

7. *Document*: After you send the pieces back, write down everything you remember happening. When you are traveling, the learning part of your brain is not active. The thoughts will go away quickly, like a dream, so hurry and write everything down. This is also helpful if the client asks a question about something you brought back since you probably won't remember.

8. *Bring the client back*: Say gently, "So-and-so, I'm back." Then, ask how it was for them and if they want to talk about their experience. Then ask if they would like to hear what you experienced. They can say no. Remind them that sometimes what you experience is in a metaphor and that it may not make sense as you explain it right now.

This is not a time for them to relive what they have been through. This is not a regression. It's not about remembering what happened to them or convincing them of what you found. Just an explanation of what you saw, the way you found it. Explain the age that they looked to you, but remind them that you do not have childhood pictures to compare, so you are estimating age. If there is sexual trauma, start by being vague and without judgment. Check your prejudice at the door. This is the doctor part of being a witchdoctor. Be clear, don't overelaborate, and don't have judgment in your statements. "I saw you at about six years old, and there appeared to be sexual trauma. I saw someone else there, an older male who appeared to me with brown hair; he was caucasian." Do not assume what you saw was "You were raped when you were six by your dad." Your assumption can destroy a perfectly good relationship, and you, in your statement, can traumatize them right then and there. They are there to get healing, not explanations from you about their past. I repeat, do not make assumptions about what you experienced. Just explain what you experienced. Be sensitive, but there is no need to edit. You can explain what they may have always suspected by phrasing things the way you saw them.

If what you experience is "I saw a dragon covered in snow, choking on ice, and while I watched, he shrank into an egg. The egg was the fragment I brought back." Or: "I was surrounded by blackness (in the upper world) and from nowhere, as I and my totem waited, there were shards, like slices of crystals, as if someone had sliced your soul into slides for a microscope. There were ten, and I brought them back. I could not look into them." It is not up to you to interpret what these mean. NEVER. You are the carrier and the healer here. You are not doing a psychic reading, you are not doing priest work, you are not here to give that guidance. Your job is to retrieve and put back, and heal. They will figure out what it means.

Remind them that they are not going to relive their trauma by having their soul back. The trauma broke the soul. The soul fragment is not their trauma, but the piece of themselves that hid or died *from* the trauma. Trauma was the cut that broke the soul. They aren't getting the 'cut,' back. They are getting the piece back.

9. *Go over aftercare again*: The first six days will be the worst. Remind them that with a complete soul, they will experience very strong emotions because their spirit is fully able to express itself. The highs will be extremely high, and the lows will be extremely low. Be careful of outbursts and encourage them to avoid doing any spiritual work or making legal decisions during this time. After that, the following week should be when brain fog lifts and their concentration improves. They will have direction in life and may be confused by what is suddenly clear. They may have new and exciting decisions to make. The following two weeks are the solidification of the integration. There can be mood

swings and more clarity, but everything will be more subtle. There can be improvements continuing for six months to two years!

10. *Answer any remaining questions:* Tell them they can reach out during the first integration portion to talk through their mind and emotional jumbles through an appropriate means of communication, one of which you designated.

Fluff's Failure or What Happens If You Don't Send the Soul Fragments Back

Characters:
Me
Fluff - A disagreeable student

During my Advanced Hawaiian Shamanic Healing course, students perform a soul retrieval on a volunteer. The students are all taught to be prepared and have all their tools ready. Everything is double-checked and triple-checked. The students may not all get fragments, but they all know how. They practice walking through the steps of telling the client what is going to happen and how everyone will be working.

In one class, I had a difficult student. This one student, Fluff, came late to class. Everyone else had come to class on time, checked their tools and steps, and layers of safety and protection, and the steps to walk the client through the healing process. When Fluff finally arrived, we were all in the middle of preparing the volunteer. The volunteer had been through a lot in his life, suffering from addictions, violence, and overwhelming letdowns. Fluff kept to herself as the rest of the students prepped the volunteer. Finally, it was time for everyone to do the soul retrieval for the volunteer. They started the drumming, prepped their space, got him to lie down, and began their journey.

The students went traveling. When the students traveled, I remained up and psychically read them. I was more productive reading the status of the students than traveling myself. This way, I could watch over the class in a trance state rather than leave my body and wander around the spirit world trying to track them all.

This class had twelve students, which is more than I can read all at once, so only half were supposed to do the soul retrieval. I figured Fluff wouldn't participate since she was late and hadn't been part of the class's preparation. My fault was in that assumption. I was only psychically reading the six students who were assigned to do the retrieval, actively not reading the others, keeping my focus on what was going on.

The students who received their pieces back sent the fragments. They all explained what they had seen. When the client left class, Fluff had said that she had found a rape incident, but didn't say anything. I reminded her that assuming it was rape is not appropriate unless she saw the actual rape happening. She said that she saw him in a closet and that there was sexual assault.

"I didn't see you send it back. How did you send it back?" I asked.

"What do you mean?" Fluff asked in a more unprepared and inattentive way. The other students were wide-eyed in shock, remembering the big lecture I gave on the importance of sending back the pieces (That is the whole point, after all).

"You have to send the soul piece back, Fluff! How did you send it back?" I said.

"Oh, I just visualized giving that kid a hug." She said.

"No! That is not an actual technique. Visualization is not active. Blow, sticks, push into a gift that you'll give him... You must have a physical response to get it out of your body. What are you going to do? You need to get it out. He needs that back." I was panicked.

"Ok, ok, I will blow or something," she dismissed me.

"You need to do it now," I pressed. The students were amazed by her brazenness. She left the class, and based on her future behavior, we know she did not send the lost fragments back.

A month later, Fluff was acting like she had lost her mind. Fluff used fake names to email me, telling me I was a piece of shit. She emailed places I was on the board of directors, left fake reviews on my social media, and cyberstalked. Fluff harassed me for almost five months, sending me bullying emails at least once a week, threatening me, calling me names, and questioning my character. Under her fake name, Fluff even made the mistake of sending her harassments from her government-issued computer. We traced her IP address, revealing her government information. Fluff was willing to risk her job for the sake of harassment. This is not someone of sound mind, and had willingly disregarded instructions.

She made threats to my marriage, my children, and my parents, and made vulgar comments about my being gay in harassment emails and messages. Fluff had become a hate crime assailant, consistently sending attacks weekly.

Why? What happened? Because she was hosting our volunteer's traumatized soul from class. She would need an extraction to take that piece out. Her soul now had a foreign body in it. The piece that someone else needs in order to heal is a poison to her emotional state, inspiring her to act out in illegal, impulsive, and damaging ways. And the poor volunteer still isn't whole.

She was the example for all students to send back the soul fragments.

Wala'au or Stay Sick

In Hawaii, we wala 'au (vala ouch, just no ch). Contextually, wala 'au means to talk story. We share what is going on in our lives. The importance is in purging and cleaning. Think about your life as a cyst. You've got to lance it, drain it, clean it, and then cover it to keep it clean. Talking about what is going on in your life does just that. Break it open, talk about everything that has happened to you, figure out how to keep your energy clean, so you don't get infected again, and then mend.

I strongly believe in therapy for the exorcist and the client. I don't know what I would do without my wonderful therapists over the years. Yes, they know what I do, and what I do scares them, as it should. However, I still need to talk about it. I need to heal from the psychological wounds from the work I do, and so will you.

When it comes to finding a therapist, remember that 1) not everyone graduates at the top of their class, 2) some therapists are suffering from empathy fatigue and aren't emotionally available to you, even if their calendar is open, and 3) some are prejudiced. When it comes to your mental health, if you don't fit with a therapist, fire them. I am not saying that you should always be comfortable. Therapy should be uncomfortable at times; you are healing, after all. But if you feel you can't be yourself and talk about what you've been through, then that therapist is not for you. At one point, I met with seven different therapists before I finally landed on one. Meeting all those therapists and starting the intake was time-consuming and frustrating, but I don't want you to settle either. Once you have your therapist, you can encourage your client to also talk to someone, as well.

Talking doesn't have to be with a professional therapist, however. The client could talk to you, and in that case, they are paying for your time and advice, not your licensure. Talking and listening doesn't mean that you are giving counseling (which will be covered in another book in the series), but you are providing a safe place for your client to feel they can talk about what has happened.

I recommend eight consecutive weeks of talking about what had happened to them spiritually, ensuring that they continue to use words in the past tense. Normalize, tell the stories about it, and heal.

I aim to establish a clear boundary. There are individuals who consciously or unconsciously choose to remain in a state of illness. These individuals, whether afflicted with physical or spiritual ailments, cannot be effectively assisted until they separate their self-worth from the identity of being sick. This process typically requires psychological counseling. Attempting to address their healing or possession issues without addressing this fundamental attachment to illness is likely to result in failure or short-lived success, leading to a recurrence of their problems or possibly even more severe issues. Their deep entrenchment in their illness or possession has become the basis of their identity, necessitating a dismantling and rebuilding of their foundation before meaningful progress can be made. They must receive alternative forms of assistance first.

Neglect

I am deeply concerned about the impact of neglect and the lack of care provision. Human beings require essential elements such as food, shelter, love, attention, safety, identity, purpose, and a sense of belonging. When these fundamental needs are unmet, individuals may adapt their lives to seek care from others to fulfill the void neglected earlier in life. Neglect can occur not only in childhood but also within relationships, workplaces, educational settings, and friendships. The absence of meeting these basic needs can result in psychological harm.

A mental health practitioner plays a pivotal role in addressing and repairing the psychological wounds through therapeutic interventions, often referred to as wala'au (talking story) or therapy. Failure to address and heal these psychological wounds can lead to the manifestation of somatic illnesses. It is important to understand that somatic illnesses are genuine conditions experienced by patients in a very real manner. However, individuals coping with these conditions require care and support from others to overcome their illnesses. When this care is provided, they may fear being abandoned by their caregivers. Somatic illness can be seen as the spiritual self (aumakua) afflicting the physical self (uhane).

Therefore, individuals who have endured a history of neglect may resist healing efforts, seeking continued illness to receive the care and attention they were deprived of in their past neglectful experiences, in an attempt to avoid feelings of abandonment. They may feel a sense of dependency on others due to the obligation of care. Effective assistance for these individuals is contingent upon addressing and processing the psychological scars and injuries stemming from neglect. They must confront and work through their experiences of neglect before true healing and progress can occur.

Identity

I encourage my clients to envision themselves five months ahead, sitting on a porch, sipping iced tea, reflecting in the past tense about the period when they were troubled by possession. Can they visualize a life free from this spiritual affliction? Do they eagerly anticipate all the possibilities awaiting them once they are liberated from the entity that haunts them?

Alternatively, are they firmly entrenched in a cycle of lamenting their troubles, deeply ingrained in their self-identity as someone possessed? Do they possess a clear vision of what their life could be like without these burdens? For individuals struggling to disentangle their identity from their spiritual affliction, the concept of Life Balance can offer valuable support.

Those who cling to the idea of possession as an intrinsic part of themselves are inadvertently allowing their spiritual guardian (aumakua) to maintain a hold on the spirit haunting them. The client must embark on a journey of self-discovery, focusing on celebrating their abilities and accomplishments, thereby altering their personal narrative. Otherwise, by remaining attached to the identity of the possessed, they risk unwittingly inviting back the spirit into their lives.

To achieve success, individuals must distance themselves from the notion of being possessed. As a healer, you cannot intervene directly in their willingness to let go of this identity. If the client remains deeply intertwined with the spirit, breaking this symbiotic relationship becomes a challenging task.

Fear

Fear triggers a hormonal response that leads to heightened arousal in the body. Prolonged exposure to cortisol, due to fear, can have negative impacts on overall health. As an exorcist, it is essential to address and manage your own fears effectively. Engaging in discussions with your clients about their fears and fear-driven thought patterns can help determine if the fear is something they can navigate through or a source of debilitating distress.

If the client is receptive to engaging in shadow work to dismantle any dependency on fear-based thinking, you can provide valuable assistance. However, if the fear is deeply ingrained and causes catastrophic thoughts or contributes to a panic disorder, they must seek professional mental health support. Encourage them to understand that seeking help from a mental health professional should not carry any stigma.

It is important to normalize the idea of seeking mental health care in the same way we seek treatment for physical health issues. Just as we visit an orthopedist for a broken bone or bone disorder, individuals experiencing grief, trauma, panic disorders, or catastrophic thinking should seek professional support to address and heal their mental wounds. For those who require regular medication to manage anxiety, proper treatment can pave the way for effective intervention and assistance from you as the exorcist.

What Do You Do?

Refer them, help them get the help they need, and then you can do your part.

I'll Talk, But No Therapy

Thomas is sitting across from me during our "Spiritual Life Coaching" session. He doesn't like to call it therapy, even though that's what we are doing.

"Therapy manifests more negativity," Thomas says.

"Why do you think that?" I asked him. "Teach me."

"Well, I work on a higher vibration, so I recognize that when you work on a higher vibration, if you spend time in therapy, it lowers your vibration."

"Ok," I waited.

"Yeah, by going to some quack and complaining about your childhood, you are putting out into the universe that you want more of that. And what's a therapist going to do anyway other than take your money so you can continue to have bad problems and fill up his chair for eternity." Thomas was set in this philosophy.

"How are things with your wife?" I asked.

"Terrible..." he said. Thomas went on to talk about the struggles he was having in his marriage. I listened, validated him, and pointed out when he was untruthful. I related, but for the most part, he did the talking. He purged, like he did every week, all of the problems and obstacles he was facing.

He didn't like to call it "Spiritual Counseling," remember?

Healing with Stories: Catharsis

In the fast-paced, and frankly stressful world we live in, finding solace and healing for our minds are hard to come by. One powerful source of comfort and rejuvenation comes from the world of stories, movies, songs, dances, and entertainment. The ability of narratives and performance experiences to heal, inspire, and uplift the human psyche is undeniable.

Stories have been an integral part of human culture since the times of sitting around a fire as the only means of warmth. Stories have the remarkable ability to transport us to different worlds, allowing us to escape reality, if only for a moment. Whether through books, movies, TV shows, or other forms of entertainment, stories engage our imagination and emotions, providing a much-needed break from the demands of everyday life.

One of the most significant ways in which stories heal the human psyche is through emotional catharsis. Watching a character overcome challenges, face their fears, or find redemption can evoke powerful emotions within us, enabling us to process our own feelings and experiences. In a way, stories serve as a mirror to our own lives, helping us make sense of the world around us and offering insights into our own journeys.

Stories have the capacity to instill hope, resilience, and empathy in us. By witnessing characters navigate through adversity and emerge stronger on the other side, we are reminded of our own inner strength and capacity for growth. Stories can also foster empathy by allowing us to see the world through the eyes of others, promoting understanding and compassion for different perspectives and experiences.

In addition to providing emotional healing, stories, movies, and entertainment can also serve as a form of therapy. Whether it's through the comfort of familiar characters, the inspiration of a hero's journey, or the solace of a happy ending, these narratives have the potential to soothe our troubled minds and nourish our spirits.

The healing power of stories, movies, and entertainment on the human psyche is profound and multifaceted. From offering emotional catharsis and fostering empathy to instilling hope and resilience, these narratives have the ability to uplift, inspire, and heal us.

In indigenous cultures around the world, storytelling has always held a sacred and central place in community life. The traditional narratives passed down through generations are not just tales for entertainment, but powerful tools for healing, connection, and preserving cultural identity. Within these societies, storytelling serves as a means to remind individuals of their shared humanity and to heal the collective spirit of the tribe.

In many indigenous communities, storytelling is seen as a way to bridge the past, present, and future. Through myths, legends, and oral histories, elders impart valuable wisdom and knowledge to the younger generations, ensuring that cultural traditions and values are preserved and passed on. These stories often carry moral lessons, guiding community members on how to live harmoniously with one another and with the natural world.

Storytelling in indigenous cultures has a profound healing impact on both individuals and the tribe as a whole. Through the art of storytelling, community members are able to process shared traumas, grief, and struggles, fostering a sense of understanding and solidarity among them. By speaking truths through allegory and metaphor, storytellers can help individuals confront difficult emotions and experiences in a safe and supportive environment.

Furthermore, storytelling serves as a mechanism for unity and connection within indigenous tribes. When stories are shared in communal gatherings or ceremonies, they create a sacred space where individuals can come together, bond over shared experiences, and strengthen their sense of belonging to the community. These narratives often emphasize the interconnectedness of all living beings, promoting empathy, compassion, and respect for diversity within the tribe.

Through the art of storytelling, indigenous cultures heal and unify. These narratives remind individuals of their roots, their values, and their shared humanity, fostering a sense of belonging and interconnectedness within the tribe. By preserving and honoring traditional stories, indigenous communities continue to nurture the spirit of their people and pass down the legacy of wisdom and healing for generations to come.

Consider helping with the healing of someone's mind with a story, something someone can relate to, or receive a catharsis that releases the pain and begins the healing process of regenerating the healing of the soul.

Stalkers on Maui

The concept of celebrity stalking is as intricate as it is alarming. Although our obsession with performers has existed for centuries, technological advancements now allow us to be more intimately connected with the actors and their curated personas. A growing number of fans develop unhealthy attachments to certain actors, often those who have an uncanny ability to elicit a wide range of emotions from their captivated audience.

At the core of stalking lies a psychological phenomenon known as parasocial interactions. These are engagements and connections that are one-sided, where an individual builds a bond with a performer through their public appearances, performances, and personal narratives. This bond often transcends the boundaries of normal social interaction and can lead to idealization and overidentification with the celebrity in question.

What drives stalking is the longing for escape. In the context of storytelling, singers, dancers, and actors possess the ability to transport audiences to another world - a world filled with excitement, passion, and healing. A person who feels lost or disillusioned in their own life might turn to these performers as symbols of their ideal self or a form of temporary relief. The intense emotions these actors can evoke become entangled with their fans' own feelings of dissatisfaction or yearning.

The characters portrayed by skilled actors also influence the development of unhealthy attachments. Characters that embody goodness, courage, or other admirable qualities often attract fans who seek these attributes in their own lives. Over time, this fascination can morph into infatuation or fixation, leading stalkers to believe that a close relationship with their favorite actor is not only possible, but crucial for their own happiness.

The first time I was stalked, I was performing in *Little Shop of Horrors* as Seymour. For such a little person, I have a pretty strong voice, and there was a man walking past the side theater door while I was singing *The Meek Shall Inherit*. I had on a baseball hat, which would be similar to the one I would wear in the show. The three women singing behind me were at a pause to discuss their harmonies, while I was given some direction on how to play with different riffs. Back then, I wasn't likely to say anything about the man watching; it was good advertisement, right?

"Let's take it from 'I sign these contracts.' Aly, are you ready?" The musical director asked.

"Yep."

"Ladies?"

They nodded. The pianist gave me my pitch, and with a nod, I started singing. I couldn't take my eyes off the man outside, growing a little more uneasy. He turned his body from watching profile to facing me full front. As I continued singing about Audrey, I turned my body away from him so I could focus on the acting. "Good," I was interrupted. "Can you riff down after 'lovely,' on that 'Audrey?'" She asked.

"Yes. No problem," I turned to see if the man was still there, and he had walked into the theater. I looked over at our assistant director, who saw my unease and stood.

"What is this?" asked the man.

The assistant director replied, "We are rehearsing for *Little Shop of Horrors*. The show opens in a month, and tickets are available online already. If you…"

"Who's that?" He pointed at me.

"Aly. He's the lead. He plays Seymore. He is adorable, you should come see him."

He paused. "I'd like that," he said leeringly.

That night, when I went to my car, he was standing behind a bush, watching me. I waved, got in my car, and quickly drove off.

That man stood outside after every rehearsal and show, and because of that, one of the male cast members or crew walked me to my car every night.

Four years later, I was singing in a Christmas concert in the same theater. I was rehearsing late with only the stage manager, so she could work on lighting cues to my song. From the front entrance, the same man walked in, stood there, and watched me, leaning against the wall. I stopped singing and announced, "Sorry, the theater is closed," and at that, the stage manager was already moving towards him.

In my performing career, people became enamored with what I put out on the stage. All because we sometimes need to have someone in our lives who we believe is strong, needs to be taken care of, or to covet.

Life Balance

The ultimate goal of health is balance.

Many of the reasons we are sick have to do with an unbalanced life. In an allopathic culture, we treat the wound, but not how it got injured. I personally believe in balance with holistic and allopathic techniques. Think of allopathics as if there is a hole in the dam. We put our finger in it to stop the leak, and we may even patch it up, but how did it happen in the first place? Can we prevent it from happening again? What are we doing that caused the break? Let's address those things in all forms of sickness, injury, and dis-ease.

By having a balanced life, we can keep the physical body healthy.

Symptoms of an Unbalanced Life

- Excessively acquiring material things
- Selfishness & greed
- Deceit
- Detail
- Spotlight Syndrome: Over-emphasis on the self
- Isolation
- Expendable people/environment
- Obsession with the importance of youthfulness
- Inability to recognize the importance of tradition & history
- "Whoever has the most, wins."
- Rudeness, arrogance, aggression
- Excessive emphasis on completing tasks
- Doing vs. being
- Bragging, showing off, challenging others
- Superficial relationships

To heal these environments that affect your aumakua, we must look at the areas of life's balance. Our goal is to even out the areas with a strong foundation of spirituality.

First, your foundation is your spirituality. In indigenous practices, spirituality isn't a part of yourself separated from everything else. Your connection to spirit and your faith should be the foundation that leads or supports the other six areas.

Spirituality: Mana

Since the beginning of human consciousness, we have always been connected to spirit in some way, and no matter how philosophies or establishments try to stop people from believing in spirit, belief in the supernatural, in the spiritual, pervades. More people believe in spirits than in anything else. We all could literally come together as one cooperative species based on that principle. If we put that aside and everyone connected to their belief in spirit, we would have a more balanced life.

Your spirituality doesn't require you to have a doctrine, a church, a deity, or any defining aspect other than one thing: belief in something bigger than yourself. What is something that makes you feel safe, makes you get up in the morning, and causes you to attempt to be better with every breath?

The next question is this: Do you allow your spirituality to drive or support the other aspects of your life? If not, why? If not, why not change that?

Spirituality is not something you pick up one day a week. We breathe it with every breath, and we move with it in every action. Do you listen to your gut instincts? Do you spontaneously connect with a god, meditation, spirit, or family traditions? Or do you limit your interaction by scheduling it? Do you feel heard by your higher power? Does your religion give you comfort instead of obligation or fear? Do you believe in something?

Mana is the spiritual aura that resides in all things. Recognize and connect your mana to all that is around you.

The Six Areas of Life Balance:

Sense of Self: Hanohano

Who are you? What is your identity? This is your self-esteem, things you enjoy, personality characteristics, strengths, and weaknesses. Some people define themselves by what has happened to them or what they've done in the world instead of descriptors that indicate the *kind* of person they are. Describe yourself today. Can you? If not, why?

Without a sense of self, we can develop depression, anxiety, and somatic illnesses. We may create illnesses from life habits that are created as a means to mask the pain from this area being weak, like sugary foods, drugs, or other excessive escapist choices.

There are personality tests, astrological charts, and profile assessments, which all help you define yourself. Find what works for you, what you identify with, and hold tight. Also, allow yourself to evolve and change. Then surround yourself with the following areas, which can support and not break down this sensitive area.

Are you confident and comfortable with who you are? Do negative thoughts get the better of you? Do you believe in yourself?

Hanohano is honor and dignity. Enhance and protect your own spirit with your breath. Remember that it is yours.

Job/Money: Pa'ahana

How satisfied are you with your financial security? How do you feel about your current financial situation? Do you waste your money, or are you investing in your interests or other areas? Is your compensation too low for the quality of life you require? Are you willing to take risks to generate more income? Do you like your job? Can you use generosity to others?

Compensation is how the world tells you of your value. If you don't like that world, why not change it? Why not move to make that change? How you invest most of your time also affects your mental health. If you don't enjoy your job enough to keep going, why not apply for something else? Is something other than yourself preventing you from having a more enjoyable life? Does your job believe in you?

Pa'ahana means industry. Having purpose in our life through the production of our will or labor, and receiving compensation and recognition, builds the thickness of our disposition.

Nature/Community: Ho'okipa

Do you get out in nature at least once a week? Do you socialize three times a week? Do you have a creative outlet? Do you have something that gives you a sense of belonging? Do you feel you don't belong because of your local community's view on race, sexual orientation, appearance, disability, gender, or employment? Do you belong to a club or group?

What about around the house? How are your home responsibilities? Do other people's comfort matter over your comfort? Do you like the state or city you live in? Do you feel connected to the culture of those around you?

This area is your literal foundation. Your home, your community, and your environment. Do you feel you thrive in the soil of your area? If not, why? What's missing to help nurture you? And how can you make a change? Do people in your neighborhood believe in you?

Ho'okipa means hospitality. Sharing your love without the purpose of impressing, by offering what is around you. Share and offer to nature, your community, and the spirits.

Health: Ma'ema'e

Is your physical health important to you? Are you happy with your physical health? What about your physical appearance? If you think about how you handle stress or how stress handles you, do you like the plan you have? Does stress affect you more than fleeting? Are you able to enjoy physical things at least once a week? How is your stamina? Your sexual health? Do a physical check of your body as a whole. How are we doing?

See a doctor, move, eat well, and sleep. If you don't have those basic needs, are you healthy? Will your body hold up so you can do everything you want to do?

Ma'ema'e means to take care of your body, spirit, and mind by means of authenticity. Authentic food, authentic words, authentic action with a commitment to avoiding negativity, confusion, and to cleanse ourselves of diseases.

Interests/Education: Ho'okuku

How do you feel about your achievements? How fulfilled are you by your interests, hobbies, or how you spend your time? How much do you look forward to your day? Do you enjoy learning? If so, what topic? If not, why haven't you found a topic that interests you? Do you feel you are advancing your interests?

This part of our lives is the section where we invest in ourselves. If you only put out time and energy, and you don't reinvest your money, energy, or time into yourself, you are telling yourself that you aren't worthy. Your interests matter. Do you believe your interests matter?

Ho'okuku means competitiveness. Challenge your potential within oneself without purposefully bringing down others. This is an internal competitiveness.

Friends/Family: Ohana

This is your connection to those closest to you. Do you accept them? Do they accept you? Is the relationship with your close friends or family important to you? In indigenous cultures, family extends outside of your direct bloodline. Family is made up of those who support and care for you. So, in this case, close friends are family. Spouses are family, and their families are family. Friendship should not be diminished because of a lack of genetics. If you didn't know you weren't related, you would believe that family friends are your relatives based on their actions, right? That's why in Hawai'i, we call our family friends (and anyone with respect who interacts in our lives) with the same titles as relatives.

Do you reach out to your family, and do they reach out to you? Are you satisfied with your romantic relationships? Does someone in your circle believe in you?

What to Do Now

Your life doesn't have to be great. It has to be balanced. If everything is at about 50%, you're doing fine. Nudge each area when you can to make them even with each other. But if any areas are shallow, they need immediate attention. Think urgent like instant surgery urgent. What is wrong? What do you need to do to fix it? What obstacles are in your way so you can fix them? What do you have to do to break down those obstacles? What can be sacrificed in your life to spend time breaking down those obstacles? Stop what you are doing, make a plan, and change that area today. Bam.

Although spiritual warfare may seem like the most crucial action, it's equally important to help your client achieve life balance. A life out of balance leaves them vulnerable and more likely to experience trauma or overwhelming experiences, which lead to a soul fracture and, in turn, spiritual attack. You see? Holistic. I will tell you that most of my clients have refused this part of the work. They don't want to deal with addictions, changing their job, or joining a kayak team. They want you to allopathically remove a spirit and expect that their unbalanced lifestyle (for which caused them, or at least put them in vulnerability in the first place, to get into a spirit attack) will not likely allow for it to happen again.

Teach them they must look at the plan with a "Yes, And" attitude only. We add and figure out the plan; get creative and get them on the right path in their life. Any spiritual attack may be because they have been at zero in one of these areas. Maybe they need help finding a new faith so they have the foundation to build everything upon. Maybe they need help with a new resume so they can interview for a new position. If it were a broken leg, they would be forced to get a cast. If other areas in their life are broken, they need to be taken with the same importance. They have to be willing to participate in the wellness and betterment of their life as well, however. Your client can't expect you just to tell them what to do; you are not them. You are not living their life, so you don't know all the nuances.

If Your Life Had No Meaning, Would You Let A Demon Drive?

Once there was a woman. She was average in almost every way. She lived a life where she got up in the morning by swinging her bare legs over the side of her bed to engage with the wood floor as she pulled her phone from the charger and made her way into the bathroom. She asked her smart home to turn on music while she brushed her teeth, leaving her phone on the sink. Grinding coffee grounds was cheaper than buying them pre-pulverized, and sipping crème and sugar was cheaper than the fancy flavored stuff. She made her coffee and stared into the distance, realizing that while her mind was unanchored, she could return to her phone.

Leaving the coffee pot to work in servitude, she went back into the bathroom to retrieve her boredom device. When she looked at her phone screen, the banner to seven different shopping applications painted and decorated her screen with tickled delight, promising accessories for her broken life. They'd at least make her feel real and seen, right? Things are nice. Things create a world around her where she can be kind to herself. She can love herself, and loving herself is the highest form of self-esteem, completion, and self-care. She spat out her toothpaste, threw off her oversized shirt onto the floor, and turned the shower water on, all the while scrolling through the banners of discounts, highlighted garments, home decorations, and the newest cat litter training device on her smartphone.

In the shower, she stared at her body. The steam curled around her limbs like a quiet veil. Her body was neither a source of pride nor of shame. It served. Her eyes glided over her form. Each inch marked time passed. Her thighs had pressed against office chairs, park benches, plastic train seats. Her shoulders had carried purses and disappointments. Her belly held foods that didn't answer the question, "Am I important?" The curve of her calves remembered childhood play and stairwells to doctor visits. Her body was only useful as an archive of the average living. She turned in the mirror and nodded.

She washed. She dried. She dressed with the practiced rhythm of someone who has tried every combination and memorized which ones communicate effort without overreach. Her fingertips tapped her banking app as she chewed the inside of her cheek. The numbers lined up like obedient soldiers who have spent 40 years in the monotony of subordination. No aspiration breathed behind those numbers. They simply upheld the present moment. Rent would be paid. Groceries could be bought. The balance was sufficient for existing, not for expansion. The account, like her, endured.

Her job filled the hours between sunrise and dinner. You, the reader, don't need to know what she did for work. It should matter as much to you as it does to her... not at all. It existed in cubicles and emails, in spreadsheets and scheduled calls. The work asked very little. It folded itself into her days like a familiar song, one with many verses but no chorus. She arrived at her desk and greeted her coworkers with a smile. They exchanged small offerings of humor and observation, trading warmth like tokens. She thought that in her dying days, she wouldn't have a single moment of substance to recall in an annoying storytelling to a scrub nurse. No grand conversation stirred in the air. Yet they each played their roles with grace. When all she will have are memories to tell her roommates at the old folks' home, as she soils her adult diapers, she will only be able to say, "We were pleasant."

When her lunch break arrived, she reopened her shopping app. Her thumb swiped gently, reverently. Each image felt like a whisper: new curtains could make the apartment feel refreshed. A diffuser with lavender oil could settle her nerves at night. A sleek kitchen appliance could fulfill a longing for gourmet transformation. These items promised a nearness to beauty, to ease. They became sacred messengers of comfort. When her purchase was finalized, a thrill passed through her, like a chime at the edge of consciousness. A package on the way meant a future. It meant anticipation. It meant possibility. We know it doesn't. It's an addictive lying demon who spouts that these things will give her something fulfilling. The meanest kind of lies. Lies that promise hope, but won't deliver. The fucking abusive lies of shopping.

Her friends, like pearls scattered across velvet, shimmered softly from the edges of her life. They met for drinks and took pictures in front of murals. They shared playlists and forwarded memes. Their presence, though light, shimmered with affection. They did not penetrate to the marrow of her days. Like pearls, they only sit on the outside as a decoration. We need sand to create something within our oyster of a soul. Her pearls liked each other's photos. They texted hearts and laughter. No secrets passed between them, nor did hopes, dreams, or arguments, but their company gave a sense of togetherness, like a string of pearls adorned on Deborah, the rich bitch from her Netflix Housewife show.

She bought a book, one with a cover that promised illumination. Its title hinted at transformation, and the author had once spoken on a podcast she admired. She carried it home and placed it beside her bed. The weight of it felt noble. It joined the quiet library of intentions she gathered, where wisdom could rise like yeast in dough. Though she never cracked the spine, its presence blessed her space.

Later, she opened her dating app. The men's profiles flickered past her eyes like faces in a dream. Some smiled with certainty. Some posed with pets or displayed curated hobbies. She tapped and swiped with the rhythm of habit, her thumb moving in search of a face that would echo a feeling inside her. She matched with several. Their messages landed in her inbox with polite curiosity. She answered. She smiled. She kept moving forward. Each profile held potential, like unopened doors, though she sensed no particular one would open. Like the collection of pearl-friends, uncracked book spines, and work pleasantries, she collected profiles of men she might one day open packages from Amazon with.

She even agreed to a date. He wore polished shoes and listened with attention. They spoke of travel, of music, of the way certain foods comfort the soul, all fake surface plumage. She paid for the meal, her card offered with grace. In that gesture, she leveled the field. She affirmed her sovereignty. She sought neither dominance nor dependence. Her equality glowed between them like a candle. She won't see him again.

Her family lived across states and seasons. They texted updates about the weather and the children. Her mother sent recipe videos. Her father forwarded articles. She replied with warmth and emojis. Love remained, though distance grew. Holidays anchored them, giving shape to the passage of time. She looked at their photos and felt both tethered and adrift. They existed in a parallel rhythm, and that rhythm hummed quietly alongside hers.

One day, she purchased an expensive coffee from a small corner café. The barista called her by name. The foam held a delicate swirl of caramel and cinnamon. She sat by the window and sipped with reverence. The cup warmed her palms, and the sweetness rested on her tongue like a hymn. The indulgence felt like an embrace. It blessed the ordinariness of the day.

At home, the light in her apartment softened. It fell gently over furniture arranged for functionality. The shelves held things, objects chosen for utility or charm. She sat on her couch and turned her gaze toward them. Each item had arrived with purpose. Each one had promised transformation. Together, they formed a mosaic of intention, a temple of consumer devotion. And yet they remained silent, offering no song beyond their surface.

In the corner of the room, something stirred. It did not announce itself. It rose from the floorboards and ceiling paint. It took its shape from the stillness of air and the murmur of electric hums. It was provocative. Something exciting... for once. It hummed with willingness. The woman turned toward it. Her eyes met its form. She offered no resistance. She made no demand. She simply allowed it.

The presence stepped forward. It didn't speak. Its voice existed in the rustle of receipts and the thrum of old appliances. It held a longing older than language. The longing to *become*. The longing to *fill*. The longing to *mean*.

It sat beside her. She sat, like she did when she didn't read a book, like when she doom-scrolled, like when she watched a show about fake people... Honestly, she didn't sit like she was depressed or dejected... she sat with an abundance of apathy. Her breath remained steady. Together they sat, the woman and the presence, both shaped by the same clay of yearning. It extended no promises. She made no bargains.

It simply reached forward and touched her hand.

At that moment, her hand was just received. Her gaze remained steady. The presence enveloped her gently, the way dawn envelops the sleeping hillside. It offered to drive. To lead. To carry her across days and years with purpose.

She nodded. The demon, needing a home, asked with body language if it could drive. She thought, *You'll probably do a better job than I. Maybe, you'll give me something... us something, to actually live for. Yes, you drive.*

It stepped inside. She was now possessed by something that could give her something to fight over, fight with, or fight for a buffet of attention, meant something to something.

The woman stood. She moved through her apartment with a new awareness. Her limbs carried the quiet knowledge of being chosen. Chosen by something real. Something present. Something ready to live her life fully, if she welcomed it.

She dressed in her warmest coat. She stepped outside. The wind touched her cheeks. The air carried the sound of passing voices. The sidewalk welcomed her feet.

Each step drew her forward.

Each breath welcomed the presence deeper into her bones.

She no longer swiped for men. She no longer waited for deliveries. She no longer refreshed her inbox, her apps, or her balance.

She walked into the morning with a spirit that had shape.

She had chosen.

The demon lifted its voice for the first time, and on the fall night, under the gaze of the streetlight, they yelled with her voice, "FUCK YOUUUUUUUUUU!"

Ho'oponopono & Healing Your Crowd

Peer pressure isn't the only reason why we make poor choices regarding our health, although peers are the most significant reason. We trust our friends to support us, give us great advice in solving our problems, and we look to them for how we should behave in all social situations. More than that, we, as humans, strive to be right, good, just, and well-liked. We determine these things from our mentors, but most of all, from our social groups.

This sounds great, right? You would think that the world would be a wonderful place because of these psychological truths. However, what if a random guy came up to you and tried to convince you to do drugs? To stop eating? To engage in dangerous behavior? We would all assume that we wouldn't because it's some crazy person, and that we would do the right thing.

Why then do we engage in dangerous behavior that our friends encourage? The need to be well-liked and right (in each social norm) is higher than the need to be good or just!

It's true. We make bad decisions because the situations in which we are currently engaged require us to fit in.

Example: When test subjects were put into an environment where everyone answered a question out loud incorrectly, the subjects also answered incorrectly because of peer pressure. Look up the data yourself!

Think about it. Have you ever experienced a situation (or witnessed) when someone was booed by one person, and suddenly a bunch of people are booing? If you've experienced this, you probably can think back to that moment and realize that you really didn't need to boo or be mean in that situation. It's because you were influenced by a social deviant.

A deviant refuses to conform to social norms because those people don't feel that they have important bonds to conventional society (don't try to help them! They need a professional). Certain cultures, like drug cultures, some arts companies, and even classrooms, promote values that attract deviant behaviors.

Time to engage in De-friending!

It's time to get rid of those poisonous people who may convince you to make poor choices. The love and adoration you receive from social deviants IS LESS than the love you can give yourself by making new friends. Find out if your friends are social deviants by noticing these characteristics:

- They hate your ambition

- They blame others

- They hate those who take responsibility for their actions

- Make fun of achievements

- Theft

- Irrational planning

- Always want instant gratification

- Refuses to use manners or politeness

- Can't control physical aggression

- No respect for others' property

- Laughs at 'wholesome' recreation

How do I get rid of my toxic friends?

It's in your power! Do things that make you feel good, be with people who support your self-esteem, avoid social deviants by making yourself busy, and know that you always have the decision.

Practicing Ho'oponopono the Traditional Way

Ho'oponopono is a sacred process for restoring balance within families and communities, as well as within the self, making the access and utilization of the ritual important to Hawaiian culture. The word itself carries profound meaning. "Ho'o" means to cause or to make. "Pono" means right, balanced, or in alignment. When repeated as "ponopono," it emphasizes complete harmony and order. To practice Ho'oponopono is to make things right, to restore proper alignment in relationships and in life.

At its core, Ho'oponopono is not about placing blame or creating division. It is about taking responsibility and seeking true healing through prayer, discussion, forgiveness, and unity. The practice has been handed down through generations of Hawaiian families and guided by kahuna, or elders who carry the wisdom of healing. Today, many Hawaiians still practice it in its traditional form. While modern adaptations exist, the authentic steps provide the deepest understanding of how families have healed and reconciled for centuries.

This chapter will guide you through the traditional Hawaiian steps of Ho'oponopono, while also explaining the cultural spirit that surrounds it. We will begin by exploring the meaning behind the process, then walk carefully through each stage. You will see that the practice begins with prayer, ends with prayer and food, and includes mediation, confession, forgiveness, and release. Every element has its place, and together they weave a ritual of profound beauty.

The Meaning of Ho'oponopono

In Hawaiian thought, all relationships are part of a web of life. When relationships are in harmony, life flows with aloha, with joy, with love. When conflict, anger, or misunderstanding enters, the flow is disturbed. This disturbance is between individuals and within the spirit of the family, the community, and even within the natural world. Ho'oponopono is the method by which this imbalance is corrected.

To practice Ho'oponopono is to accept responsibility for what is within one's life. This responsibility is not limited to the self alone. It extends to family, ancestors, and the living spirit that connects all beings. To heal, one must acknowledge their place in the web and take part in restoring it to harmony.

It is prayerful. It is guided. It is conducted with respect, intention, and care. The kahuna or elder would traditionally lead the family in the ritual, ensuring that everyone had a voice and that the spirit of the ancestors was invited into the circle. In this way, Ho'oponopono is both practical and spiritual. It brings people together in honesty and compassion, while also inviting divine assistance to transform hearts.

The Structure of Ho'oponopono

The practice follows a clear structure. It begins with pule, which is prayer. This opening prayer calls upon divine presence, asking for guidance, clarity, and blessing upon the participants.

After prayer, the facilitator leads the family into discussion. This is where the source of conflict is named and spoken aloud. Each person has the opportunity to share openly, without fear. The facilitator ensures that voices are heard and that communication remains clear and respectful.

From there, the steps move into confession, forgiveness, and release. Each stage is essential. Without confession, the truth is hidden. Without forgiveness, the heart remains closed. Without release, the past continues to weigh upon the present.

The practice concludes with a closing prayer. This seals the healing, restores alignment, and calls upon divine blessing to maintain the harmony achieved. Finally, the ritual ends with the sharing of food. Eating together symbolizes that unity has been restored, that the bond of family is whole again, and that all have returned to a state of pono.

Step by Step Practice

Step One: Preparation and Gathering

Before the ritual begins, the family or group must be gathered together. Traditionally, this would be within the home or a sacred space chosen for the practice. The facilitator, often a kahuna or elder, prepares spiritually through their own prayer and alignment. Participants prepare themselves with humility and the willingness to open their hearts.

The gathering itself is already part of the healing. By agreeing to come together, all participants acknowledge that harmony is desired. They recognize that the process is important enough to set aside time and energy.

Step Two: The Opening Prayer

The practice formally begins with pule, the opening prayer. The facilitator prays aloud, asking for divine guidance. The prayer invites the ancestors, the family guardians, and the spiritual presence of the divine to witness and bless the work.

This prayer is essential because it reminds everyone that the process is sacred. This is healing in alignment with spirit. The words spoken are heard by those present and by the unseen world that surrounds them.

Step Three: Naming the Issues

Once prayer has been offered, the facilitator introduces the purpose of the gathering. The issue that has created imbalance is spoken aloud. This could be conflict between family members, misunderstandings, resentments, or even larger community disagreements.

The facilitator ensures that the naming of the issue is done with respect. It is not about accusation. It is about clarity. By naming the issue, the family brings what is hidden into the light.

Step Four: Discussion and Confession

Each person involved has the opportunity to speak. This is the time for confession, for expressing feelings, for acknowledging mistakes, and for bringing truth to the surface. The facilitator ensures that everyone is heard, one at a time, without interruption.

Confession is about honesty. It is about allowing the heart to express what has been carried. It may include admitting wrongs, acknowledging pain, or recognizing where one has not been pono.

During this stage, deep emotions may surface. Tears may come. Anger may arise. The facilitator's role is to keep the space safe and sacred so that all can be expressed without harm.

Step Five: Seeking Forgiveness

After confession comes the seeking of forgiveness. Each person who has spoken takes responsibility for their words and actions. They ask for forgiveness from those they have hurt. They also open their hearts to forgive those who have caused them pain.

Forgiveness is central to Ho'oponopono. Without it, the spirit remains bound to past wounds. With forgiveness, the heart is freed. Forgiveness is a cleansing of the entire web of relationships, including the ancestral lines.

Step Six: Release

With forgiveness spoken, the next step is release. In Hawaiian, this is called kala. To release is to let go completely, so that the burden no longer clings to the heart. The facilitator may lead a prayer or chant to mark this release.

Release is the turning of the spirit back to alignment with pono. It is the recognition that the past is no longer binding the present.

Step Seven: Closing Prayer

Once forgiveness and release have taken place, the facilitator leads a closing prayer. This seals the process. It calls upon divine blessing to maintain the harmony achieved. It thanks the ancestors and the spiritual guardians for their presence and guidance.

The closing prayer ensures that what has been spoken does not remain open and unsettled. It completes the ritual in sacred balance.

Step Eight: Sharing of Food

The final step of Ho'oponopono is the sharing of food. This may seem simple, yet it carries profound meaning. Eating together is a symbol of restored unity. Food nourishes the body, and sharing it nourishes the bond between people.

By sitting together at a meal after the ritual, the family affirms that the conflict is resolved, and that they return to daily life in harmony. The act of eating is a grounding of the spiritual work into physical reality.

The Spirit of Ho'oponopono

While the steps of the practice are clear, the spirit in which they are carried is equally important. Ho'oponopono is approached with reverence, not haste. It is guided by the values of aloha, respect, humility, and truth.

The facilitator must carry wisdom and compassion. The participants must carry sincerity and openness. Together, they create a space where healing can occur.

It is also important to remember that Ho'oponopono is about maintaining harmony. Families may practice it regularly, even when no great conflict has arisen, as a way of keeping the relationships aligned and the spirit of aloha strong.

Pele and Kamapuaʻa

Characters:
Pele - Goddess of the Volcano and Fire
Kamapuaʻa - Pig God and of the Rainforest
Lono - God of Agriculture

The earth trembled softly, and the wind carried the scent of roots split open. That night, the mother of Kamapuaʻa cried out in relief that she no longer was carrying him within her womb. Her son emerged already marked by the gods; his back strong, his skin thick as bark, and in his eyes, the flicker of an untamed animal.

"He was no ordinary child," the people whispered. They saw him eat roots no human could chew, wallow in red mud without falling ill, and speak to the clouds as if they were his cousins. He laughed at thunder and grunted at priests. His name became his shape, Kamapuaʻa, the child-god who is a pig. His kupua body could shift and melt, bone bending to will. He became boar with hunger. He became a man in desire. He became mist when chased, and rock when struck.

By the time he reached manhood, the taro fields lay ruined behind him. Walls collapsed beneath his temper. The sweet-potato mounds had been trampled in his pursuit of lovers. His presence brought fertility or ruin. Chiefs could neither bless nor banish him, for he obeyed no law save his own hunger. He stole wives, stole fruit, and danced among trees. The priests said he had no kapu. The old women said he had no shame. The land, however, didn't care about the opinions of old women. Wild pigs followed him. Rain answered him. The forests deepened in his wake.

One night, Kamapuaʻa stood at the edge of a cliff in Koʻolau, his chest bare, his face smudged with roots. Below him, the ocean swallowed the moon. Behind him, the hills exhaled a single, hot wind. It carried her name, Pele.

He had heard of her, the woman of fire, the one who carved bones into islands. Her skin was said to glow. Her voice shattered stone. She who had crossed from Kahiki (Tahiti) in a canoe of flame and claimed Hawaiʻi as her own. She burned what displeased her. She who hid her ember-body inside the mountain.

Kamapuaʻa grunted once, standing on a plateau overlooking the ocean towards the direction of the mountain volcanoes that hosted the fire goddess. "A woman like that," he said, "must be taken."

He summoned the wind. He blew into the shell of the pu. He slapped the mountain with his open hand. The ridges echoed. Birds flew from their perches. He began the journey across the islands.

When he landed in Hawaiʻi, the rain came with him. The rivers swelled. The forest groaned as if remembering something ancient. With confident authority, he walked into Pele's land as if it were already his. In Puna, the people watched from their huts, mouths full of poi, mouths full of awe, mouths full of gossip.

He was tall. His chest gleamed. His legs were thick with root power. And yet he smelled of pig. Even as he bathed in the waterfall, the scent lingered, earthy, pungent, the kind of smell that belongs to something raw.

Pele saw him before he reached her cave. She sat among her sisters, her feet curled into the warm stone, her hair trailing into the embers of her hearth. Her eyes narrowed.

"There is a man approaching," she said.

Her sisters giggled. "A man with shoulders like logs and eyes like fire."

"He is no man," said Pele.

"He is handsome," said another.

"He is hunger wearing skin," said Pele.

Kamapuaʻa walked into Halemaʻumaʻu as if he had been invited. He didn't bring an offering... well, kind of... He brought his body. He brought his voice. He brought his storm.

"Woman of fire," he said, "I have come."

Pele rose. Her hair caught flame. The cavern walls glowed.

"I did not call for you," she said.

"You did," he answered. "Your name blew across the water. It sang into my bones."

"Then my bones will burn you," said Pele.

Kamapuaʻa laughed. His body swelled. Bristles rose from his arms. His face thickened. His tusks slid from his gums like promises.

"Will you burn the forest that feeds you?" he asked. "Will you burn the rain that cools your throat?"

Pele stepped forward. "You stink of roots and filth."

He said. "Do you scorch all your lovers?"

She lifted her arms. Flame gathered behind her shoulders. Lava hissed. The mountain awoke.

He lifted his voice. Rain fell. The wind turned cold. Thunder rolled in from the sea.

Their first battle.

He chanted of her eyes, red-rimmed and swollen from too much fire. She chanted of his breath, foul from rotting bark and pig's guts. He chanted of her hair, falling like ash after an eruption. She chanted of his skin, thick and calloused from wallowing in mud.

The words cut. The words healed. The words fated.

But beneath the rage, they watched one another. Beneath the insults, their eyes locked. Pele tilted her head.

"You are ugly," she said.

"You are dangerous," he answered.

"You are stubborn."

"You are mine."

She laughed. The laugh cracked stone.

"You will die," she said.

"Then let it be in your arms," he said.

She raised her hands. Fire shot from her fingers. It danced toward his face, trailing cinders. He stood his ground, and when the fire reached him, it licked his chest, and hissed because water rose from his skin, steam bloomed, and smoke curled around his shoulders. He stood there, silent, still, until the flames faded.

He stepped forward.

He took her hand.

Kamapuaʻa bent his head and pressed his mouth to Pele's wrist.

She closed her eyes. Then they disappeared into the heart of the mountain.

And the rain fell, and the fire slept.

For a while.

The days after their union were thick with silence. Rain clung to the canopy, and lava curled deeper within the mountain. The people in Puna whispered of thunder from beneath their feet and saw no smoke rise from Halemaʻumaʻu. The birds stilled their wings. The trees, even the hau, bent lower, holding their breath.

Inside the great cave, Pele and Kamapuaʻa slept together with the intensity of two gods who could never belong to the same world. For a time, they danced.

Kamapuaʻa brought her ginger from the mountain, petals still wet. He pressed the flowers into her hair, and her heat did not wilt them.

Pele gifted him fire wrapped in kapa cloth, the ember taken from the mouth of the caldera. He placed it on his tongue and did not cry out.

They laughed, they lay together, and they consumed each other like tide and reef.

But love built on opposition can't hold.

It began when Kamapuaʻa asked for her land.

"I will grow gardens where your lava has hardened," he said. "I will bring back the vines."

"You will not touch what I have claimed," she answered. "I buried my brothers beneath these stones."

"They are bones now," said Kamapuaʻa. "The land must breathe."

"You would turn my altar into pig wallows?" Her voice cracked with flame.

He stood: "I would give life where you have only taken it."

She rose. Her hair caught fire. The stone floor rippled with heat. "I am not one of your roots to be pulled!"

"And I am not one of your lovers to be burned!"

They shouted. The walls split. The mountain stirred.

And then they warred.

The flames rose from the crater's mouth. Lava spilled into valleys and chased the trees.

Kamapua'a called for the rains. He lifted his arms to the heavens and grunted the sacred syllables of his lineage. His boar form swelled, thick with forest mana. The rains obeyed and poured over Puna in sheets. Rivers burst. Water steamed as it struck the lava, and mist bloomed where fire met flood. The land became a battlefield of elements. Forest versus flame. Root versus stone.

Fire hissed.

Rain howled.

Clouds turned black.

They met at the rim of Kīlauea, Pele with her hands glowing red and her eyes like coals, Kamapua'a with his body steaming, mud on his face, and rage in his chest.

She struck first. Fire burst from her chest, a rope of flame coiling toward his throat. He leapt, shifting mid-air from man to boar, tusks catching the flame and tossing it into the rain.

She screamed and sent more. He charged and tore the lava flow apart with his hooves. She called on the wind. He answered with thunder. All of Hawai'i heard them. The elements clashed and locked. The mountain shook. Trees snapped. Rivers changed their course. Birds flew in circles and forgot their names.

She chased him with lava and cornered him at a cliff. Kamapua'a launched himself into the ocean, afraid that Pele's shark brother Kamoho'ali'i might be at the edge waiting for him.

As he crossed the veil of air into water, he transformed into humuhumunukunukuapua'a, the fish with the face of a pig, with skin tough enough to withstand the heat of the chasing lava, which followed him and solidified into the water. His brilliant colors taunted Pele to let her know exactly where he was and that the pig god could not be killed by her vengeful persistence.

He stepped out of the water and walked back onto land to continue to fight for the land.

For days and nights, they fought. Until one night, as the mist thickened and no stars could be seen, Lono appeared. He came with the silence of rain that falls in the uplands. His cloak was the grey of smoke, and his staff grew from living wood. He stepped between fire and rain, between tusk and flame, and he said one calm word: "Enough."

The mountain stilled. The rain slowed. Pele stood panting, her skin blistered but proud. Kamapua'a crouched low, chest heaving, body bleeding steam.

Lono simply looked at them both.

"You are gods," he said. He walked to Pele. "You forget that fire without water is only destruction." Then he walked to Kamapua'a. "And you forget that water without fire grows rot." He raised his staff. Rain fell upon the lava, but this time, it cooled gently. Steam rose like a prayer. "You love each other because you are the same," he said. "You hate each other because you will never be alike." He pointed to the land, scarred by lava and rain. "This is your child, and you will share it fairly. Pele, you will burn down one side of the island only, and you may claim the windward side as yours. Kamapua'a, you grow your rainforests on the leeward side of the island. You may both now grow your land... our land... and it is my wish that you two, in your viciousness, will not meet again."

Pele turned her face away. Kamapua'a lowered his tusks.

Lono nodded, "Say goodbye." And then he disappeared.

They stood in silence. The storm had ended. Only mist curled around their feet.

Pele stepped back. "You will not have me," she said.

Kamapuaʻa turned toward the forest. "Your fire will burn forever," he said. "But it will burn alone."

She turned to the crater.

"Your forest will grow tall," she whispered. "But no root will reach me again."

And so the war ended. But the scar remained.

In the uplands of Puna, there are places where the forest stops suddenly, as if cut. There are groves where the trees lean away from the mountain. There are ridges where no plant will grow, and the stones are red with memory.

These are the places where fire met rain.

Where gods made love, and then made war. The land held its breath.

This story teaches us something that many people forget in modern spiritual culture: your mana grows best among your own people. There is a lot of pressure right now to follow novelty. People chase every new workshop, new teacher, new method. They leave behind their crowd, their community, their lineage, their grounding, to chase something they think will give them more power. But it does not work that way.

Mana is not gained by collecting experiences like souvenirs. Mana is cultivated through rootedness.

This is the lesson: You must know your crowd and grow there.

That does not mean your crowd is always right. That does not mean you are never challenged or stretched. But it does mean that you are seen. When you belong, your mana has a place to move, to be mirrored, to be received.

Know your crowd. Stay on your side of the island. Don't try to overtake someone else's with your know-how. That is how you become medicine.

Notice Others

Healing in the Hawaiian tradition is more than medicine, herbs, or physical therapies. It begins in the unseen, in the subtle exchanges between human beings, in the threads of connection we weave through everyday gestures. The Hawaiian way teaches that to heal the body, one must also nourish the spirit. One of the simplest and most profound ways to do this is to *notice others*.

When we notice another person, truly see them, we affirm their place in the world. In that moment, we acknowledge their humanity, their presence, their worth. This simple act is medicine for both giver and receiver. In Hawaiian culture, this is woven into the practice of aloha, a word that holds the essence of love, respect, compassion, and mutual regard.

The Healing Power of Eye Contact

A glance can be transactional, but eye contact with intention is transformative. When you meet someone's eyes, you create a moment of shared humanity. In that exchange, your nervous systems speak to each other, signaling safety and connection. This calms stress responses and supports the body's natural healing processes.

Eye contact sends the message: *I see you, and you matter*. In Hawaiian healing, the soul is nourished when it feels seen and valued. The soul, in turn, communicates to the body, easing tensions that may have been carried in the muscles, calming the heart rate, and softening breathing. Over time, this contributes to the body's vitality.

Making eye contact as you thank a driver who lets you cross the street is more than politeness. It is an offering of presence. The driver, often a stranger, experiences that acknowledgment as a gift, and their spirit lifts. You, too, carry the lightness of that exchange forward into your day.

Waves, Greetings, and Simple Courtesies

In Hawai'i, small courtesies hold great weight. A lifted hand in thanks when a car pauses for you is an act of connection. A warm "Aloha" to a passerby opens the doorway to a shared smile. Saying "Excuse me" when you move around someone in a store creates space for both of you to exist comfortably.

These gestures may seem small, yet they ripple out. They create micro-moments of harmony that feed the soul. When harmony flows in the spirit, the body relaxes into its natural rhythm. Stress, which often manifests as inflammation, muscle tightness, or fatigue, loses its grip. The physical body thrives in an environment of kindness and connection.

The Feedback Loop of Aloha

Aloha, expressed genuinely, sets in motion a healing loop. You offer kindness, and the other person receives it. Often, they mirror it back in some form, a smile, a wave, a softened posture. Your heart registers this response, and the joy of being connected floods you with warmth. That warmth is not metaphorical; it is biochemical. Your brain releases oxytocin and endorphins, your immune system strengthens, your blood pressure balances, and your mood lifts.

The beauty of aloha is that its power multiplies. Every time you offer it, you also plant seeds of healing in others. This creates a living circle where health, joy, and well-being move between people like ocean currents, returning to each shore they touch.

Healing the Soul to Heal the Body

The human body listens to the soul. When the soul feels isolated, unseen, or disconnected, the body responds with signals: fatigue, tension, and imbalance. When the soul is nourished through acts of connection, the body receives signals of safety, belonging, and peace. These states allow the body's natural repair systems to function at their best.

In Hawaiian healing, the soul is the navigator, and the body is the canoe. When the navigator is at ease, the canoe travels smoothly. When the navigator feels joy, the journey becomes effortless. Every "Hello," every wave, every moment of presence is a course correction toward balance and vitality.

Everyday Practices to Notice Others

You do not need a special ceremony to bring this healing into your life. It begins with everyday choices:

- Greet the morning with aloha. As you step outside, offer a smile to the first person you see.

- Acknowledge kindness. Wave or mouth "thank you" to anyone who gives you space, time, or patience.

- Make space for others. Move aside with grace when sharing a narrow path and offer a friendly acknowledgment.

- Connect with your eyes. Meet the gaze of cashiers, servers, and strangers with warmth, letting your eyes convey that you see them.

- Share a wave with strangers. Whether on the beach, on a trail, or in your neighborhood, lift your hand as a sign of shared presence.

These actions are the seeds of aloha. They require no extra time, only awareness and willingness.

Aloha as a Daily Healing Practice

Think of aloha as a living energy you carry within you. Each time you express it, you strengthen its presence in your own life. Over time, this practice becomes part of your way of moving through the world. You begin to notice more: the person who needs a smile, the elder who appreciates your wave, the child who lights up when you greet them.

This awareness heightens your sensitivity to connection, which feeds your soul's desire for belonging. That sense of belonging is a powerful antidote to stress, loneliness, and disconnection, the very conditions that wear away at the body's vitality.

The more you practice aloha through noticing others, the more you will feel its effects on your own health. You may find that your breathing deepens, your shoulders relax, and your mind feels clearer. This is the body's natural response to a nourished soul.

Living the Spirit of Connection

In the Hawaiian worldview, healing is never a solitary act. It is a weaving together of relationships, with people, with the land, with the ocean, with the unseen. Every time you notice another person, you strengthen the weave. You say, "We are in this life together," and that truth becomes embodied.

Your gestures, words, and eye contact send ripples far beyond the moment. They touch the other person's spirit, and they return to you magnified. Over time, this ongoing exchange creates a life filled with ease, joy, and health, the hallmarks of a balanced spirit and body.

To notice others is to honor the shared journey of life. In Hawaiian healing, this is a sacred practice. A glance, a wave, a kind word... these are the threads that bind soul to soul, creating a fabric strong enough to carry health and joy through generations.

When you move through the world with aloha, you invite healing into your own life and into the lives of those around you. In doing so, you become both healer and healed.

Part 5

Uhane & The Body

Breath in Polynesian Philosophy: Energetically Designed to Heal

There are things we need to hold true: We have the nature to grow old and cannot escape growing old. We will have ill health and cannot escape it either. We will die, and everything dear to us, like the flowers on a vine, will eventually die; we can't hold onto people or items, as we will eventually be separated from them. We see it in nature and are its custodians of nature.

In many Polynesian traditions, life is understood as a living network of energy, spirit, and body, woven together with intention and care. This worldview holds that human beings are inherently designed to heal. Healing is a matter of physical recovery and a restoration of balance across the energetic and spiritual dimensions of the self. At the center of this design is the breath, which is more than a biological process. Breath is the carrier of mana, the sacred life force that connects each person to the gods, the land, and the lineage from which they come.

The breath is the bridge for the flow of mana out of us. In Hawaiian, the word *ha* means both breath and life force. The very name Hawai'i contains the syllable ha, reflecting the recognition of breath as the source of vitality. In the spiritual practices of kahuna, breath is the primary means by which mana is gathered, focused, and directed. It is through breath that prayers gain power, intentions take form, and healing is made possible.

Traditional breathing practices are designed to draw mana into the body, to guide it where it is needed, and to release what no longer serves. One such practice is the complete breath, which begins deep in the belly and rises smoothly through the chest until the lungs are filled. After a brief pause, the breath is released slowly and steadily, contracting from the abdomen outward. This deliberate cycle creates calm and restores clarity to the mind.

In these traditions, breath is far more than oxygen exchange. It is the vessel that draws in mana from the surrounding world, from the sea wind, the forest air, the mountain mists. With each breath taken in awareness, a person gathers vitality from the land, the ancestors, and the unseen realms. With each exhale, the body releases tension, emotional burdens, and spiritual stagnation. In this way, breathwork clears blockages that prevent energy from flowing freely through the aka cords linking the three selves.

When these cords are strong, the unihipili, uhane, and aumakua can act in harmony. The subconscious is no longer burdened with unprocessed emotion, the conscious mind becomes focused and at ease, and the higher self can guide without obstruction. This alignment is the essence of Polynesian healing philosophy. The breath is the means by which such alignment is both established and maintained.

Breath is also deeply integrated into other healing modalities. In la'au lapa'au, the use of medicinal plants, the healer will often breathe prayers into the remedy, imbuing it with mana. In lomilomi, the traditional massage practice, the practitioner's breath guides the rhythm of their hands, and they may synchronize breathing with the person receiving the treatment. This creates a shared flow of energy that supports the release of physical tension and the restoration of spirit.

Breath also holds a ceremonial role that extends beyond personal healing. In the traditional Hawaiian greeting, the honi, two people press foreheads and noses together, exchanging the ha.

To share breath is to acknowledge one another as family, to honor the sacred essence within each person, and to establish a bond of trust and mutual respect. The honi is still practiced in cultural and ceremonial contexts, and its exchange of breath reflects the deep understanding that healing and relationship come from the same root: the flow of life force between beings.

The breath appears in origin chants as a primal act of creation. In the Kumulipo, the great Hawaiian creation chant, the unfolding of life begins in darkness and deep water, and breath appears as the animating element that awakens the first forms. The first inhalation marks the arrival of consciousness; the first exhalation offers a return to the universe. Breath is the sacred threshold where spirit becomes embodied. The very gift of life given to the first humans in Polynesian creation stories often comes through a god leaning down to breathe into them, just as in Hawaiian tradition, the high god Kane breathed ha into the nostrils of the first man, giving him life. That same breath flows within every descendant, unbroken through time.

In voyaging traditions, the breath is carried in chants that guide the canoe across the ocean. Navigators chant to the stars, the swells, and the winds, timing their breath to the rhythm of the sea. The breath becomes a way of syncing the body with the natural world, of entering into deep awareness of the forces that guide and sustain the voyage. Healing is present here as well, for the navigator who breathes with the ocean learns to release fear, maintain balance, and trust the living network of land, sea, and sky.

To live with awareness of breath is to live in constant conversation with the forces that sustain life. The air becomes a gift of the ancestors, a reminder of the original breath given at creation. Each inhale is a renewal of that gift; each exhale is an offering in return. In Polynesian thought, to breathe consciously is to take part in the eternal exchange between self, spirit, and world.

In Polynesian philosophy, healing begins with the recognition that the human being is a vessel of life force. This life force flows through the body like a current through the ocean. It animates the bones, warms the blood, and stirs the mind into awareness. It is present at birth with the first breath, and it departs at death with the last exhalation. The Polynesian understanding of this current sees the breath as a sacred link between the seen and unseen worlds.

The Story of the Ipu

Characters:
The Woman Who Chanted Beautifully
The Husband
The Fisherman

There lived a young great woman upon the wind-worn lands of Ka'u on the Big Island, where the southern plains reach toward the ever-moving, restless clouds. She was beloved. The people spoke of her in chants long before her death, for her presence soothed the restless. She sang, and they all revered.

Hapai (pregnant), her womb had turned full before her time on earth had ended. She died before the child stirred, and the grief that followed was loudly lamented, rising like surf in the bones of her people, crashing against the walls of the hale, soaking through kapa, and laced in the very sweat that fed the fire. For ten days, the skies above Ka'u held the moaning of a thousand bones, and every wind that blew from Mauna Loa's shoulder carried with it a cry that was too heavy to name.

Her husband, hollowed by sorrow, wrapped her body in tapa soaked with the tears of their family, and laid her to rest within a cave that opened only to the sea wind. He rolled a great stone across the mouth of that cave, and he placed his hands upon it as if to say goodbye. When he turned, he did not look back.

But the earth is never finished with those who carry songs within them.

From the place where her body returned to Milu, a vine grew. It came first as a tendril, slick and green, pushing from her navel like a whispered breath. Each night the vine lengthened, winding around the stone like fingers searching for a way home. It crept through the crevice of that grave with a hunger that knew immortality. Its leaves were wide and glistening with mana. Its length was unnatural. It stretched over seven districts, and at the very border of Kona, the vine paused. A single white flower bloomed there. A breath later, the petals loosened and fell. In their place: an ipu (gourd), round and shining like a child's dreaming.

It grew beside a fisherman's house.

The fisherman had no name worth remembering, but he had eyes that watched the sea and hands that knew how to untangle nets in the dark. One afternoon, as the tide sighed against the rocks, he looked toward his garden and saw a glimmer among the grasses. He rose from his place and stepped outside, brushing sand from his knees. When he reached the ipu, he smiled.

"You are a fine thing," he said aloud. "Yes. You will grow round, strong, a true gift for me. I will place my fishhooks on you. My line. My lures. You will hold the works of my life."

He bent beside the gourd and began his labor. He gathered three sticks and made a frame, lifting the gourd from the earth so it would not grow flat. He brushed stones from beneath it. He made a cushion of soft grass so it would not bruise. A nest.

He whispered to it. He placed his own shadow between it and the noonday sun, and in the months that followed, he watched the ipu swell until it was nearly the size of a calabash used by chiefs.

Each evening, he visited it, humming to himself as he checked its skin. He thumped it with his knuckles and waited for the sound. Each time, the gourd answered with a low and empty thud. He would pinch it gently. Turn it slightly. Adjust the frame and settle it again like a mother soothing a sleeping child. Then he would go back inside and dream of the sea.

"No," he would mutter. "You are not ready yet. Not yet."

One night, the chiefess stirred.

She rose in spirit, still adorned in her kapa, still swollen with life never born. She came to her husband in a dream that was so sharp it cut through the veil like a fishhook in the mouth of a shark. Her face was darkened by pain. Her voice was hoarse with complaint.

"My husband," she said, "I have been thumped. I have been bruised. He pokes and tests and does not see that I am already ripe. You must find me. You must bring me home!"

With sweat, he awoke, and the image of her face clung to the lids of his eyes. Without waiting, he ran to the cave where her body had been laid.

The stone was as he had left it, but the vine had curled through the cracks.

He fell to his knees. He touched the vine where it met the mouth of the cave and followed it with his hands, crawling into the dark.

Inside, he found her. His wife. Her body still wrapped, still whole, as if the cave had preserved her. From her belly, the vine rose, alive, full, and green with the mana of something neither plant nor child.

He wept beside her. He held her cold hand and pressed it to his forehead.

"I will find you," he whispered. "I will bring you home."

He set out at once.

The vine showed him the way. Over hills, through districts, across dry earth and old trails, he walked where it led. It took him across the Ka'u, through the groves of koa, across the lava fields that cut like broken teeth. The sun rose and fell and rose again before he reached the place where the vine ended, and there, cradled in its curl, was the ipu.

He knelt beside it, tears already welling in his eyes. He placed both hands on its skin and felt a warmth there, as if it had been held by a fire long banked.

But as he prepared to lift it, the fisherman returned.

"Hey!" he shouted. "That gourd is mine! Put it down!"

He rushed forward, anger flashing across his face like a wave breaking against a rock. He seized the gourd and pulled. The husband held it tighter.

"Stop," he said. "Please, listen. This is sacred. This gourd is not yours. It is my wife. It is my child."

The fisherman froze. He stared at the man, confused, panting from the struggle. Then, the husband told his story. He told of the death. Of the burial. Of the vine that grew from the grave. He told of the flower. Of the dream. Of the spirit who had begged for return. And as he spoke, his hands cradled the gourd gently, rocking it as one would a child freshly born.

The fisherman fell silent. His anger melted like wax before the sun. At last, he bowed his head and said, "If this gourd is your wife, then I have tended her well. I raised her like one of my own. You may take her. May she bring you joy."

The husband thanked him. He wrapped the gourd in a soft kapa and carried her home. All the way, he spoke to her. Whispering. Singing. Remembering. It had been nine months since his wife had died, and no decay, only the womb of Lono's vegetation remained.

When he reached the burial cave, it was already night. He did not return her to her grave. Instead, he brought her into their hale and laid her gently upon the mats. He unwrapped her and placed his hands upon her smooth, roundness. Then, too weary to remain awake, he lay beside her and fell into the deep sleep of the truly burdened.

By morning, the gourd had changed.

It had split clean down the center. Within the folds of the kapa lay two seeds. He reached down with trembling fingers. The seeds were warm. And as he touched them, they moved. A flutter. A pulse. A stirring like wind in a bird's throat.

And then... they split! From each seed, a tiny girl emerged.

They were so small at first that they did not seem real. But even as he blinked, they grew. Inch by inch, the children took on flesh and bone, filling the air with their breath. In moments, they were infants, swaddled in the remnants of the gourd's warmth. They opened their mouths and cried. He fell to his knees and wept.

"My beloved," he said aloud, "you have returned to me in double measure. This is the gift of the gods, and I will never fail them. I will raise them as you would have. I will teach them to honor you with every step they take."

He pressed his face to their hair. He felt their tiny hands grip his fingers.

And so they lived.

The girls grew as girls do. Their hair was thick. Their legs were strong. They ran through Ka'u's grass with feet that never stumbled, and their voices carried far over the dry wind. The people came to love them as they had loved their mother, and their father watched them with the pride of one who has seen the dead reborn.

More than anything, their song sang. They were the children of the gourd. The ipu holds music, the ipu holds fish, care, tools... knowledge. The ipu *is* Lono's reminder of what we can hold. So the sisters sang, the sisters held, the sisters supported, and the sisters gave birth to more children. They became women. They bore children. Their children bore children.

They settled where the vine had once crept. They planted ipu of their own and taught their children to tend them with reverence. Their descendants called themselves *Na Pua o ka Ipu*: the Children of the Gourd.

They stretched from district to district. They became farmers. Chiefs. Midwives. Priests. They carried the memory of the gourd in their chants. They carved its shape into stone. They painted its story upon kapa. Every birth among them was said to echo the first. Every time a woman was hapai, an ipu gestated at the same rate as the incoming baby.

This is the story of the gourd. Even now, when the ipu grows round and smooth upon the land of Ka'u, the people look upon it with reverence, like a newly born baby.

Herbs, Medicine, Nutrition

I have been a professional dancer since I was fifteen, just turning sixteen. I have done incredible damage to my body, and the stress of being a child performer did a lot of damage to my mind. However, there are ways to heal those things. This section is, of course, not all-encompassing, but it should be enough to get you started. Your client will need to have proper care, so I recommend finding resources you can give your client in any of these areas.

I, in no way, certify you with the book's reading as an expert or someone who should prescribe for clients. This part of the book is for informational purposes, and you should either acquire the necessary certifications and insurance to give medical advice. Please always consider that there may be allergies to things that you/they have not come in contact with.

Natural Medicine and Herbs

AHCC - A strong immune support that is derived from shiitake mushrooms. When the pandemic hit, this was the only thing I could think of that might naturally help people to fight the Coronavirus. However, this does not take the place of vaccines. AHCC was sold out the first week of the pandemic in 2020 because all of us naturopaths thought the same thing: to help our immune systems have a fighting chance.

Aloe (Panini 'awa'awa) - this cactus's juice is used to help with stings and burns, especially sunburns and heat burns. Digested, it helps heal the probiotic layers of your system.

Apple Cider Vinegar - is an astringent and can help pull toxins out of your body through the water in your body. People always think that this is for weight loss, but all that is happening is you're losing toxic waste. If you don't have the toxins and are overweight, this isn't going to work. Apple cider vinegar is excellent for baths to help draw out toxins and make you feel better. I recommend an apple cider vinegar bath at least once a month.

Astragalus, Echinacea, Golden Seal - Your body builds a resistance to the efficacy after about two weeks, but these elements help build and protect the immune system.

Awa or *Kava* - This is a root with swollen joints. This would be ground up, and the root would be massaged through a cheese cloth to create a drink. It's good for nervousness, wetting the bed, insomnia, headaches, pain, and rashes.

Cinnamon - helps to regulate blood sugar.

Coconut Oil - helps fight kidney stones and helps to whiten teeth.

Elderberry - This is also an immune system supporter and safe for babies and young children (pending they aren't allergic to it, like my daughter).

Fish Oil - Good for hair, nails, immune system, and skin.

Garlic and a Warm Washcloth - place (don't shove or put deep) a half of a garlic clove resting in your ear (literally on the surface) and put a warm washcloth over it. The oils will seep into your ear to help with ear infections.

Hapu'u Pulu - This fern has smooth, brownish, silky material and is used in a boil to treat bad breath, and skin ailments.

Hau (Hibiscus tree) - The flowers, when pulverized and added to water, are a laxative.

Kalo (taro) - This is so nutritious that if a mother cannot produce milk, poi (fermented taro) can be given to a baby! Chewing it before cooking it can be bad, though. This can help with all kinds of ailments: cuts, boils, infections, and diarrhea.

Macadamia Nut Oil - heals skin problems, including dermatitis

Manuka Honey - the honey pollinated from the tea tree family. Some studies determined Manuka honey has repaired esophageal and stomach lining injuries. Manuka honey can also keep a wound from reinfection, help heal a wound, and will help to prevent scarring.

Mint - helps to aid in digestion.

Olive Leaf - This is one of the most natural remedies against MRSA. It is a potent way to build your immune system so you can fight viral loads, especially in the nasal spray.

Papaya leaves - The sap on the skin is healing for stings and wounds.

Potato - put on a cyst, and it should help raise it to the surface (it's the starch).

Salt Water - gargle for mouth and upper throat repair

St. John's Wart - the exorcist's favorite! Mood improver, spirit reducer.

Tart Cherry - Strongest responder to sore muscles and the natural removal of lactic acid.

Teatree Oil (pepa) - Disinfectant and removes blemishes. Also suitable for canker sores and to prevent bugs from biting.

Ti Leaves - This ceremonial plant has medicinal uses, including helping with earaches and fever blisters.

Vitamin C - This is water-soluble. Get an extended-release if you are going to throw this at your body.

Volcano Oil - put on your temples, can stop migraines

When taking or educating others about these things, be sure to read the recommended doses and to have a medical professional oversee any interactions with medication or other health observances that need to be overseen.

Nutrition

Your body holds fats for two reasons: protection or excess.

You need enough nutrition to function. If you are not behaving in a way that gives you the flexibility to do what you want in your life (either by being underweight, not strong enough, or being overweight and being held back by your weight), you need to adjust your nutrition.

I don't believe in diet food. I believe in food. First, I think all the food you eat should be delicious. If you decide that you only eat food that tastes good *and* is good for you, then you automatically limit yourself to the food you put in your body.

Second, if you want to be a different weight, let's look at food intake:

Write out what you think someone eats who weighs what you want to weigh. Write out their life in meal plans. Now, is that what you want? I look at some models and think, *man, they rarely get to eat cheesecake*, and I am reminded that I don't want that body. However, I like the weight I am at, so I'm not going to change my diet by increasing or decreasing how much I eat—looking at the lifestyle of someone who weighs what you want to weigh will tell you exactly how to do it.

Your body is the way it is based on what you've done to your body (pending hormonal irregularities). If you do something new to your body, your body will eventually adjust to its new lifestyle.

Learn about spices. Spices make healthy food more delicious than junk food, and you don't have all that refined sugar; plus, the spices you use are ingredients in spells.

Instead of sitting in the mentality that you need to "diet," just become who you want to be in 5 years, and your body will become that. Don't deviate. Just adjust. Literally live the life you want to be in five years, and your body will become that.

Massage

There are several benefits of massage, including:

1. Reducing stress and promoting relaxation

2. Relieving muscle tension and soreness

3. Increasing circulation and boosting the immune system

4. Improving flexibility and range of motion

5. Enhancing athletic performance and reducing the risk of injury

6. Helping to alleviate symptoms of anxiety and depression

7. Improving sleep quality

8. Lowering blood pressure and reducing the risk of heart disease

9. Reducing headaches and migraines

10. Boosting overall mental and physical wellness.

Massage can have several spiritual benefits, including:

1. Relaxation: Massage helps to reduce stress and induce deep relaxation, which can lead to a more peaceful and calm state of mind.

2. Increased awareness: As you receive a massage, you become more aware of your body, how it feels, and how it moves. This can help you be more present in the moment and increase your mindfulness.

3. Emotional release: Massage can help to release emotional blockages that are stored in the body, helping you to feel more emotionally balanced and centered.

4. Connection: As you receive a massage, you are connecting with another person and experiencing a sense of touch and nurturing.

This can help you feel more connected to others and build a sense of community.

5. Spiritual growth: Massage can be a powerful tool for spiritual growth and personal development. It can help you connect with your inner self and gain a deeper understanding of yourself.

In the Polynesian tradition, healing through touch is considered a sacred exchange of energy. It is a meeting of two spirits, a conversation carried through the hands, guided by the heart, and blessed by the ancestors. Among the Hawaiian people, two practices stand as profound examples of this: *lomi lomi* and *kahi loa*.

Lomi lomi is more than a massage technique. It is a prayer in motion. The practitioner calls upon the divine and upon their own healing spirits, asking that the work be guided for the highest good of the one receiving. The hands move with rhythmic, flowing motions, like the ocean's waves against the shore. Each stroke works to release tension, to encourage the blood and lymph to flow freely, and to awaken the body's own ability to heal. In lomi lomi, the body is seen as a reflection of the mind and spirit; tightness in the muscles may mirror old grief, fear, or unspoken words. As the practitioner works, they offer both physical release and the clearing of the energetic pathways that carry mana.

Kahi loa, often called "the gentle touch," is an even more subtle form of healing. This practice uses light, graceful contact over the body, connecting the receiver with the elements of nature. Traditionally, kahi loa follows the cycle of the elements: earth, water, fire, air, plants, animals, and spirit, each one addressed through intention and guided touch. The practitioner moves in harmony with the breath of the receiver, inviting the energy of each element to flow through them. It is a way of reminding the body that it belongs to the greater world, that it draws strength from the land, nourishment from the waters, vitality from the flame, clarity from the winds, and connection from all living things.

Both lomi lomi and kahi loa recognize that touch is more than a physical act. It is a bridge. Through it, the healer can help restore harmony, awaken memory in the cells, and call the spirit home to the body. In the Polynesian view, illness can sometimes arise when the soul feels distant from the body. Healing touch serves as an invitation for the soul to return, for mana to flow, and for balance to be restored.

When touch is offered in this sacred way, it becomes more than technique, it becomes a prayer of the hands, a song of the spirit, and a living conversation between healer, receiver, and the divine.

Exercise

In the world of all-or-nothing, people try to do exercise activities and then give up. From giving up, people then go into a need for comfort and sit and hide away. The need to sit on the couch instead of exercising comes from wanting to feel better about not exercising.

Find four things that you enjoy that are physical. I don't enjoy picking items up and putting them back down. Weightlifting is never going to be something I enjoy doing. Therefore, why would I get a gym membership? Also, I don't particularly appreciate running anymore. I used to, but since my knee injury, I don't run. The gym can be a great way to mind dump or work through what is going on in your life. It's a place to think and process. I like to do that with a massage.

I like to kayak, garden, dance, have sex, enjoy Tai Chi, and go for walks.

Exercise means you need to move, somehow. So does your client. Get up and move. You don't have to do CrossFit to check the box, but you need to do something. Many people perceive exercise to be something that is daunting and time-consuming. Look at exercise as a physical activity instead of a physical chore. What activities do you enjoy that are physical? Bam. You just checked the box of exercise.

Medicine

Go to the damn doctor!

I don't understand mainland American culture, where people choose a sports team for everything. People are either Western medicine or Natural medicine. They are either spiritual or scientific. Why can't you be both?

If someone is under spiritual attack, they will need help from the trauma of what has happened to them. Spiritual attack does not mean healing can only be either spiritual healing or mental healing. Spiritual attack means both are necessary. We must help the client from all avenues.

Get a therapist.
Get a primary care doctor
Get vaccinated.
Talk to a goddess.
Forest bathe.
Take your vitamins.
See the oncologist.
Take your AHCC.
Get your insulin shots and take cinnamon.
Listen to your spirit guides.

How the Work of Plant-Healing Came To Be

Characters:
Lono - God of Agriculture
Laka - Goddess of Inspiration
Hiʻiakaʻakapoliʻopele (Hiʻiaka) - Goddess of Healing and Dance

Hawaiʻi sat naked beneath the firmament, and the plants slept beneath cold stones. There was no healer yet, no *laʻau lapaʻau*.

Then came Lono, descending on the wings of rain-clouds and the scent of ripening taro. His presence was slow as island dawn, soft as the rising mist, and as certain as the call of the coqui frog at night. No trumpet thunder, no rightful announcement, just the hush that follows the first drops of rain on dry earth.

He stepped onto the volcanic slopes, and the ground greened beneath his feet. Fern curled upward. Taro leaf unfurled. He brought with him the spirit of *Hoʻoulu Laʻau*, the turning of seed into leaf, stem into remedy. Rain filled the valleys. Seedpods swelled. The world exhaled into life.

Across valleys and ridges, Lono whispered: "Holo ka wai. Holo ka ola."(The waters move. So moves life.)

But life needs guidance. Life needs ceremony. Life needs the still hand and the sacred chant.

When Lono had made the land fertile, he called to Laka, whose domain is the forest, the gathering of materials, and the shaping of ritual. She answered from within the palms and the ti leaf. She came as a green, weighty plumage of vines and ferns that tickle the wind.

With customary care, Laka created places for gathering, for respecting, and for medicinal work. She wove hula beneath the canopy and painted the dance of healing from branch to breath. Every lei she braided carried the meaning of kapu, of pono, of pono loa, right balance.

Under her guidance, the people learned when and how to enter the forest. They learned to ask permission. They learned to lay bark cloth at the roots before harvesting. They learned to chant the name of each plant and to honor the akua that dwelled within it. Without Laka, the plants might cease, or the meditational chant might fail, or the medicine might spoil in its own mana.

She taught life that extends through lineage, and through protocols so old even the stones remember.

But still, there was no healer, only the groundwork of growth (Lono) and the pathway of inspiration (Laka). Healing cannot manifest without daring to journey into the unknown. So Lono and Laka called to Hiʻiaka, chaperone of the sacred flame, wielder of chants that tie the living with the unseen.

She answered by collecting plants that no one else could see: mamaki, ko, ʻahuʻawa, kukui, lauaʻe, alaheʻe… each named by her chant and each guided to healing by her breath.

Hiʻiaka placed her foot upon lele koa and hopped across steaming stones. She entered realm after realm, sometimes sea-deep, sometimes mountain-high, and always returned with leaves and roots, past chants and cures, stories and possibilities. She tested each plant on the broken, the wounded, the lost in dreams. She sang pale ana to chase away illness, oli mau to anchor balance, and hoʻola ʻiʻa (the chant of rebirth) over the dying.

She merged the power of Lono's growth and Laka's weaving of what moves, and she enacted the final transformation. From her hands, midwife between spirit and leaf, the art of *laʻau lapaʻau* was born.

On the vast plain of Waipiʻo, a traveler fell ill. Fever roared through his blood. His body shrank beneath sickness. The shamans fed him food and chants, but nothing held. A girl found him and brought him to her mat.

Then came wind from the uplands, the scent of wet stones and trees' shadows. Lono's rain fell across his brow. Fern and ti leaf freshened his breath. Laka's inspiration came when a girl knelt in the forest, whispered the plant name into the breeze, and wrapped a leaf of hala over his hair and shoulders.

Meanwhile, Hiʻiaka emerged with healing songs, placing her hand under his head and opening his mouth. With Lono growing the plants, Hiʻiaka's knowledge, Laka's inspiration penetrated the girl's mind.

The girl named the plants: "'Olena.ʻAwa. Kukui. ʻAlae. Hinahina." She chanted them three times. She wove them into a poultice. She wrapped it in kapa. She pressed it on fevered skin.

The fever broke. The traveler exhaled long. The redness drained back into his bones. When he opened his eyes, the rain still fell. He saw Lono's blessing in the droplets. He felt Laka's wisdom in how the girl cared for him. He heard Hiʻiaka's blessings in his sudden recovery.

From that day, the story of healing was not just the plants, nor only the rites, it was always the union of Lono, Laka, and Hiʻiaka. A healer, kahuna laʻau lapaʻau, brought seeds to the rain (Lono), took them with respect and inspired how to treat her (Laka), and used them with devotion (Hiʻiaka).

In later generations, priests and practitioners built hale laʻau lapaʻau in valleys where these akua were strongest. They placed altars for Lono to ensure rain, leafy offerings for Laka to ensure a respectful harvest, and chant-stones engraved with the name of Hiʻiaka to guide the healing.

Aromatherapy

As you read this, you're going to be "team lemon," because you'll find out how many things are treatable with the aromatic properties of the lemon. Interestingly enough, in modern witchcraft, many newer spells call for the use of lemon as a banishing ingredient. This is a common mistake. Lemon is 'cleaning you' of the person in question, not sending them away. It doesn't "sour the relationship." Lemon will treat, cure, and make well. Be careful how you use it.

Remember that smells that are foul make us sick; they make us physically ill. Fragrances that waft can be healing as well, like the incredible use of Vic's VapoRub.

Aromatherapy has a long tradition of healing. Many people will utilize essential oils in their daily lives to help with anxiety, depression, or focus, but did you know you can cure other ailments of the body? Unfortunately, there isn't a lot of scientific investigation as to how aromatherapy works, but we have excellent reason to believe it does because of repeatable positive outcomes.

To add, with the wonders and amazements of healing, also include the reactions to aromatic essences, which can cause distress, like dizziness, tightening of the lungs, nasal drainage, or even nervousness. Why? Because your body wants you to leave the environment where the smells are present. In many cases, certain perfumes or colognes may have a synthetic or repulsive quality to our physical body, even if we find the smells pleasant. One can also develop skin disorders from continued exposure to aromas that are counter to the needs of the person.

The vapors of certain oils have antiseptic powers by impeding the development of microbial cultures, strengthening elastic membrane molecules that combat developing germs. The strongest to weakest in order are lemon, thyme, orange, bergamot, juniper, clove, citronella, lavender, peppermint, rosemary, sandalwood, and then eucalyptus.

For instance, lemon essence has shown the ability to help fight meningitis, staph infections, strep, scarlet fever, rheumatoid arthritis, and to help quicken the healing of wounds, according to Dr. Jean Valnet's *The Practice of Aromatherapy*.

We can also appreciate the significant improvement in smell when using toothpaste. There are bactericidal qualities when adding clove, camomile, and peppermint to toothpaste, helping the qualities of hydrogen peroxide in fighting bacterial infections in the mouth.

Essential oils help aid in soaps as well, aiding in the healing process. Pine, thyme, lemon (I know!), and cinnamon help to break down the viral load of the flu. During the holidays, keep those seasonal candles going through February. When we use aromatic essences, healing takes place quickly.

Lavender, mint, and geranium have pesticidal properties, keeping mosquitoes, wasps, and moths at bay, and can help in the treatment of bites and stings.

Ylang-ylang helps with sexual difficulties, and camphor helps as an aphrodisiac. Cypress and lemongrass help with hormonal deficiencies in women, while rue, basil, cinnamon, lavender, and thyme can help to normalize a menstrual cycle.

Remember that these treatments are to be utilized like medicine, with purposeful exposure. Not a one-night use of a lemon-scented candle and boom, you have killed strep-throat.

Let's look at a few others specifically for the healer exorcist. These problems leave the body feeling vulnerable, and therefore should be used continuously while adapting the life balance:

Antiseptics: basil, bergamot, citronella, clove, eucalyptus, juniper, lavender, lemon, orange, peppermint, rosemary, sandalwood, thyme.

Antitoxin: lemon

Arthritis: lemon, garlic

Chronic Diarrhea: clove, garlic, geranium, lemon, nutmeg

Infection: Borneo camphor, clove, eucalyptus, juniper, lavender, lemon, pine, thyme

Migraine: lavender

Obesity: lemon, onion

Pain-relieving: camomile, cinnamon, clove, coriander, garlic, geranium, ginger, lavender, nutmeg

Parasiticides: caraway, cinnamon, clove, eucalyptus, garlic, lemon, peppermint

Sedatives: camomile, lavender, lemon, thyme

Sexual Dysfunction: cinnamon, clove, juniper, lemongrass, pine, rosemary, sandalwood, thyme, ylang-ylang

Stimulants: basil, clove, coriander, eucalyptus, juniper, nutmeg, rosemary, pine, savory, tarragon

You're Not Sick, The Doctor Is Making You Sick

Characters:
The Menehune - The little people of Hawai'i
The man - A man over-medicated

    The Menehune are a legendary people in Hawaiian mythology, known for their small stature, supernatural craftsmanship, and nocturnal activities. They are often described as ancient builders who lived in the deep forests and hidden valleys of the Hawaiian Islands, particularly on the island of Kaua'i. While modern retellings sometimes reduce them to childlike fairies or mischievous elves, traditional Hawaiian perspectives view the Menehune with a mixture of reverence, caution, and mystery. Their presence in oral traditions points to deeper cultural truths about ancestry, memory, and the power of unseen forces.

    In many Hawaiian stories, the Menehune were the original inhabitants of the islands, skilled and intelligent beings who lived in harmony with the land before the arrival of the Polynesian voyagers. Some legends portray them as a distinct race of beings who predated the first settlers from Tahiti. Others suggest they were an early human population, possibly an ancestral group, who chose to live in isolation as later waves of migration brought new chiefs, new gods, and new systems of rule.

    Across the islands, tales of Menehune tend to follow a consistent pattern: they are expert builders who work swiftly at night, completing massive construction projects in a single evening. Their works vanish with the sun unless they are undisturbed during their task. If they are seen, interrupted, or mocked, they abandon the project and disappear. Because of this, Menehune are often credited with the construction of impressive ancient structures whose origin is unclear, such as the Alekoko Fishpond (also called the Menehune Fishpond) on Kaua'i, or ancient heiau whose stones appear too massive or precisely placed to have been made without divine assistance.

Menehune are deeply connected to nature and spirituality. In many traditions, they are associated with mana, particularly the kind that comes from knowing how to live properly with the land and elements. Some stories describe Menehune as spirit-guardians of sacred places, or as ancestral builders who worked in the service of the gods. Their invisibility to most people speaks to a spiritual truth: only those who live with respect and humility may perceive or benefit from the work of the Menehune.

Menehune choose when and to whom they reveal themselves. They appear most often to children, to those near death, or to people in need of healing who have exhausted all other paths. In this way, they serve as protectors of the old knowledge, keepers of medicine, chant, and structure long forgotten by the modern world.

In contemporary times, the image of the Menehune has often been commercialized or misrepresented. Tourists may encounter cartoonish depictions of them as playful sprites or mischief-makers. While the cultural memory of the Menehune has remained alive in Hawaiian storytelling, it is important to distinguish between authentic mo'olelo (oral traditions) and modern appropriations. True stories of the Menehune are rooted in spiritual depth, ancestral lineage, and the understanding that not all wisdom reveals itself to the loud and proud.

Whether remembered as ancestors, spirits, or a lost race of builders, the Menehune embody a core Hawaiian truth: that those who live close to the land and serve with humility may do great things, even in secret. Their legacy endures in stones, in dreams, and in the hidden folds of the forest, just beyond the place where most people stop looking.

The man had forgotten how to breathe.

He had not been born that way. In his youth, his chest had risen and fallen with the tides. His body had known the salt winds and the shimmer of moonlight on skin. He had stood in streams without fear of leeches or shadow.

But something had happened.

Perhaps it began with the swallowing of the first white pill. Perhaps it began when the needle pricked his arm and he looked away, trusting a man with a badge instead of a kukui salve. Perhaps it began before all that, when his breath first learned the rhythm of buildings instead of trees.

He became tired. Then heavy. Then slow. His mind lost clarity. His body swelled and sagged. The pills were meant to help, but they stacked upon each other like stones upon his chest. When one failed, another was given. When that one failed, it was doubled. And soon, he lived in a fog where birds no longer sang and time no longer mattered.

The doctors were white-coated and hurried. They spoke with mouths shaped by another land. They told him that healing would come if he endured, but healing didn't come. Something in him broke. It was quiet. But it broke. One day, he looked into the mirror and saw... no one.

That day, the Menehune began to whisper.

At first, he heard them in the roots beneath the house. He had moved to the forest edge, hoping the quiet would help him sleep. However, it was probably a noisier life in the aina's hem than if he had stayed in this apartment in Manoa.

He heard scratching. He heard tapping. He heard laughter so small it might have been wind, except it followed him even when the air was still.

That night, he dreamed of hands. Small hands. Brown and thick with dirt. They reached into his body without harm. They pulled strands from his liver. They lifted shadows from his lungs. They untied the knots from his stomach. He awoke with sweat pouring down his spine and the taste of red clay in his mouth. He got up, drenched in his nocturnal shower, and went back to the mirror, looking over the moon-lit sink. He could see a version of himself. Really see... someone.

He stopped taking the pills.

The shaking came first. Then the sickness. Then the screams. He curled up on his bed and bit into his blanket until blood came. He heard the doctors in his memory telling him to go back. Telling him he was dying.

Each night, the Menehune returned. They sang with vibration. They hummed into his joints. They placed leaves upon his eyes. They pressed his tongue with a root that burned and then cooled. He slept, and in the morning, he would sweat. Each day, a little more darkness left his bones.

One night, his spirit left his body and followed them.

He woke in the dark, and the air smelled of awa and moss. He saw a flicker outside his window. When he stepped barefoot into the night, the forest opened without protest. The vines parted. The stones shone with dew. A trail lit itself before him, pulsing like a heartbeat.

He followed without question.

They led him deep into the trees. Deeper than the oldest paths. Deeper than human memory. The forest grew thick, then thin, then thick again. He passed between trunks so wide they held the names of ancestors. He stepped over roots that moved to let him through. At last, he came to a clearing where the moon sat low and full.

There they were.

They stood no taller than his knee. Their eyes were round, black, and glistening like lava rock wet from the sea. Their hair was wild. Their skin was dusted with ash and fern. They wore nothing but belts of ti leaf and kukui bark. They were older than he was, older than his grandfather, older than the cliffs that cradle the bones of the dead.

The tallest among them stepped forward.

He said nothing. He pointed to a stone.

The man sat.

Then the Menehune came forward in silence. They touched his limbs. They opened his mouth. They pressed behind his ears. They smelled his skin. Then one by one, they reached into small pouches and pulled out medicine. Bark. Slivers of bone. Ash from a sacred fire. A tiny gourd that glowed when opened.

They placed their medicine upon him.

One wrapped his belly in wet kapa. One chewed a root, opened the man's mouth, climbed onto his lap, and placed the paste beneath the man's tongue.

They laid him down, and one climbed his back and pressed down between his shoulder blades until he gasped. One sang into his ear a sound that made the earth shiver.

He wept, but they did not comfort him. They let the tears come. They let his mouth stretch open in wailing. They waited until the grief had passed, like rain moving through a valley.

Then the tallest one spoke.

He said, "You were poisoned. But not by the plant. Not by the drug. You were poisoned by forgetting. Forgetting how to breathe. Forgetting how to kneel. Forgetting how to ask."

The man lowered his head. The Menehune touched his chest.

"This is your altar," he said. "You buried it beneath pills. You buried it beneath pride. Now you must uncover it."

Then the Menehune faded. They dissolved like mist. The clearing still breathed with their presence. The stone still held his warmth. The air still rang with their chant.

He stood, and the path lit itself once more.

When he returned to his house, the sky was beginning to shift. The stars were dulling. The birds had begun their rustling. He gathered water from the stream. He built a fire with care. He placed his hands on the ground and thanked the roots for lifting him.

He awoke. From that day forward, he changed. He grew thin but strong. His eyes cleared. His voice became low and steady. He grew his own food. He made his own medicine. He sang chants his grandmother had taught him when he was small. He spoke to his ancestors again. He fed the altars. He sat with the wind.

He did not return to the hospital. When people came to ask how he had healed, he said only, "There are beings who live beneath the roots. They remember what we forget."

Some laughed at him. Others listened. But those who listened began to heal, too.

They came quietly. They left their shoes outside. They brought offerings of awa, of taro, of moʻolelo. They learned to sit without speaking. They learned to breathe again.

Part 6

Unihipili & Past Life Healing

Maui Slows Down The Sun

Characters:
Maui - Demi-god of Pure Will
Hina - The Goddess of the Moon
The Sun

The mountain held its breath while the village slept. Dew cooled the palms. The sea kept its shape. The people lay with their mouths quiet, the hard work pressing behind their eyes like a debt. Days flew like birds with no nest. The Sun ran across the sky and left the world unfinished.

Maui walked through the village and listened. He saw kapa half-dried and women weeping quietly at the river. He watched fishermen pull nets full of fish that would spoil because light had rushed them raw. He touched the shoulder of a man whose breadfruit had turned in the heat before anyone could finish peeling it. The complaint was the same in every tired voice. The Sun moves too fast.

He went to his mother. Hina lived where the moon rides low and the tides tell secrets. Her house smelled of salt and wrapped mats. She saw the way his jaw set and the way his hands curled like someone holding a stone too long.

"What will you do, child," she asked, "when the gods themselves move faster than the hands of people?"

"I will stop the Sun," Maui said. His eyes knew the cliff faces and the seam of the reef and the old prayers that keep a canoe from capsizing.

Hina opened a woven box as if she had been waiting her whole life for this exact moment. She handed him ropes plaited from her hair. Each strand carried her mana, woven from her hair. Each loop held the hush of ocean nights. "Listen," she said. "The ropes remember the names of the winds. They will not break." Then she set before him the hook that had been in the family for generations. It was carved from a bone older than most stories, curved and black, its point worn like a promise. This hook had carried islands up from the bottom of the sea. It had been called Manaiakalani. It had fished for land. It had lifted stars in other versions of the tale. "Take it," Hina said. "This will hold what your arms alone cannot keep."

Maui lifted the hook. It fit his hand like a thought he had been waiting for. He pressed his forehead to Hina's and took the mana of her voice. He climbed.

He climbed slowly so that the mountain would not hear him as a trespasser. He crept up Haleakala, the red earth sweating under his feet, until he reached a stone rim where the world opened like a mouth. The rope lay coiled like a sleeping serpent. The hook lay beside it, dark and heavy as a moonless sea.

When the horizon paled, the Sun pushed up in its usual fierce hurry. It came like a hot god in motion, blazing the clouds, wanting always to hurry on. Maui waited until its rim hung at the lip of the sea. Then he heaved his hook.

The hook flew like a spear and struck into the arm of daylight. It caught the Sun as if it were a fish, that great bright body snagged by bone and rope. The Sun roared, and the heat came down like a shout, but the hook held. Maui tied the ropes to the hook and wrapped them around a great stone and around his own waist. The ropes sang with Hina's voice.

The Sun thrashed. It tried to tear away from the hook. It sent blinding light down the rim, and Maui's skin blistered where the heat struck, but he would not yield. He planted his feet and pulled. The ropes cut into his hands, and he smiled because that was the work of a man made desperate for his people.

"Who binds me?" the Sun thundered, its voice like drums in caves.

"I am Maui," he cried back, "son of Hina. You race like a thief and leave us no work to finish. You lift the days from our hands. You will slow."

The Sun strained. The hook groaned. The ropes burned but stayed. Maui heaved again and again, clicking the hook if the light tried to slip, and the Sun sagged. It felt the muscle of the mountain beneath Maui's feet. It felt the stitch in Hina's hair in the rope. It felt like every voice from every house below was calling for more time. The Sun quieted a fraction. The world held a new breath.

When it could, the Sun demanded a bargain. It asked why a man should tie it and command the hour. Maui answered plainly. "We make our days by the sweat of our hands. Give us time to do our work, and we will sing for you. We will offer thanks. We will plant and harvest and remember you."

The Sun had been hurried for eons and was proud of its path. It looked at Maui's eyes and saw the faces of people who had nothing but the day, and it felt the hook that had fished islands from the deep, and it gave up its sprint. It lengthened its step. It decided to move slower so the kapa would dry so that the fish would cure, so mothers could finish plaiting their hair.

Maui slackened the line but did not let it go. He watched the Sun arc across the softened whole sky. The light moved like a measured drumbeat. Down below, the village rose with the careful efficiency of people who had enough time. They patted wet kapa, they split breadfruit, they sang while they worked because the day came at a proper pace.

When Maui came down from the rim, he did not march like a conqueror as you would expect. He walked with dust in his hair and burnt rope on his hands. The people met him and pressed leis into his shoulders and gratitude to his ears. They told the children so the story would not die. Remember the hook. Remember the ropes. Remember Hina's hair. Remember the man who dared hold the light.

Years come and go, and the Sun still moves with a care it did not have before. Mothers point at the slow rise on the eastern rim and say the name Maui. Grandmothers tap the rope they keep beside the grindstone and tell the story of the hook and how a human hand can hold a god when it carries the right song. The children play as they play all over the islands, running under light that lasts long enough to finish the day and begin the night with stones stacked upon dry kapa.

We say it for a reason. The story holds the teaching. Do not let the work of one life be swallowed by haste. Bind the day with purpose. Tell the tale so the ropes will remember the names. The hook was a tool. Hina's hair was a womb of blessing. Maui was a man who would not allow his people to lose what they needed.

If you walk to Haleakala at dawn and press your ear to the red earth, you might still hear the faint click of the hook where it caught the Sun. You might feel the old rope in the wind. And if you listen as your mothers listened, the story will travel on. You will learn to braid your own ropes and to pass the hook, in word, in song, in the work you finish before night falls.

Just remember, the deal is to sing for the sun. While the sun shines, sing.

Trigger Unihipili Healing with Past Life Regression: The Akashic Records

A Past Life Regression is remembering what had happened to you through your unihipili. The parts of your psychic self were so affected by your physical and mental self that there are still footprints taking you back through time. These are also known as your akashic records.

When we die in terrible ways or are forced to do things in our past lives, we sometimes carry those into our current lives. Learning about it can set you on the path to understanding yourself and then making the changes appropriately so as not to repeat history. These traumas in a past life have fractured and infected our reincarnatable soul into this life. Unfair? Probably, so let's fix it.

Why is this important for you to know? Those who are debilitated by phobias, addictions (including to people), blockages that then turn to life imbalance, or chronic pain where your client wants to give up, leave them vulnerable to possession through the unihipili part of their soul.

How do you benefit from doing a Past Life Regression?
- Clarity as to your phobias
- Clarity as to why you repeat things you know are bad for you
- Are you pulled to unexplainable places?
- Do you have a fascination with time periods or cultures?
- Do you have fears or avoidances of certain kinds of people?
- Are you good at something you didn't need a lot of training in?
- Do you repeat the same kind of relationships?
- Do you have addictions?
- Do your possessions break often?
- Do you suffer from night terrors, nightmares, or have trouble sleeping, AND they aren't linked to what you're going through currently?
- Are there blockages in every area of your life for no reason?
- Are you experiencing unexplained sickness, aches, and pains with no diagnosis?
- Have you been diagnosed with one thing after another?
- Does death surround you? Are most of them unexplained?

Steps to Past Life Regression:
1. Breathe
1.5. Do the bonfire version of the journey. I have learned it helps to do the bonfire section here and then take a small flame from the bonfire and go to the steps.
2. Steps and Mind Dump

3. In the foyer, walk to the left this time. Off to the left, there is a well. Look deep into the well. See that this well is a tube, a tunnel that will go past the markers of rebirth. This underground tunnel will bypass the amnesiac part or rebirth and take you to the memories and experiences of your past lives. The sooner you jump out of the akashic current, the closer the life is to your current life. The longer you ride the current, the further you are in time from your current life. Can't see the well at all? Welcome! This life is your first incarnation, you new soul! That means that this form of healing will not work for you.

Stand on the edge of the well, looking down at your feet, down into the cosmic-colored tunnel. When you jump down, you will jerk and jolt around. You will have to consciously push yourself out, feeling like you will fall into nothingness, to experience a life.

Once you push yourself out of the akashic current, wait for everything to come into light. What are you wearing? What language are people speaking? What is your gender? Skin color? Is there electricity? What is the weather like? Any notable environmental features or structures? How old are you? Stay for a while. Just ride the life. Feel the moments from moment to moment. Do you fast-forward to other notable parts of your life? Try to move from one memorable moment and only a little bit further in the life. Take your time. Stay for as long as you can.

Come back by repeating your current name if you don't naturally come back on your own.

Nuumite can help with past-life travel. It helps clear up the visuals. I just keep it about two feet in front of me, and I'm good.

Blasphemous Blogger

I talked with one of my teachers at BearBridge Academy of Witchcraft and Psychic Development: she sent me an article from a woman who lives near her, "I'm struggling with this," she messages me. "Can you decipher what she is talking about and reframe it?"

I read the article. The author says she had a past life regression. From that regression, she states that her past self had trauma from WWII. When she got back, she was so upset by the regression that she carried those emotions from that time with her.

Then she said she was a living "Horcrux" because her past life self was haunting her. So, she and this other version of herself smoked pot, got high, and did a soul retrieval on herself. And you, too, can hire her for 30 minutes and $30 to receive this grade-A level help.

I was angry when I finished.

My response to my teacher was this: "This is bullshit. Past life regression turned possession from an alternate her and then getting high and calling it soul retrieval is a mockery of shamanic healing modalities."

That woman is the reason why people from indigenous backgrounds want to gate-keep. She is a spiritual opportunist, taking advantage of those who may actually need healing. She was writing about something she had no authority to do, and taking innocent people's money while getting high, stealing these poor victims' money, and losing trust in us, authentic healers. And let's throw in some easily recognizable *Harry Potter* pop culture to tickle the familiar bone.

First, if she had a successful regression, then that regression should give her insight into the unexplainable habits, life patterns, and phobias she is experiencing, including likes and dislikes. Or if there are odd repetitions that her body keeps having as illnesses from a previous life that were linked to her psychic self. A regression points out answers.

Second, if something attached to her for real, then it was something pretending to be her past self. Or perhaps she created an artificial elemental of herself to possess herself, or even worse, she has the beginning symptoms of D.I.D. (see Diagnosis section).

You can't be possessed by you from another life. You are already in possession of yourself.

Third, you can't do a soul retrieval by getting high and meditating.

A soul retrieval from a past life is simply not done because it requires many skills and stones.

Because of my outrage, I'm going to walk you through the information on past life healing, but I will gate-keep the details. Along with those who have taught me, there is a responsibility to do Past Life Healings. Basically, if someone says they do it, they are probably lying. The best thing you can do is have a regression and then talk about those things in a therapeutic environment.

Past Life Healing

Breakdown of an Actual Past Life Healing

1. Be able to do your own past life regressions and be able to verify them with historical information. I find it interesting that people from America only come back from lives where they spoke English. Ha! Red flag. Or if the timelines don't match up. Or if they are someone famous who would not have reincarnated because they are a master. Ha!

2. Once you can do that, you also have to be psychic enough to read someone's mind. Yep, that's the next skill. I know... Why? You have to know you are reading the correct person's mind when you are connecting to someone for their past life reading. Then you have to do *their* regression. You have to do a regression of someone else's past life. You have to channel a living person and ride through *their* akashic records. Again, this should be verifiable and repeatable. Watch for red flags in historical information, prejudices, and easily found information.

3. If this is all verifiable and the person is trained enough to do past life regressions and then to channel a living person and ride through their client's past life, then they would have to have enough control to be able to stop their travel in their akashic records at the life they need healing. I mean, they will have to be able to pause what they are experiencing.

4. If that is successful, then you have to find a moment when they are asleep after the said trauma (yeah, then they have to land precisely after the trauma or be able to move through that timeline to a place where they are sleeping). Imagine needing to find the part of someone's past life *after* a trauma, and then finding them asleep. Tricky aiming.

5. If you can get that far, you have to leave that life and head to the Otherworld from that point to do a soul retrieval. You are in spirit form, connected to another person, that person has been through the trauma, then they go to sleep, then you have to spirit-walk *from that point* to the Lower World, going deeper and further away from yourself. You have to have a strong enough sense of self to then sit with the sleeping person in the past to leave yourself further. You go up the stairs, and you have to cross to the Spirit Current from that person's past mind and then go to the Lower World from that point.

6. In the Lower World, find the pieces of their trauma, and understand what you're doing, but you're so removed from yourself, you cannot even function. You have to get the pieces from that life's trauma, come back to that timeline, stop there, and integrate them into the other person. You have to hope that you picked a time that they aren't going to do drugs or drink alcohol for twenty-four hours, and then finally make it back into you in the time that you are now.

7. My teachers also told me I had to acquire the seven stones (this is what I'm gatekeeping) that would help me not die in the process. You have to "wear" those stones. So, I have a specific belt with a holder made out of leather that goes around my torso. The leather is touching my skin, and the stones touch the leather the entire time. If I disconnect from that belt, I'm done. These stones (which I will continue to keep a secret until I have a student who has demonstrated all of the previous skills mentioned with repeatable accuracy) are all specific to help with that distance focus, amplification of psychic senses, ultra-grounding, and cord connecting.

8. Here is the worst part: you die a little while you're gone. There is no waking you up. You're just gone. And worse: you want to know what happens if your client gets up and moves while you are traveling? Coma. You see, their current body is the only anchor you have to come home. If they move, you are brain-dead. Oh, did I mention that you lose your power-animal on the cross over to the Spirit Current from the past life's location? Yep, you're on your own. No help. You aren't going to the spirit world from your own body, so your psychic self is not with you. Your power-animal is back at home base. So, if you lose your way, you have nothing to help you find your way back, and you don't have your spiritual self to make sure you don't end up somewhere spiritually dangerous. If your client gets up to use the bathroom while you're under, you are basically brain-dead. Braindead done; you're stuck in the Other World hundreds of years ago.

I have done two Past Life Healings. They are so dangerous that I don't do them because I have to trust the client with my very life. Those two clients were people I trusted with my life. They needed it. There was so much damage in their past lives that they were repeating the same life. One of the clients was so complicated. She was a friend for decades. While I was doing the healing, I had to keep getting back into the akashic flow to another life and fix from that life, then another life, then another life. I was gone for two and a half hours, my body parched and aged from being dead for two hours.

She said, "I didn't know where you went, but I felt like you had really gone... like, gone gone. I watched the screen, and your body fell over, collapsed onto the mat. I was too afraid to move, though. I remembered what you said, and when I saw you fall, I knew that you were trusting me with your life and all, to help fix mine. So, I sat still and waited. I wanted to get up and get my phone and call 911, but risking getting up was not worth it. I told myself that after three hours, I was going to yell for help. I'm so glad you came back."

Let's just clear up a few things now: this book is a manual of skills you have to practice. You have to master these things (or have viable substitutions) in order to help someone or yourself. This book isn't an easy recipe book you can just pick up. There are some advanced skills to be undertaken seriously, with diligence and mastery.

There are plenty of books with quick ways to do things. There is no shortcut to mastery. There is no shortcut or easy weekend away to get a certification in this work. Practice, repeat, practice, learn, practice, repeat, practice, learn, and master it.

Please, regarding seeing that anyone who says they do Past Life Healings, I implore you to ask for a Regression and see what happens first. Get proof. And anyone who does a Past Life Healing and isn't a fearful practitioner is probably someone stealing money.

I hope with your education and commitment to mastery of the subject of being a witchdoctor that you share my outrage, caution, and alternatives. Our voices, especially if you have privilege, need to be used to talk about indigenous practices because these people who are charging spiritually hurt folks so they can sit on their couch getting high need to be overshadowed by truth.

With all that said, a Past Life Regression should do the trick, and Past Life Healing is rarely needed. You can heal from the regression. Do that instead.

Pele and Poliahu: Fire and Snow

Characters:
Poliahu - Snow Goddess
Lilinoe - Goddess of fine, delicate mist on Mauna Kea
Waiau - Goddess of cold waters and cleansing
Kahoupokane - Goddess of Snowstorms
Pele - Goddess of the Volcano

Poliahu sat among her companions, her white feather cloak spilling across the ground like a fall of snow. Beside her were Lilinoe, Waiau, and Kahoupokane, their cloaks glimmering with the colors of clouds, dew, and storm.

They laughed together as they readied their holua sleds. The hills stretched before them, smooth and green, their slopes running toward the valleys like streams of grass. The wind caught at their hair and cloaks as they raced, their laughter carrying across the wide mountain.

Poliahu's sled cut through the grass like the glide of an 'io hawk through the air. Lilinoe was swift, her hair streaming like mist. Waiau leaned low, her eyes bright with the joy of the race. Kahoupokane's laughter rose behind them, deep as the voice of a waterfall. They were sisters in spirit, each of the mountain's cold breath made flesh.

As they returned to the top of the slope, a woman stood waiting. She was tall, her skin warm with the light of the sun, her hair flowing in black waves. Her skirt shimmered as though threads of fire had been woven into its folds. Around her shoulders rested a cloak of red and gold feathers, gleaming like the wings of the ʻiʻiwi bird.

"May I join you?" she asked, her voice smooth and bright as a shell held to the ear.

"You may," Poliahu said. Her eyes held curiosity. "Have you ridden a holua before?"

"I have," the woman replied, smiling. "And I will gladly race with you."

They set their sleds side by side. Poliahu and her sisters leaned forward, and the stranger crouched low. At the signal, they pushed off together. The grass whispered under them. Wind sang in their ears. The stranger's sled shot forward with startling speed, and she laughed, her voice ringing like molten rock striking the sea.

Race after race followed. At first, the joy of the game carried them. The stranger laughed with them, her eyes bright with the spirit of play. But as the sun moved toward the west, a shadow passed between them that was not cast by any cloud.

The stranger's gaze lingered on Poliahu with something sharper than admiration. Poliahu felt it like the first sting of heat upon snow. She sensed in the woman an ancient force, one that breathed from a place far below the skin of the earth.

"You ride well," Poliahu said, her voice even.

"And you," the stranger replied, "are swift. The mountain favors you." Her eyes flicked to the snowy crown high above. "But the mountain's favor is never given forever."

Lilinoe drew close to Poliahu. "Sister," she whispered, "do you feel it? The breath of fire hidden behind her words?"

Poliahu's gaze did not waver from the stranger. "I feel it."

When they began the next race, the stranger did not wait for the signal. She lunged forward, her sled cutting the grass like a flame through dry leaves. Poliahu gave chase, her companions close behind. At the bottom of the slope, the stranger sprang from her sled and turned to face them, bursting into flames.

"You have raced with me," she said, "but now you will face me. I am Pele of the fire. These slopes are mine."

The air trembled. The ground beneath them stirred as though some great heart had begun to beat. Heat rose from the soil, carrying the scent of stone just before it shattered. From the earth's skin, a red glow began to seep.

Lilinoe's voice cut through the air. "Sister—"

"Go," Poliahu said.

They fled up the slope. Behind them, the ground split, and molten rock surged upward, spilling into the grass. The heat struck Poliahu's back like a blow. Her cloak flared around her, and turned to a mighty blanket of snow. Her feet carried her toward the white crown of Mauna Kea.

"Pele!" Poliahu cried over her shoulder. "Your fire has no hold here!"

"I will melt your throne!" Pele's voice roared. "I will burn your grass, crack your stones, drink your rivers in steam. I will leave only my black rock behind!"

The air shimmered with heat. Poliahu's breath came fast, the thin wind of the mountain filling her chest. Her sisters ran beside her, the frost of their power spilling from their cloaks. Lava rolled behind them, bright as the heart of the sun.

At last, Poliahu reached the cold heights. She turned and raised her arms to the sky. "Mauna Kea, my home, hear me. I send cold. I send ice. Cover my slopes in white."

The mountain, the sky, and the air around answered. From the summit, clouds gathered thick and heavy. The wind sharpened, cutting like a blade. Snow began to fall, at first in drifting flakes, then in torrents. The air froze between breaths.

Pele's fire struck the wall of frost. Steam screamed into the sky. Lava hissed and cracked as it met the ice, darkening to stone. Pele surged forward again, her flames bright against the snow, but each wave of fire cooled beneath the onslaught. Black rock lay in her path, stripped of heat, unable to rise again.

Poliahu stepped forward, her voice calm. "Your fire has its place, Pele. It brings warmth, it shapes the land, it feeds the roots of life. But here, the mountain needs the touch of snow. Without the cold, the streams below will dry. The grass will wither. The fish in the rivers will vanish. Even your forests would fade."

Pele's eyes blazed, but her fire slowed. The snow swirled around her, clinging to her hair, her cloak, her skin. She looked toward the horizon, where the dark flanks of Mauna Loa lay beneath the clouds.

"Then we will share these islands," Pele said at last. "Your snows upon Mauna Kea. My fires upon Mauna Loa and Kīlauea. But never shall we step freely into each other's realm."

"Agreed," Poliahu replied. "For each is needed. The cold for rest and renewal. The heat for growth and creation. The people need both to live well."

The snow eased. The clouds thinned, letting the sun spill once more upon the slopes. Pele turned and strode down the mountain. Her steps cooled to black rock that marked her path. Poliahu stood upon the high slope, watching her go.

Lilinoe came to her side. "She will return, will she not?"

"She will," Poliahu said. "For fire always seeks new places to burn. And snow will always be here to answer."

Below, the people of the island learned the story. They saw the dark rock where lava had flowed and the white snows that guarded the summit. They knew then that the land's health came from both forces. The warmth of Pele's fire brought the soil that fed the taro and the sweet potato. The cold of Poliahu's snow fed the streams that watered the loʻi and filled the fishponds.

So it has been since that day. Mauna Kea wears her white crown, sending her rivers down to the valleys. Mauna Loa and Kīlauea send their fire to make new land, black and shining, ready to be softened by rain. The people live between these powers, taking warmth in winter and coolness in summer, their lives bound to the balance of fire and frost.

The elders teach this truth to the children: seek the heat that gives life, and the cold that grants rest. Do not take one and reject the other. For a land of only snow is barren, and a land of only fire is ash. Life grows strongest where the two meet, each keeping the other from excess.

And so when the people stand in the warmth of the lowlands, they honor Pele with chant and dance. When they climb to the heights and feel the kiss of snow, they honor Poliahu with gifts of kapa and lei. In this way, they remember that healing comes from many kinds of nature. Fire to awaken, snow to soothe. Heat to open the body, cold to let it mend.

Music in Healing: Power of Song, Prayer, and Dance

As you've learned that ho'upu'upu can be harmed with the words of someone hateful, the power of prayer, song, and dance can heal, dismantle those spells, and rejuvenate those who are harmed, including yourself. The power of music is extraordinary.

The spiritual power of listening to music can vary. Music has been known to have a positive impact on mental and emotional well-being. When individuals listen to specific music, their mood will change, decrease stress and anxiety, and improve focus and concentration. In some spiritual practices, music is used as a form of meditation or prayer, allowing individuals to connect with a higher power or a sense of inner peace. Additionally, music can bring people together and create a sense of community and shared experience. Ultimately, the spiritual power of listening to music may be found in its ability to provide a sense of connection, hope, and inspiration.

Hawaiian culture recognizes music as something more than entertainment. Music is a profound vehicle of healing, deeply interwoven with spirituality, identity, and connection to land ('aina). Drawing on rich traditions of chant (oli/ mele), hula dance, and native instrumentation, Hawaiian music embodies mana. Through sound, movement, and story, Kanaka Maoli (Native Hawaiians) access healing on physical, emotional, and spiritual levels.

Playing Instruments as Extensions of Land and Spirit

Traditional Hawaiian instruments, such as ipu (gourd percussion), pahu (sharkskin drum), nose flute, ukulele, and slack-key guitar, carry symbolic ties to the land, gods, and ancestral knowledge. The ipu, for example, is made from gourds cultivated with ritual care. Its planting follows lunar protocol, often by a "pot-bellied man" reciting chants to ensure growth and spiritual alignment. The ipu is more than percussion; it is a fertility symbol and vessel of mana, linking performer, earth, and healing rhythm.

Similarly, the god Lono, associated with agriculture, fertility, and rain, is invoked through musical practices. In rituals, meke (chant and dance) draw on Lono's generative energy, creating balance and harmony in individuals and the community.

While formal studies of Hawaiian instruments are limited, parallels can be drawn from research on sound healing traditions. For instance, studies on Native American flute playing have shown increased heart rate variability, slow-wave EEG patterns, and emotional calm in listeners and players alike. Hawaiians intuitively value the vibratory effects of sound: the low frequencies of pahu and ipu, and the gentle tone of slack-key guitar or ukulele, are believed to soothe nerves, release emotional blockages, and restore balance (just go listen to Hapa or Jake Shimabukuro).

In Hawaiian healing practices, sound is used intentionally alongside herbal poultices, prayer, and massage. Chant and instrumental tones support healing protocols, aiding in the alignment of spiritual and physical energies in a holistic manner.

Individuals learning to play in this way often describe profoundly meaningful, transformative experiences. The daily practice, ceremonial offerings, and kahu guidance create an environment where psychological stress dissolves, identity is anchored in ancestral wisdom, and community support fosters healing.

Singing & Chanting (Oli and Mele)

At the core of Hawaiian musical healing lies oli, the sacred chant. Hawaiian linguistics holds "I ka 'olelo ke ola, i ka 'olelo ka make": In the word is life, in the word is death.

Words carry real force and chanting them shapes spiritual, social, and environmental outcomes. Chants involve deep ritual protocols: oli komo (entering), oli kahea (calling), oli mahalo (gratitude), each with specific tone, breath control (ha'i), and kaona (layered hidden meaning) that convey genealogy, identity, and intention. Chanting is vibrational cartography, a way to negotiate spiritual presence, mark respectful entry to new space, or align personal mana with place and ancestry. By chanting with intention, practitioners tap into ancestral energies, invoking healing influence upon mind, body, and community.

When mele is combined with hula, it becomes a melodic, rhythmic composition still infused with meaning and intent. These sacred songs preserve creation myths, genealogies, environmental lore, and ancestral memory. They unite sound, story, and movement in a dynamic framework that heals through connection and identification.

Chant is frequently shared in a communal context, between kumu hula and haumana (students), family genealogies recited in group gatherings, chants exchanged at canoe arrival rituals, and in ceremonial contexts where individuals and land exchange identity and recognition. These communal chants reinforce relationships, restore collective well-being, and reaffirm ka'aina aloha: love of land, rooted in mutual interdependence and cultural care.

During times of stress or trauma, historically or in modern contexts, chants and mele are used to foster inner peace, restore emotional balance, and generate communal solidarity. At the University of Hawai'i, Native Hawaiian healers have incorporated mele pule (prayer chant) into mental-health seminars and workshops to support pandemic-related anxiety and trauma among students and staff.

Music as Hawaiian Healing

As you'll notice in many of the stories, song, dance, or music is integral to the magic of Hawai'i. Hawaiian music is healing because it activates mana, cultivates connection (to ancestry, land, self, and community), and enables holistic alignment (spiritual, emotional, physical). Whether through the resonant vibration of an ipu, the flowing gestures of hula, or the sacred power of chant, musical traditions offer an integrated path toward ola (life, health, and balance).

Fundamentally, Hawaiians believe that sound is not separate from spirit, and that by weaving music into intentional cultural practice, individuals can access ancient channels of healing and strength. Music becomes a bridge: to gods (like Laka and Lono), to ancestors, to the land, and to one's own heart. In this way, every song (even every breath of chant) is a prayer for well-being, and every dance is a medicine for body and soul.

Shamanic Power Song

A shamanic power song is a song or chant that is used in shamanic practices to help connect with spirits, increase spiritual power and energy, and facilitate healing. It is often created and used by shamans during their journey or ceremony. The song may be composed of words or sounds that have significant meaning and power for the shaman or community, and it is believed that the repetition of the song can create a powerful resonance that can aid in the shaman's communication with the spirit world.

A shaman may find their power song through meditation, journeying, or experimenting with different sounds and tones. A power song is a special song that can be used for healing, protection, and manifestation during shamanic ceremonies or rituals. It is believed to carry a specific energy frequency that helps to connect a shaman with the spirit world, guides, and ancestors. To find their power song, a shaman may need to sit in silence, connect with their inner voice, and listen to what vibrations resonate within them. Alternatively, they may journey to the spirit world with the intention of receiving this song from their guides or spiritual allies. Once they have found their power song, they may work with it, practice singing or chanting it, and allow its healing energy to permeate through their body and spirit.

Healing Prayer

The healing purpose of prayer can be interpreted in different ways based on religious, spiritual, or personal beliefs. Many people believe that prayer can help with physical, emotional, or spiritual healing by providing comfort, hope, and strength. Some may believe that prayer can help to redirect energy and promote positive changes in the body and mind. Additionally, prayer can offer a sense of connection and support from a higher power or community, which can contribute to a feeling of well-being and resilience. Ultimately, the healing purpose of prayer may vary from person to person and is often a deeply personal and subjective experience.

The bridge from the divine and our soul's consciousness is the holy act of prayer. Prayer changes our vibration (to lower and calm or tighten) through rituals, ceremonies, and full committed gratitude, sometimes accompanied by gifts, offerings, or the sacrifice of time or the burning of a candle.

Prayer strengthens our spirituality and is the bridge of our soul consciousness (aumakua) to our primal way of healing and connecting (unihipili). Rituals and ceremonies are incomplete without prayers, especially if they aren't done with full commitment and intention. What's interesting is that when the kahunas noticed the Christian priests and missionaries praying, they noticed that there was no intimate connection to their breath in their prayer. There is no mana traveling on the ha to ignite the connection to the divine.

Dance: Hula as Healing in Motion and as Spiritual Practice

Hula embodied prayer and oral history. It connects dancers to gods such as Laka (goddess of hula and forest regeneration) and Pele (goddess of the volcano and creative power), weaving creation myths into each gesture. Before hula is taught in a sacred space (halau), protocol requires chants to Laka, offerings at the altar (kuahu), and spiritual alignment. The dance becomes a conduit through which Laka's energy flows through the dancer.

From a healing standpoint, hula integrates body, breath, word, and intention. Each movement aligns with mele (songs or chants) recounting genealogies, nature, or historical events, creating an experience of wholeness across physical, emotional, and spiritual planes. The rhythmic swaying of hips and arms mirrors ocean tides, breezes, and flora motions, fostering resonance with one's own internal rhythms.

Health professionals and wellness practitioners have recognized hula as a form of expressive therapy: participants often report enhanced mindfulness, decreased anxiety and depression, and stronger social connections. The disciplined coordination of movement and chant creates avenues for emotional release and self-awareness while fostering a deep sense of cultural belonging.

In the Hawaiian worldview, telling a story through hula is itself healing. It situates an individual in a broader lineage, with ancestors, myths, and the land ('aina). Hearing and embodying tales of creation, chiefs, voyagers, or natural phenomena grounds the person in ancestral resilience, renewing identity and self-worth.

Also, hula is framed within protocols of pono (balance and righteousness). When hula is performed in alignment with good relationships to self, others, and nature, it becomes a restorative art, promoting holistic well-being.

Dance is a common practice in shamanic traditions and is used for various purposes, including:

1. Connecting with the spirit world: Shamanic dance can be used to enter a trance state and connect with the spirits. The movement and rhythm of the dance can help to shift the consciousness and open the dancer up to spiritual experiences.

2. Healing: Dancing can be used to help heal physical and emotional wounds. The movement and energy of the dance can help to release blockages and promote healing.

3. Celebration: Dance is often used in shamanic traditions as a way to celebrate important events, such as births, weddings, and harvests.

4. Journeying: Shamanic dance can be used as a form of journeying. The movement and rhythm of the dance can help the practitioner to enter into a meditative state and journey within.

Overall, dance is an integral part of shamanic traditions and is used for a variety of purposes, including spiritual connection, healing, celebration, and journeying. Dancing was regarded as a way to honor the supernatural, or at least connect to it. Sacred dances could help the crops grow, help it rain, or scare away the demons that caused strife, disease, or misfortune. The connection of dance to the supernatural, who could make the clouds move, was profound and done throughout the world in indigenous cultures.

> **Even at times of burial, we dance, we sing, and we pray, to heal the mourning, and to give peace to those who have transitioned from their living life and journey to the world of the spirits.**

Step Kick

"Start with back-flap-toe back-flap-toe. Okay? 5,6,7,8," and the music starts a seductive rhythm of notes while an assortment of dancers begin to become characters of the song. With so many different kinds of people, the choreographer must shape a dance that gives life to the music and to the dancer, weaving steps, rhythms, and emotions together. Each time I watch the same dance, I notice something new, which makes it exciting every time. The more energy (don't confuse "energy" with freneticism; something calm can be full of energy) a dancer brings, the more the performance reaches the audience. I have always loved to dance, and since the age of ten I have wanted to entertain, to create.

To dance for a living, it has to be for pure satisfaction, because dancers have to love it in order to do it. I believed it had to be the only thing I was allowed to truly care about in my life, with everything else falling to the back of the closet, relationships, hobbies, pop culture, social life, health, other interests... If it isn't the only thing you want, then it's a sure chance of failure. I didn't have to worry about that because I loved dance more than anything in the world.

"The most important thing, when you go out into the world to dance, is to remember who you are, don't forget who you are, for they are going to tear it out of you," my high school dance instructor explained with extremely honest words of wisdom that could have only been said from experience.

I was first introduced to the world of dance through the grace and discipline of classical ballet, the rhythm and precision of classical tap, and the exuberance of classical jazz. Each style offered a different lens through which I could explore movement, and each left an indelible mark on both my body and my spirit. The pursuit of mastery in these styles shaped my early years, instilling in me a foundation of strength, flexibility, and artistry.

I moved to New York City, like most dancers do, at the age of 17. My expertise in dance was far from over, as I ventured into the realm of musical theater, where the choreography of Bob Fosse and Jerome Robbins captivated my imagination. I studied their techniques with fervor, dissecting their work in order to understand the unique language of gesture, line, and rhythm that they used to bring stories to life on stage. My passion for storytelling through dance only grew stronger as I delved deeper into theatrical choreography, learning to embody characters and convey emotions through the transformative power of movement.

At 19, I had my first dance company. I had choreographed 7 productions, and I was the youngest to receive the dance teacher training at Broadway Dance Center (back then, now anyone can join those trainings). My true evolution as a dancer, however, came under the tutelage of Luigi, whose wisdom transcended technical mastery. With Luigi, I discovered that dance was no mere exhibition of tricks and rehearsed postures, but a subtle exploration of pressure and resistance along soft lines. This revelation allowed me to access a deeper level of grace, one that extended beyond physical expression and into the realm of emotional resonance. Dance became a means of communication, a way of connecting with others and expressing my innermost thoughts and feelings. It's with his brilliance that he gave me the ability to be as captivating on stage as I was, no matter the discipline.

The freedom I found in dance could not be confined to a single style, as I ventured into African dance and learned to release my body in new and unexpected ways. The uninhibited movement that characterized African dance allowed me to forge a new connection with nature and the earth, teaching me the importance of honoring the rhythms and cycles of life. I studied dances from throughout the continent, their history, and rhythms, taking me into Afro-American dance and how the slave movement affected the dance we have in America.

As I continued my exploration, I discovered the healing power of modern dance, particularly the techniques developed by Martha Graham and Lester Horton. Modern dance encouraged me to delve into the depths of my own emotions, using movement as a means of self-discovery and catharsis. Through the practice of modern dance, I was able to confront and transform my own pain, loss, and fear, ultimately emerging as a brilliant choreographer.

Throughout this journey, I also reconnected with my cultural roots by learning traditional European partner dances, such as the polka, various waltzes, and the tango, alongside partner dances like the cha-cha and swing.

Because of my light eyes and pale complexion, I was not allowed to learn hula. I'd like to point out that there was a bigger issue with me having green eyes than being strictly white presenting. You see, in the local races represented in Hawaii, you have many mixed people, and intrinsically, Portuguese, which is a "local" race, is actually white. The issue was that my white-ness was accompanied with green eyes. Back then, on Maui, this meant that I did not have the privilege to learn hula. In my late twenties, I took it upon myself to use my prodigy mind and body to learn secretly with private lessons and guidance to incorporate the ways of my culture into my knowledge and practice. With my own performing arts school in Maryland, I was able to step into the role of a kumu hula, finally being able to wear my culture fully, with my halau, Ka Hui 'O Hula 'O Ho'okoa Kaenalu, I had come full circle teaching my culture, language, and practices with the love of dance and storytelling.

By striking a balance between these diverse styles, I cultivated a rich understanding of movement that transcended individual techniques. By the time I was 25 years old, I was one of five people in the country who were considered a master choreographer, as an expert in eighteen forms of dance. How was this possible? Sacrifice. In my spare time, I danced, I learned, I rehearsed. I didn't watch TV, I didn't go out with friends, and I didn't do much of anything other than dance.

In addition to embracing the physical aspects of dance, I also recognized its power as a means of storytelling. Through movement, I could remind the audience of our shared humanity and the universal emotions that bond us together. This realization fueled my passion for performance, as I became increasingly adept at weaving intricate narratives with my body.

As I began to appreciate the transformative potential of dance, my body became a powerful vehicle for both self-expression and connection with others. Although I became an expert in 18 distinct dance styles, my true mastery lay not in the mere execution of these techniques, but in the ability to evoke deep emotions within the hearts of those who witnessed my movements. In this way, dance served as a remarkable tool for healing, continually pushing my boundaries and illuminating new pathways to understanding.

In the realm of spiritual healing, dance serves as a potent medium through which a witchdoctor can channel their mystical power. By weaving tales through movement and allowing their body to become a conduit for the stories they seek to share, a witchdoctor can tap into the deepest recesses of the human psyche, breaking down barriers that impede emotional and spiritual wellness. Through this powerful form of storytelling, one can experience catharsis, release pent-up energy, and unravel the intricacies of their own interconnectedness with the world around them.

As a practitioner of dance-infused healing, the witchdoctor can summon the teachings of their ancestors, incorporating indigenous dance forms that reflect their cultural heritage. Harnessing the timeless wisdom passed down through generations, they weave together an intricate tapestry of movement that resonates with the very core of their being. This connection to ancestral knowledge provides a foundation for the witchdoctor to create a sacred space in which they can guide their subjects on a transformative journey, enabling them to rediscover their sense of self and spiritual wholeness.

In engaging with the power of dance, I, the undercover witchdoctor, could also draw upon the innate healing properties of rhythm, melody, and movement. As witchdoctors and shamans skillfully manipulate their bodies to music with the intention of a story, they can channel the raw energy of the universe, harnessing its restorative potential. In this way, the witchdoctor serves as both a gifted storyteller and an accomplished healer. By weaving together the threads of their cultural heritage and harnessing the restorative power of dance, they can offer their subjects a profoundly transformative experience that transcends the limitations of everyday reality.

As a young dancer, this prodigy grew to comprehend the delicate and robust balance between movement and emotion, which allowed me to tell stories through dance that resonated with audiences on a profound level, triggering cathartic reactions and fostering a sense of relatability. As I matured, my innate ability to heal through movement led me to embrace the responsibility fully as a witchdoctor. Here, I could harness natural talents to deeply impact the lives of others and promote emotional growth.

With the wisdom of teachers and ancestors, I've learned to call upon the ancient power of dance to mend spiritual wounds in a spectator. Through captivating performances, other dancers and I guide you and them towards healing, unity, and self-discovery. As a witchdoctor, this young child had found his true purpose, where the sheer power of dance and the profound wisdom of witchcraft intertwined, strengthening the transformative potential for those fortunate enough to experience a few mesmerizing performances.

Releasing into Water and Receiving from Trees

In Polynesian understanding, water is a living presence that receives, transforms, and carries away the energies we no longer wish to hold. Water remembers the mountains it has touched, the rain clouds that birthed it, and the deep ocean currents that cradle it. When a person enters the sea, stands beneath a waterfall, or immerses in a river, the body and spirit enter a sacred exchange. The water moves over the skin, and with each movement, it gathers the heaviness from the heart and the thoughts that have grown stale. Polynesian healers speak to the water during such moments, offering words or chants that name what is being released. The release is intentional. Once given to the water, the energy changes form. It becomes part of the great movement of tides and rain cycles, no longer lodged in the body or the mind.

Fresh water has a different voice than the sea. A stream may hum a gentle song as it winds through stones. A waterfall roars with vitality. The ocean breathes in long, rhythmic pulses. Each has its own way of helping the body reset and the mind become clear. In this way, water does more than cleanse the skin. It clears the pathways of energy so mana can move without obstruction. This practice remains alive in many islands, where people enter the water at dawn to begin a new day, or at sunset to release the work and emotions gathered since morning.

Just as water carries away, trees replenish. In Polynesian thought, the forest is a place where life force thrives in abundance. Trees stand rooted in the earth, drinking deeply from the soil while their leaves gather light from the sun. They offer this stored energy freely to those who approach with respect. Leaning against the trunk of a tree or resting in the shade beneath its branches creates a silent connection between human and tree. Breath deepens naturally in such places, and the heart slows its pace. The air beneath trees carries more than oxygen. It carries the subtle vitality of living green things.

Forest bathing, as it is now called in many lands, mirrors practices that Polynesian people have known for centuries. Moving slowly through a grove, touching the bark, inhaling the scent of leaves warmed by sunlight, the body receives the healing balance of nature. Each inhalation draws in the forest's energy. Each exhalation offers the body's rhythm back to the trees. The relationship is reciprocal. In the presence of tall and ancient trees, a person feels their own smallness and their belonging at once. Energy flows more freely, and the spirit grows steadier.

By combining these practices, one can live in balance. Water clears. Trees restore. Together they create a cycle of release and renewal. To walk from the shore into the forest is to move from cleansing into replenishment. To journey from the mountains to the sea is to follow the natural flow of life itself. Polynesian philosophy teaches that healing happens when we live in harmony with these cycles, allowing ourselves to give and receive as naturally as the tides and the wind.

The Japanese health practice of forest bathing, also known as Shinrin-yoku, involves immersing oneself in the natural environment, specifically forested areas, for therapeutic and wellness purposes. This practice is believed to promote relaxation, reduce stress, boost the immune system, and improve overall well-being. People who practice forest bathing typically take slow walks through the forest, practicing mindfulness, and deliberately taking in the sights, sounds, and smells of the natural environment. This practice is gaining popularity worldwide as a way to help people connect with nature and improve their mental and physical health.

Shinrin-yoku Benefits
1. *Reduced stress:* Shinrin-yoku has been shown to reduce levels of the stress hormone cortisol.

2. *Improved immune function:* Forest bathing appears to boost the immune system, helping the body fight off illness.

3. *Lower blood pressure:* Spending time in nature has been linked to lower blood pressure levels.

4. *Reduced anxiety and depression:* Shinrin-yoku has been shown to reduce symptoms of anxiety and depression.

5. *Boosted creativity:* Being in a natural environment can help clear the mind and promote creativity.

6. *Enhanced focus and attention:* Studies have suggested that spending time in nature can improve focus and attention.

7. *Improved sleep:* Shinrin-yoku has been linked to better sleep quality.

Overall, spending time in nature can have a wide range of mental and physical health benefits.

Ocean Benefits

1. *Physical exercise:* Swimming in the ocean gives a full-body workout, works the muscles, and aids in burning calories, which helps in losing weight.

2. *Stress-relief:* The ocean's rhythmic movements and calming sound can bring a sense of peace and reduce stress.

3. *Increased blood circulation:* The saltwater in the ocean can help improve blood circulation throughout the body, which can support metabolic processes.

4. *Vitamin D:* Swimming in the ocean can help the body produce Vitamin D because the sun's rays reflect on the water.

5. *Mental health:* The ocean is a natural element that can help with feelings of relaxation, peace, and calmness, helping to alleviate depression or anxiety symptoms.

6. *Spiritual awakening:* Being in the ocean's presence brings a sense of interconnectedness with nature, leading to spiritual growth and greater understanding.

The Story of Laka and The Gift of Hula

Characters:
Laka - Goddess of Inspiration
Pele - Goddess of the Volcano and Fire
Kane - Sky God
Kanaloa - God of Magic and the Veil between the Ocean and the Underworld

Long ago, the gods saw that the people of Hawai'i needed a way to honor the divine, preserve their stories, and express their gratitude for the beauty of the land. Among the many gods, it was Laka, the goddess of hula and the forests, who took on the task of creating a sacred dance that would weave together spirituality, nature, and storytelling.

Laka was known for her grace, creativity, and connection to the plants and animals of the land. Her journey to create hula would take her across the islands, where she gathered inspiration and wisdom from the natural world.

Laka traveled to the lush forests of Hana, Maui, and ascended the sacred mountain of Haleakala. There, she communed with the gods and spirits of the land, seeking their blessings for her endeavor. Laka spent days observing the natural world, the sway of trees in the wind, the rippling of waves on the ocean, the flicker of fire, and the gentle flow of streams. She realized that these movements reflected the rhythm of life and could be translated into a dance.

With her arms full of sacred plants, Laka wove a beautiful altar, called a kuahu, as a tribute to the gods. She prayed to Kane, the god of life and creation, and Kanaloa, the god of the ocean and the underworld, for their guidance. She also invoked Pele, the goddess of volcanoes, asking for her fiery inspiration to infuse the hula with passion and energy.

Once she had perfected the movements, chants (oli), and prayers, Laka descended from the mountains and brought her gift of hula to the people. She taught them the sacred dance, showing how each movement told a story: A swaying hand mimicked the motion of the ocean. A downward sweep of the arms reflected the falling rain. Stomping feet imitated the rumble of the earth...

Through her teachings, Laka emphasized that hula was a sacred act of worship. She instructed the people to build altars dedicated to her, adorned with the plants she had gathered, and to offer prayers and chants before performing the hula. These rituals ensured that the dance would remain a connection to the divine.

Laka's gift of hula transformed the way Hawaiians honored their gods, told their stories, and connected with the land. She became known as the goddess of hula, and her spirit is invoked in every halau hula (hula school) and performance to this day.

Altars to Laka, adorned with maile, lehua, and palapalai, are still central to hula ceremonies. Her sacred journey is remembered through chants and dances, and her teachings are passed down from one generation to the next.

This story of Laka highlights her role as a nurturer and creator, forever tied to the beauty and spirit of Hawai'i. Every time hula is danced, Laka's legacy comes alive, connecting the past with the present in a living expression of Hawaiian culture.

The Stone in the Jar, Grief in Hawai'i

Some stones live inside us forever. They fall, sudden and heavy, striking the deepest part of the spirit. These stones enter when someone beloved dies, when a bond breaks, when a path closes that cannot open again. From the moment grief enters, it presses against the soul, seeking a place to rest.

In Hawaiian thought, the soul has three parts: the aumakua, the uhane, and the unihipili. These three move together like braided cordage. When one strand suffers, the entire cord strains.

Grief affects all three. The unihipili, the root soul that remembers everything, the higher knowing that carries us between lifetimes, may become quiet for a time. The uhane, the body, physically aches with the memory of touch, scent, voice. Even the aumakua struggles to choose direction, no longer walking beside the one who once offered guidance.

Grief reaches through every layer of our being. It shows that love existed, that connection mattered, that something sacred took root in us. Instead of seeking to remove grief, we learn to carry it with wisdom and strength.

Imagine your soul as a jar made of clear glass. When grief first arrives, it is a stone that drops into you, the glass jar. At first, the stone takes up the entire space. You may feel unable to move or breathe, suffocating from the pressure of grief. Over time, the stone remains unchanged, but your jar begins to grow. Your soul expands around the grief. You discover space for other feelings, other experiences, other kinds of love. The grief does not vanish. You become larger than it. That's our goal: to expand and not ignore.

This is the path of Hawaiian healing. We do not strive to erase sorrow because sorrow reminds us to love life; we cultivate our capacity to live fully while holding it.

The Place Where Grief Lives

In traditional times, when someone passed from this world, the people expressed grief openly. They wailed and chanted, sometimes through the night. They called out the names of the departed. These expressions marked reverence. The voice became a vessel. The body releases through movement. The tears returned love to the earth.

The elders knew that unspoken grief settles into the body. The belly, the chest, the back of the neck, all these become homes for emotions that were never released. The unihipili absorbs what we refuse to speak. It stores every moment, every goodbye, every ache left unnamed.

In our tradition, healing begins when grief receives permission to move. Tears carry power. Sound carries mana. Silence, when used with intention, holds presence. When used to hide suffering, it becomes a weight the soul must bear alone.

Our ancestors wailed so their children would not have to. They chanted so the earth could absorb what they could no longer hold.

When the Soul Wanders

Grief sometimes causes the soul to wander. In the first nights after a loss, the uhane may drift away from the body, lingering near the place of parting or searching the winds for signs. A grieving person may stop eating, forget simple tasks, or stare into the distance. Elders would say, "His soul walks with hers." When this happened, loved ones gathered to call the soul back of the grieving. They might place cool water on their forehead. They might chant into the ear of the sleeper. They might whisper, "Come home. I see you. You are needed here."

Even though grief remains, the soul must return to the body. The living must eat. They must walk. They must care for others. Though grief sits within them, the soul must stay rooted.

The forest teaches this. The ʻōhiʻa lehua tree, born from a love both tender and sorrowful, continues to bloom. Its red flowers rise from black lava, even as stories say the rain falls when lovers are pulled apart. The tree flowers anyway.

You also may bloom again.

Rituals of Holding

Healing in Hawaiian practice begins with acceptance and integration. When grief enters, the spirit does not push it away; instead, it creates a place for it. A ritual of holding invites the grieving person to say: "I recognize this pain. I will not let it control me, but I will learn how to carry it."

One such ritual begins by choosing a stone. The person wraps it in white kapa cloth, naming the sorrow or the loved one who has passed. They press the stone to their forehead, allowing their tears to fall. Then they return the stone to a sacred place, the ocean, the base of a tree, or the mouth of a cave.

This act gives the grief form. It grants it a shape, a body, and a resting place.

We do not cast grief away. We honor it. We allow it to rest in the world around us so it does not become trapped within us.

Another ritual is to simply create a lei for the departed. Flowers are not meant to be permanent. They are meant to remind us that the beauty of life is fleeting, to stay present. Giving a gift of flowers to the departed is to recognize the beauty of their life and to accept that it can wither away. And that it's ok. Create a lei, take it to the ocean, and lay it in the water so that Kanaloa, the guide between the worlds, can deliver the fleeting gift to the departed.

The Expanding Jar

With time, the stone does not change; the jar grows.

You learn when the weight presses harder, on anniversaries, during certain seasons, when a song begins to play. On those days, you choose to pause. You light a candle, walk to the ocean, or speak their name aloud. Living with grief becomes a rhythm. A mother may lose a child and still find a way to laugh again. Her laughter does not replace her child. It honors her own life. A brother may chant at sunrise to remember a sibling. His voice becomes a bridge between this world and the next. An elder may return to the path once walked with a beloved, leaving flowers along the trail. These petals carry memory. Each one whispers, "I carry you with me." This is the transformation: grief becomes a companion. You no longer fear its presence. You walk beside it.

Ancestral Stones

Traditionally, bones held great mana. Families carried the iwi of loved ones until they found a place suitable for resting. They wrapped them carefully, sang over them, and treated them with reverence. The bones represented legacy and presence. They continued to guide. Grief also becomes part of this inheritance. When we carry grief with respect, we allow it to shape us without hardening us. The stone becomes part of our lineage. We tell stories about it. We pass down its lessons.

The Homecoming of the Soul

Sometimes, grief grows too heavy, and a person forgets who they are. They forget how to eat, how to sing, how to rest. In these times, the soul may need guidance to return. Families may call upon a kahuna or an elder to lead a ceremony. Sometimes they use water and salt.

The chant calls to the uhane:

"O soul, return to the body that feeds you. Return to the name that shelters you. Return to the hands that hold you. Return to the breath that loves you."

The person remains exactly as they are, grief included. But their soul comes home to them again.

The body begins to rise with breath. The memory begins to find a rhythm. And the stone in the jar finds its place among everything else the soul now holds.

A Sacred Way of Living

To grieve is to love fully. To carry grief with courage is to live as our ancestors lived. In our way, we do not ask, "Are you over it yet?" Instead, we bring food. We walk together. We chant. We say, "I see you. You are still here."

These simple gestures call the soul back into the body. They strengthen the jar so it can hold the stone. You may cry today. You may cry in ten years. Each time, you honor what matters. Grief does not measure weakness. It confirms love. When that love no longer has a physical place to go, it transforms. It sings. It grows trees. It raises children. It dances into the world as remembrance.

A Closing Chant

We offer a chant that speaks to both the departed and those who remain:

E hoʻi ana ka ʻuhane i ke kino.
E hoʻi ana ke aloha i ke alo.
E hoʻi ana ka ʻuhane i ka lahui,
i ka ʻohana, i ka ʻiwi o ke ola.

The soul returns to the body.
Love returns to the face.
The soul returns to the people,
to the family, to the bones of life.

This is the legacy: we carry it as evidence of a life intertwined with others. Our jar grows. Our breath deepens. Our hearts learn how to live with weight and still open wide.

The stone does not define us; the way we carry it does.

Ohia Lehua

Characters:
Ohia - A handsome man who loves only Lehua
Lehua - A winsome woman who loves only Ohia
Pele - Goddess of the Volcano
Laka - Goddess of Inspiration

Sometimes the gods speak in red blossoms and in the ache between lovers who have touched hands for the last time. This is one such story. The kind that enters your bones.

Ohia was a young man, upright and strong, with the broad shoulders of a warrior. His feet walked purposefully, and his heart loved with just as much purpose for Lehua, the girl who moved like a breeze between the trees. She was beloved by the forest and the people alike. Her touch made the ti leaves lean toward her, and when she danced, it was the kind of joy that even the birds watched in silence.

They loved each other. The kind of love that already remembers loss.

Pele saw him, and with her amorous desire and her consistent character, she decided she would make him hers.

She had risen early that day, smoke weaving through her hair, a skirt of flame wrapped about her hips. She walked among her lands, watching for changes, watching for anything beautiful enough to match her power. Then she saw Ohia standing in the clearing, shirt off, eyes skyward, enjoying the rays that caused brown hair to redden, breathing like the trees, still and sure.

Pele appeared before him as a young maiden in white.

He turned, knew that this was Pele, and bowed.

"Ke aloha," she said, low and sweet.

He nodded but did not return it.

She offered him the world. Promised him lava trails to walk, clouds to sleep on, bones that would never ache, and her immortal hand to hold.

Knowing that he would surely perish for denying her, he held stern and strong. Keeping a strong stance, hiding his weakness, knowing his answer was both a death sentence and the last words he would utter, he chose carefully. He squared himself and made no expression on his face. This would be his goodbye. Ohia's eyes met Pele's, and a tear fell down his expressionless face. He answered with only one word.

"Lehua."

Pele's face hardened. Her mouth turned to stone. She had been refused before, but never by someone so young, so alive, so worthy. She simply lifted her hand, and as the witch-goddess of fire and form did… Ohia fell.

Roots burst through his spine. His arms stiffened into branches. His skin hardened into bark. His voice silenced beneath the weight of her curse, and there in the clearing, where once he stood with breath and promise, a tree rose crooked and pained, twisted and blackened.

Lehua, feeling that her love was gone and the sudden stones of grief filling her up, came running.

Lehua saw what remained of Ohia and fell to her knees. She cried out at Pele. Lehua tore at the ground. She called Pele by name and begged her to return him, but the goddess of flame had turned her face away. Her wrath had cooled into something worse. Indifference.

But Lehua's tears did not go unanswered.

The other gods came quietly. Laka watched from the edge of the forest, the goddess of inspiration and care. She could not undo what Pele had done. Pele's word had already become law in the bark of the tree. But Laka could do something else. Lehua's soul danced between the trees, so it was only fitting to give Lehua the connection to her love, permanently.

The goddess of inspired dance touched Lehua. She gasped once, and in that final breath, Lehua understood that her grief would transform her. Lehua became blossoms the color of blood.

Lehua's body softened. Her limbs rose. Her soul stretched like morning light and flowed upward into petals. Red. Brilliant. Shaped by longing. Lehua became the blossom: Ohia, the tree. The two who were lovers in life, and Laka made them become one in form. Since that day, they have never been apart.

The Ohia Lehua tree is sacred now. It grows where lava once consumed the earth, the same way love can rise after ruin. Its blossoms are not to be taken except by women (for a man taking Lehua away from her mate is kapu). Even if a woman plucks lehua, the sky mourns, and rain comes. Those are the god's tears, lehua rain. She grieves for the brief moment she is pulled away from him, but she, in her grief, will grow love back.

People call it the Ohia lehua, a form made of sorrow and choice and the kind of love that will not break even when the gods themselves bend it.

Final Thoughts

The Proof Is In The Fruit

When the fires in Lahania, Maui, happened in August of 2023, I sat in my Austin apartment, helpless and devastated. Naturally, the homes, the people, the helpless carnage that overtook the mountainside were horrifying. I couldn't go home to help because if I had, I'd be taking up a bed, supplies, and resources for people who needed them locally. Instead, I took out a legal pad and started a list of people. I could bring a little control and help by having mainland friends, students, family (and some strangers) call me, and I would locate their missing family. I did this for a week, keeping pages and pages of notes that people were safe (or still missing).

The hardest tragedy that still brings tears to my eyes is the burning of the Banyan tree. This one tree covers almost an entire acre. Its branches are supported by 16 major trunks (yes, one tree - the vines drop and root and create support trunks), and it was planted in 1873.

This tree could not be replaced or rebuilt, like homes do and can. Its roots witnessed hundreds of thousands of people's steps, visitors, and maoli alike. Its branches watched over us, shaded us, and allowed for our silly shenanigans. Imagine all it has seen and covered since 1873 to 2023. Take a pause and think.

THE PROOF IS IN THE FRUIT

And in the course of this tragedy, many of us cried. It was like our world tree. A staple to Maui culture. The Banyan tree represented more than just a tree. She was our longest living relative.

It took six months before the arborists and botanists from around the world gave us the signal that she was going to survive the fire. Again, I cried.

I had wanted to go back and just heal her. There were so many doctors, volunteers, organizations, and healers who were helping with the people, and all I wanted to do was get to that tree, and help sew her soul… give as much mana as I could pour into her, as minuscule in comparison to what she needs and what she once had.

In writing this book, I'm reminded that even the oldest things can be taken from us. It's Pele's entire persona, right? And in destruction, we are reminded of the urgency in keeping things well, as long as we have them.

Healing expresses itself in many ways. A person living with cancer may receive treatments such as surgery, radiation, chemotherapy, changes in diet, and time for rest. Yet the journey may also call for conversations that help bring understanding and meaning to the experience. True healing can include recognizing how this illness belongs within the greater path of the soul, inspiring shifts in priorities, perspectives, and ways of living. It can involve clearing stagnant energy, restoring balance within the body's energetic systems, and renewing the connection with the Source of life.

From a spiritual view, where the growth of the soul is central, healing can still take place even if the body does not survive the illness. By engaging in this inner work, a person gives themselves the fullest opportunity for physical recovery. This renewed state can include stronger health as well as the creation of a new life story, one that honors the lessons learned and supports continued vitality.

True healing is about bringing someone to their wholeness, not their origin.

I don't know how to tell you to pause before you begin. The problem with resurrecting old ways and applying them is opportunistic. The Hawaiian culture was almost eradicated. Many want to protect it and keep it only for themselves. However, there aren't enough from within the community who care enough about enacting the old ways, spreading them, and teaching them. So, we have to risk keeping them alive by reaching out to those who are not culturally or ethnically Hawaiian.

However, by making culture more accessible, you'll find that there will always be the opportunists, the culture vultures, who dive into the profitable portions of someone's culture, put on a costume, and try to sell it for an easy-to-make-a-buck product, instead of really healing people.

I don't think it's healthy to question every person you come across who is attempting to learn and practice, and benefit from these old ways of healing.

I don't think it's healthy to gate-keep something that wasn't a gate-kept modality.

I think we just need to see proof in the fruit.

You can put a label on a plant, but it isn't an orchid until it shows us proof. Real proof. And with that, please feel the patience of allowing space for someone who is learning, perfecting, and actually mastering the Hawaiian healing ways to fail, struggle, and learn, without the expectations that they will always get it right. Mastery takes failure. Just because someone fails does not mean that they are a charlatan.

It's a six-sided blade of confusion to navigate.

I wrote this book because I feel it is more important to bring more healers into the world than to let it die by not teaching anyone, and to risk that we will get some snake-oil salesmen out of it.

The proof is in the fruit.

The humility is in the struggle.

The spirits will help us weed out the fakers.

Go heal something.

La'amaomao and Passing The Wind

Characters:
La'amaomao - Goddess of the Wind
Paka'a - Her Son, the Steward of the Ipu

The winds belong to La'amaomao. They move at her will. She keeps them in her sacred ipu, the gourd that holds every breath that runs across Hawai'i. The cold winds that sweep from the mountain peaks, the warm breezes that carry the scent of hala, the sudden gales that churn the sea into white chaos, all rest in her keeping until she chooses to let them free.

Her son was Paka'a, born with the sound of the wind in his ears. La'amaomao taught him the secret names of the winds, the soft call that draws the gentle breezes, and the sharp command that sends the fierce squalls racing. She placed the ipu in his care, for he was wise and steady, a man who knew how to listen before he acted.

Paka'a became steward to the chief of Hawai'i Island. When the chief wished to cross the seas, Paka'a would open the gourd and call the wind that would serve them best. The canoes would fly over the waves, swift and sure. The chief trusted him. The people praised him.

But trust breeds envy in small hearts. The chief's jealous advisors whispered lies, and the lies grew like mold in a dark, abandoned closet. They said Paka'a held the winds only for himself. They said he plotted against the chief. Paka'a heard the rot spreading. He did not wait for it to poison everything; he left, carrying the ipu of La'amaomao back to his own homeland, where the winds knew his name. When people make up their minds about you, leave.

Years passed. When Paka'a left, the sea turned against the chief. Storm after storm battered his fleet. The waves rose high, and the sky lowered black. He remembered the one who had once commanded the winds for him. He called for Paka'a to come back home.

Paka'a came. He took the gourd in his hands, called to the winds in the old way, and they obeyed. The seas smoothed. The clouds broke. The canoes slid over quiet water toward safety. The chief saw the truth in Paka'a's actions, the fruit of his actions. Paka'a was restored to his place.

The gift of La'amaomao was never just the gourd. This story is more than the tale of winds and warriors. It is the breath of our ancestors carried on the trade winds. It is the voice of the gods whispered in the rustle of leaves and the roar of the sea. It teaches us to respect the forces that move around us and within us.

We are part of the world, bound to its rhythms. The lessons passed down by La'amaomao and her son Paka'a remind us that power comes with responsibility. Jealousy and deceit break the harmony of the community, but loyalty and honorable pa'ahana restore it.

The winds hold these stories, just as we hold them in our hearts. They teach us to listen to the voice of the land, the call of the sea, and the guidance of our ancestors... to pass these stories forward is to keep the winds alive.

In sharing the tale of La'amaomao and Paka'a (and the rest of these stories and so many more), we carry their mana, their knowledge, and their respect for the balance of all things. We learn that to move forward, we must honor what came before. The winds are always moving, always changing, but their story remains. It is ours to tell, again and again, so that all who hear may know this sacred dance.

And so the ipu of La'amaomao turns to you: Use the winds of your breath to continue the story.

Author Bio

Aly Cardinalli is an accomplished witchdoctor, performing arts specialist, psychic, and master educator with over twenty five years of experience in his fields. He has dedicated his life to promoting traditional practices and spreading knowledge about culture.

Born a dark medium and oversensitive psychic, Aly grew up surrounded by spirits and natural remedies that were used to cure both physical and spiritual ailments. He learned from various family members the art of healing, witchcraft, and spirituality, gradually developing a deep passion for indigenous and creolized practices.

As a young man, Aly decided to pursue a career in the performing arts. He studied music, dance, and theatrical directing, and quickly made a name for himself as a talented performer, exceptional choreographer (an expert in over eighteen styles of dance), and an award winning director. His unique knowledge of the arts and culture, along with his exceptional stage presence, made him an instant hit with audiences across the globe, artistically influencing over 135 productions and performing in over 200.

Despite his success in the performing arts, Aly continued to practice traditional shamanic techniques. Aly has also developed an innovative training and classification system for psychics, mediums, and sensitives. Because of his genius and prodigy youth, his knowledge and aptitude in the inclusive disciplines of culture, healing, spirituality, mysticism, and storytelling is unmatched.

Over the years, Aly has gained immense popularity as a master educator in his fields. Aly has been the dean of education for a performing arts school, a teacher trainer, the headmaster at a witchcraft and psychic development school, and the education director for a healing arts institute.

Thanks to his dedication and hard work, Aly Cardinalli is now widely recognized as a commodity to cultural education. His talent, passion, and expertise have inspired countless people to embrace rich and vibrant culture and to embrace the power of spiritual arts and ancient cultural expression.

BIBLIOGRAPHY AND CITED SOURCES

Apostal, Virgil Mayor. *Way of the Ancient Healer, Sacred Teachings from the Philippine Ancestral Traditions.* Berkley, CA: North Atlantic Books, 2010.

American Psychiatric Association. *Diagnostic and Statistical Manual of Mental Disorders, Fifth Edition DSM-5.* Washington, DC: American Psychiatric Publishing, 2013.

Berney, Charlotte. *Fundamentals of Hawaiian Mysticism.* Berkeley, CA: Crossing Press, 2000.

Bryan, Jessica. *Psychic Surgery and Faith Healing.* Newburyport, MA: WeiserBooks, 2008.

Cowan, Tom. *Shamanism as a Spiritual Practice for Daily Life.* New York, NY: Crown Publishing, 1996.

Crawshaw, Ralph. *Compassion's Way: A Doctor's Quest into the Soul of Medicine.* Bloomington, IL: Medi-Ed Press, 2002.

Cunningham, Scott. *The Complete Book of Incense, Oils & Brews.* Woodbury, MN: Llewellyn Publications, 1989.

Cunningham, Scott. *Cunningham's Guide to Hawaiian Magic & Spirituality.* Woodbury, MN: Llewellyn Publications, 1994.

Cunningham, Scott. *Hawaiian Religion & Magic*. St. Paul, MN: Llewellyn Publications, 1995.

Diadochus, Proclus. *The Hymns of Proclus - Ernst Vogt: Procli Hymni*. (Klassisch-Philologische Studien, Heft 18.) Pp. 100; 4 plates. Wiesbaden: Harrassowitz, 1957

Eliade, Mircea. *Shamanism Archaic Techniques of Ecstasy*. Princeton, NJ: Princeton University Press, 1964.

Ellwood, Taylor. *Walking with Spirits, How to Work with Spirits and Get Consistent Results*. Portland, Oregon: Magical Experiments Publication, 2020.

Fortune, Dion. *Psychic Self Defence, A Study in Occult Pathology and Criminality*. Naples, Italy: Albatross Publishers, 2018

Guiley, Rosemary Ellen. *The Encyclopedia of Demons & Demonology*. New York: Visionary Living, Inc, 2009.

Greer, Carl. *Change the Story of Your Health: Using Shamanic Techniques for Healing*. Scotland, UK: Findhorn Press, 2017.

Grimassi, Raven. *Grimoire of the Thorn-Blooded Witch, Mastering the Five Arts of Old World Witchery*. San Francisco, CA: Weiser Books, 2014.

Hall, Manly P. *The Secret Teachings of All Ages, An Encyclopedic Outline of Masonic, Hermetic, Qabbalistic, and Rosicrucian Symbolical Philosophy*. Mineola, NY: Dover Publications, Inc., 2010.

Hanh, Thich Nhat. *Fear, Essential Wisdom for Getting Through The Storm*. New York, NY: Harper One, 2012.

Harner, Michael. *The Way of the Shaman*. New York, NY: Harper One, 1980.

Helvin, Natasha. *Russian Black Magic, The Beliefs and Practices of Heretics and Blasphemers*. Rochester, Vermont: Destiny Books, 2019.

Hoffman, Enid. *Huna, A Beginner's Guide*. Atglen, PA: Whitford Press, 1981.

Horne, Roger. *Folk Witchcraft, a Guide to Lore, Land, and Familiar Spirit for the Solitary Practitioner*. Moon Over Mountain Press, 2019.

Illes, Judika. *The Encyclopedia of Spirits: The Ultimate Guide to the Magic of Fairies, Genies, Demons, Ghosts, Gods, and Goddesses*. New York, NY: Harper Collins, 2009

Ingerman, Sandra. *Soul Retrieval, Mending the Fragmented Self.* New York, NY: Harper Collins, 1991.

Inkwright, Fez. *Folk Magic and Healing, An Unusual History of Everyday Plants.* Turkey: Liminal11, 2019.

James, Matthew B. *The Foundation of Huna, Ancient Wisdom for Modern Times.* Kailua-Kona, HI: Advanced Neuro Dynamics, Inc., 2014.

King, Serge Kahili. *Instant Healing.* New York, NY: St. Martin's Publishing Group, 2020.

King, Serge Kahili. *Kahuna Healing.* Wheaton, IL: Quest Books, 1983.

King, Serge Kahili. *Urban Shamanism.* New York, NY: Fireside, 1990.

Konstantinos. *Summoning Spirits, the Art of Magical Evocation.* Woodbury, MN: Llewellyn Worldwide, 2002.

Krauss, Beatrice H. *Plants in Hawaiian Culture.* Hilo, HI: University of Hawaii Press, 1993.

Lee, Pali Jae, and Koko Willis. *Tales from the Night Rainbow.* Honolulu, HI: Night Rainbow Publishing Co., 1994.

Lecouteux, Claude. *Witches, Werewolves and Fairies, Shapeshifters and Astral Doubles in the Middle Ages.* Rochester, Vermont: Inner Traditions, 1992.

Liliuokalani, Queen. *The Kumulipo, An Account of The Creation of the World According to Hawaiian Tradition.* 1897

Long, Max Freedom. *Huna, An Introduction.* Midwest Journal Press, 2015.

Long, Max Freedom. *The Hula Code In Religions.* Marina Del Rey, CA: Delors's & Co., Publishers, 1982.

Long, Max Freedom. *The Secret Science Behind Miracles.* Blacksburg, VA: A&D Publishing, 2011.

Mack, Carol K., Dinah Mack. *A Field Guide to Demons, Fairies, Fallen Angels, and Other Subversive Spirits.* New York, NY: Owl Books, Henry Hold and Company, 1998.

Mackesy, Charlie. THE BOY, THE MOLE, THE FOX AND THE HORSE. New York, NY: HarperOne, 2019

Madden, Kristin. *The Book of Shamanic Healing.* Woodbury, MA: Llewellyn Publications, 2002.

Mantles, Doc. *Shamanism for Beginners! How to Understand and Implement a Shaman Way of Living.* CreateSpace, 2018.

Martinie, Dr. Louie. *Talking to the God with Food, Questioning Animal Sacrifice.* Cincinnati, Ohio: Black Moon Publishing, 2019.

Masters, Robert Augustus. *Spiritual Bypassing: When Spirituality Disconnects Us From What Really Matters.* Berkley, CA: North Atlantic Books, 2010.

Matthews, John, and Caitlin Matthews. *The Element Encyclopedia of Magical Creatures.* Hammersmith, London: HarperCollins Publishers, 2005.

McBride, Likeke R. *Practical Folk Medicine of Hawai'i.* Hilo, HI: Petroglyph Press, Ltd, 2014.

McBride, Likelike R.. *The Kahuna, Versatile Masters of Old Hawai'i.* Hilo, HI: Petroglyph Press, ltd, 2003.

Morrison, Dorothy. *Utterly Wicked: Hexes, Curses, and Other Unsavory Notions.* Newburyport, MA: Weiser Books, 2020.

Murphy-Hiscock, Arin. *Protection Spells, Clear Negative Energy, Banish Unhealthy Influences, and Embrace Your Power.* New York: Adams Media, 2018.

Ody, Penelope. *The Holistic Herbal Directory, A Directory of Herbal Remedies for Everyday Health Problems.* Edison, New Jersey: Chartwell Books, Inc., 2001

Oesterley, W.O.E.. *Sacred Dance in the Ancient World.* Mineola, NY: Dover Publications, Inc., 2002.

Penczak, Christopher. *The Temple of Shamanic Witchcraft, Shadows, Spirits, and the Healing Journey.* Woodbury, Minnesota: Llewellyn Publications, 2016.

Phelan, Rev. Arlene.. *Hawaiian Shamanism, Secrets of the Modern Shaman.* DM Bookpro, 2018.

Powell, Wayne Kealohi, and Patricia Lynn Miller. *Hawaiian Shamanistic Healing, Medicine Ways to Cultivate the Aloha Spirit.* Woodbury MN: Llewellyn Publications, 2018.

Power, Tomas. *Morbid Magic, Death Spirituality & Culture From Around the World.* Woodbury, MN: Llewellyn Publications, 2019.

Rezentes, William C., III. *Ka Lama Fukui, Hawaiian Psychology: An Introduction*. Honolulu, HI: 'A'ali'i Books, 1996.

Rodman, Julius Scammon. *The Kahuna Sorcerers of Hawaii, Past and Present*. Smithtown, NY: Exposition Press, 1979.

Rosean, Lexa. *The Encyclopedia of Magical Ingredients, A Wiccan Guide to Spellcasting*. New York, NY: Pocket Books, 200

Rysdyk, Evelyn C. *Spirit Walking, A Course in Shamanic Power*. Newburyport, MA: WeiserBooks, 2013.

Sarangerel. *Chosen by the Spirits: Following Your Shamanic Calling*. Rochester, VT: Destiny Books, 2001.

Scully, Nicki. *Alchemical Healing*. Rochester, MT: Bear & Company, 2003.

Simon, Ed. *Pandemonium: A Visual History of Demonology*. New York, NY: Abrams Books, 2021.

Souza, Ka'ala. *Pono, a Hawaiian-Style Approach to Balance and Well-Being*. Hi-Mountain Publishing, 2012.

Valnet, Jean. *The Practice of Aromatherapy, A Classic Compendium of Plant Medicines & Their Healing Properties*. Rochester, VT: Healing Arts Press, 1980.

Warner, Michael. *The Way of the Shaman*. New York, NY: Harper Collins Publishers, 1980.

Wesselman, Hank, and Jill Kuykendall. *Spirit Medicine, Healing in the Sacred Realms*. Carlsbad, California: Hay House, Inc, 2004

White, Gordon. *Star.Ships, A Prehistory of the Spirits*. UK: Scarlet Imprint, 2016.

www.ingramcontent.com/pod-product-compliance
Lightning Source LLC
Chambersburg PA
CBHW030330240426
43661CB00052B/1585